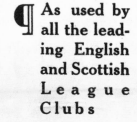

¶ As used by all the leading English and Scottish League Clubs

'Maltese Cross' Association Jerseys

'Maltese Cross' Association Jerseys are in three qualities: Light, Medium & Heavy. Vertical woven, elastic-ribbed collar and cuffs. All seams overlocked stitch, reinforced fronts, ivory finish eyelets, and silken cord lace.

'Maltese Cross' Rugby Jerseys

'Maltese Cross' Rugby Jerseys are stocked in three qualities: " A," " B " and " C." Vertical woven, all seams overlocked stitch, white collars, strengthened fronts, three buttons.

ARANTEED

Rugby

Jersey Halves

Jersey Quarters

Colours as Stripe Rugby Jerseys.

Rugby Jerseys in " B " and " C " qualities are made with extra strong reinforced tape at neck and front

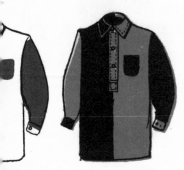

"Maltese Cross"

Hockey & Lacrosse Shirts

WINNERS
IN
ACTION

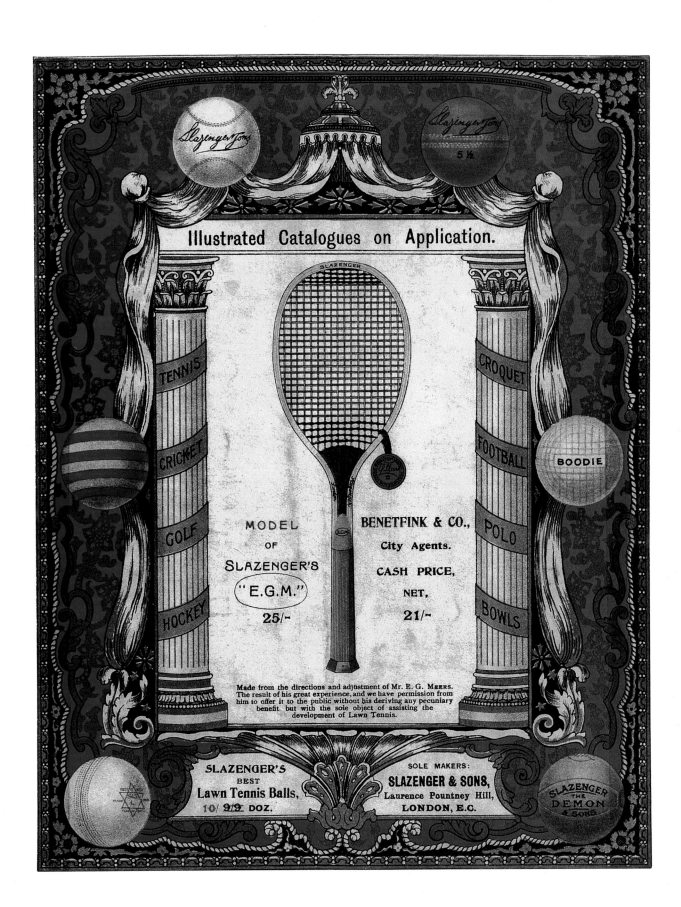

WINNERS IN ACTION

The complete story of the
DUNLOP SLAZENGER
Sports Companies

Brian Simpson

CONTENTS

	Page
Bibliography	vi
Acknowledgements	vii
Preface	ix
Chronology	xii
Introduction	1
Slazenger	11
The House of Ayres	15
William Sykes Limited	26
Gradidges	39
Slazenger	44
Dunlop	
1909–1918	99
1919–1939	110
1939–1958	143
1959–1983	158
1984–1998	201
Dunlop and Slazenger Abroad	223
Dunlop Slazenger 1998–2004	267
Inserts	*Between pages*
Wimbledon	79–82
World Cup	90–91
Masters Golf	198–200
Photos of leading players in action	*Throughout the book*
Leading Dunlop and Slazenger players	275
Index	278

BIBLIOGRAPHY

Sunday Times Illustrated History of 20th Century Sport (1996 edition) published by Hamlyn

Oxford Companion to Sports & Games, edited by John Arlott, published by Oxford University Press in 1975

Tennis, A Cultural History by Aeiner Gillmeister published by Leicester University Press in 1997

Tennis by Gianni Clerici published by Octopus Books Ltd in 1976

Wimbledon, the Official History of the Championships by John Barrett published by CollinsWillow in 2001

Wimbledon Compendium (2002) by Alan Little published by The All England Lawn Tennis and Croquet Club

Dunlop Story by James McMillan published by Weidenfield and Nicolson in 1989

Dunlop in War and Peace by Sir Ronald Storrs published by Hutchinson & Co Ltd in 1946

Slazenger, Moss and Dean – Some Pages from a Family History by Colin Dean

The Curious History of the Golf Ball by John Stuart Martin published by Horizon Press in 1968

500 Years of Golf Balls by John Hotchkiss published by Antique Trader Books in 1997

Please Play On, Biography of John McEnroe by James Harbridge published by Central Publishing Ltd in 2001

McEnroe, A Rage for Perfection by Richard Evans published by Sidgwick & Jackson in 1982

Courting Triumph by Virginia Wade with Mary Lou Mellace published by Hodder & Stoughton in l 978

Tinling, 60 Years in Tennis by Ted Tinling published by Sidgwick & Jackson in 1983

Peter Alliss' Golf Heroes by Peter Alliss published by Virgin Books in 2002

The Don, the Definitive Biography of Sir Donald Bradman by Roland Perry published by Virgin Publishing Ltd in 2000

Some Horbury Yesterdays by R S Woodall published by Horbury County Secondary School

Jumping Over the Wheel by Geoffrey Blainey published by Allen & Unwin in 1993

ACKNOWLEDGEMENTS

There is acknowledgement in the preface, and elsewhere in the book, of the enormous value of previous work on the history of the company by Colin Dean (the Slazenger family history), Professor Roy Jones and George Norton (Slazenger) and Bill Evans (Dunlop) Additionally much of the detail of this account would not have been possible without the contributions from a great many former employees and others associated with the company. These were generously provided in a considerable number of interviews and from a wealth of written and illustrated archive material.

Particularly valuable contributions were made by 'Buzzer' Hadingham, George and Gwen Carr, Peter Wycherley, Bob Howe, Pat Hughes, Bert Allam, Bob Haines, Mike Shaw, Denis Osborne, Alun and Zara Morgan, Findlay Picken, Alan Finden-Crofts, Patrick Austen, Hershel Noonkester, Graham Nicholas, Peter Warren-Tape, Len Rennocks, Cyril Bradford, Bill Peters, Robin and Dick English, Les Denman, Cyril Smith, Eric Loxton, Tony Carter, Ian Peacock, John Barrett, Rob McCowen, Allan Woodgates, John Goodman and Robert France, who made available his extensive collection of Horbury photographs. And George Somerfield and Len Thompson provided valuable insights into the history of Dunlop Footwear Ltd.

The book was originally commissioned and consistently sustained by Philip Parnell, and especially by Alan Lovell, who also proved to be a strict editor. Considerable support and practical assistance were provided by Alistair Ritchie as well as by his colleagues at the Camberley head office, notably Kristine Fleet, Yvonne Fertwig, Angela Teasdale, Cathy London and Ian Hamilton. More recently, David Hughes, at the Wakefield office, has smoothed the final stages to publication.

The chapter on 'Dunlop and Slazenger Abroad' could not have been included without the substantial input from Detlef Grosse (Germany), Dick Birch (Canada), Colin Van Jarsveldt (South Africa), John McClean (Australia), Denis Osborne (Philippines and Indonesia), David Branon, Tommy McDermott, Ron Schichtel, Doug Williams and Beth Anderson (USA), and Akiteru Fujimura (Japan).

Considerable thanks are due to Honor Godfrey and Alan Little of the Wimbledon Lawn Tennis Museum, who made their archives, exhibits and library available, and for their encouragement and support. Also to Virginia Wade and Ian Woosnam, who agreed to valuable and very interesting interviews, and to Peter Alliss for being both very encouraging and also a source of characteristically unique observations based on his association with Slazenger. Michael Cole, of Michael Cole Camerawork, was a major source of outstanding tennis photographs and astonishingly patient while his prints were retained for much longer than anticipated.

During the later stages of the project Sir Campbell Fraser and James McMillan gave generously of their time to review the draft text and their constructive comments were very much appreciated.

Throughout the process of research and writing it has been very encouraging to have the support and interest of many former Dunlop and Slazenger 'people' around the world, most notably Scott Brown, Margaret Wing, Vivienne Bedlow, Bob Hampton, Dick Dodson, John Rees, Andrew Peters, Naresh Kadiwar, Mike Casazza, Joe Moses, Tracy Brinkley and Brian Jenkins, as well as all those mentioned above.

ACKNOWLEDGEMENTS

MAGAZINES	NEWSPAPERS
Tennis	The Times
Lawn Tennis and Badminton	Sunday Times
Sports Trader	Daily Herald
Sports Trader & Exporter	Daily Express
Harpers Sports & Leisure	Daily Mail
Sports Dealer	Daily Telegraph
Golf Illustrated	Guardian
Golf Magazine	Liverpool Echo
Golf Trader	Liverpool Daily Post
Today's Golfer	Garston Weekly News
The Field	Birmingham Mail
Pastime	Wakefield Express
Land & Water	Yorkshire Post
India Rubber Journal	Yorkshire Evening Post

PICTURE ACKNOWLEDGEMENTS

	Page no.
Getty Images	All full page player pictures with the exception of Eagar and Sheldon pictures
Patrick Eagar	Full page pictures of Ramprakash, Pollock, Kallis and Waugh
Philip Sheldon Sports Picture Library	Full page pictures of Couples and Langer
Hulton Collection	63
BBC	71
Archie Handford Ltd	84
Richards (Wed) Ltd	97
Aerofilms and Aero Pictorial Ltd	146
Peter Dazeley Photography	165 (top)
Stewart Bale Ltd	177
Derek Rowe (Photos) Ltd	199 (top)
Michael Cole	191 (middle)
PH Jauncey Studio	224

PREFACE

Anyone who watches golf, or tennis, or cricket on television, or looks at newspaper and magazine photographs of the leading players in action will be very much aware of three of the world's most famous brand names: Dunlop, Slazenger and Maxfli.

That they are so visible in today's fiercely competitive and almost wholly professional sports environment is powerful testimony to the quality and performance that the products displaying these names offer to the highly skilled players who choose to use them. What is probably less well known, both to the star players and to the many millions of recreational sportsmen and sportswomen also using these golf and tennis balls, golf clubs, rackets and cricket bats, is the unique heritage of these brands, which can be traced back nearly two hundred years.

And what is so fascinating when this heritage is explored is to find that the histories of the companies that have become today's Dunlop Slazenger Group march in step with the evolution of so many of the world's most popular sports from their very small and often exclusive beginnings to the present day picture of millions of participants and billions of spectators in every country on the planet. To take 'One giant step' beyond that one of the first golf balls hit on the moon, in 1971, was a Dunlop 65, allegedly for over 1600 yards.

The history of any business is likely to be a mixture of major events, successes and failures, of its key products and most important customers, of the locations it chose for its offices and factories, and, most of all, of the people who gave it life, ambition, and achievement. The account of how Dunlop Slazenger became one of the greatest sports equipment businesses during the last 150 years easily fits that pattern. Most certainly it will show the absolutely crucial roles played by the men and women whose skills, ideas, energies and loyalties have made these brands enduringly famous and popular wherever balls have been kicked, driven, smashed, putted, potted, hooked, glanced or lobbed.

There never was a 'Mister Maxfli', although Dunlop did design a cartoon character to promote that particular brand in the 1920s, but there definitely was a Mr. Dunlop. Also introduced are several members of the enterprising Slazenger family, as well as Mr. Ayres, Mr. Sykes and his family, and Mr. Gradidge, who will all feature strongly as pioneering founders of sports businesses as far back as 1810, and which eventually merged with the Slazenger company, itself founded in 1881. In 1959 that Slazenger grouping joined forces with the Dunlop Rubber Company's sports division, which had begun making golf balls in 1908, to create the International Sports Company, later to become the worldwide Dunlop Slazenger Group. Thus the early beginnings in London by the Ayres and Gradidges, in Manchester by the Slazengers, in Yorkshire by the Sykes, and in Birmingham by Dunlop grew during the 20th century to become probably the world's best known and most truly international sports business.

These Dunlop and Slazenger companies not only established a sales and distribution organization that covered the globe but also, before the break up of the parent Dunlop Rubber Company in the 1970s and 1980s, had established nearly thirty sports equipment factories in the United Kingdom, Ireland, France, Germany, USA, Canada, South Africa, Australia, New Zealand, Japan, the Philippines, Indonesia and Malaysia. Most of these factories, certainly in recent years, concentrated on producing millions of dozens of tennis and golf balls, but, during the longer history of the business, it has manufactured a bewildering array of sports and leisure products, including indoor games, billiard tables, rickshaws, bicycles, bows and arrows, and a huge range of leather goods as well as the cricket bats, golf clubs and rackets so well known and so visible today.

Bearing in mind that the timescale of this history is nearly two hundred years from the start of the 19th century to the beginning of the new millennium, and that it gathered momentum from 1870 onwards, there is a considerable story to tell. Regrettably, but not unusually in such circumstances, no previous attempt has been made to produce a complete account of the formation and development of all of the businesses involved. There have been a number of excellent but relatively brief summaries of how the Group evolved from its various founder companies, and there are also several more detailed records dealing with individual parts of it, albeit for limited periods. All these sources are acknowledged but it is necessary to make special reference to the research carried out by Professor Roy Jones of Loughborough University, who expanded a particular interest in the Slazenger family history to write about both the Dunlop and Slazenger operations based not only on his research but also a large number of very valuable interviews with past and present employees of both companies. Professor Jones, in turn, would be the first to acknowledge the painstaking research of Colin Dean, himself a member of the Slazenger family, who has told its story from the perspective of his mother's side. It is also appropriate to make special reference to a history of the Dunlop sports business, which was written mainly in the 1970s by Bill Evans, who started a fifty-year career with the company when, in 1924, he joined the fledgling operation at the Waltham Abbey racket factory. He started, in his own words, as 'a humble office boy in the service department' but, for a number of years, held the key appointment of Manager, Stocks and Supplies at the famous Essex factory.

All these separate pieces of the jigsaw have been extremely valuable in pulling together the more complete picture that has now emerged. They have been supplemented by further research into a range of generally unsorted archives – mainly boxes of papers stored in out-of-the-way corners around the country – old price lists and catalogues, promotional material, many hundreds of photographs, press reports going back to the last quarter of the

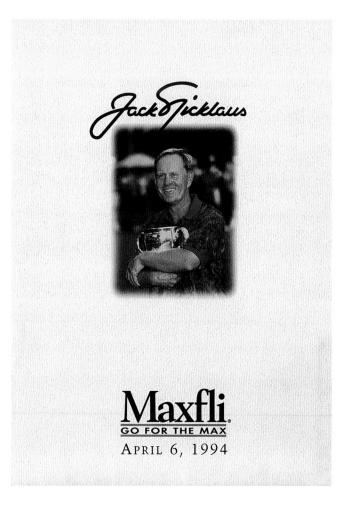

Jack Nicklaus

Maxfli.
GO FOR THE MAX
APRIL 6, 1994

19th century, a wide range of sports reference books, and, most importantly, more interviews with former employees. In the last case it has been particularly valuable to listen to personal recollections of what it was like to work for Dunlop and Slazenger as far back as the 1930s.

An additional dimension has been the scale of the international reach of the business, which was becoming evident as early as the 1890s, and that has extended the research, and the input from contributors, to overseas territories like Japan, North America, South Africa and Australia, that both grew from and later gave back to the overall development of a business that reached an annual sales level close to one billion pounds.

However, despite this considerable store of reference material, there are elements of the account where information is sparse. Because it would be worthwhile to ensure the history is eventually as complete and accurate as possible any contributions or corrections from readers that would add to it would be very welcome for subsequent incorporation.

All from William Sykes Ltd.

CHRONOLOGY

1810	F.H. Ayres founded in Clerkenwell, London
1845	Birth of Ralph Slazenger, who would be founder Chairman of the Slazenger business
	The solid gutta percha golf ball invented in Scotland
1851	Birth of Albert Slazenger, who was Chairman from 1910 to 1940
1860	First British Open at Prestwick
1866	William Sykes makes his first six soccer balls in Horbury
1867	All England Croquet Club founded at Wimbledon
1870	William Sykes Ltd. founded in Horbury
	Gradidges start making cricket bats in Woolwich
1872	Lawn Tennis invented
	First F.A. Cup Final
1873	First Cricket County Championship
1874	William Heathcote invents flannel covered tennis balls
1877	All England Croquet Club adds 'Tennis' to its name and holds its first Lawn Tennis Championship. The first champion is Spencer Gore using an Ayres racket
	First England versus Australia Test Match
1879	Ayres supplies balls and court equipment for the Wimbledon Championship
1881	Slazenger et Fils registered in Manchester as gaiters and leggings manufacturers
	First US Open Tennis Tournament
	First of six successive Wimbledon titles for William Renshaw
1883	Slazengers move their head office from Manchester to Laurence Pountney Hill, Cannon Street in the City of London
1884	First Slazenger advert for rackets appears in the trade press
	First Ladies singles title at Wimbledon won by Maud Watson
1887	Slazenger take over Jefferies tennis ball factory in Woolwich and start making their own balls there

1888	Lawn Tennis Association formed
1889	John Boyd Dunlop invents pneumatic tyre for racing bicycles and first Dunlop Company formed in Dublin
1890	First Slazenger golf clubs made by Gow of the Glasgow Golf Club
	Start of a sequence of 28 Wimbledon Men's finals (1890–1921), in which Slazenger or Ayres rackets were used by one or both finalists, 23 of them by the winner
1891	Slazenger launch their first golf ball, a 'Guttie'
	The first real golf course in USA is opened at Shinnecock Hills, Long Island
1892	Harold Hilton wins British Open with a Slazenger golf ball
	This was first time the Open was played over 72 holes and the winning score was 305
1893	Badminton Association formed
1894	United States Golf Association founded
1895	Frank Slazenger selling golf clubs in USA
	Edgar Sealey fishing tackle business founded in Redditch
	First US Open Golf Tournament
1896	William Sykes moves to larger factory in Westfield Road, Horbury
1897	Harold Hilton wins British Open with Slazenger ball
	Reginald Doherty wins first of four successive Wimbledon titles with his Slazenger racket
1899	William Sykes manufacturing military equipment for the Boer War
	Ruth Underhill wins USA Women's Amateur Golf Championship with a Slazenger ball
	Invention of wound golf ball
1900	Harry Parker starts to sell Slazenger products in Australia
	First competition, between USA and Great Britain, for the Davis Cup
1901	Harold Hilton first player since 1887 to successfully defend the British Amateur title
	PGA founded

1902   At the request of the leading players Slazenger tennis balls first used at Wimbledon – and still are the choice more than 100 years later

Laurie Doherty wins first of his five successive Wimbledon titles with his Slazenger racket

The newly invented wound golf ball begins to dominate the game and courses are lengthened to cope with the extra distance players could achieve

1903   Laurie Doherty wins the US Open Tennis

British residents build a nine hole golf course in Kobe, the first in Japan

1904   H.O. Sykes makes his first sales visit to South Africa

The winner of the British Open (Jack White) is the first to break 300 and the first champion to break 70 with a first round 69

1905   Archdale Palmer joins Slazenger as managing director

First Australian Open Tennis Championship

Eighteen year old American, May Sutton, is the first overseas player to win the Ladies' Singles at Wimbledon with a sensational 'almost knee length skirt'

Balata first used for golf ball covers

1906   Dorothea Douglas/Mrs Lambert Chambers wins the third of her seven Wimbledon Singles titles, all with Slazenger rackets

Sport achieves official respectability in the United Kingdom when the Board of Education allows it to become part of the school curriculum

1907   Australian Norman Brookes, using an Ayres racket, is the first overseas player to win the Wimbledon Men's title

First Slazenger sales agency established in Canada

Frenchman Arnaud Massy is the first overseas player to win the Open. He would later use Dunlop balls

1908   W.G. Grace retires at the age of 59. During his career he had used Ayres cricket bats

James Braid lowers the record score at the Open to 291. It remained a record until 1927 when Bobby Jones won with 285

1909   Dunlop enter the golf ball market with production based at their Manor Mills factory in Birmingham

Arthur Gore, with a Slazenger racket, wins his third Wimbledon Singles title, and at the age of 41 is the oldest Men's champion

1910   Deaths of both Ralph Slazenger and William Sykes

New Zealander Tony Wilding wins first of four successive Wimbledon Men's titles with his Ayres racket

The prize money at the British Open is increased to £125

1911   Slazenger's Limited floated as a limited company

The Dunlop Tire Company in Canada advertises golf balls imported from UK

William Larned, who used Slazenger rackets, wins the last of his five US Open titles

1912   Dunlop launch much improved '29' and '31' golf balls

First time par used for golf scoring – at the US Open

International Lawn Tennis Federation established

1913   Ladies and Mixed Doubles are championship events at Wimbledon for the first time

J.H. Taylor, who played Dunlop golf balls towards the end his career, wins the British Open for the fifth and last time and 19 years after his first victory

1914   Birth of Albert Slazenger's son, Ralph

1915   Molla Bjurstedt/Mallory, who used Slazenger rackets, wins the first of her eight US Open titles

1916   Slazenger take successful legal action against a Nottingham company that had alleged they were German and should be shut down

US PGA established

1917   First appearance of the Dunlop 'Caddie' in their golf ball advertising

1918   John Letters golf club company is founded

Litesome clothing company founded

1919   Albert Penfold joins Dunlop from the Silvertown Rubber Company and starts work on the Maxfli golf ball

All five titles at Wimbledon won by overseas players for the first time

1920   Tim Hadingham joins Slazenger as managing director

1921   The USGA and the Royal and Ancient Club agree a standard size golf ball measuring 1.62 inches and weighing 1.62 ounces

1922   Dunlop launch the Maxfli golf ball

Slazenger open their first factory in Australia, in Sydney

First Wimbledon to be held at present site, which took two years to prepare and cost £140,000

First Walker Cup match – United States beat Great Britain 8 – 4

1923   Dunlop acquires an interest in the sports equipment manufacturer, F.A. Davis

1923
(cont) Dunlop transfers golf ball production to Fort Dunlop and also starts to make tennis balls in that factory. The Prince of Wales visits the factory and inspects the golf ball line

Tennis ball production is established in the Dunlop factories in Hanau and Montlucon

Arthur Havers wins the British Open with a Maxfli ball

Vincent (Vinnie) Richards, aged 19, later to establish the Dunlop sports business in the USA, makes his first appearance at Wimbledon and loses in the third round to the eventual winner, his fellow American William Johnston

United States beats Britain 7 – 0 in the first Wightman Cup

1924 Dunlop move their sports sales office away from Birmingham for the first time, to Albany Street in London

The first Slazenger office in Canada is opened in Toronto

The US Open Men's singles is played for the first time at Forest Hills

The French 'Four Musketeers' (Jean Borotra, Jacques Brugnon, Henri Cochet and Rene Lacoste) signal the start of their domination of the major tennis championships when Borotra beats Lacoste in the Wimbledon final. Between them they will win 40 Grand Slam singles and doubles titles in the next eight years, and will win the Davis Cup for France between 1927 and 1932

Wimbledon centre court tickets subject to a ballot for the first time

1925 Dunlop Japan start to sell golf and tennis balls imported from the UK

1926 The Honourable F.M.B. (Frank) Fisher and Albert Burden become heavily involved in the management of the Dunlop sports business, which is still located in the F.A. Davis office in Holborn

William Sykes acquire the Jefferies racket making business located in Kentish Town, London

Seventeen year old Don Bradman selects a Sykes 'Roy Kilner' bat as a reward for scoring 300 for his Bowral club in New South Wales. He would use Sykes made bats throughout his career

The first 'unofficial' Ryder Cup match staged at Wentworth – Great Britain beat the United States 13 – 1

1927 Dunlop Sports Company registered as a separate business for the first time

Humphrey and Michael McMaster purchase the Gradidges company

First radio commentary from Wimbledon

First official Ryder Cup between United States and Britain is played at Worcester, Massachusetts – United States won 9 – 2

1928 Dunlop acquire an interest in Gardner Brothers, racket makers based in Waltham Abbey, Essex, launch their first tennis racket range, and introduce a dating scheme for tennis balls. Their sports sales office moves to St. James's House

Sammy Ball becomes the golf ball technical manager at Fort Dunlop

The LTA and ILTF adopt the stitchless, seamed tennis ball

1929 The Dunlop Sports Company acquires the Gardner Brothers business and moves its main office to Waltham Abbey where Guy Proctor begins the process of developing the factory into the world's best known racket plant

In Australia the Barnet Glass tennis ball operation is purchased by Dunlop

In the USA the Dunlop Tire & Rubber Company establishes a sports division with Vinnie Richards as chief executive. The division's first sales office is located in the newly built Empire State Building in New York

Don Bradman signs a contract to use a signature bat made by Sykes

Fred Perry wins the world table tennis championship

1930 In Japan Dunlop start production of golf and tennis balls in Kobe

19 out of 22 players in the Headingley Test between England and Australia use Sykes bats. In that match Don Bradman scores a record 334 and has a series average of 139.14

1931 Slazenger and Gradidges announce a joint buying scheme as a prelude to merger. Michael McMaster becomes joint managing director of Slazengers with Tim Hadingham

William Sykes expand their range of tennis rackets based on their purchase of the Jefferies company

Prince George, later the Duke of Kent, visits William Sykes Horbury factory

1932 Waltham Abbey successfully develops the manufacture of racket frames with a cold bent laminated process to produce and launch the Maxply, which will become the world's most famous tennis racket for the next 50 years

Dunlop golf ball production starts in Australia

Fred Perry switches from Dunlop to Slazenger tennis rackets

The United States win the first Curtis Cup match, played at Wentworth

The attendance at Wimbledon passes the 200,000 mark for the first time

The USGA introduces a new standard ball with 1.68 inch diameter and weighing 1.62 ounces

1933 Fred Perry wins his first Grand Slam title, in the USA

'Buzzer' Hadingham joins Slazenger's export department

Bunny Austin is the first man to wear shorts on the centre court at Wimbledon

Led by Fred Perry, Great Britain beat France in Paris to win the Davis Cup, which will be retained for the next three years

1934 Fred Perry wins the first of his three Wimbledon singles title, and it's a double success for Slazenger rackets as Dorothy Round wins the Ladies championship

Using a new ball developed by Sammy Ball at Fort Dunlop Henry Cotton wins the Open and his second round score of 65 provides the name for its worldwide launch the following year

The first Masters is played at Augusta National and is won by Horton Smith

1935 Gradidges start to make golf clubs

The Dunlop '65' is launched and immediately added to the Dunlop Japan range.

All members of the Great Britain team use the '65' in the Ryder Cup and so does Alf Perry to win the British Open

Gottfried Von Cramm is the first Men's singles finalist at Wimbledon to use a Dunlop racket (a Maxply) but loses to Fred Perry

1936 Sales of Dunlop tennis and golf balls both reach 250,000 dozen for the first time

First time there are more Dunlop rackets at Wimbledon than any other brand and Helen Jacobs is the first Ladies champion to win with Dunlop

William Sykes expands production in Horbury by moving into Albion Mill

1937 Dunlop Sports Company formed in Australia

TV cameras at Wimbledon for the first time

1938 Len Hutton, with his Gradidge bat, scores a record 364 against the Australians at the Oval

The number of golf clubs a golfer could carry in his bag limited to 14

1939 Slazenger open a factory in New Zealand

The Slazenger tennis ball factory in Woolwich is damaged by bombs but carries on

The Australian, Adrian Quist, develops the herringbone sole pattern used for Green Flash tennis shoes

1939–1945 The main Dunlop and Slazenger factories around the world, and in the UK; Fort Dunlop Horbury and Waltham Abbey; switched from production of sports goods to a huge range of products for the services.

1940 Death of Albert Slazenger, and Michael McMaster succeeds him as chairman of Slazenger

Merger of William Sykes and Ayres

1941 The F.A. Davis office and factory in Holborn destroyed in London blitz

Enemy bombs also severely damage the Slazenger and Gradidge factories

Woolwich and the golf ball plant at Fort Dunlop damaged during several raids on Birmingham

The end of golf and tennis ball production at Fort Dunlop

1942 Sykes/Ayres merge with Slazenger/Gradidge to form Slazenger's Ltd

USGA limits golf ball velocity to 250 ft. per second

1946 Slazenger tennis ball production transferred to Barnsley and the rest of Company's UK output concentrated at Horbury

Dunlop golf and tennis ball production begins at the Speke plant on the edge of Liverpool

Dunlop stage their first Masters golf tournament

Slazenger stage the first ever tournament for UK tennis professionals – the winner is Dan Maskell

Victor Barna, 15 times world table tennis champion, joins Dunlop to work in marketing and export sales

Slazenger start golf ball production in Australia

First post war Wimbledon championships – Yvon Petra wins the Men's title and Pauline Betz the Ladies'

1947 Dunlop Japan restarts tennis ball production and Emperor Hirohito visits the Kobe factory

Denis Compton and Bill Edrich score over 7,000 runs for Middlesex and England

1948 Henry Cotton wins the British Open for the third time and fourteen years after his first success at Sandwich

1949 Bill Carlton invents plastic shuttlecocks

Bobby Locke wins the first of his four Open championships using Slazenger clubs and balls

Tennis ball production resumed at Hanau

Gussie Moran wears lace panties at Wimbledon

1950 Bobby Locke sets a record winning score (279) at The Open, which he equals in 1957

1950 (cont) Horbury production of billiard tables and rocking chairs (for Ayres) ends

Slazenger in Canada expand into larger premises at Meritton

Frank Smith becomes general sales manager of the Dunlop sports business

Slazenger establishes a sports and social club in Horbury, which is still thriving

The Ladies Professional Golf Association is established

1951 Dunlop start tennis ball production in South Africa in the Durban tyre plant

Slazenger return to golf ball production with the Horbury made B51 but close down the manufacture of bowls in the same factory

1952 UK wins the Curtis Cup for the first time

1953 Slazenger annual sales reach £2.5 million

Ken Rosewall, with his Slazenger racket, wins the Australian and French Open championships

England beat Australia 1 – 0 to win the Ashes for the first time in 19 years

1954 Jaroslav Drobny, who had been the losing finalist in the 1949 and 1952 Wimbledon Men's finals, is the first to win the title with a Dunlop racket (Between 1951 and 1973 a Dunlop or Slazenger racket, or both, would be used in every Men's final, and in 12 of the Ladies' finals)

Peter Thomson, using Dunlop equipment, wins the first of his five Open Championships (1954/55/56, 1958 and 1965)

The John Letters company starts to make Dunlop golf clubs

The Dunlop Sports Company moves its head office from New Bond Street to Allington House

Arnold Palmer, aged 25, wins the US Amateur Championship and turns professional

1955 Angela Mortimer, who would be the Wimbledon Champion in 1961, wins the French Open with her Maxply

The British Open is shown on live television for the first time and the prize money for the winner is raised to £1,000

1956 Golf ball production resumes at the Kobe factory

Between them Lew Hoad (Wimbledon, Australian and French) and Ken Rosewall (US) win the Grand Slam titles with, respectively, their Dunlop and Slazenger rackets

1957 Dunlop acquire John Letters

Frank Smith becomes General Manager of the Dunlop Sports Company

The Queen Mother visits the Speke factory, including the golf and tennis ball departments, and the Duke of Edinburgh visits the Horbury and Barnsley factories

Lew Hoad wins again at Wimbledon, with Maxply, and Althea Gibson is Slazenger's first Ladies Champion since the end of the war

Slazenger in Canada add the Ping range to their golf assembly unit, which already produces Hogan clubs

Great Britain win the Ryder Cup for the first time in 23 years

1958 Jack Morton takes over from Frank Smith as General Manager of the Dunlop Sports Company

Garfield Sobers scores a Test record 365 not out against Pakistan

Great Britain win the Wightman Cup for the first time in 28 years

As the year ends the Slazenger board accepts the Dunlop takeover bid

1959 Death of Vinnie Richards, who had been in charge of the Dunlop sports business in the USA since its formation in 1929

Maria Bueno wins the first of her three Wimbledon and seven Grand Slam titles

Following the announcement of the Dunlop and Slazenger merger in the UK the same process is applied in Australia and South Africa, in the latter case the new company is named Sports Equipment International

Nineteen years old, and unseeded, Rod Laver reaches the Wimbledon Men's final

Another nineteen year old, Jack Nicklaus, wins the US Amateur Championship

1960 Dunlop acquire the Edgar Sealey fishing tackle business

Dunlop introduce the newly designed 'Flying D' logo

Slazenger beat Dunlop in the Wimbledon and US Men's finals when Neale Fraser beat Rod Laver on both occasions but Laver had been the victor in the Australian Open and would win at Wimbledon in 1961 and 1962

Dunlop open a new golf ball plant in Westminster, South Carolina

Margaret Smith wins the Australian Open, the first of her 62 Grand Slam singles and doubles titles

The larger size American golf ball is used for the first time in a UK event, the Ballantine at Wentworth

1961 Angela Mortimer beats Christine Truman in the first all-British Wimbledon final since 1914 and is the first British winner, with her Maxply, since Dorothy Round had won, with her Slazenger racket, in 1937

Drobny joins the Dunlop Tennis Department

Slazenger acquire Litesome

Number of golfers in USA reaches 10 million

1962 The Slazenger head office in Cannon Street is demolished and they move to Mitcham Road, Croydon

George Carr becomes General Manager of Dunlop Sports Company

Slazenger acquire Pennsylvania Sporting Goods in Philadelphia and establish their own company in USA

Rod Laver wins his first Grand Slam

Arnold Palmer wins the British Open with a record score of 276, which will stand until 1977

The last match between the Gentlemen and Players held at Lord's

1963 Slazenger register their Panther logo and begin to develop a more extensive clothing line

All Dunlop and Slazenger golf ball production concentrated at Speke and all tennis balls at Barnsley

In the USA golf club production starts at the Westminster plant

Arnold Palmer signs to play Dunlop clubs and the 65 in Europe. He also becomes the first player to win $100,000 in a single season on the US PGA Tour

Start of one day cricket with the first Gillette Cup competition

1964 Formation of International Sports Company (ISC) with George Carr as its General Manager. Annual sales of the new group were £7 million

John Letters set up production of Maxfli golf clubs in the Kobe factory in Japan

Jack Nicklaus signs to play Slazenger clubs in Europe

The first World Matchplay Championship at Wentworth is won by **Arnold Palmer in an 'all 65' final with Neil Coles**

1965 Michael McMaster retires and is succeeded by his twin, Humphrey, as Chairman of Slazenger

Dunlop open a golf ball factory in Ireland

Carlton move to a new factory at Saffron Walden

Jonah Barrington wins the first of his six British Open Squash titles

Slazenger in Canada acquire the Raymond Lanctot ski equipment business

On the same day as the Great Train Robbery Peter Thomson wins the last of his five British Opens. He would continue to play in this tournament until 1984

A combined UK, USA and Canadian team develops racket purchasing from Far East sources, mainly Taiwan

1966 Slazenger soccer balls are selected for the 1966 World Cup

Dunlop golf ball factory opened in New Zealand

Carlton start to manufacture badminton rackets

Annual production of golf balls in the USA is estimated to reach 16 million dozen

Jack Nicklaus wins first of this three British Opens

1967 Tony Jacklin wins the Dunlop Masters and scores the only hole in one in the history of the tournament

In Australia the Dunlop and Slazenger sports businesses merge under the Slazenger brand

John Newcombe is the last amateur to win the Wimbledon Men's singles title

The attendance at Wimbledon passes 300,000 for the first time

1968 ISC acquire Carlton, who are now making 11 million shuttlecocks per annum

In the USA Dunlop open a second golf ball plant, at Hartwell in Georgia

Virginia Wade wins the US Open

Colin Cowdrey is the first cricketer to play in 100 tests and Garfield Sobers the first to hit six sixes off an over – against Glamorgan

In Canada Sportlines International formed to combine the Dunlop and Slazenger businesses

The Royal and Ancient Golf Club adopts the larger, 1.68 inches in diameter, golf ball for all British PGA events

The Dupont company's 'Surlyn' cover material is used on more than 80% of all golf balls

Rod Laver and Billie Jean King are the champions at the first 'Open' Wimbledon winning, respectively, £2,000 and £750

1969 Rod Laver wins his second Tennis Grand Slam and collects total prize money of £51,605 during a 32 week period, which includes those four major titles

Tony Jacklin wins the Open

Dunlop sell the Edgar Sealey fishing tackle business

Production of Slazenger soccer balls at Horbury is stopped

Dunlop Germany purchase the Erbacher ski factory

First appearance of metal framed rackets at Wimbledon

1970   Tony Jacklin wins the US Open

Winners of Tennis Grand Slam titles include John Newcombe (Wimbledon), Ken Rosewall (US) and Margaret Court, who wins all four. In the 25 years since the end of the war players using Dunlop and Slazenger rackets won more than 80 Grand Slam titles

The tie break is introduced in tennis

Jack Nicklaus is the first to win more than $1 million on the US PGA Tour

1971   ISC receive the Queen's Award to Industry

Gary Player signs with Dunlop to play the 65 in Europe – he was already playing Dunlop balls and clubs in USA

The two piece golf ball first appears on the scene and will soon become dominant

Opening of the first squash court with a glass back wall

1972   Dunlop open a second golf ball plant in the UK, at Normanton

Virginia Wade wins the Australian Open

Because of a dispute between the ILTF and World Championship Tennis many of the professional players did not appear at Wimbledon

1973   With ISC sales increased to £16 million George Carr retires and is succeeded by Findlay Picken

In Japan Dunlop Sports Enterprise is established as a separate division for Tournament management and promotion

Wimbledon is again disrupted by a dispute between the players and the game's ruling bodies, and 81 of the leading professionals withdraw

Composite racket frames appear at Wimbledon for the first time

1974   In USA tennis ball production starts at the Hartwell plant

Bjorn Borg wins his first Grand Slam title, the French Open

The larger, 1.68 golf ball used for the first time at the British Open

1975   Dunlop open a golf ball plant in Malaysia

The Australian Blade iron launched in USA

Wimbledon prize money increases to £114,875

1976   The company makes its first two piece ball at Speke

Slazenger opens its Batley warehouse to handle the growing clothing line

Humphrey McMaster retires and is succeeded, as chairman of Slazenger, by 'Buzzer' Hadingham

Slazenger introduce their graphite 'Phantom' racket

Jack Nicklaus is the leading money winner on the US Tour with $226,438. Seve Ballesteros leads on the Europe Tour with £39,504

The USGA introduces its Overall Distance Standard setting the maximum distance of 296 yards for balls hit by their mechanical hitting machine

1977   Dunlop begin development work on the injection moulded racket

Slazenger announce link up with Puma for UK marketing of clothing and footwear

Virginia Wade is Wimbledon champion in the Queen's Silver Jubilee year

Wimbledon prize money rises to £218,385 and John McEnroe, aged 18, is the first unseeded qualifier to reach the semi-finals

Ball girls in action at Wimbledon for the first time

Kerry Packer attracts 66 of the World's leading players to his World Series Cricket

1978   Production starts at the Philippines tennis ball plant

Opening of Dunlop and Slazenger sourcing office in Hong Kong

Geoffrey Boycott signs for Slazenger

New Research and Development Centre opens at Horbury

Sumitomo Rubber Industries acquire a majority holding in Dunlop Japan

Total prize money on the US PGA Tour exceeds $10 million for the first time

1979   Closure of both Speke and Waltham Abbey

Seve Ballesteros wins his first Major, the British Open, and is the youngest ever champion

Fuzzy Zoeller wins the Masters at Augusta on his first appearance there

The Dunlop Germany Erbacher factory makes graphite rackets

Death of Humphrey McMaster

Great Britain and Ireland joined by Europe to contest the Ryder Cup

1980   Dunlop launch the 150G injection moulded racket

The DDH golf ball is launched in the USA

Seve Ballesteros, at 23, is the youngest winner of the Augusta Masters

Bjorn Borg beats John McEnroe in one of Wimbledon's greatest Men's finals

1981   John McEnroe signs for Dunlop and beats Borg in the Wimbledon final

The DDH golf ball launched in the UK

The 150G racket wins the Design Council Award

For the first time the number of wooden rackets used at Wimbledon is overtaken by the total of graphite and metal frames

1982 The DDH golf ball wins the Design Council Award and is launched in Japan

Dunlop launch the 200G injection moulded racket

The last Dunlop Masters golf tournament is held at the St. Pierre club

Dunlop open a new distribution centre in Wakefield

Sumitomo Rubber Industries acquire Dunlop France, including its sports business

Alan Finden-Crofts is appointed director of the Dunlop consumer businesses including Dunlop Sports Company and Slazenger

Wimbledon prize money is close to £600,000

The world's first all transparent squash court was used for the World Masters in Leicester, greatly increasing TV coverage of the sport

1983 John McEnroe switches from his Maxply McEnroe wooden racket to the 200G

Creation of Dunlop Slazenger International, which includes Dunlop Footwear

Retirement of 'Buzzer' Hadingham 50 years after he joined Slazenger

1984 The John Letters golf club business sold back to the Letters family

Dunlop and Slazenger players continue to capture major prizes – John McEnroe wins Wimbledon and the US Open, Seve Ballesteros wins the British Open and Fuzzy Zoeller the US Open

Dunlop in Japan becomes 100% Japanese owned

Sir Michael Edwardes becomes chairman of Dunlop and as part of his restructuring of the company gives worldwide control of all sports operations to Dunlop Slazenger International, including a newly established North American region

Wimbledon prize money moves close to £1.5 million

1985 BTR acquires Dunlop

The 200G receives the Queen's Award for Technological Achievement

Sandy Lyle, playing with Dunlop equipment, is the first British winner of the Open since Tony Jacklin in 1969

After the USA's 28 year reign Europe win the Ryder Cup

1986 Establishment of David Geoffrey and Associates as the Slazenger Golf business in the USA

Closure of the Horbury factory

Yellow Slazenger balls used at Wimbledon for the first time. The Men's Championship played for the 100th time – Dunlop or Slazenger rackets used in 65 of the finals

Wimbledon attendance passes 400,000 for the first time and prize money is more than £2 million

1987 Patrick Austen succeeds Alan Finden-Crofts as chief executive of Dunlop Slazenger International

Steffi Graf, with the 200G, wins her first Grand Slam title, the French Open

Laura Davies is the first British winner of the US Women's Open

Europe win the Ryder Cup in the USA for the first time in the 61 year history of the contest

Ian Woosnam is the first golfer to win more than £1 million in a year

1988 Dunlop Slazenger head office moves from Croydon to Leatherhead

Steffi Graf wins the Tennis Grand Slam and Olympic Gold

Another 'big year' for Dunlop and Slazenger golfers – Sandy Lyle is the first British winner of the Masters, Seve Ballesteros wins the British Open and Curtis Strange the US Open, as well as being the first to win more than $1 million on the US Tour in a year

At Wimbledon it is the first year ever no player has used a wooden racket

1989 Dunlop Slazenger changes from regional to product management

Curtis Strange again wins the US Open

The manufacture of Dunlop and Slazenger golf clubs in the UK stops

1990 The company's sourcing operation in the Far East is expanded and the regional office moves from Hong Kong to Kuala Lumpur

Maxfli is established as the lead brand for the golf business

1991 Ian Woosnam wins the Masters

1992 Closure of the Hartwell tennis ball plant and transfer of its equipment to the Philippines

National Golf Foundation estimates the USA has 25 million golfers and that golf ball production has reached 45 million dozen per annum

1993 Patrick Austen moves to Liberty plc and for a year the company operates without a chief executive

Stuart Surridge acquired

Bernhard Langer wins the Masters and is the eighth European to do so during the last 14 years. Jose-Maria Olazabal will make it nine the following year

1993 (cont) The Dunlop sports operation in France becomes part of Dunlop Slazenger

This is the year of the 100th Ladies Championship at Wimbledon – Dunlop and Slazenger rackets have been used in 51 of the 85 for which the racket details have been recorded

1994 David Jacobs becomes chief executive of Dunlop Slazenger

Tim Henman, at the age of 21, makes his first appearance in the Wimbledon Men's singles

1995 David Jacobs stages the 'Way Ahead' conference, which charts the future for the business

Steffi Graf continues her winning ways with the 200G, taking the Wimbledon, French and US titles

Dunlop Footwear operations are transferred to licensees

The Dunlop Japan factory in Kobe is virtually destroyed by an earthquake and golf ball production there comes to an end. New plants are brought on stream later in the year

Early discussions take place with Cinven regarding a management buy out of Dunlop Slazenger

1996 The Dunlop Slazenger management buy out from BTR is completed early in the year

The greatly expanded Philippines tennis ball plant comes on stream

Sir Michael Perry becomes chairman of the newly established Dunlop Slazenger board

The company's organisation structure is changed from product to functional Management

Having won three successive US Amateur Championships, Tiger Woods turns professional and wins three of the seven Tour events he enters

1997 The Dunlop Slazenger head office moves from Leatherhead to Camberley

The Sportlines operation in Canada is absorbed into the Greenville based USA organisation

The Maxfli urethane covered Revolution golf ball is launched

Tiger Woods, at 21, becomes the youngest ever Masters champion

Wimbledon has a new record attendance of 436,351

1998 Philip Parnell succeeds David Jacobs as chief executive

The Westminster plant takes over the supply of Maxfli golf balls to the Australian company

Tim Henman reaches the semi finals at Wimbledon and will do so again in 1999, 2001 and 2002

1999 The Puma UK business, which was first operated by Slazenger in 1977, returns to its German owner

The Dunlop, Maxfli and Slazenger operations in North America are streamlined and concentrated into Dunlop Slazenger Group, Americas

Steffi Graf wins the French Open – her 21st major singles title – and retires

Wimbledon attendance hits a new high of 457,069 and the prize money passes the £7.5 million mark

2000 The Normanton golf ball plant is closed

Wimbledon stages its Parade of Champions when 64 singles and multiple doubles winners were presented on the Centre Court. 27 of those champions had used Dunlop or Slazenger rackets

2001 A licensing agreement signed with TaylorMade-adidas for the distribution of Maxfli and Slazenger golf products

2002 The Barnsley and Hanau tennis ball plants closed and all production concentrated in the Philippines factory, which has become the most versatile and modern in the industry

Wimbledon and Slazenger celebrate 100 years of Slazenger balls being used at this great event

A licensing agreement signed with Resilience Capital Partners of Cleveland for Slazenger golf in North America

2003 As has been the case for nearly 10 years, Slazenger cricket bats and other equipment highly visible throughout the Summer and especially when used by leading players on both sides during the England and South Africa Test series

The Slazenger 'S' symbol previously seen on the racket strings of such players as Bjorn Borg, John Newcombe, Ken Rosewall and Margaret Court, reappears at Wimbledon on Tim Henman's racket

The company's new focus on the Dunlop brand is confirmed by the launch of new golf and tennis ranges, including a urethane covered 65u golf ball and a completely new 200G racket

John McEnroe endorses the Dunlop tennis ball and racket range

TaylorMade-Adidas purchase the Maxfli golf brand

As Wimbledon attendance moves towards 500,000 and prize money well over £9 million the winners of leading events on both the US and European Golf Tours receive cheques for £1 million or more

2004 Sports World International acquire Dunlop Slazenger

INTRODUCTION

Today's Dunlop Slazenger Group of worldwide sports equipment businesses and brands is the 21st century embodiment of nearly 150 years presence on the playing fields and major sporting arenas of the world. The foundation of this heritage was laid in the 100 years between 1810 and 1910, when its far-sighted founders were quick to see the enormous potential of the growing demand for the equipment required to enjoy the ever widening variety of indoor and outdoor games then being devised to occupy the available leisure time.

In those early years, and long before the 37$^1/_2$ hour working week with four weeks annual holiday, the majority of the population had much less time for leisure and sport, but by the end of the 19th century many of the major sports had become formally organised into associations with governing bodies and rule making responsibilities. And by then they were attracting many thousands of participants as well as hundreds of thousands of spectators.

The 1860s saw the first moves to establish what was to become the Football Association, and the first cup final was played at the Oval in 1872, when two thousand saw the Wanderers beat the Royal Engineers 1 – 0. The Lawn Tennis Association was formed in 1888, which was eleven years after the first championship staged at The All England Croquet Club in Wimbledon with twenty-two entrants competing for the men's singles title and a twenty-five guinea prize presented by *The Field* magazine. The spread of golf had begun to gather momentum in the 18th century, when the first local clubs were formed, including, in 1754, the Royal and Ancient at St. Andrews, which in 1919 was to become the supreme authority on the rules of the game. The pace of that growth is reflected by the increase in the number of clubs in the UK from 17 in 1850 to 2330 by 1900. The game had spread to the USA in the 1880s where the United States Golf Association was formed in 1889.

The 18th century had also seen the real beginning of cricket in the form in which it is played today. During the 19th century the Marylebone Cricket Club, even then located at Lord's, drew up a new set of laws which gave the game a formal structure and was the platform for subsequent revisions. The county championship was properly established in 1873 and the first test match with Australia was played in Melbourne in 1877.

In 1863, forty years after William Webb Ellis is reported as having picked up the football at Rugby School, there were twenty clubs in the London area

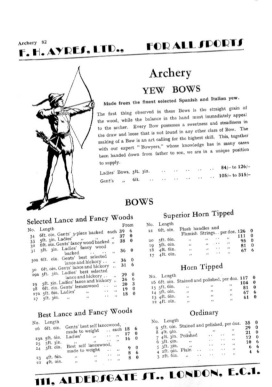

A typical entry from an Ayres catalogue in 1938 with the emphasis on their archery range

and the Rugby Football Union was founded in the Pall Mall restaurant in Cockspur Street, London. The first home international matches were played in the ten years from 1871 when England's home ground was either the Oval or Blackheath.

It's likely that table tennis began in the 1870s, as a miniaturised version of the lawn tennis game then being developed for outdoor play, and F. H. Ayres, eventually to become part of the Slazenger grouping of companies, offered equipment for the game in an 1884 catalogue.

Squash was being played at Harrow in 1850, though it was 1928 before the Squash Rackets Association was formed. The first croquet sets were made by John Jaques in 1857, the Hockey Association was founded in

Bat making at Horbury in the 1950s – left to right Brian Hepworth, Don Ward (who made Don Bradman's bats), Joe Parkinson and the actor, Michael Rennie

1886, and the Badminton Association in 1893. The origins of bowls can be traced back for more than a thousand years, and Sir Francis Drake was certainly familiar with the game in 1588, but it took until 1849 to set down the first rules of the game for level greens, and it was 1873 before the first crown green championship was held in Blackpool. Archery, which as the bow and arrow had been a thread through history for thousands of years, for the most part as a hunting or battlefield weapon, became an official competitive sport in 1844 and in 1861 the Grand National Archery Society was formed.

It is at least reasonable to think that in these early days sports equipment manufacturers based in the UK would have been able to take some advantage from the fact so many of the associations being formed to organise all these games, and, frequently to provide specifications for the equipment to be used, were also located in England or Scotland. It is certainly clear that the rapid development and expansion of these and other new leisure pursuits caught the attention of the companies that would eventually evolve into Dunlop Slazenger. Appropriately archery, the sport with probably the longest history, became a particular speciality for the F. H. Ayres company, which was established in Clerkenwell in 1810 and was, by some distance, the oldest of the four main businesses that would become Slazengers Ltd. The other three were Gradidges, founded in Woolwich in 1870, William Sykes of Horbury in Yorkshire, which started by producing soccer balls in 1880, and Slazenger et Fils, which was first registered in 1881 as a manufacturer of gaiters and leggings with premises in Manchester, but moved two years later to a new office and factory at Laurence Pountney Hill near Cannon Street in the City of London.

While these companies were obviously in the vanguard of those quick to see the opportunities developing during the Victorian formative years of popular sports, the Dunlop Company, founded in Dublin in 1889 as the Dunlop Pneumatic Tyre Company Limited, was not quite so quick off the mark. Not surprisingly it was initially preoccupied with the explosion of motorised transport but it did take its first steps into the sports market when it started golf ball production in the corner of a Birmingham tyre factory in 1909. However, once the upheaval of the first world war had been overcome, its rapid worldwide expansion, and great strength in rubber technology, provided the basis for a hugely important and innovative worldwide source of golf and tennis balls, as well as a wide range of other sports products.

While there may be a perception at the start of the 21st century that social and business environments are facing an increasingly frantic pace of change, it is easy to forget the scale and rate of change during the last 150 years. In many ways those earlier changes were more radical than those more recently experienced and made possible the increasing sophistication of life at the start of the new millennium.

When F. H. Ayres started to make games and sports equipment in 1810, his workforce would have relied almost entirely on relatively simple, hand-operated tools. Their correspondence and invoices would have been hand-written and their customer deliveries, mainly in the London area, would have been made either on foot or in horsedrawn vehicles. The battle of Trafalgar had been fought only five years earlier and Waterloo was still five years ahead. George III was king and the throne would be occupied by George IV and William IV before Queen Victoria was crowned in 1837.

Her reign was to be one of the most remarkable in English history and spanned a period of change which is unlikely ever to be matched. The country was just beginning to recover from the Napoleonic wars, was starting to reap the economic benefits of the Industrial Revolution, and was laying the foundations of the British Empire. Against that momentous background which, as has already been shown, included the emergence of a large number of now formally organised sports, the founding fathers of the Dunlop Slazenger companies began to build the new businesses, which would become synonymous with the growth of the games that would ultimately be played and watched by so many millions around the world. It can also be claimed, with considerable substance, that their ingenuity, skill and vision contributed very significantly to both the growth and enjoyment of those games.

Even as late as the 1880s, when both Slazengers and Sykes had just begun in the sports business and were following in the footsteps of the well-established Ayres and Gradidge companies, working conditions were still relatively primitive. A brochure published by Slazengers in 1931, to commemorate their first fifty years, noted that 'In the year of grace of 1881 there were no tube trains, no wireless, no motors, no aeroplanes. Electric lights and telephones were in their infancy, and it is very hard to visualize now the inconveniences and difficulties of organising a business at that time.' They drew on contemporary writers to describe the City of London at that time as 'A fat and sleepy city, a city of riches and veiled splendour, a city cloaking its gold guineas in shadows of dim lights, a capital of aristocrats and red carpets.' It was an environment where 'The weekend holiday as we know it did not exist' and where 'Businessmen remained in the City on a Saturday until one or two o'clock whilst their clerks worked for hours later.' Thus 'In these circumstances and under these conditions Slazengers commenced the making and selling of sports goods in 1881.' It is true the business did start trading in 1881, but two years later it transferred from Manchester to 'The City of riches and veiled splendour.'

The growth and spread of the British Empire during the 19th century was to be an immensely important factor for these new businesses, and was probably even more crucial in shaping the development of Dunlop sports operations in the first half of the 20th century. Although the Sykes and Slazenger

1963

1967

1978

1996

The four stages in the evolution of the Panther logo between 1965 and 1996 companies had been quick to see the potential for sports equipment in overseas countries, the Dunlop policy of establishing multi-product factories, usually based around the initial tyre plant, meant that the company was frequently the first to introduce large scale and efficient golf and tennis ball production in countries like Australia, South Africa, Canada, France and Japan where demand for those products was expanding as rapidly as in the UK.

The steady expansion of both the sports and the companies whose products fuelled these new passions was abruptly halted by the first world war. By then Dunlop was beginning to recognise the value of its relatively new golf ball operation as an extension of its tyre business, but it was obvious to the management that, at least temporarily, it had become much less important. However, production did not stop completely as it was decreed, presumably by the appropriate Government departments, that golf ball manufacture should continue on a limited scale because officers of the army and Royal Flying Corps found that, when the opportunity offered, a game of golf provided welcome relaxation. A contemporary account recorded that 'Dunlop golf balls were to be seen wherever our armies were.'

That particular Dunlop contribution to the 1914-18 war effort, however important for the morale of the golfing officers, would have

John Boyd Dunlop

been relatively small compared with the flow of military items pouring from their own, and from the Slazenger, Sykes and Gradidge factories. The wide range of skills they had by then developed applied not only to virtually every type of ball for every sport but also, and more importantly in relation to supplying the military, to woodworking and leather. The Sykes company had considerable previous experience of supplying the British army as they had been official Government contractors during the Boer War.

Although the war largely halted all production of sports equipment the foundations of these new, worldwide businesses had been laid before Europe was overwhelmed by hostilities. Dunlop had already accumulated five years experience of making golf balls and was rapidly acquiring a strong market position. The Slazenger factories in the City and Woolwich were producing top quality tennis rackets and balls, as well as a huge range of other items, and they had secured the Wimbledon ball adoption (from Ayres) as early as 1902. Gradidge bats were market leaders and the huge Ayres range covered every known leisure pastime. Sykes were expanding rapidly from the base of a much larger factory they had built in Horbury before the turn of the century, and both they and Slazengers had established thriving overseas markets, most notably in South Africa, Australia and North America. An early Slazenger gutta percha ball had not only been used by Harold Hilton to win the 1897 Open at Hoylake, but also by Ruth Underhill to win the 1899 USA Women's Amateur Championship in Philadelphia.

Between the wars, and developing steadily from these early foundations, the founder companies of the group, and the rapidly enlarging Dunlop sports division, combined their separate expansions with a series of mergers and acquisitions, which enabled them to establish dominant positions in their key markets of golf, tennis and cricket. And through all that period, despite the impact of the severe worldwide trade recession, all these sports continued to attract more and more players and spectators. In 1932 the attendance at the Wimbledon championships passed 200,000 for the first time. Just under one million watched the 1937 test series between Australia and England when Don Bradman was so dominant with his Sykes bat. In 1930 there were 1000 entrants for the US Open Golf championship compared with the eleven who had contested the first at Newport, Rhode Island in 1895. The winner of that first US title, an English professional, Horace Rawlins, took home $335. In that same year Frank Slazenger had started to sell golf clubs in the USA from his New York base.

While sport was becoming an increasingly large part of everyday life, and being helped in this direction as films, radio and television extended their coverage of the major events – as early as 1938 the cup final, the Derby and the first rugby union international appeared on TV – so war clouds again gathered around the world. In 1932 Japan invaded China, by 1936 the Spanish civil war was raging, and 1939 brought the start of the second world war. Once again the Dunlop and Slazenger factories 'went to war' and by now their much larger plants around the world had a significantly bigger part to play than twenty years earlier. And this time they were right in the front line as bombs fell on the Fort Dunlop factory in Birmingham, severely damaging the golf ball department, and also badly damaging the Gradidge and Slazenger plants in London. In the case of Slazenger the virtually complete loss of its Woolwich factory to German incendiaries was the major factor in bringing about the 1942 merger with William Sykes and the subsequent development of their large-scale manufacturing base in Yorkshire centred on Barnsley and Horbury.

The fifty years from the end of the war, that provided the timescale for the transition of Dunlop and Slazenger from five separately distinguishable businesses and brands into the single private company that became the Dunlop Slazenger Group, also covered a period in the evolution of sport quite as dramatic as the earlier 19th century in the scale of participation. Then the very few and often elite expanded to the millions of players and spectators either engaged in or watching the major sports for the first time. Now the change was of a different kind involving even greater awareness of the leading sports, and, more radically, the injection of huge amounts of money into their promotion and presentation, including unimagined rewards for the leading players. These factors were to provide both opportunity and challenge for Dunlop Slazenger.

An early golf ball wrapping machine at Fort Dunlop in 1928

During the immediate post-war years massive change was neither evident nor imagined. Bradman, Hutton and Compton again wielded their Sykes and Gradidge bats as they returned to Lord's, Headingley and the Sydney Cricket Ground. Yorkshire won both the 1939 and 1946 county championship titles. Thirty-two of the entrants for the 1946 Wimbledon men's singles title had played in the first round seven years earlier and John Bromwich won both the 1939 and 1946 Australian Opens. Three winners of the golf majors in the first few years after the war had also been winners just before it started. Most notably Henry Cotton's last two British Open titles, won with Dunlop balls, spanned an eleven year gap between 1937 and 1948. And to add another Dunlop Slazenger star, the incomparable Joe Davis, who promoted Sykes products, won both the 1939 and 1946 billiards world championships.

Cricket in England and Wales still recognized amateur Gentlemen and paid Players. Tennis, apart from a small group of famous champions and coaches, who had turned professional, was an amateur game and the winner of the

The golfers – an 1820 print

main golf titles still only banked a few thousand pounds. But encouraged by the rapid growth of TV and other media coverage, attendances at most major events were rising steadily. Golf courses hosting the majors were rapidly improving their crowd handling techniques and with the Dunlop Masters Tournament leading the way in the UK, laying down temporary roadways for cars. It wasn't very long before Wimbledon was attracting 400,000 spectators, more than twice the pre-war numbers.

As the media spotlight intensified, and millions worldwide watched the great sporting occasions, many for the first time, so the promotional potential of sport exploded and began to attract ever larger investments, initially in the events themselves but soon also in the leading performers. The spectacular rise in the earnings of the leading players, combining prize money and endorsement contracts, has been well documented but just two examples with Dunlop Slazenger connections help to make the point. Under the headline '£1000 a week sports stars' the Slazenger sports newsletter reported, with obvious amazement, in 1970, that 'it was nice work if you can get it' when 'in just thirty weeks of competition Rod Laver, and his Dunlop Maxply racket, had won no less then £51,605 in prize money'. That included the four wins of his second Grand Slam, which today would bring closer to £2 million. And in 1987 a lifelong user of Dunlop and Maxfli golf equipment, Ian Woosnam, became the first golfer to win more than £1 million in a single year – only ten years after Jack Nicklaus had won just £150,000 as the leading money winner on the US PGA tour. In that same year, the top money winner on the European tour, Severiano Ballesteros, had won £39,000.

Against that background the stage was set after the war for the still separate Dunlop and Slazenger sports companies to build on the powerful operations they had established by the end of the 1930s. Dunlop moved its main UK manufacturing base for golf and tennis balls from Fort Dunlop to the Speke factory on the outskirts of Liverpool, which had only just stopped turning out Halifax bombers. Within the next few years ball plants were established, or recommissioned, in North America, Japan, Australia, South Africa, France and Germany, most of which were located within tyre factories operated by the local Dunlop subsidiary companies. At the same time the company's Waltham Abbey factory in Essex, freed from virtually one hundred per cent concentration on the war effort, rapidly expanded and modernised its racket production, including the now all conquering Dunlop Maxply that was to dominate so many Grand Slam and other major tournaments for the next thirty years. Its only serious rival during that period was the Slazenger 'Challenge' racket.

While the Dunlop post-war momentum was gathering pace the final stages of the combination of Slazenger, Gradidge, Sykes and Ayres was taking shape to form, as described in that group's 1946 brochure to celebrate this new strength, 'the final combination of all these resources and experience in one great joint undertaking'. Although this judgement was to prove premature, in terms of subsequent smaller acquisitions it certainly did bring together four of the most famous and longest established UK sports manufacturers, who between them had provided an enormous range of products for all forms of sports and leisure activities for well over one hundred years. And, at the same time, contributed significantly to the development of these activities both in the UK and overseas.

In 1959 that Slazenger led group was acquired by the Dunlop Rubber Company but continued to operate as Slazengers Limited as a very definite competitor for the sports division of their common parent. In 1964 Dunlop set up the International Sports Company as an umbrella organisation to co-ordinate the activities of its two main companies together with a number of smaller businesses operating in specific sectors of the sport market. These included the Edgar Sealey fishing tackle business in Redditch, the John Letters golf club company in Glasgow, the Litesome business for athletic sports and clothing, and, in 1968, the Carlton badminton business. In 1977 a Slazenger initiative secured the UK distribution rights for the Puma brand of sports footwear and sports bags, which was later extended by a licence to market that famous brand on a UK designed clothing line.

Arnold Palmer tries his new Dunlop clubs in 1964 after signing to play them, and the 65, in Europe

The International Sports Company organisation, which was primarily a combination of these UK-based companies, and a very substantial export operation servicing both overseas distributors and the overseas, locally managed, Dunlop sports businesses, was unchanged until the dramatic period covering the end of 1984 and the early part of 1985. These months first saw a major restructuring of the struggling Dunlop company, led by Sir Michael Edwardes, and then the BTR takeover of what had by then become a largely non-tyre operation.

For the first time all the Dunlop-owned sports businesses were pulled together to form Dunlop Slazenger International Limited with a single management team responsible for worldwide sports operations. This single responsibility replaced the previous mixture of the International Sports Company and the overseas operations reporting to the local Dunlop territory management. Whereas the International Sports Company had certainly been responsible for liaising with the overseas operations, and had provided a degree of technical and marketing leadership, the newly established single leadership and responsibility had a crucial capability, for the first time, to direct all the avail-

Back Row (Left to Right): Goran Ivanisevic, Fred Stolle, Ken Rosewall, Kurt Nielsen, Peter Fleming, Pam Shriver, Helena Sukova, Hana Mandlikova, Darlene Hard, Gigi Fernandez, Natasha Zvereva, Rosie Casals, Frew McMillan, Owen Davidson, Tony Roche, Ken Fletcher, Bob Hewitt, Ken McGregor. Middle Row (Left to Right): Michael Stich, Stefan Edberg, Pat Cash, Boris Becker, John McEnroe, Bjorn Borg, Jan Kodes, Stan Smith, John Newcombe, Manuel Santana, Roy Emerson, Rod Laver, Neale Fraser, Alex Olmedo, Ashley Cooper, Tony Trabert, Frank Sedgman, Dick Savitt, Budge Patty. Front Row (Left to Right): Bunny Austin, Sidney Wood, Jana Novotna, Conchita Martinez, Martina Navratilova, Chris Evert, Ann Jones, Margaret Court, Maria Bueno, Pauline Betz-Addie, HRH The Duchess of Gloucester (Honorary President LTA), Shirley Fry-Irvin, Angela Mortimer, Billie Jean King, Evonne Goolagong-Cawley, Virginia Wade, Steffi Graf, Bob Falkenberg, Ted Schroeder, Vic Seixas, Jaroslav Drobny.

able worldwide resources and to co-ordinate the combined skills and experience of a very strong group of managers in all the key functions, notably research and development, manufacturing and marketing. At this time these resources included more than 3000 personnel operating twelve factories and two research centres, as well as a very large sales and distribution organisation in Europe, North America and the Far East. For reasons related mainly to overseas regional management accountability, the new Dunlop Slazenger International operation was also responsible for manufacturing and marketing the famous Dunlopillo foam and bedding brand in Thailand and Indonesia, where the two product lines operated in shared facilities. The international spread of the new operation was not as complete as it had been in the past because the parent company's difficulties had led to the divestment of several of its major overseas units, including the sports elements, in Australia, New Zealand, Japan and France.

The newly-formed Dunlop Slazenger International marketed four main brands – Dunlop, Slazenger, Maxfli and Carlton – and in the UK not only continued to operate the Puma distributorship and licence, but also became responsible for the long established Dunlop Footwear Company. The new sports 'conglomerate' generated sales close to £300 million. The Dunlop and Slazenger sports operations that continued under the direction of their new owners in those countries from which the parent company had withdrawn, were selling another £400 million of clothing and equipment, and a developing licensing business, based in the UK, would soon generate worldwide sales of equipment, footwear and clothing close to £100 million. An important feature of this new, truly international, organisation, involving both the new Dunlop Slazenger and the locally owned overseas sports businesses, was the considerable amount of continued technical and marketing co-operation, which provided a substantial degree of uniform brand and product presentation around the world.

Dunlop Slazenger had become a BTR-owned business in March, 1985 and would remain as a major element of that company's group of consumer product activities for the next eleven years. Contrary to a certain amount of apprehension among Dunlop Slazenger employees, BTR, which was overwhelm-

The 2000 Parade of Wimbledon Champions – No fewer then 27 of those pictured in Wimbledon's Parade of Champions in 2000 had played Dunlop or Slazenger rackets during their careers

ingly oriented towards industrial product manufacture and marketing, injected considerable management and investment resources into the business. The BTR style, which was to allow the managers of each of its business units, who were expected to be the best judges of how to succeed in their own particular markets, to run their operations to meet objectives and targets agreed on an annual basis. The key, and controlling factor in this approach was the stringent level of financial control applied to each business, based on a detailed monthly reporting system.

Within this framework Dunlop Slazenger sales grew by well over 50% during the next ten years with the main increase by product in the Golf market, and by region in North America and the Far East. A key factor was the new owner's willingness, and ability, to invest substantial capital sums in an overdue modernisation of manufacturing plant, again primarily in the Golf sector and in the main golf ball plant in North America. Although they were also prepared to agree to a higher level of promotional expenditure than had been possible in the latter years of Dunlop ownership, this was to become an area of increasing pressure for the business as competitors in the sports equipment and clothing markets around the world hugely increased their media and player contract spending levels, especially the latter. Nevertheless, evidence of the BTR view of the importance of its sports and leisure business was the prominence it gave to its activities and successes, most notably in its corporate advertising and annual reports. This would suggest it is not inconceiv-

Peter Alliss – always a great supporter of Slazenger

able that what had been essentially a hugely successful industrial conglomerate relished the 'glamour' provided by the presence of its sports products on the world's biggest sporting stages.

In the mid-1990s BTR's strategic policy moved to a focus on its core industrial businesses, which meant that Dunlop Slazenger was one of a number of operations, including all their other consumer product companies, to be divested. During the second half of 1995 intensive negotiations took place between BTR and the venture capitalist, Cinven, to secure a management buy out of the business. These negotiations were complicated by the intricate structure of the numerous individual Dunlop Slazenger companies around the world, including several with local partners, but were eventually concluded in February, 1996.

Since the MBO the business has completed a major restructuring and rationalisation programme, which was largely driven by the urgent need to create a much simpler and more market-oriented organisation than that bequeathed by the Dunlop and BTR years. The most significant steps in this programme have been the sale of the Maxfli golf brand to the TaylorMade–adidas Group, and the licensing of the Slazenger brand for sales of golf products in North America, the UK and Asia Pacific. In both cases Dunlop Slazenger will continue as the golf ball supplier from its plant in Westminster, South Carolina. These moves allowed the Group to focus on a smaller, less complex brand portfolio, which has the particular benefit of creating the opportunity for a powerful redevelopment of its classic brands in the worldwide sports market. This positioning for the future has been given an enormous boost by the February, 2004 acquisition of the company by Sports World International, who have announced their commitment to relaunching the Dunlop and Slazenger brands.

This brief review of the organisational history of the business from its variety of beginnings to its current position, and of some of the background influences, during nearly two hundred years, will be expanded as the stories of the individual companies unfold.

These separate accounts will look at a number of the most important individuals who shaped the growth of the total company, at the extraordinary scope of the international element of the business, at products which achieved worldwide and enduring success, and at some of the world's greatest ever sportsmen and sportswomen who enjoyed enormous success with these products.

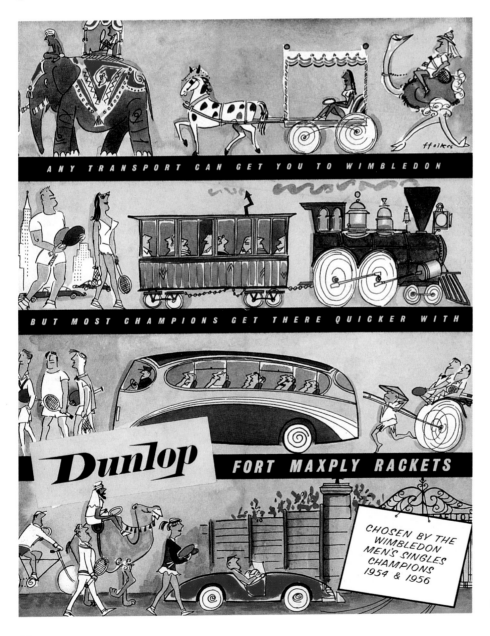

A Dunlop racket advert in 1957

SLAZENGER

Ralph Slazenger, the older of the two
brothers who founded the business

THE SLAZENGER COMPANIES

Ralph Slazenger, the elder son of one of the two brothers to found the Slazenger sports business in 1881, once described it as 'rather a small, friendly company, despite its international operation.' He also reflected that his father, Albert, 'had an excellent eye for selecting splendid agents to represent us around the globe, which tended to give the impression that we were a very large organisation, but we were not.'

Several elements of that assessment were particularly appropriate. It certainly never became a giant corporation, and it is clear it always was a 'friendly' company blessed with a powerful combination of a family feeling amongst its employees and a huge enthusiasm for all things sporting. It is definitely true that from its very earliest beginnings both the Slazenger brothers, Ralph as well as Albert, were very alert to the huge overseas potential for sports goods and their ability to select those 'splendid agents around the globe' turned that potential into solid business. One of those agents was their own brother, Frank, who established a golf agency in New York before the end of the 19th century.

Many of those agents became close friends of both the Slazengers themselves and the managers involved with the export business, and so joined 'the Family'. And that skill in building lasting and personal relationships, which also served the business very well, extended to many of the players who used the company's products, and who still recall their association with Slazenger with considerable affection. Peter Alliss, who had a particularly close relationship with the company, and has vivid memories of many of its people he knew well over thirty years ago, confirms that thought with the recent comment, 'My times with Slazenger were always happy and they looked after me very well.'

In the 115 years between the company's foundation in 1881 and the 1996 management buy out of Dunlop Slazenger from BTR, the Slazenger business has had its ups and downs. It had to endure two world wars – the second bringing destruction to its main factories – it had to work through a long period of trade depression in the 1930s, and it had to deal with the impact of the Dunlop takeover in 1959. Nevertheless as a sports brand it had maintained, through all of that, a sufficiently strong and favourable presence to feature prominently in the thinking of the new owner/management team that began to plan the future of Dunlop Slazenger from 1996 onwards.

One of the key objectives of the new team was the re-definition and re-launch of all the company's principal brands. This underlined the fact they were aware they should play to the strength of one of its most valuable assets, specifically the brands Dunlop, Slazenger, Maxfli and Carlton. Of these four, Slazenger stood out as the senior brand with its well over one hundred years focus on purely sports and leisure activities. So began the process of restoring Slazenger to the position that Peter Alliss has observed it had achieved before and after the second world war. 'It was,' he says, 'simply THE brand for most sporting equipment and its strength was quite enormous.'

What follows will describe how it reached such a powerful position and also why, for a period, it lost some of its lustre. What is interesting to note now is that the 1996 management team took the view that the brand image they wished to project for their Slazenger asset, essentially one of style and quality appealing to true sportsmen and women, was very largely a re-statement of a heritage and customer perception established one hundred years earlier by Albert and Ralph Slazenger. As recently as 1981 a press release to mark the centenary of the business celebrated the fact that 'Slazenger's name will always go hand in hand with top players all over the world, which reflects the consistently high quality, reliability and sophisticated design that makes more and more sportsmen and women rely on Slazenger.'

How appropriate then that the Slazenger style and image so powerfully evident at Wimbledon as the 19th century gave way to the 20th, when the Renshaws and Dohertys were so dominant, again in the 1930s when Fred Perry was a triple singles champion and Don Bradman and Len Hutton were finding new batting boundaries, and in the post-war years when Denis Compton, John Newcombe and Margaret Court paraded their skills, should again be so elegantly visible at the start of the 21st century in the hands of such modern 'top players' as Mark Waugh, Jacques Kallis, Shaun Pollock, Alec Stewart, Mark Butcher and Tim Henman.

The same Ralph Slazenger, who recalled the spirit and style of the company founded by his father and his uncle, was the last member of that family to be involved with the business. He played a key role in the 1958-59 negotiations, which led to the Dunlop Rubber Company purchasing Slazengers. At the time a *Sports Trader* leading article described 'the Dunlop and Slazenger fusion' as 'one of the most momentous happenings the trade has ever seen … which may have a profound effect on the trade as a whole.'

While that 1958 view was appropriate at that stage in the history of the UK sports trade, it was only acknowledging the latest chapter in the story of the much longer fusion process that had created the Slazenger business about to become a prized addition to the Dunlop portfolio of companies operating across a wide range of both industrial and consumer sectors. The Slazenger that Dunlop then acquired was itself a fusion, indeed a multi-fusion of very considerable sports businesses, at least one of which, William Sykes of Horbury, had been just as much a force in the land as Slazenger prior to their merger in 1942. The other two companies involved in this process were Ayres, which had been acquired by Sykes in 1940, and Gradidges, who had 'formed an alliance' with Slazenger in 1931. The *Sports Trader* verdict on 'this important fusion' – 'fusion' appears to have been a much favoured word in the vocabulary of that journal – was that, 'The sports trade is now supplied by one of the most powerful groups in the country and dealers are offered outstanding advantages by the combined organization of the well-known constituent companies. The policy of the

Albert Slazenger, younger of the two brothers to found the company

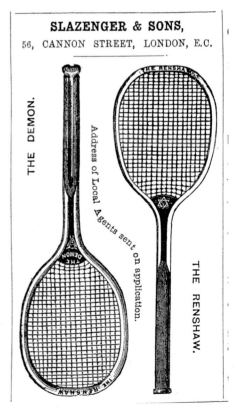

One of the very first Slazenger advertisements in *Pastime* (1884) for the Demon and Renshaw rackets

W. G. pulling a ball.

W. G. Grace
(and see the list of
other Dunlop Slazenger
'greats' on pages 255-7)

Arnold Palmer

SLAZENGER & SONS,

56, Cannon Street,
LONDON.

THE GUINEA

DEMON

LAWN-TENNIS
RACKET.

Every one guaranteed strung with
18-strand gut, and perfect in every
detail.

EVERY GUINEA "DEMON" BEARS THE
SIGNATURE—

"SLAZENGER & SONS,"

AND IS NUMBERED FOR REFERENCE
AND WARRANTED.

Extract from *The Field* :—"In the combination of power with lightness, we have seen none
equal to the 'Demon.'" Made by

SLAZENGER and SONS,

56, CANNON STREET, LONDON.

A larger advertisement in the *Pastime*
(1885) for the 'Guinea Demon' racket

alliance is "support the trade" and its travellers will carry samples of both firm's goods.' The magazine was confident the trade would agree with their wish for 'success and prosperity to this new enterprise', which is slightly at odds with the concern they expressed seventeen years later, when Dunlop and Slazenger joined forces, in their reference to 'whether the concentration of the productive side of the industry into fewer hands is for the betterment of the trade is open to argument.'

What is absolutely clear is that the Slazenger company owed much of the pre-eminence in the sports equipment market acknowledged by Peter Alliss's reference to it being 'THE brand' to the benefits derived from the earlier fusion process, between 1931 and 1942, that combined the skills, strengths and reputations of Ayres, Sykes and Gradidges with those of Slazenger. Most notably Gradidges were to add strengths in cricket and golf, and Sykes their expertise in leather products – especially soccer and rugby balls – a long tradition of cricket excellence and their remarkable Horbury factory to the outstanding strength of Slazenger in racket sports and especially tennis. It is also clear that Slazenger had always been strong on the sales and marketing side and that may go some way towards explaining the eventual disappearance of the other brands after the war and the exclusive use of the Slazenger brand across the combined product line. As early as 1946 it was announced that Slazenger would open the new tennis ball plant in Barnsley – virtually in Sykes's backyard – and in 1950, when the company opened its new sports club in sight of the Horbury factory, it carried only the Slazenger name. And still does today as a flourishing and independent club providing excellent facilities for cricket, tennis, soccer and hockey – as well as an excellent social centre – for the Horbury district. In terms of maintaining brand awareness, certainly in South Yorkshire, the Slazenger name appears over and over again in every issue of the weekly local newspaper as it reports the successes and failures of the club's numerous teams.

Before looking more closely at the histories of the four, originally separate businesses that became Slazenger's Limited it is well worth looking at *Sport and its Industry* which the company published in 1946 to provide 'a record of constant progress between 1810 and 1946' by what was described as 'the Associated companies of Slazenger, Sykes, Gradidges and Ayres'. The new tennis ball plant in Barnsley was a major feature in this brochure, which also celebrated the past, present and forecast future virtues of all four of the companies with each given virtually equal prominence in a presentation that made an excellent promotional piece. Because of its timing it can be seen as marking that phase in the overall history which saluted the records and traditions of the four companies that had now become 'one great joint undertaking', and would develop under the Slazenger banner for the next twelve years leading up to the Dunlop acquisition.

The brochure opened with a commitment to service based on 'a resolution passed at a meeting of the directors held at Laurence Pountney Hill, London, E.C.4 the 4th day of July, 1945, at 10.30 o'clock in the forenoon' and which set out the following sales policy:

As a broad principle of sales policy that the aim of the associated companies should be to provide the finest sporting goods at the fairest possible prices, while at the same time maintaining the full quality of all products and rendering the maximum possible service to the trade and to the public. With this end in view steps should be taken immediately to keep selling prices at the minimum consistent with the financial position of the company and the welfare of its employees. After considering the matter, the Board expressed its unanimous approval and authorised the managing-directors to proceed on the lines indicated.

Then follows an introduction, which draws the reader into the background of the 'Associated Companies':

In the heyday of Queen Victoria's reign, not long after the triumphant success of the Great Exhibition had shown to the world the pre-eminence of Great Britain in commercial enterprise of every description, three manufacturing firms were founded, each of which in its principal products exemplified a characteristic preoccupation of the typical Englishman – his love of sport. These three businesses, founded in the 70s and 80s of the last century by Mr. Albert Slazenger, Mr. William Sykes and Mr. Harry Gradidge, originally manufactured implements for the then increasingly popular pastimes of lawn tennis, football and cricket. Their productions now include implements for almost every known form of sport, their manufacturing resources are second to none, and their overseas organisation, which spans the globe, has everywhere fostered the development of sports and games, and ensured the worldwide use of British sports goods.

'Championship of the World' tennis rackets – a 1910 advertisement

The extent of the union of the companies which by then was well developed, is reflected in the list of directors and senior managers shown in the brochure. The three executive directors of group were Michael and Humphrey McMaster, who had brought Gradidges to Slazenger in 1931, and joined the board of the latter, and Bill Dunning, who as both production director at Horbury and chairman of Sykes had been the driving force in that company in the pre-war years. The senior sales managers were based at the Slazenger offices in London, and were a combination of mainly Slazenger and Gradidge executives. Most of the senior manufacturing and operating managers, based at Horbury, were largely drawn from the Sykes team with the notable exception of Slazenger's Norman Groves, who had come from London to Barnsley to set up the new tennis ball operation.

While later press releases and general publicity material, right through to the start of the millennium, have not forgotten to mention the four separate roots of the business, the Slazenger brand quite quickly became the prime promotional focus and the corporate link for the other brands as they were gradually removed from actual products. In the case of Ayres, and as shown in the 1946 brochure, this element of brand rationalisation had already reached the stage where the only product reference in the text was for archery equipment, which was a sad postscript for the company that, among the four, had led the way in the early days of sports manufacture and marketing.

What follows will describe how each of the four grew to prominence from their very small beginnings and how, eventually, they became 'one great joint undertaking'.

THE HOUSE OF AYRES

Although the 1946 Slazenger-Sykes-Gradidge-Ayres brochure relegated the Ayres brand to a relatively small archery section it did acknowledge the company had flourished for over half a century before the other three were founded. It had been in 1810, five years before Waterloo, that Edward Ayres established himself in Clerkenwell. He started a cabinet-working and wood-turning business with a particular interest in the production of equipment for indoor games. The choice of Clerkenwell could have been influenced by the fact that it was then a part of rapidly growing London that was home to literally thousands with skills related to watchmaking, which would have been very relevant to many of the quite complex mechanics of the games and toys to be produced by the House of Ayres.

In 2002 it was one hundred years since Slazenger tennis balls were first chosen by the All England Club for their Wimbledon Championships. Dunlop Slazenger and Wimbledon celebrated this unique relationships between a product and a world famous event, but thanks to the Ayres company the link with Wimbledon goes back even further than 1902 – almost to the first championship held at the original Worple Road site in 1877. On that very first occasion fifteen dozen new balls were supplied by Jefferies and Company of Woolwich to meet the specific request that 'the flannel covers be sewn by hand with unbleached heavy thread and with uncrossed stitches'. The weight of the balls could vary only from $1^{1}/4$ to $1^{1}/2$ ounces. That specification applied only to the match balls: the practice balls were supplied by the gardener. The balls were kept in canvas 'wells' at the side of the court. These were hammock-like structures suspended from a wooden frame and although Ayres didn't supply them in 1877 they did appear in their catalogues soon after as 'Lawn tennis wells and ball carriers', which they claimed were 'indispensable to every lawn tennis court, by which all stooping for balls is avoided, and the game not interrupted, and also most convenient for carrying balls to the court.'

The flannel covering required for the balls used in the first championship had been introduced to lawn tennis by John Moyer Heathcote, who, in 1875, had been the instigator of a commission to establish a new set of rules for the game, which could be universally adopted. He had maintained, in an 1874 letter to *The Field* magazine, that he had 'found advantage in covering balls with white flannel, which made them bounce better, while they were also easier to see and control'. Compared with the uncovered India rubber balls then generally used, the flannel cover was providing air resistance, reducing the speed of the balls, stabilising their trajectory and making them heavier. Heathcote's enthu-

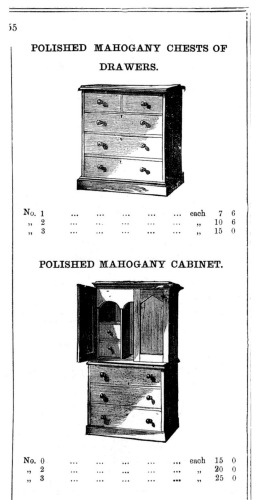

POLISHED MAHOGANY CHESTS OF DRAWERS.

No. 1	...	...	...	...	...	each	7	6
„ 2	...	...	...	...	...	„	10	6
„ 3	...	...	...	...	...	„	15	0

POLISHED MAHOGANY CABINET.

No. 0	...	...	...	...	...	each	15	0
„ 2	...	...	...	...	...	„	20	0
„ 3	...	...	...	...	...	„	25	0

Ayres mahogany office furniture in an 1896 catalogue – the company had started in cabinet making

siasm for the flannel cover could have been due to his Real Tennis experience of using balls made with compressed rags with stitched flannel covers. Certainly some of the flannel used for these balls was produced in Melton Mowbray, which is a likely explanation for the subsequent description of top quality covering cloth as 'Melton'.

The Ayres company, by now trading as F. H. Ayres and located at 111 Aldersgate Street between St. Paul's and Clerkenwell Road, and in the process of adding equipment for the new outdoor games to its huge range of indoor products, had been quick to see the potential of the growing popularity of lawn tennis. It is also likely that, as a business that had become one of the most experienced in England in providing games and sports equipment, they had also spotted the promotional value of being associated with what had become the undisputed 'World Championship' of lawn tennis. That first tournament in 1877 really did signal the arrival of a game that would soon become one of the dominant international sports, and only two years later Ayres were supplying the Wimbledon balls. So while the connection between the world's premier tennis event and Slazenger balls with their unequalled reputation for consistently high quality, is now over one hundred years old, the relationship between the Dunlop Slazenger Group and the Wimbledon tournament can actually be traced back 125 years.

It is probable that in the early years of the Ayres relationship with Wimbledon that the actual ball supplied was 'The Wimbledon', which was retailed in the 1880s at 12s per dozen as being made of 'superior stout rubber covered in fine Melton cloth, cemented and sewn, a good reliable ball suitable for club use'. However, by the mid 1890s 'The Wimbledon' price had been reduced to 9s 6d, which made it considerably cheaper than the patented 'Perfect Seamless' rubber ball at 15s per dozen, and the company's top quality cloth covered 'Championship' ball at 13s 2d, which was presented in their catalogues, 'As used in the principal tournaments throughout England, Ireland, Scotland, America and Australia ... this is further confirmed by the fact that it has been selected for use in all the great tournaments that have taken place not only in the United Kingdom, but in all foreign countries where the game has any votaries.' It was further claimed that, 'The most flat-

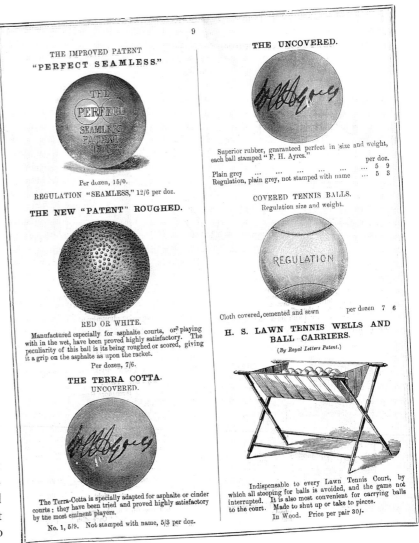

The Ayres tennis ball range in the 1896 catalogue and the patented tennis well to hold and carry the balls. Their 'Championship' ball was used at Wimbledon from 1879 to 1901

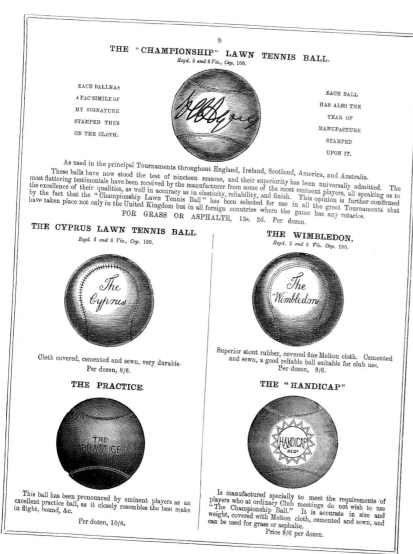

THE "CHAMPIONSHIP" LAWN TENNIS BALL.

Regd. 5 and 6 Vic., Cap. 100.

EACH BALL HAS
A FAC-SIMILE OF
MY SIGNATURE
STAMPED THUS
ON THE CLOTH.

EACH BALL
HAS ALSO THE
YEAR OF
MANUFACTURE
STAMPED
UPON IT.

As used in the principal Tournaments throughout England, Ireland, Scotland, America, and Australia. These balls have now stood the test of nineteen seasons, and their superiority has been universally admitted. The most flattering testimonials have been received by the manufacturer from some of the most eminent players, all speaking as to the excellence of their qualities, as well in accuracy as in elasticity, reliability, and finish. This opinion is further confirmed by the fact that the "Championship Lawn Tennis Ball" has been selected for use in all the great Tournaments that have taken place not only in the United Kingdom but in all foreign countries where the game has any votaries.

FOR GRASS OR ASPHALTE, 13s. 2d. Per dozen.

THE CYPRUS LAWN TENNIS BALL.

Regd. 5 and 6 Vic., Cap. 100.

Cloth covered, cemented and sewn, very durable.
Per dozen, 8/6.

THE WIMBLEDON,

Regd. 5 and 6 Vic. Cap. 100.

Superior stout rubber, covered fine Melton cloth. Cemented and sewn, a good reliable ball suitable for club use.
Per dozen, 9/6.

THE PRACTICE.

This ball has been pronounced by eminent players as an excellent practice ball, as it closely resembles the best make in flight, bound, &c.

Per dozen, 10/6.

THE "HANDICAP"

Is manufactured specially to meet the requirements of players who at ordinary Club meetings do not wish to use "The Championship Ball." It is accurate in size and weight, covered with Melton cloth, cemented and sewn, and can be used for grass or asphalte.
Price 9/6 per dozen.

tering testimonials have been received from some of the most eminent players, all speaking as to the excellence of its qualities, as well in accuracy as in elasticity, reliability and finish.' The 1896 catalogue featured no less than ten completely different ball specifications to suit every pocket, all skill levels, all surfaces and even weather conditions; the patented 'Roughed' ball was not only specially suited to asphalt courts but also 'highly satisfactory in the wet'.

This attention to tennis – which extended well beyond balls to include more than thirty different rackets in most of their ranges, a bewildering choice of posts and nets, eight mechanical line markers, eight racket presses, scoreboards, umpires' chairs, racket bags, tennis shoes and fourteen different boxed sets of all the equipment required to set up a court and to play the game – reflected the evolution of the Ayres approach to sports and games during the 19th century. What had started out as a business devoted to indoor games had recognised the Victorian explosion of interest in organised and regulated outdoor activities and introduced not only this comprehensive tennis line, but also equally complete product ranges for cricket, golf, bowls, croquet, hockey, lacrosse, badminton and, of course, archery. The brand emphasis was placed very firmly on 'F. H. Ayres' with the sub brand 'International' applied to premium products across both indoor and outdoor equipment. However, there was one interesting exception to this pattern, the 'Julian Marshall' junior tennis racket. Julian Marshall, like John Moyer Heathcote, had been a member of the commission that had formalised the rules of lawn tennis just in time for the first Wimbledon tournament. Previously, in 1872, he had codified the rules of Real Tennis, and is credited with being the principal advocate of changing the shape of the tennis court from its original hour glass configuration to the rectangular shape still used today. The Ayres company did well to acknowledge his unique contribution to the game in this way.

As with tennis so with the other main outdoor games in their catalogues, Ayres offered everything required to build the playing area and then all the necessary equipment to play each game. In the case of cricket the basis of the range was a selection of nineteen men's and boys' bats, including a 'Broomstick' line offered in either ash or willow for play in the backyard, and a choice of 37 balls with the top line 'International – specially dyed by a scientific process *through* the leather to keep the colour as long as the ball lasts'. In addition to their own brand the ball line also included, at the highest price, four Duke's balls, the very best at £4 16s per dozen. Add to these 11 varieties of stumps, available in each case either plain or polished, 21 types of bails, batting and wicket keeping gloves, 22 types of batting pads, nets and matting pitches, bags, scoreboards and scorebooks, pitch measuring tapes, cricket boots, umpires' coats, and, possibly best of all in confirming their comprehensive approach, either pony or full size horse boots for pulling the rollers, and you really do have everything required for the game.

Croquet gets the same treatment. The catalogue illustrates or describes 53 different half or full sets of everything required to set up a croquet lawn, the most expensive being just over £4. All the individual items, like mallets, arches and balls, were also available separately as well as 20 different stands for the mallets. As was the case with both Slazenger and Sykes golf doesn't get quite so much attention. However, the basics were covered with a set of 15 hickory-shafted clubs, 7 different golf balls, ranging from 8s 6d to 21s per dozen, a combined umbrella, walking stick and club rest, caddie bags and the ingenious 'Golfer's Compendium' for 'painting balls, with paint brush, calipers and zinc tray at 3s each'. Technology was beginning to appear in the 1890s in the shape of the 'Perfect' golf club head, which was made by 'the insertion of cork in the face of the head and celluloid front thereto', and which 'provided greater driving power, less liability to break and jarring reduced to a minimum'. Ayres's general enthusiasm for producing miniaturised versions of both indoor and outdoor games, like croquet, tennis and billiards, extended to Garden Golf sold in a box complete with mallets, cups, flags and balls for 49s 6d per set, and which they claimed had been introduced 'For the purpose of enabling players to enjoy the exhilarating amusement of the ancient game of golf in spaces that from their circumscribed area do not admit of the extended tract of country inseparable from the links.'

Immediately following the golf section is the fascinating entry for 'The old English game of Knurr and Spell'. Its positioning in the catalogue is very appropriate because this ancient game was sometimes known as 'Poor Man's Golf'. Its origins are thought to be either Teutonic or Norse and in the UK it had mainly northern, and, above all, Yorkshire associations. The Knurr, in the catalogue, is a round lignum vitae, wood or pottery ball, which is spring-released from the Spell, or frame, holding the spring arm and is struck by the player's bat into a marked field of play, usually downwind on waste ground or moorland. Hits of two hundred yards were common and a distance of well over three hun-

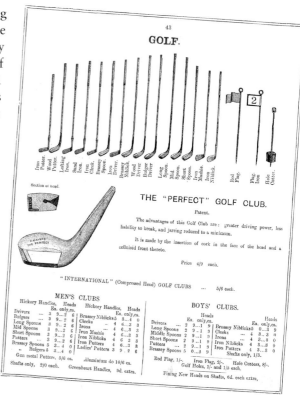

Ayres golf clubs in 1896 and a sample of their golf accessories

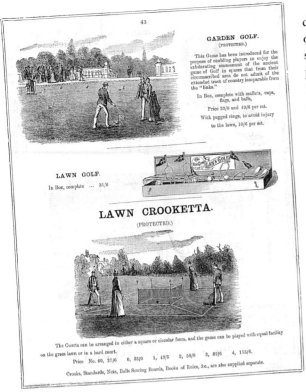

Miniaturised outdoor games for the country house lawn

dred was recorded in 1899 with the help of a freak bounce off a stone wall. The half ounce Knurr had a hand-carved surface giving it a striking resemblance to the modern, dimpled golf ball and the bats, or sticks, were usually about four feet long made out of ash, hickory or alder with a striking head about two to three inches wide made of boxwood, hornbeam, sycamore or maple, compressed to half its volume in a steel frame. The shafts of the sticks had fabric or rubber grips, which again evokes comparison with golf. Indeed steel golf shafts were tried but proved unsuccessful because they lacked the necessary whip. The Ayres catalogue tells the reader, 'This is a revival of the old North Country sport, which requires good judgement and furnishes capital exercise to the muscles without creating too great a demand on the physical system.' They offered a choice of four sets, the most expensive, at £3, providing an iron spell, metal spring and adjuster, two brass cups, two clubs, twenty-four lignum and twenty-four pottery balls, and a set of rules.

Other outdoor sports catered for included hockey, lacrosse, soccer, rugby, bowls, skittles, badminton (indoor and outdoor), and, of course, archery. Far removed from the brief reference in the 1946 brochure the catalogues in the 1890s featured 42 different bows, 24 types of arrows – with peacock feathers 2s per dozen extra – 11 targets, ladies and gents gloves and armguards, and quivers and quiver belts. The company's pride in its archery tradition, and maybe a reason why it was the last product to carry the Ayres name, is evident in the foreword to one of their last (1936) archery equipment catalogues, which tells the enthusiast for that sport that 'Fletchers and Bowyers are very rare, but the craftsmen who make the bows and arrows listed in these pages can trace their descent back to the seventeenth century, and ever since those days the trade has been handed down from father to son together with the cunning secrets which enable them to produce the perfect arrow or the best casting bow.'

The Ayres approach to outdoor games is impressive enough but pales in comparison with how they dealt with the combination of indoor activities and the range of products based on their original cabinet-making and woodworking skills. And it is relevant to make the point that when the business started in 1810 there would not have been much demand for the equipment for the outdoor sports that later became so important to them. At that time they hardly existed in the popular sense and it would have been much more appropriate to concentrate their skills on games and other products to be used inside the homes of the more prosperous.

A version of billiards was played as far back as the

An Ayres boxed set of badminton equipment from the 1897 catalogue

16th century, but, like so many of the other sports supplied by the Dunlop Slazenger companies, it was given substance and rules by the Victorians, ever keen to organise both their work and their play. In this case the first Billiards Association was formed in 1885 and it is quite clear from the Ayres catalogues, published only a few years later, that they had targeted this particular indoor sport as having major potential for their skills and experience. Their range offered 14 full-size tables – with a choice of four different styles of legs for each – ranging in price from £13 to the top line £100 model 'of superior design and finished in the best style complete with extra thick slate bed, improved fast India rubber cushions, covered with superfine West of England cloth and supplied with twelve cues, two butts, two rests, a set of ivory balls, a marking board, six chalk cups, cue rack and butt hooks, iron, brush, a Holland cover and with rules in a glazed frame'. Then add eight variations of a miniature table, eight table tops, three styles of portable tables (with all the accessories), eight games of portable billiards, which 'formed a ready and convenient substitute for the more ponderous and expensive regular tables', table billiards in three forms and two sizes, a reversible billiard and dining table in three sizes plus, of course, every conceivable accessory including 'Chalks, superior', and then a large range of bagatelle boards. Just to complete this category they offered German Billiards, which was a version of pin ball, Tobogganette – another version of pin ball – and Cockamaroo, which was pin ball with a cue instead of a spring release for striking the ball.

Today a common and very powerful factor across most industries and markets is to continuously seek to reduce the number of product lines. In the second half of the 19th century it is quite clear that the number of different inventory items in any one company's range was dictated by a competitive thrust to offer as many products and variations by size, colour and design detail as it was possible to make, or buy in, distribute and list, very graphically, in relatively huge catalogues. And it should not be overlooked that in the very earliest of these catalogues most of the ranges offered for the main sports, like tennis, cricket, golf and croquet, included products, as appropriate, sized for boys and ladies.

Within the total Ayres range the 'huge choice' approach is most evident in the 35 tightly and well illustrated pages devoted to indoor games. These offer physical and mental challenges as complex as 'Gwalior', at 33s each, 'a new and interesting game, depending somewhat on the skill of the player, aided by the operation of certain ingenious mechanical contrivances. The board is of polished mahogany and represents a series of drawbridges and moats or fosses. A top is spun and on its safely crossing these drawbridges and knocking down various obstructive pieces depends

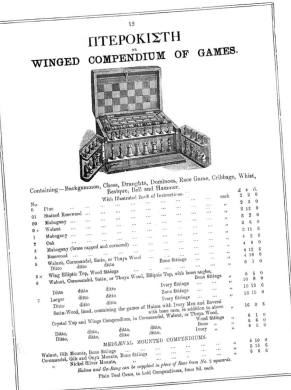

Examples on this page and opposite of the huge range of indoor games in the 1897 catalogue

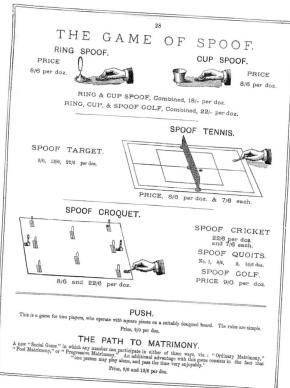

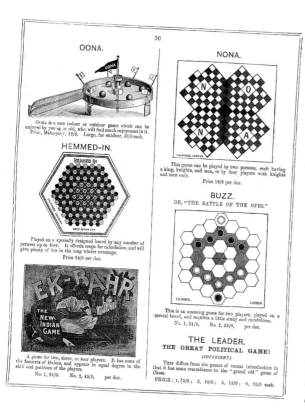

the victory' – or as simple as 'Parlour Aunt Sally', at 1s 9d each, 'savouring more of green-fields and outdoor frolic but her genial presence and radiant face is made to contribute to the jollity and mirth of every fireside'. 'Aunt Sally' was a miniature scarecrow figure with a clay pipe and the jollity and mirth was evoked by trying to throw small rings over the end of the pipe.

It is impossible to do full justice to the extraordinary range of games available but the £44 'Fall Front Compendium of Games' provides a flavour of the Ayres style in offering a selection including chess, draughts, backgammon, dominoes, a race game, table croquet, halma, reversi, whist cribbage, bezique, euchre, ecarte and other card games with either wood or bone men in a choice of mahogany, rosewood, walnut or coromandel cabinet with ivory fittings. 'Parlour Aunt Sally' appears again in a combination set of parlour games, which also includes croquet, Ton Ton, Go-Bang, Expert Angler, Snails, Trails, Puff and Dart, Germana Tactics, Spellicans, Ball Solitaire, Fox and Geese, Circular Bagatelle, Magic Skittles and Mysterious Mallet. Most of these exotically named games could be purchased separately along with twenty variations of dominoes and seventy of chess/draught boards. The game of 'Spoof' – based on tiddlywinks – could be played with either the usual cup or an elevated ring as the target and also in variations to allow 'Spoof' cricket, tennis, croquet, quoits and golf to be played on a table top. The familiar Snakes and Ladders and Ludo appear among the not so well known Roquet, Romette, 'the New Indian game Ek-Bahr', Fanorana – 'a game of Eastern origin though not an absorbing pastime yet affords a great deal of excitement' – the thought reading 'Pytho', which 'determines the simplest and most efficient means for the communication of automatic, telepathic and spiritualistic messages providing a never-ending fund of wonder and amusement'. 'Parlour Decapitated Head' is suitable for two or more persons and, perhaps most intriguing, 'The Path to Matrimony', in which 'any number can participate in either of three ways, viz: ordinary matrimony, pool matrimony or progressive matrimony and has the additional advantage that one person may play alone, and pass the time very enjoyably'.

The range of 'Jinrikshas', or Japanese cars extended to twenty-three models priced from a very basic 7s 6d to nearly £3 for a relatively luxurious Gig fitted with best carriage cloth upholstery and a cashmere-lined hood and patented folding shafts. The range, all of which would have required one human driver, or puller, between the shafts, also included accessories that provided a play table in front of the passenger, a bed rest adjustment and optional wide (six or eight inch) rubber tyred wheels.

Wooden office furniture and accessories from paper

Two of the many models of gigs and chaises

knives to desks and mahogany storage cabinets, take up another eleven catalogue pages and again reflect the company's woodworking origins as does the huge range of exercise equipment for indoors and outdoors, and which includes complete gymnasiums. Most impressive in this section is the 'Compound Chest Machine', which is 'A highly finished and effective gymnastic contrivance containing upwards of one hundred different exercises, all the movements acting upon set of weights, so that as the gymnast becomes stronger the weights can be gradually increased.' Puzzlingly it was presented as being 'Invaluable in hospitals and schools but more especially for Ladies.'

Their rocking horse range appears to have been very popular and production was maintained, along with the billiard tables, right through to the 1950s, by which time the business had been absorbed into the Sykes and Slazenger operations in Yorkshire. And, on top of all that, their range expansion policy in pursuit of the market for the new leisure activities developing during the second half of the century took them into the personal transport sector with a collection of 'High Grade Cycles', backed by every conceivable accessory from the oil can to the saddles and including no less than six different bells and fourteen lamps. The cycles included tandems for both men and women, racers, semi-racers, roadsters and tricycles priced between £23 and £40, all fitted with the newly invented pneumatic tyres including those supplied by the very young Dunlop company then operating out of Dublin.

If Ayres were among the leaders in the marketing of cycles, it also appears they were one of the very first equipment companies to offer a clothing line. The evidence for this activity, possibly short lived, is an early 20th century poster showing, in vivid colours, the 'Maltese Cross' range of shirts for soccer, rugby, lacrosse and hockey plus 'Knickers for all sports', goalkeeping sweaters, running vests, elastic supporters and football socks.

Having started out in Clerkenwell the company later moved a short distance to Aldersgate and finally, in the early 1940s and about the time they were being absorbed by William Sykes, to 1 Old Street, which would only have been a very short distance away and still within the Clerkenwell telephone exchange. By then the range, not surprisingly had been considerably reduced but they still covered the major sports that had been featured in their earlier catalogues and still provided most of what was required to set up the cricket pitch, croquet lawn and lawn tennis court, as well as the playing equipment. As late as 1941, which would have been after the merger with Sykes, the catalogue blurb for their 'Championship' tennis ball would have been as powerful as those for any of their competitors:

Leading as they did with one of the earliest plugless and chemically inflated cores, Ayres have now made a further step forward by greatly increasing the percentage of pure rubber in the core, which,

94

COMPOUND CHEST MACHINES.

A most highly finished and effective gymnastic contrivance, containing upwards of 100 different exercises, all the movements acting upon one set of weights, so that as the gymnast becomes stronger, the weights can be gradually increased. Some of its movements are Rowing, Walking, or Running, Top and Bottom Sawyer, Chest Expanding, &c. It is invaluable in Hospitals and Schools (more especially Ladies'), and large Families.

Price, from £5 to £50

The Compound Chest Machine from the 1897 catalogue

F. H. AYRES, Cycle Manufacturer.

MODEL A RACER.

Price—Fitted with Dunlop-Welch, Palmer, or Clincher Path Racing Tyres, £21 15 0

The "INTERNATIONAL" Semi-Racer.

Racer bicycles from the same catalogue

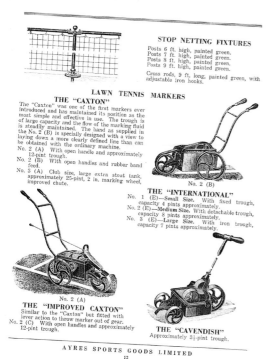

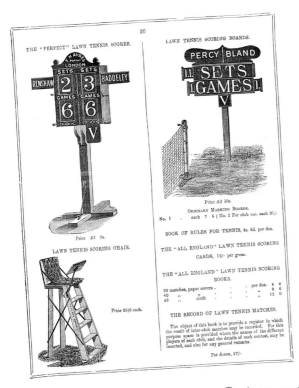

Lawn tennis line markers from Ayres
1939 catalogue, the designs virtually
unchanged since the 1890s

in addition to giving greater elasticity of life has made it possible to reduce the actual weight of the core and increase that of the cover by twenty per cent. With this margin in hand exhaustive experiments were made to find a cloth worthy of covering the most accurate and longest lasting core yet produced. Ayres SUPAPILE – the finest cloth yet used on a tennis ball – supplied the answer … and Ayres latest seaming cement, again the outcome of prolonged experiments, provides the finishing touch to THE PERFECT BALL.

It is interesting to see that the style of the 1941 catalogue illustrations had not changed from those appearing fifty years earlier, in fact several could have been produced from the same printing blocks. In the case of the indoor games the product line has been enormously reduced and while billiard tables are still prominent the games are limited to darts, skittles, quoits, a much expanded and up-to-date range of table tennis equipment and, harking back to earlier days, puff billiards, which involves blowing a ball around a 38-inch board 'by means of the puffers provided'.

While it is reasonable to assume that Ayres had found it increasingly difficult to compete with the numerous sports equipment companies that had followed them into the market, and also that their presentational style had not moved with the times as quickly as companies like Slazengers and Sykes, it is

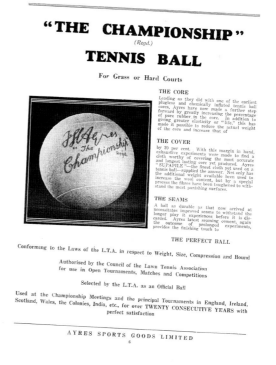

Tennis accessories and the Championship
Tennis Ball from the 1939 catalogue

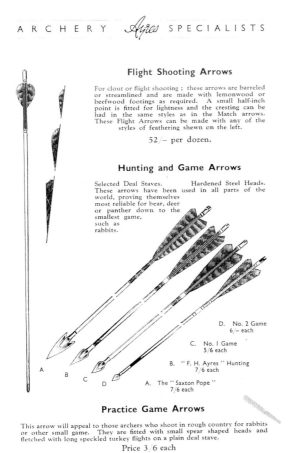

ARCHERY *Ayres* SPECIALISTS

Flight Shooting Arrows

For clout or flight shooting; these arrows are barreled or streamlined and are made with lemonwood or beefwood footings as required. A small half-inch point is fitted for lightness and the cresting can be had in the same styles as in the Match arrows. These Flight Arrows can be made with any of the styles of feathering shewn on the left.

52/– per dozen.

Hunting and Game Arrows

Selected Deal Staves.   Hardened Steel Heads.
These arrows have been used in all parts of the world, proving themselves most reliable for bear, deer or panther down to the smallest game, such as rabbits.

D. No. 2 Game
6/– each

C. No. 1 Game
5/6 each

B. " F. H. Ayres " Hunting
7/6 each

A. The " Saxton Pope "
7/6 each

Practice Game Arrows

This arrow will appeal to those archers who shoot in rough country for rabbits or other small game. They are fitted with small spear shaped heads and fletched with long speckled turkey flights on a plain deal stave.

Price 3/6 each

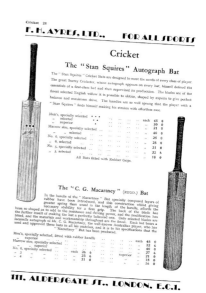

A GROUP BY *Ayres* Archery Specialists

Ayres archery catalogue in 1939

also obvious that by the 1930s they were no longer heavily involved in woodworking. By then consumers were much more interested in outdoor sports than passing the time at home with the myriad of ingenious games for which they had been famous during the first hundred years of their existence. In that context the merger with Sykes made sense, especially as the onset of war virtually killed off, for the duration, the requirement for sports goods. Nevertheless, the final disappearance of the Ayres brand, so soon after the war, must have been a disappointment for the employees of a business that had, in many ways, been a pioneering force in the sports industry.

Among the Slazenger quartet of companies Ayres had led the way, and by a distance, in establishing a formidable sports and leisure business and had been unique not only in the scope of a range that had included the bewildering array of indoor games, cycles and furniture, but also in their early marketing style of producing, or wholesaling, simply everything that was required to play the newly popular sports. They were supplying balls to Wimbledon two years before Slazenger started in the sports market and had a full range of products for nearly every known sport while Sykes were getting going with mainly leather products and a limited cricket range, and Gradidges were focused almost entirely on cricket. Dunlop entered the market with their first golf balls almost exactly one hundred years after Edward Ayres set up shop in Clerkenwell. It is also

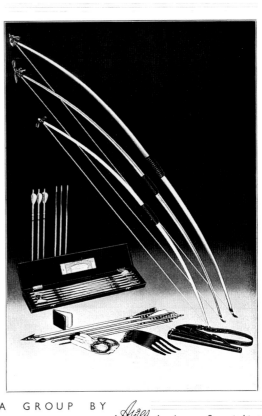

The International cricket bat from the same catalogue

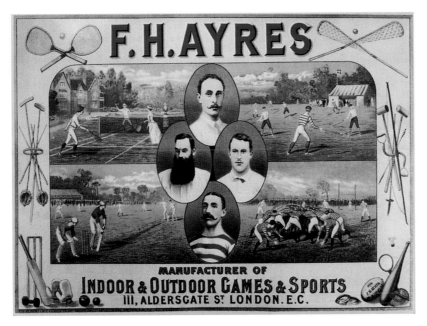

William Renshaw and W. G. Grace
featured in an Ayres advertisement in
the 1880s

reasonable to assume that Slazenger in particular, and to a lesser extent Sykes, would have learned from the Ayres comprehensive approach to marketing sports products. Slazenger's 1909 catalogue, with its emphasis on croquet and tennis, reflects the Ayres approach, though already with a more attractive presentation, and Sykes certainly learned quickly to be just as complete with their cricket, tennis and leather ranges.

And as early as the 1880s they were producing high quality colour advertisements. There is a very vivid illustration of a cricketer with his 'International' bat, and also a composite, and possibly earlier, advert with detailed action scenes of a country house doubles court, a lacrosse game and well-attended cricket and rugby matches. In the centre of this advertisement are four sports 'Stars' presumably representing the activities in the action scenes. It is not clear who they all are, but the face of W. G. Grace is unmistakable and the tennis representative is almost certainly William Renshaw, who won seven Wimbledon titles between 1881 and 1889. Another of these advertisements shows a family gathered around a magnificent Ayres billiard table with an enormous amount of detail in the furnishings and around the room and in the clothes worn by the adults and children in the scene. Here again, 120 years ago, is the evidence of the early strength of the House of Ayres and its influence in the formative years of the UK sports industry. Not so well known these days as Slazenger or Dunlop, but for many years the leading company of those that ultimately became the Dunlop Slazenger Group.

Nothing emphasises more the early importance of this company, or its claim to sports equipment fame, than the fact that the winner of the very first Wimbledon men's singles championship, in 1877, Spencer Gore, used an Ayres racket, as did Norman Brookes and Tony Wilding, who, between them, won the tournament six times between 1907 and 1914.

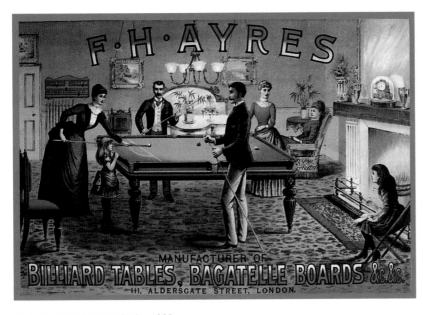

An Ayres advertisement in the 1880s
for billiard tables and bagatelle

WILLIAM SYKES LIMITED

William Sykes, the founder

Within the 'Big Four' companies – Slazenger, Sykes, Ayres and Gradidge – that eventually became Slazengers Limited, it is arguable that the Yorkshire-based William Sykes contributed the most potent element, certainly in terms of manufacturing skills and capacity. The Sykes centre of operations was in the town of Horbury, which lies a few miles down the M1 motorway south of Leeds. This is an area where the main industrial activity in the second half of the 19th century was signalled in the 1875 edition of the local business directory by the reference to the existence of 'extensive woollen and worsted mills'. In fact with a population of less than 4000 the town was then home to nine woollen manufacturers and at least six other businesses associated with the wool industry.

However, among the list of other traders and businesses in the town, shown in the same directory, was one saddler. This was William Sykes, who, in 1866, as a teenage apprentice, had, quite by chance, made his first acquaintance with sports products. By the time he died, in 1910, the apprentice had become the chairman of one of the very largest sports equipment manufacturers in the country, probably also in the world at that time, operating from an up-to-date and very large purpose-built factory – 'The Yorkshire Athletic Manufactory' – on a four acre site in the centre of Horbury.

Returning to the young apprentice, and 1866, that was a period when, for the first time, factories were closing on Saturday afternoons and the churches and chapels were encouraging their young men to join the newly-formed football clubs that were now possible because of the extra leisure time available. Leather footballs were still rare, certainly in the North of England, and not to be found on retailers' shelves. Responding to this growing interest in football the superintendent of a local Sunday School, anxious to provide a new activity for his pupils on the Whitsuntide holiday treat, gave the young William, who was a member of his class, a piece of leather to make a football. There were no instructions and no model to work from but at Whitsuntide the boys played with the first two Sykes-made balls, and certainly with the first two leather balls made in Yorkshire.

From that very small beginning – and for some years it seemed nothing more would develop from it because William didn't give much thought to making any more footballs – the House of Sykes eventually evolved. When he finished his apprenticeship he became a journeyman saddler for his master at 24s per week, and two years later, aged twenty-three, very much against the advice of his father and without a penny from him, he married. He bought the saddler's business in Horbury with his and his wife's savings, the premises, stock and goodwill costing them £19.

After less than three months trading in his new business, the young entrepreneur had paid off all his bills and sat down to count his cash. There was exactly £1, in four crown pieces. He used to say that he there and then decided that if he put those four crowns away, he would always be worth at least

William Sykes's first saddlery shop in Horbury

£1. So they were put away and were found among his effects after his death forty years later.

That first venture was typical of his character and the methods he used throughout his career. It may have been a risk to start his own business, and certainly his father had told him he was a fool to leave a steady job to be his own master, but William Sykes was ready to take risks – carefully. After a couple of years of continued concentration on saddlery he began to think about expansion, and again took a risk. It is worth remembering that at this time cars were still unheard of and there was nothing to suggest that the dominance of the horse as a means of personal and at least short distance haulage would not continue to make saddlery the safest business in Europe. But William had other ambitions for his future that were too big to be sustained by saddlery alone.

He had observed the rapid growth of sport among the general population, and he remembered the footballs he'd made for the school treat. Putting these two thoughts together he made six dozen footballs and within two years William Sykes was established as a leading maker of footballs with saddlery as a diminishing sideline.

Now the expansion gathered pace and extended beyond his basic expertise in leather. He began selling cricket bats, at first buying them from other makers but always intending to start his own production. Once a steady cricket trade had been established the bat making department was set up, 'with the aid of some of the best craftsmen in England', and, shortly afterwards, tennis racket production was started. All of this extra activity necessitated a move from the original saddler's shop to his first, albeit small factory in an old stone-built mill in the centre of Horbury. By now the business employed 60 craftsmen skilled in leather and woodworking, and had begun to take on apprentices. The transition had been made from the first two footballs to 500 per week, plus the bats and rackets. William Sykes was now emerging as one of Horbury's principal employers.

In those days of generally smaller businesses it could have been argued that further expansion was undesirable, and could even put at risk the Sykes reputation for personal service and first-class craftsmanship. If that was a risk, and William might have agreed with that view, he was ready for the next stage provided he moved, as usual, carefully. So in 1895 the move was made to a new, four-acre site, again in the centre of Horbury, and work started to transform what had been wasteground into the Yorkshire Athletic Manufactory. But the locals weren't convinced he'd done the right thing and they christened the new factory 'Sykes's Folly'.

But he had been careful. He had made sure of the money for the new building by paying for years into a building society. To secure the reputation for craftsmanship he had made sure that his two sons, Henry and William, who were to become joint managing-directors, could be relied upon to maintain the traditions he had started. Proof of the extent of his achievement is very clear in the pictures of the interior of the Manufactory in a 1903 catalogue. These show the attention to quality in the shots of the separate departments for

The Sports Trader.   June, 1907.

SPORTS TRADERS.

No. 6.—Mr. H. O. SYKES,
Of The Yorkshire Athletic Manufactory, Horbury.

William Sykes son, Henry

leather and wood products, of the ambition to expand further in the extensive areas devoted to export packing, and of the advanced technical nature of the Sykes approach shown in the immaculate and obviously up to date engine and dynamo house.

The scope of the business is also clear in the 1903 catalogue. From those early beginnings of a few footballs William Sykes, 'manufacturers and patentees of all kinds of athletic goods and billiard tables', were now offering very complete product ranges for tennis, croquet, bowls, cricket, badminton, polo, soccer, rugby, hockey, boxing, billiards, exercise equipment and table tennis. Very similar, indeed, to the Ayres range at that time. Their premium tennis racket, the 'E.D.B.' was 'made from the instructions of the well-known player, E. D. Black, champion of Yorkshire'. The 'E.D.B.' was supported by more than twenty other rackets ranging from the 'Wonder' at 4s 6d, which was 'a real wonder of cheapness and durability', to the 'Special' version of the 'E.D.B.' at 17s 6d with 'the shoulders greatly strengthened by being bound with specially selected gut instead of silk' and its stringing improved 'by having two extra strands through the centre from top to bottom'. Their number one tennis ball carried one of their most used sub-brands, 'The Electric', and was the only premium type available in this category, but, like Ayres and Slazenger, their tennis range included all the items required for both setting up the court and for the player. 'Electric' appears again in the croquet and cricket sections and, in the latter case, they offered an even larger range of boots for the roller horses than Ayres. Their leather history shows in the number of variations offered in cricket bags, batting pads and wicket-keeping 'Gauntlets'.

William Sykes Junior

Those leather origins show even more strongly – certainly much more so than with Ayres and Slazenger – in the range of boxing gloves and especially an enormous choice of soccer and rugby balls, including the top-of-the-line 'League Champion' ball, as used by Sheffield United, the 1902 F.A. Cup winners. The catalogue offers 44 footballs and 22 shin guards and, still in the football section, moleskin and buck ear caps, and, intriguingly, 'Flesh Gloves' for the soccer player. There was no sign of footwear in the tennis or cricket pages but they did offer seven types of football boots from 4s 11d per pair to the 'MacGregor' at 8s 6d, modestly described as a 'superb boot'. Billiards get a small section but 'Electric' table tennis was already a big item for Sykes with fourteen sets ranging in price from 1s to 13s 6d, plus separately listed high-quality, cork-faced bats at £1 per dozen.

As William said in his introduction to the 1903 catalogue, 'I believe you will find it replete with illustrations and prices of all kinds of implements used in the sporting world. My factory contains the latest machinery, and each department is under the control of a thoroughly competent foreman, subject to my immediate personal supervision, and by strict attention to detail I am enabled to produce better results at far less cost than my competitors.'

By this time the company could state it was a contractor to the War Office – it had supplied material for the Boer War – and its export activities were supported by offices in Hamburg, Sydney, Cape Town and Auckland. William himself made his first selling trip to South Africa in 1904, Henry was to visit North America 27 times in the next twenty years,

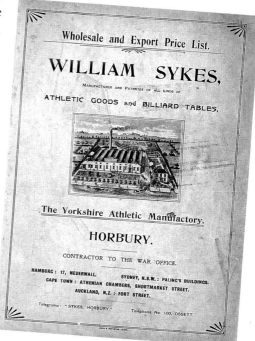

The front cover of William Sykes 1903 price list featuring the Yorkshire Athletic Manufactory opened in 1896

28

Jack Nicklaus

Sandy Lyle

Hand sewn footballs in the Horbury factory

and William 'Junior' spent four months in South Africa consolidating the business there. Striking evidence of both their foresight and attention to detail appears in a post first world war catalogue issued from their Lombard Street office in Toronto, which shows a range entirely devoted to North American sports, including ice hockey, basketball, volleyball and 'American Rugger Football'.

In 1907 the *Sports Trader* visited the Horbury Factory. The writer remembered the earlier factory in Twitch Hill as 'a little building, which, not many years ago provided ample facilities for their trade, and out of which the idlest dreamer would hardly have dared to foreshadow that the present magnificent works could grow'. Apparently he was also aware of the local reaction to the opening of 'Sykes's Folly' in 1895 when 'the inhabitants of the little village of Horbury were open-mouthed with astonishment – a place of such magnitude could never be kept running, and even if Mr. Sykes secured the whole of the sports trade certain failure was predicted as a result of building such a big works'.

The account of the visit goes into considerable detail about the layout of the factory and the range of products being manufactured. Not surprisingly its tone is favourable but what emerges most clearly from the article is the recognition that William and his sons are developing their business not only by the most modern methods but also with a great deal of thought for the welfare of their employees, which was not a uniform approach in the early years of the 20th century. There is reference to the firm keeping their own 'Foreign Correspondents' and the introduction of the most up-to-date methods in office equipment. The magnificence of the billiards showroom leaves a huge impression, which reflects the importance of this product in the overall range, and the main room in the factory is described as 'a very large place admirably arranged for the various branches of the business which are conducted there'. As well as billiards this room is the location of the soft goods department, where 'women and girls' were producing boxing gloves, leg guards, gauntlets and batting gloves with 'a trained staff of cutters employed to keep this army of women going'. Further evidence of the Sykes determination and ingenuity in building their business appears in the reference to the fact that 'Mr. Sykes is just on the point of taking a factory in Woodstock, Oxfordshire to cope with the considerable demand for hand-made, soft leather goods'. Apparently that was the only part of the country at that time where the necessary skilled hands could be found for this

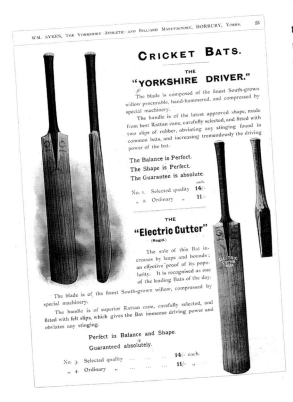

Sykes bats – the 'Yorkshire Driver' and 'Electric Cutter'

type of work.

'A long avenue of sewing machines' was producing the machine-sewn footballs while another part of the room was devoted to hand-sewn football making, which was regarded as one of the most important parts of the business as 'Mr. Sykes is to be numbered amongst the largest manufacturers of these goods, his turnover being well over 100,000 footballs per year'. Certainly a long way from those first few balls he shaped from the piece of leather given to him by the Sunday school superintendent. It didn't escape the writer's notice that many of the machines used for stitching footballs had been made specially by Sykes's engineers, and that some of them were 'so ingenious as to produce a football which it would puzzle even an expert to say whether it was hand or machine sewn, for not only are the stitches of the same length and character but the same kind of thread can be used with the machine'. The football department was fitted up with several ingenious contrivances for labour saving and contained 'a huge clicking machine, which chops out sections of the footballs from the hides as quickly as one can count'. One man was seen doing nothing else but testing footballs, before sending them into the warehouse, using a steam driven pump which inflated them at enormous speed.

As the visitor moved to the woodworking department he noticed the polishing shop, which had been partitioned off to make it perfectly dustproof. The woodworking area itself was divided into two sections. The first was used for hand labour and fitted with benches and vices where 'practical craftsmen give form and shape' to cricket bats, hockey sticks and tennis rackets, and was sealed off from the adjoining machinery section with its dust and mess to ensure that 'the men are not only working under better conditions but the articles produced come out cleaner and smarter than would be the case if they were being produced in an atmosphere of sawdust'. That probably explains his observation that 'it is not often that one finds utility and humour go hand in hand but this does in a very marked degree in this department'. However, not everything was completely modern because in the centre of this room was a huge cauldron 'presided over by a sharp youth and reminiscent of anything but an up-to-date sports factory'. This was the firm's 'Glue-pot', which was regarded as both more satisfactory and a considerable economy rather than for each man to have his own kettle of glue and gas jet on his bench. The other section in this area was the stamping room, which, surprising to the writer, had been set apart for branding the goods manufactured and where several hands were continually employed.

The remarkable scale and versatility of the factory unfolds as the writer moves on to the leather drying houses, which used either steam heat or natural air, and into the tannery, which it is reported has been made three or four times larger in the last two years. There the curriers were impregnating leather with the various chemicals necessary for football manufacture and using powerful machines that could produce the effect of crocodile hide

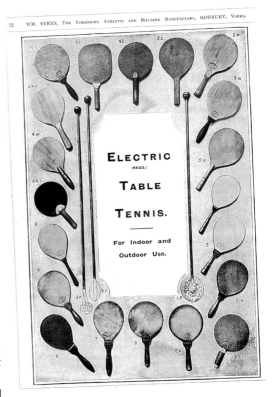

Indoor and outdoor table tennis bats

The 'E.D.B.' tennis racket in Sykes range for many years

POLO.

Polo equipment

and other fancy leathers. The other departments visited included the section that produced the top quality 'Tuphine' leather, which had been 'dressed by a special secret process to provide exquisite suppleness and toughness', the new 'American Staking machine' which made chrome leather soft and pliable, the Chrome Laboratory which resembled 'a chemist's shop with a number of bottles of various coloured liquids and powders', the spacious timber sheds, a section containing an ingenious bending machine, invented by a Sykes engineer, for producing tennis racket frames, the boiler-house where they produced all their own gas and electricity, a brand new woodworking department lit by huge electric arc lamps and fitted with 'the latest and most ingenious contrivances irrespective of cost', and a new golf club department producing the 'Select' and 'Eclipse' ranges. The tour ends in a spacious stock-room where goods are kept in a semi-finished state, 'Cricket bats ready for wrapping and finishing, tennis racket frames in the process of seasoning ready for stringing, and other stock lines to be brought up to a certain stage of manufacture during the quiet months and which are all the better for being kept and finished when required.'

The writer, clearly overwhelmed by all the wonders he had inspected, apologised for his 'feeble attempt to portray the ramifications of this huge business'. His report ended on a sad note with reference to the fact he had not been able to meet the founder of the business as he was away recuperating because his health had not been the best for sometime. However, it was clear that his sons, Mr. Harry and Mr. Willie, who were now supervising the business, were to be congratulated 'on the way in which the place has gone ahead under their auspices'. Even more sadly their father died only three years later – the same year as Ralph Slazenger died – but he would have been content with the verdict of this report that his Yorkshire Athletic Manufactory was a 'magnificent works'.

This rock solid foundation of the business, based primarily on the obviously outstanding Horbury factory and the continuity of leadership by William and his sons, was the springboard for further expansion after the first world war when the company had continued limited production of sports goods while again placing all its manufacturing skills at the disposal of the War Office. One of their own publications includes the quotation, 'The other side of an emergency is an opportunity', and it is easy to imagine that they used the 1914-18 emergency when the Government asked them to produce new products for the war effort, to refine and develop their manufacturing tools and systems, which would have put them in excellent shape once hostilities ceased.

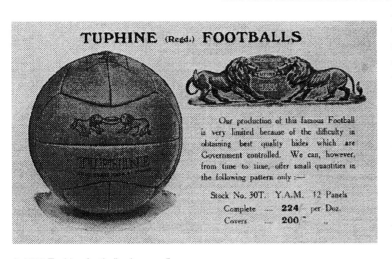

TUPHINE (Regd.) FOOTBALLS

Our production of this famous Football is very limited because of the difficulty in obtaining best quality hides which are Government controlled. We can, however, from time to time, offer small quantities in the following pattern only :—

Stock No. 30T. Y.A.M. 12 Panels
Complete ... **224** per Doz.
Covers ... **200** "

A 1918 Tuphine football ad – supplies still limited by government control

Abbreviated price lists produced by Sykes during the war make reference to a 'London Works' at Blythe Street in Bethnal Green, but early in the 1920s that disappears and is replaced by the 'London Works and Showrooms' at Fortress Road, Kentish Town. That had been the location of another racket manufacturer, Jefferies and Company, who had started a woodworking business there in 1820 and, at some stage, begun to manufacture frames to meet the rising demand for this new product. For a short period during and after the war the price lists also mention additional factories in Birmingham and Manchester, but by the start of the 1930s the business appears to have settled down with just the two plants in Horbury and Kentish Town.

A new product introduced in 1916 was polished, blocked leather leggings manufactured on a newly installed large and up-to-date plant and made in 'the latest approved shapes'. That venture into the fashion trade doesn't seem to have lasted very long and, in any case, was rather at odds with the special notice in a 1918 list, which announces that, 'In consequence of further serious depletion of staff consequent upon the needs of the army and because of the employment of semi-skilled and unskilled labour in the manufacture of footballs we have decided to adopt the policy of manufacturing Wartime Standard Footballs'. The notice went on to explain that by eliminating all intricate and difficult patterns, requiring highly skilled labour, it would be possible to considerably increase output. Another of their special notices at this time drew attention to 'the abnormal increase in prices for boxing gloves brought about by the extreme shortage of glove leather consequent upon Government requirements, and by the abnormal increase in price of this raw material, some of which has increased by as much as 250%'.

Despite these difficulties, large and small, Sykes kept their product line more or less intact, so would have been quick to get back into their stride after the war. By the mid 1920s their catalogue was larger and more attractive than ever, and included a much stronger tennis line incorporating the Jefferies rackets. The 1927 list includes up-to-date photographs of the Horbury plant, including the rapidly expanding tannery, and a shot of the company's stand at the 1927 British Industries Fair showing both the Sykes and Jefferies names on the fascia. By now they had overseas agents in Toronto, New York (Fifth Avenue no less), Copenhagen, Shanghai, Nairobi, Hong Kong, Berlin, Paris, Colombo, Auckland, Cape Town, Buenos Aires and Istanbul – plus representatives in 28 other overseas territories. Their sales director is a Mr. Sam B. Weaver, who they 'poached' from Slazenger.

Their separate summer and winter catalogues reveal an immensely strong product line with a very clear emphasis on tennis and cricket in the former and soccer and rugby in the latter. In both books their strength and heritage in leather is also very apparent. Both the Sykes and Jefferies brands appear in the rack-

An advertisement for Jefferies rackets in the 1903 Sykes catalogue

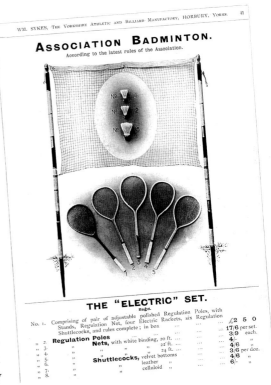

The 'Electric' badminton set

et illustrations and the long-lasting Captain Black's 'E.D.B.' frame, which has certainly outstayed the Captain himself, is now joined by such splendid sub brands as 'Aristocrat', at 67s 6d the premium product, 'Senior Service', 'Gold Medal Ruby' by Jefferies, 'Blue Riband', 'Ensign', 'Drake', 'St. George', and in case it was needed to underline pride in home-produced products, the 'B.K.O.' (British Knock Out). As already seen in the Ayres range they also offer every conceivable accessory for the game, including a book of rules, and use their racket brands, 'E.D.B.', 'Senior Service' and Jefferies 'Autograph' for tennis balls, 'undoubtedly the most perfect balls now produced'. All, of course, covered with first quality Melton cloth (without the Mowbray).

The Sykes 'Roy Kilner', which was Don Bradman's first new bat

As might be expected from a Yorkshire-based company, cricket is obviously very serious business for Sykes. The 1926 catalogue majors on a premium quality line of 'Roy Kilner' bats, pads, and batting gloves. Roy was a well-known Yorkshire and England all-rounder, who achieved the double of over a thousand runs and one hundred wickets for his county in three seasons – and was a key member of the Yorkshire side that won the county championship in four years from 1922 to 1925. The strength of the Sykes association with Roy was such that even though he died at a tragically young age in 1928 his name, 'by arrangement with his widow', continued to appear on the company's bats well into the 1930s.

Maurice Leyland, another very famous Yorkshire and England cricketer, was 'so satisfied with the performance of his Sykes bat that he allowed the company to associate his name with its production'. But most significant of all, and it would be difficult to measure the impact if it had happened in recent years, was the Sykes association with the greatest batsman the world has ever seen. In 1926 a seventeen-year-old Australian, playing for the Bowral club in New South Wales, scored 300. This was by no means the first three figure innings by the young batsman but his mother had promised to buy him a new bat if he hit a century in this particular game. So he duly travelled to Sydney with his father and, after very careful consideration, selected a Sykes 'Roy Kilner' bat. He continued to use Sykes bats as his career and fame steadily increased and in 1929, during his first test series in the Australian side, he agreed to let Sykes use his name on their number one bat.

The cricket section in the 1932 catalogue opens with two pages devoted to 'Don Bradman' bats and gloves and proudly records that 'Mr. Don Bradman has used no other bats than those manufactured by William Sykes Limited throughout the whole of his cricketing career, and Sykes-made bats were used by him in compiling the world's record score (452 not out), the world's record test score (334), and the world's record season test aggregate (974).' It was probably due to Bradman's influ-

Some of their cricket balls

ence that a remarkable 19 of the 22 players at the 1930 Headingley test between England and Australia used Sykes bats.

The relationship between these famous players and Sykes is mentioned to highlight the fact that the Horbury-based business was very much in the lead in using famous players and major events to endorse its products. In addition to the great cricketers already mentioned, Arthur Dolphin of Yorkshire and England, H. B. Cameron of South Africa and Ken James of New Zealand form an international trio of wicket-keepers endorsing gloves and pads, and they recruited well-known stars to promote hockey, table tennis, water polo and crown green bowling products. Another of the all time 'Greats', Joe Davis, endorsed their billiards range. And their catalogues frequently referred to the fact that their soccer balls were used at F.A. Cup Finals, and their rugby balls in Rugby League Challenge Cup Finals.

When it came to office systems and procedures, Sykes ingenuity was again apparent. They operated a cable and telegraphic code to simplify the ordering process 'for the convenience of Colonial and also Home customers'. The code consisted of a ROOT WORD to denote a particular article, e.g. 'Bravr' stood for a size 5 Junior Bradman bat, and an Affix to be added to the root word to indicate the required quantity, e.g. IS for two items, ERO for 18. Thus an order for two size 5 Junior Bradman bats would be transmitted as BRAVIS. In this way a quite complex order for nine completely different products, each with a different quantity required, would be cabled to Horbury using just nine code words.

Visible evidence of the company's growth and success, a new head office building, was opened in 1930 at the front of the factory site, and, even today, it is an imposing and modern looking structure. Its impact in 1930 was such that 'many visitors to the town mistook it for the Town Hall, recognising that it was by far the most impressive piece of architecture in the district'.

At the same time the company records show that its 500 employees were producing 300,000 footballs per annum, 60,000 cricket bats, 50,000 tennis rackets, 30,000 hockey sticks, and 25,000 sets of boxing gloves as well as what must have been hundreds of thousands of units across the vast range of accessories, and then smaller quantities for the more specialist sports like bowls, croquet and table tennis. Although William 'Junior' died in 1931, expansion in the eight years running up to the start of the second world war continued to be impressive. In 1935 the company purchased what was probably the largest industrial building in Horbury, the Albion woollen mill built in the 1870s. Until its closure in 1986 this building was the largest manufacturing unit first for Sykes, then for Sykes and Slazenger, and eventually for the International Sports Company, which was the forerunner of Dunlop Slazenger International. During the peak periods of

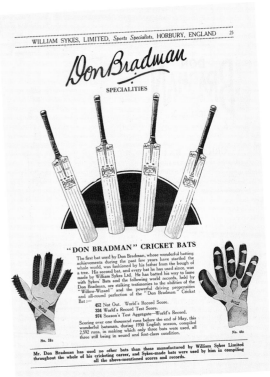

The Don Bradman page from Sykes 1932 catalogue

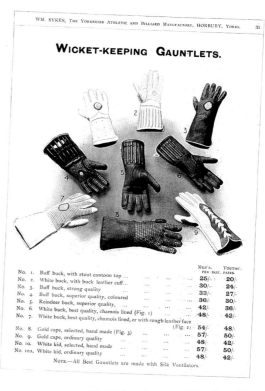

Wicket-keeping gauntlets – from 25s per dozen!

its activity, and on top of producing a huge range of finished sports products, the Albion mill plant included a tannery with an annual capacity of one million square feet. Today's visitor to Horbury will find most of the 1895 Sykes 'Manufactory' and its 1930 head office still standing, and also most of the Albion mill complex, which has been split into a number of separately owned small and diverse manufacturing units.

By the time of the merger with Ayres in 1940, at least 700 were employed at Horbury and once again it was necessary to switch from bats and rackets to meet a fresh demand from the Government. This time virtually the entire range of the company's production capacity, and its many skills in engineering, woodworking and leather processing, were devoted to the war effort. By the time the factory reached the maximum output level for its 'Military' range, nearly 1000 were employed producing an astonishing variety of products in huge quantities. These included snow shoes, flags, bayonets, ammunition boxes, gloves, belts, rifle slings, skis, balloon stabilizers, fuse cylinders, three million snow and sand goggles, rocket tail components, officers' kit bags, 300,000 pairs of drivers' gloves and 120,000 pairs of workmen's gloves for the U.S. forces, dinghy leak stoppers, pilot's knee writing pads, 50,000 kits of tank waterproofing equipment, seventeen and a half million detonator caps and, not forgetting the recreational moments allowed to the armed forces, fencing equipment, medicine balls, Indian clubs, boxing gloves and, of course, several hundred thousand footballs.

Possibly the most notable item of military hardware produced was the more than one million sets of rifle furniture and 80,000 machine-gun butts. Although the

Making rifle furniture at Horbury

workforce was very experienced in woodworking processes, the manufacture of rifle butts required the introduction of a large number of ultra-modern, special machines, jigs and tools, which were largely designed and built by the factory's own drawing office and engineers. Rifle furniture production started in March, 1941, at the rate of 500 sets per week and rapidly built to a peak of 11,000 sets by the end of 1942. The company's special brochure describing its wartime contribution proudly reports that, 'It will be seen that although weekly output increased 22 times, the actual labour force increased little more than four times – a striking testimony to modern methods, improved machinery and the incentive of a bonus scheme.' Interesting, too, to see that the specially constructed storage sheds for seasoning the wood used in making cricket bats proved ideal for preparing the walnut, birch and beech for rifle butts.

The factory was considered sufficiently important to be visited by Ernest Bevin, the wartime Minister of Labour. This occasion fell roughly half way between two other very notable events for Horbury. In 1931, Prince George, later the Duke of Kent, visited the older factory and its brand new head office. He had been advised by his Yorkshire hosts to see the famous factory that made the bats for Don Bradman, and also the office buildings so grand as to be regularly mistaken for a town hall.

William Sykes's extensive factory at Horbury

Just over a quarter of a century later, the Duke of Edinburgh visited both Horbury and Barnsley, by which time the Slazenger name was over the doors of both plants. The Duke, who was very impressed by the smartness of the Horbury station and the factory, both of which had been newly painted for the occasion, was accompanied by Michael McMaster, chairman of Slazengers, and during the visit he met Len Hutton, who introduced him to Donald Ward, who was then making his bats and had previously made them for Don Bradman. Before leaving the Duke was presented with a pair of boxing gloves specially made for Prince Charles by Mrs. Edith Steele of Gervase Road, Horbury. *Harpers Sports and Games*, who covered the visit, reported that, 'The spontaneous cheering with which Prince Philip was so often greeted was a sincere tribute to the interest he had taken in everything he saw, and a heart-warming demonstration of the genuine loyalty, affection and esteem in which he is held. It was indeed a great day for Slazengers.'

The history of this remarkable company, which had a completely separate existence for nearly seventy years before its merger with Slazenger, is very much a testimony to the virtues and commercial skills of the Sykes family and to the community of Horbury. Major buildings, that housed its production equipment and provided the platform for its expansion, still stand and, very appropriately, an extremely vibrant factor in the community is the Slazenger Sports Club, which was set up by the company in 1950 and now, as a flourishing and financially independent organization, provides high quality and up-to-date facilities for cricket, tennis, bowls, soccer and hockey – as well as an excellent social club – for hundreds of local sports enthusiasts including many youth teams.

The foundation of the success of William Sykes Limited, laid down by William in the 1870s, was the tradition of quality and service he instilled into his sons and also all his employees. At its heart was the continuity of both its management and its policies primarily maintained by the Sykes family but also by a workforce and management that lived mainly in the area and, many of whom, like William and his sons, followed each other into the business. One of the most notable examples of that pattern was the Wycherley succession of grandfather, father and son, all of whom worked initially in the tannery. Peter, who was the last member of the family to join the company, started at Horbury in 1953 with Slazengers and before retiring in 1993 held a number of senior management positions in Slazengers, International Sports Company and Dunlop Slazenger International, including a spell in New Zealand. His father, who was a senior production manager for both Sykes and Slazenger, designed the first laceless football launched after the second world war and also invented the 'Sykeometer', which was a device to measure the pressure of a football and ensure a consistent bounce. And his grandfather, who was a key member of the management team during the company's hugely successful growth period between the wars, invented the twelve-panel 'Zig-Zag' football, which was a premium product for nearly thirty years.

Both Ralph Slazenger and William Sykes died in 1910. They would have been competitors since Slazengers entered the sports trade in 1881 and their companies continued to be among the leading UK manufacturers until they joined forces in 1942. Then Slazengers, and their subsidiary, Gradidges, acquired the share capital of both Sykes and Ayres to create the largest sports group in Europe. Although enemy bombers had deprived them of their London factories, which made the acquisition of a manufacturing base in Yorkshire very attractive, the Slazenger brand and marketing capability remained extremely powerful. So the union of these southern and northern sports giants made immediate sense as well as preparing them for future growth after the war. Whether or not the outcome would have been the same if the Slazenger board had been obliged to negotiate with either William Sykes, or his sons, will never be known, but in the event it wasn't very long before only the Slazenger name appeared on Horbury products and the Sykes name, along with Ayres and Gradidge, faded from the sports scene it had embellished for nearly seventy years.

It is appropriate to close the Sykes chapter by drawing a paragraph from one of the brochures published by the company just before the outbreak of war, and which set out the enduring principles of the business as they had been established by William, and main-

Joe Davis endorsed Sykes miniature billiard tables

tained by his family and employees throughout the life of what had become probably Horbury's best known company:

Neither mere chance nor especially fortuitous circumstances could produce such outstanding proof of supremacy in every branch of sport. It is evidence, evidence beyond dispute, that today, under the high speed and pressure at which every game is played, Sykes experience, stretching back nearly three-quarters of a century, enables them to produce sports goods of an unassailable quality, sports goods in which age-old craftsmanship is combined with the latest scientific developments. The result is a range of sports goods supreme the world over. This is no idle talk or boastful statement. It is proved to you by the use of Sykes British-made sports goods in games throughout the whole world. So why think further about your choice of equipment? Time is all too short and money is far too valuable to be spent and wasted in trying many makes. Follow the lead of the leaders and insist on Sykes better aids to better sport. All the knowledge and care of Sykes's years of experience can be yours today. And Sykes sports goods cost no more than ordinary sports equipment. But what a lot more you get for the same money. Confidence born of the knowledge that Sykes British-made sports goods will not only never fail you but will actually help you in your game through their accuracy of design and soundness of construction embodied in the age-old craftsmanship and the modern scientific developments of today. Our dealers throughout the country will be only too glad to help you in your choice of Sykes sports goods – the British-made sports goods that you will use tomorrow. But which you can use today.

6 WILLIAM SYKES LIMITED, Sports Specialists, HORBURY, ENGLAND

FOOTBALLS
18 PANEL DESIGNS

Patent No. 236389—1924.
"ZIG-ZAG 18"
See Page 7.

Patent No. 292196—1927.
"ZIG-ZAG 18 INVERTED"
See Page 7.

Patent No. 301714—1928
"Y.A.M. 18"
Models "B" and "C"
See Page 7.

"FACILE PRINCEPS"
"SYKRAFT A"
See Page 8.

"B.K.O. 18"
See Page 8.

"ELITE 18"
See Page 8.

Some of Sykes famous soccer balls from the 1935 catalogue

Sykes ball leads Sheffield Wednesday on to the pitch at the Wembley Cup Final in 1935

GRADIDGES

An 1890 advertisement of H Gradidge of Woolwich – 'All Tennis Bats Strung with Best English Gut'.

Some nine years before the Sykes and Ayres merger in 1940 Slazengers and Gradidges had 'formed an alliance', which was the first Slazenger – and McMaster – inspired step towards the creation of an 'association of four outstanding firms to pool their resources for the specialist production in peace of sports products of all types, to the manufacture of which they could bring such unrivalled knowledge and experience'.

Having examined what Ayres and Sykes brought to this sports coalition, it is now appropriate to look at the Gradidge contribution. In product terms, and at the time of the merger with Slazenger, they brought a very powerful cricket presence and, subsequently, in 1935, the Gradidge brand and expertise, still operating in separate premises, opened the door for Slazenger to operate in the golf market more effectively than ever before. And, in addition to the product impact, possibly of greater importance had been the arrival on the scene of the owners of Gradidges, the twin brothers Michael and Humphrey McMaster.

But to revert to the beginning of the Gradidge story. Cricket has been described as 'casting a ball at three straight sticks and defending the same with a fourth'. For the most part the history of Gradidges is about the 'fourth stick', the bat, which in the very early years of the game was very similar in shape to a hockey stick. The present shape evolved around 1775, but more than fifty years were to elapse before its construction began to resemble the modern bat. Then ash handles were spliced into the bat and in 1860 the first whole cane handles were produced. Although bowlers were pitching the ball up in the 18th century, it would be many years before batsmen gave any thought to wrist play. So long as the drive was the principal shot, bats continued to be heavy. With the eventual popularity of wrist play and more skilful technique, accurate balance, lightness, resilience and strength became all important factors in bat design and manufacture. Something more was then needed than the rough and ready methods of a more primitive age.

Responding to this growing demand for more sophisticated equipment, Harry Gradidge started making bats in Woolwich in 1870, which was five years after W. G. Grace's first class debut and the same year that the Kent county set up was reorganised after an earlier start in 1859. Kent is mentioned because a strong connection

Harry Gradidge surrounded by his racket and bat makers

developed between Gradidges and the county side, which was to provide a rich list of star players to use their products – bats, pads and gloves – notably Frank Woolley, Leslie Ames, Brian Valentine, Arthur Fagg, Godfrey Evans, Colin Cowdrey and Alan Knott. The foundation of the company's success in the cricket market was Harry Gradidge's determination, right from the start of production, to employ only the most skilled craftsmen and to produce bats that would exactly meet the requirements of the most skilled exponents of this rapidly maturing and expanding game. He took the same approach to cricket balls, which he made in a small separate factory in Tonbridge. Again the 'Kent connection'.

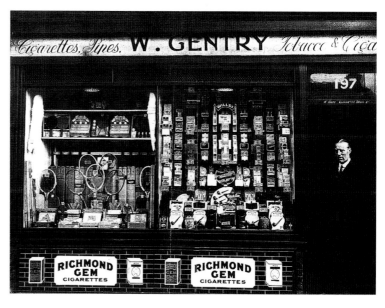

Shop window in Plumstead about 1900 packed with Slazenger rackets and balls and Gradidge bats

The emphasis on cricket is still very apparent seventy years later in the make-up of some of the last catalogues produced by the company before the start of the second world war. Although their product line then included tennis, hockey, lacrosse, badminton, squash, rackets, fives, soccer and rugby balls and boxing gloves, two-thirds of the catalogue is devoted to everything required for cricket. And by this time the link with Kent has been augmented by no less than Yorkshire's Len Hutton. The centrepiece of the cricket section is a page devoted to the 'Four Rose' quality bat, with which he scored his record 354 against the Australians at the Oval in 1938. He is pictured being congratulated by his batting partner, Joe Hardstaff, and by the Australian captain, Don Bradman, who, on this occasion, hadn't been able to use his Sykes bat during his side's response to the England total of 903 for 7 wickets because he'd broken his ankle while bowling. A later, post war addition to this list of remarkable Gradidge batsmen was Denis Compton (soon to be switched to Slazenger) and, as will be seen later, the connection between the Slazenger companies and the very best of the world's cricketers has been maintained right through to the new millennium with the Panther branding carrying on the tradition of excellence established by Harry Gradidge in 1870.

In 1935 Gradidges entered the golf market with a range of steel shafted clubs. As Harry Gradidge, sixty-five years earlier, had been quick to see the potential for a more sophisticated design for cricket bats, so the company was now quick to recognise that the legalising of steel shafts by the Royal and Ancient in 1929 was having as sweeping an effect on the game as the wound ball when it first appeared in 1902. The new shafts gave golfers the extra length they always look for and

A 1921 Gradidge advertisement featuring the famous 'Imperial Driver' bat

Bobby Locke in action with his
Gradidge driver

slowly but certainly steel replaced hickory. This meant that much of the work to produce the shafts, which had previously been done by hand with immense care and artistry – and in many cases by descendants of the great club making families – now moved from the professional's shop on the course to new factories.

So club manufacture started at the Woolwich factory. Gradidges clubs very quickly established an excellent reputation and only a year later Alf Padgham used them to win the 1936 Open at Hoylake. Henry Cotton won in 1937, with Dunlop '65' balls, but Gradidge clubs were in the bag of the 1938 champion, Reg Whitcombe. Both in 1938 and 1939 the Woolwich-made clubs were used to win a large number of major tournaments, including the Open championships in Ireland, France, Holland (both years), Scandinavia, Belgium, New Zealand (both years) and South Africa (also both years). And in 1939 the British and French Amateur championships were also 'Gradidge wins'. After the war, and the formation of the enlarged Slazenger group, the clubs were marketed under the Slazenger brand and with great success. Among the leading players to use them were Bobby Locke, who had originally played them as Gradidge clubs and went on to win four British Opens, Ben Hogan, Jack Nicklaus, Johnny Miller and Seve Ballesteros. The period between 1934 and 1958 was extraordinarily successful for the Dunlop and Slazenger/Gradidge combination at the British Open. Of the nineteen championships during that period no fewer than sixteen were won by players using either clubs and/or balls produced by these companies – seven went to Gradidge/Slazenger and twelve to Dunlop.

The inspiration for the Gradidges move into golf was Humphrey McMaster, a scratch golfer who had won the South African amateur title. He and his twin brother, Michael, also an accomplished sportsman, had bought Gradidges in 1927 following the death of Tim Gradidge, the son of the firm's founder. The McMasters were born in Porlock, Somerset, in 1896. Both had distinguished naval careers in the first world war – Humphrey had served in the same ship as the future King George VI – and shortly after the war ended they moved to South Africa where they worked together in the sugar trade before buying Taylor & Ellis, a well-known sports company.

In 1930 the *Sports Trader* had paid tribute to the achievements of the McMasters, who 'although they have not been in Woolwich very long had proved themselves real good sportsmen, young men of initiative and enterprise and to be trusted to continue the fine traditions of the House of Gradidge'. The occasion for this tribute was a luncheon to mark the opening of an extension to the Woolwich premises 'to cope with the steadily increasing demand for the Gradidge service'. To further celebrate the event the brothers were presented with silver cigarette cases; the one given to Humphrey was inscribed to the 'Outside Smasher', and the other to Michael to the 'Inside Economics'. Years later interviews with those who had worked with these remarkable twins, both to be chairmen of Slazengers, confirmed the aptness of these inscriptions. Humphrey was regarded as an outstanding sales and marketing man with a

Len Hutton and the Imperial Driver he
used to score 364 against the
Australians in 1938

great capacity for building lasting relationships with key customers, and Michael was seen as an extremely skilful businessman.

The 1931 sale of Gradidges to Slazengers was negotiated by the McMasters with a Slazenger board that included one of the company's founders, Albert Slazenger, and its joint managing-directors, Archdale Palmer and Tim Hadingham. There is more to say about this very distinguished trio in the Slazenger section of this history but it is important to note this very crucial moment in the whole story as the three Slazenger directors joined the Gradidge board, and the McMasters, who would eventually pilot the Slazenger ship for nearly forty years, joined that company's board. This early reference to the Slazenger line of succession draws attention to the fact that throughout the nearly one hundred years of its existence, either as a separate company or as a clearly identified operating entity within the Dunlop organisation, only three names – Slazenger, McMaster and Hadingham – were attached to the role of chairman.

1930 *Sports Trader* sketches of Michael and Humphrey McMaster

The Gradidge range included fives and rackets equipment

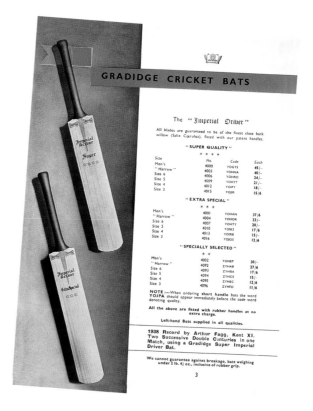

The 'Imperial Driver' featured in the 1939 Gradidge catalogue

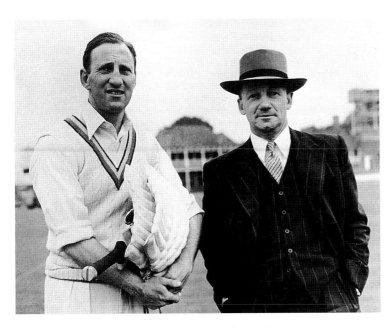

Len Hutton (Gradidge) and Don Bradman (Sykes) in 1953

Gradidge's separate existence within the Slazenger group effectively ended in 1940, when the Woolwich factory was severely damaged by German bombs. After the war both golf clubs and cricket bats were produced at Horbury, in the latter case involving craftsmen transferred from London. The clubs were quite quickly re-branded Slazenger, but the bats, enhanced by the Gradidge pedigree, evolved through a more gradual process of showing first Gradidge only, then Gradidge with a small Slazenger and, finally, to Slazenger only. By then both the Ayres and Sykes brands had also disappeared.

SLAZENGER

During the 1930s Slazenger introduced a new tennis racket, 'The Victory', which was named after Nelson's flagship, and to promote its launch put a full-page advert in the *Daily Mail*. Not only was that almost certainly a first in promotional terms for a sports product but this racket was also the first to carry a logo, stencilled on the strings, in the shape of a diamond. This marking was designed to encourage the best results by hitting the ball in the middle of the racket. During that same period the company started using the slogan 'Keep your eye on the ball – and see it's a Slazenger'. Keeping your eye on the ball has become a commonly used phrase for all sorts of situations requiring focus, which is certainly highly appropriate during the Wimbledon fortnight when, every year, the world's best players try their hardest to keep their eyes on Slazenger balls.

In no sense does this reference to the 'Victory' racket, with its logo and slogan, reflect the whole Slazenger story but it does serve to highlight several of the key elements of this remarkable business. Perhaps the most important point to pick out is the connection with tennis, which has always been the most important of the sports for which the company has produced high quality equipment for 120 years. Against that overall tennis background has been the key factor of Slazenger tennis balls, widely acknowledged as the best in the world for many years and, most appropriately, linked with the Wimbledon tournament as the 'World's Championship Ball' (an early claim) for 100 years. Add to that the innovative promotional approach adopted more than seventy years ago and there are some of the clues to why the Slazenger name has achieved such durable fame as one of the great sports equipment brands.

The earlier accounts of how Ayres, Sykes and Gradidges made their distinctive marks on the UK and worldwide sports scene during the span of well over 100 years also showed how much they brought to what eventually became just Slazengers. All of them were in business before Slazengers started their sports business in 1881 and, in their various ways, made unique contributions to the development of sports goods manufacture and marketing. However, Slazengers were quick to catch them up, certainly in the early years of the 20th century, and before the second world war brought a near total halt to sports manufacturing they had become the dominant force of the four companies. In fact by the end of the 1930s it would have been the relatively much younger Dunlop sports business that would have been offering the greatest challenge to Slazenger, and particularly so in the tennis market.

The 'Victory' and 'Queen's' rackets appear in the 1933 Wimbledon programme

Archdale Palmer, a key figure in the development of Slazenger

Edward (Tim) Hadingham, managing-director of the UK business and later chairman of the South African operation

To search for the reasons for the success of Slazengers is to find that it was very largely, if not entirely, due to the energy and vision of a relatively small group of outstanding leaders. And, equally important is the fact that they were successfully involved in the business, over a 100 year period, two or three in any one stage in its development, and in each case for at least ten and up to forty or fifty years. This provided a solid line of succession particularly adept at maintaining the strong principles and traditions established at the very start by Ralph and Albert Slazenger. To those founding brothers also goes the huge credit for having the foresight to see the potential for a high quality sports business and to take the decision, very early in its history, to maximise that potential by transferring the location of its head office and factories from Manchester to London. The latter would have been much closer to the strongest centres of demand for their key tennis and croquet ranges. After Ralph's early death in 1910 the business was driven forward by Albert with the assistance of two key figures, Archdale Palmer and Tim Hadingham, both of whom were managing-directors. In 1931, when their company, Gradidges, was purchased by Slazenger, Michael and Humphrey McMaster brought an injection of more youthful leadership as successive managing-directors before and after the 1959 merger with Dunlop. Finally, and while the company still maintained a separate identity within the Dunlop organisation, the leadership baton passed to 'Buzzer' Hadingham, who had joined the company in 1933 and served it with considerable distinction and energy as European sales director, marketing director, managing-director and chairman.

All these Slazenger leaders were either accomplished or enthusiastic sportsmen and spent virtually their entire working lives in the sports business. In particular this meant they all built very strong personal relationships with their most important customers around the world, which was to prove a lasting strength for the business, and is still recalled today by many of the present Dunlop Slazenger distributors. And the same personal approach certainly enriched the company's relationships with many of the famous players who used their rackets, cricket bats and golf clubs. This was especially so during those years when the quality of both that relationship and the products was probably much more important to the players than the relatively small sums of money involved. So it is fair to say that the Slazenger style, still recognisable today, was shaped by those formidable and charismatic directors who were in charge for over 100 years. Having highlighted the management principles of the business, both internally and externally, it is now appropriate to return to the 19th century to see how it all began.

A history of the Slazenger family would, very easily, provide the basis for a separate book and has already been the subject of considerable research both by Professor Roy Jones and by one of its members, Colin Dean, who in 1987 produced an account of his findings. The excellent and quite fascinating material produced by Roy and Colin has provided the basis for the details in this history of those members of the family who founded and developed the sports business.

A Manchester directory, published in 1800, included the name Mordecai Slazenger, and his address, 4 Millar's Lane. Four years later this listing, in the same directory, is expanded to add 'Umbrella Maker'. Mordecai's origins are not clear but it appears he came to England towards the end of the 18th century, possibly via Ireland, because it is known that his wife, Isabella, was born in Dublin in 1775. Slazenger is an anglicised version of Schlesinger, which meant from Silesia in Poland, though members of the family believe they may originate from Scandinavia.

It is known that Mordecai was living in Manchester by 1795 because that is the birth date recorded there of his first son, Henry, who was the second of six children. Four of them were boys and they all, for all or part of their lives, worked as tailors in their father's successful retail business. After Mordecai died in 1819 his widow changed the fam-

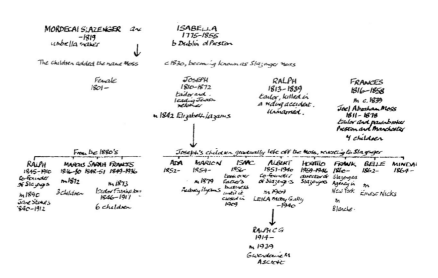

Part of the extensive Slazenger family tree, which includes Ralph, Albert, Frank, Horatio and also Albert's son, Ralph.

ily name to Slazenger Moss, so it was as Joseph Slazenger Moss that their fourth child started his working life as a second-hand clothes dealer in Warrington. In 1842 Joseph married Elizabeth Lazarus, the daughter of an itinerant trader, and by 1844 he had at least two tailor's shops, one in Lancaster and the other at his Warrington home, which was the birthplace, in 1845, of his first child, Ralph, who was to become one of the founders of the Slazenger sports business.

Joseph and Elizabeth had twelve children between 1845 and 1864, and three of his other sons, Albert, Horatio and Frank, would eventually join Ralph in the sports business. Joseph himself, who died in 1872, built a very considerable tailoring and woollen business and became a leader of the Jewish community in Manchester. After his father's death twenty-six-year-old Ralph, who had been educated at Manchester Grammar School before learning the tailoring business, took over J. S. Moss and Sons and immediately acquired two additional premises. By 1877 he had five shops in the Manchester area and his advertisements gave the first hint of the future direction of the business by proclaiming, 'J. S. Moss and Son, makers of four-in-hand driving coats and sporting clothes, military tailors.' One of the five shops, located at 23 Market Street, was 'Slazenger et Fils, importer of French fancy goods', and it was this company that, in 1881, having moved to 14, 16 and 18 Corporation Street, Manchester, was newly registered as 'Gaiter and Leggings manufacturer with factories in Manchester and Paris'. Ralph, himself, ran this part of the business, Albert was the commercial traveller, Frank worked in the warehouse and Horatio looked after the shirt and hosiery interests.

In 1883 Ralph and Albert moved the business, described in their Jubilee brochure as then 'a mere infant', to Laurence Pountney Hill, 56 Cannon Street in the City of London, which that same brochure described as 'that fat and sleepy city of riches and veiled splendour'. The building, which would be the Slazenger head office until it was demolished in 1962 to make way for the new road along the Thames embankment, had originally been a tea warehouse. At first they described themselves as India rubber goods manufacturers, but by 1890 the Post Office directory for London listed Slazenger and Sons as 'India rubber goods manufacturers, waterproofers, lawn tennis rack-

Betty Gutt, who worked in the Woolwich tennis ball factory in the 1890s

The Slazenger tennis ball factory in Woolwich as it was in 1910.

ets and appliances, cricket bat makers, football and football boots, legging and gaiter manufacturers', with a factory in Holland Street, Woolwich.

As suggested by the 1890 directory listing, the pace of expansion had quickened and the future direction of the business had begun to emerge. It seems reasonable to assume that the move to London coincided with a decision by Ralph and Albert to move very strongly into the newly expanding sports equipment markets where Ayres, Sykes and Gradidges were among a large number of companies to have already established flourishing businesses. From 1884 onwards *Pastime* magazine carried their adverts starting with the 'Demon' and 'Renshaw' rackets for one guinea and 12s 6d respectively. The 'Guinea Demon' was 'guaranteed strung with 18-strand gut and perfect in every detail'. Each racket carried the signature of Slazenger and Sons and was numbered for reference and warranty. One of these adverts is next to the announcement of the first issue of the *Lawn Tennis Magazine*, which it promised would contain 'two excellent portraits of lawn tennis celebrities [they would be the Renshaw brothers, both early Slazenger players] original articles and interesting news', and which further emphasizes the growing interest in the game. Other rackets soon followed, notably the 'Lawford', the 'Ich Dien' and, in a range extension move so frequently copied in later years, the 'Special Demon', which *The Field* reported 'has more drive than any we have yet tried'.

The Slazenger factory in Woolwich, now a private residence and office, as it is today.

The brothers were also revealing their innovative skills. An 1886 patent application by Ralph described a new game to be called Badminton Tennis, which involved a Tivey, or shuttlecock, being struck by 'tennis bats' over an elevated net with two movable courts, one each side of the net, preferably formed of Japanese paper or any similar material that would emit a sound when struck by the Tivey so that the opponent would know whether or not it had landed in or out of his adversary's court. A year later Albert, still calling himself Slazenger Moss, applied for a patent for woollen tennis balls made impervious to moisture 'by the introduction of a chemical preparation for the purpose of waterproofing fabrics'.

This year, 1887, saw the start of tennis ball production, which was possibly the most important decision made during the early days of the business. The Holland Street factory wasn't large enough to contain the new production line so new premises were found in Lower Wood Street, Woolwich.

Amazingly the building still exists and is largely unaltered in appearance, though part of it is now a private residence. Mr John Goodman, who lives in the area, and whose grandmother, Betty Gutt, sewed tennis ball covers in the new factory in the 1890s, has provided intriguing insight into the working conditions between the wars based on the published recollections of Cissie Gouldson, who remembers her experiences when fitting covers to the balls:

The work, from 9.00 to 5.30 at piece-work rates, was tiring and repetitive but by 1930 she was able to make £3 a week whilst her husband, Arthur, also a Slazenger employee but doing less skilful work, was only earning 19s a week. The cover fitting was carried out on the first floor. The glued balls and covers were brought up on a lift from the ground floor and using an awl, the girls stripped the edges of the cover and then fitted them closely to the ball, making a fine closure seam. They were then inspected, some balls selected to be sent out for hand-stitching and some were not. Cissie's husband, Arthur, then loaded the boxes of balls into the lift, operated much like a dumb-waiter. After collecting them downstairs he loaded them onto a barrow to trundle them across the street to another part of the factory where they were 'baked' and flight-tested.

The 'baking' referred to might well have been the heat application of latex applied to the seam and although Cissie cannot recall what method was used for testing, she strongly recalls that the factory manager in the 1920s was a Mr. Groves, who was well able to afford to run a car! Cissie also recalls the pungent smells of the naptha fumes, which caused girls to regularly faint. This chemical was used to protect the 'duck-cloth' from moths and sometimes small sachets of crystals were packed in with the completed balls when boxed. She also remembered that red tennis balls were exported to India because the white balls could not be seen in the strong, Indian light. The girls were only allowed to work on them for limited periods as the colour was considered bad for the eyes.

The enthusiasm for waterproofing appears again in an early advert for the 'Reliance' waterproof football, which 'will not vary in weight in any weather and will not become greasy or difficult to pick up'. The 'Repellant' football was made from the same treated leather. By 1888 the steadily larger racket range had been joined by equipment for setting up the court and an 'All England' tennis shoe made of 'fibrous rubber of a very durable nature, and is brought out at a moderate cost'. As for the Lower Wood Street tennis balls they seem to get off to a shaky start as *Pastime* recommended its readers 'to settle for themselves by trial the vexed question of their merits'. However, despite awarding the title 'Father of lawn tennis balls' to Ayres, who were still supplying the balls to the Wimbledon tournament, the same magazine did concede that Slazenger balls were being made 'with great care and minute accuracy' and 'that it was curious and interesting to see how each ball, taken at random from a promiscuous heap, was exactly balanced in weight and severely tested for uniformity of bound.'

In 1889 the 'Whip' cricket bat is introduced embodying 'a genuine novelty – at the spot where the right hand grasps the handle this is slightly hollowed out, a piece of whalebone being inserted to compensate for the weakening of the cane'. In 1891, Albert, now signing his name with the Moss,

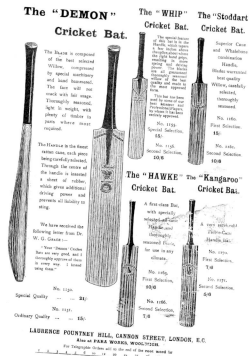

The 'Demon' brand was also applied to cricket bats

wrote to *Golf* magazine about an incident that occurred while he had been playing at the Chingford club. After landing his ball in the mud his opponent had attempted to move it with a niblick, which only made matters worse as the ball adhered in a mass of mud to the head of the club. He solved his problem by carrying the ball, attached to the club, and placing it in the hole, claiming there was no rule to prevent him doing so. It is not clear how the matter ended on the course but in response to Albert's request for a ruling on the validity of this method of holing out the editor was very firm in pointing out that 'to carry a ball any distance at the end of a club and then drop it into a hole is not Golf!'

By now Albert's interest in golf had become much more than purely recreational. In 1890 the company had advertised in *Golf* magazine for club-makers to supply them and they subsequently entered the market with products made by a number of Scottish professionals: Gow of the Glasgow club, Fairful of Larbert and Gibson of Kinghorn in Fife, who supplied the clubs to be sold in the USA. In 1891 they introduced their first golf ball, the 'Truflite', made of gutta percha and favourably noted by *Golf* as 'a hard, well-moulded, finely nicked ball, capable of withstanding much hard usage, and painted with so much care to secure immunity from chipping'. Not content with that assessment, a year later they launched the 'Slazenger', again made of gutta percha, and now *Golf* went into overdrive:

> In all externals it has all the characteristics of the 'Truflite', though not so heavy. By a series of elaborate processes in the manufacture, which, of course, are a trade secret, the material is refined in such a way as to cast aside all impurities while preserving the MAXIMUM of elasticity. It is as hard as a bone, does not hack with the iron, always preserves its shape, and springs off the wooden club at the tee with great initial velocity. We have recently subjected the ball to a severe test in play, as well as to other experiments. Playing with this ball the other day over a course replete with difficult hazards to clear, the round was accomplished in 79, on one stroke below scratch. We found the ball, instead of losing its travelling power at the end of the upward flight, and dropping to the ground in a semi-perpendicular fashion, continued its course, and gradually descended like a scarcely perceptible curve of an elongated arch. In this way the carrying power of the ball was greatly extended. One often finds, however, that a ball which drives well is treacherous on the putting green, springing off the face of the club with too great a velocity, thereby over-running the hole, and generally being very difficult to control. Contrary to expectation, this defect was absent from the Slazenger ball. It ran true, with no embarrassing vivacity. Another point which we noticed in this ball being compared with a variety of balls by well-known makers of high repute was this. Every one of the Slazenger balls floated in water, while all the other balls sank, including the 'Truflite' of the same makers, thereby showing the superiority of the new ball in elasticity and buoyancy. Again, the rebound of the ball on being dropped on stone in competition with all kinds of first class balls was at least from a foot to a foot and a half higher. Messrs. Slazenger probably do not expect that their new ball will become so popular for ordinary play as the cheaper balls now in vogue, but certainly for important matches and tournaments, either among professionals or amateurs, it may be said without the slightest divergence from the truth that, like the well-known and extensively advertised pills, they are worth 'a guinea a box'.

Early tournament successes for the golf range were achieved by Ruth Underhill with the clubs – at the 1899 USA Women's Amateur Championship – and by Harold Hilton with the ball – at the 1892 and 1897 British Opens. However these early triumphs were not maintained. Although the golf range continued to offer a limited club line, the balls were withdrawn early in the new century in the face of the all-conquering new wound balls.

Slazenger did not return as a real force in this sector until Gradidge golf clubs were introduced in 1935, and the Horbury-made B51 golf ball was launched after the second world war. The name 'Truflite' survived into the new century when it was switched to soccer and rugby balls.

Meanwhile important family affairs were occurring. In 1890 Ralph married Jane, the widow of Robert Stokes of Hawkes Bay, New Zealand. It has been said that she was very wealthy and it is likely that the additional funds she brought to the family helped to finance the expansion of the business. Albert, as co-founder, had been alongside Ralph from the very start, and in the 1890s the younger brothers, Horatio and Frank, joined them. Horatio moved to London as a director

A 1999 Wimbledon poster recalling a 1920s scene

mainly concerned with sales and marketing and remained on the board until his death in 1946. Frank, who was the youngest of Joseph's sons, and twenty-five years younger than Ralph, moved to New York, probably in the mid 1890s, where he was soon selling golf clubs under the name of Frank Slazenger. He was also active in the purchasing area as in 1896 he was one of the first to buy Persimmon heads from Crawford, McGregor and Canby of Dayton, Ohio, presumably for shipment to the UK.

The company's catalogues for 1904 and 1910 show the extent of the success in building an extremely attractive and comprehensive range, albeit with that consistent emphasis on the flagship tennis line, and, to a lesser extent, on croquet. And by now both the catalogues and the products illustrated are prominently displaying the company's trademark based on the Star of David with 'S & S L' in the centre supported by 'Best is Best' across the top and 'Thro the World' across the bottom. And a fiercesome 'Demon' had been developed to highlight this premium racket line. Cricket, golf, hockey, badminton, football and 'other games' are also listed with comparatively small-

The famous 'Best is Best' Slazenger and Sons trademark incorporating the Star of David

The dramatic Demon advert

er ranges, but the overall product line approach being pursued as they entered the 20th century would have made them a potent competitor for their longer established rivals, Ayres and Sykes. The 1910 catalogue is a remarkable publication featuring complex multi-colour theme pages for the main sports, which would have a sensational impact if issued today, not least because of the huge range and variety of products offered. This marketing approach, common to most of the leading sports manufacturers, remained the norm right through to the start of the second world war.

Expanding on some of the key features of the 1910 range, it included 33 tennis rackets with the 'Doherty' frame at the top end at 30s, supported by the proud boast that, 'The World's Championship had been won no less than fifteen times between 1890 and 1908 with our rackets, of which the highest honours in single-handed lawn tennis were secured with the Doherty racket for the eleven consecutive years ending 1906, while the World's Championship 1908, and both the Covered Court Championships, 1908, have been won with our new production – the "Slazenger"'. Among the bewildering array of other rackets the special two-page treatment given to the 'Demon' stands out and includes the ringing endorsements of both *The Field* and *Land and Water*, the latter declaring, 'For genuine good service we have not heard any racket better spoken of than this, as it is a fine driver, and stands wear well.' The early attention given to building business abroad is reflected by the inclusion of the specially made 'Colonial' and 'Kangaroo' rackets for the 'Australasian' trade, and the 'Cato' and 'Viceroy' specially made for the Indian market 'and other tropical climates'. The latter had originally been called the 'Kaiser-I-Hind', but by 1910 it was obviously deemed appropriate to think in terms of the British, rather than the German Empire. The overseas theme is repeated in the multi-coloured ball section, featuring the 'Colonial', which was 'for all countries situated at a great distance from where the ball is made, and where extremes of temperature have to be contended with', and the 'Tropical' – available in thirteen two-colour combinations plus any other combination of colours desired – and 'specially suited for hot climates or when the sun is very glaring'. The star product in the ball section is clearly the 'World's Championship Ball', at 15s 6d per dozen, which can now claim to have been selected for nine Wimbledons, five Dwight-Davis international competitions and the 1904 and 1908 Olympics. The tennis-shoe range has now expanded to twelve different styles, and, of course, there is absolutely everything required for the court from the line tapes and score books to the stop netting, plus five complete, boxed sets for the game and a host of minor accessories.

Croquet is given the same treatment as tennis, though in this case 13 complete sets are available for the game. There are 10 Badminton rackets, no fewer then 16 hockey sticks, 6 qualities of rugby and soccer balls, 16 cricket balls and 8 bats. Notably, the 'Demon' bat boasts the approval of no less a figure than Dr. W. G. Grace, who is quoted alongside the illustration of this premium line as saying, 'Your "Demon" cricket bats are very good and I thoroughly approve of them in every way. I intend using them'. This was an excellent, early endorsement by the greatest batsman of his day to be followed in later years, for Sykes, Gradidge and Slazenger bats, by such equally legendary figures as Bradman, Hutton, Compton and Sobers and then right through to the 21st century by present day 'Greats' like Mark Waugh, Shaun Pollock, Jacques Kallis and Alec Stewart.

The golf section is quite small and – very much in the same way as Sykes and Ayres at this stage – is based on a good range of accessories with just two sets of clubs. In 1910 Slazenger offered the 'Boodie' range at 4s 6d per club for the woods and 5s for the irons, and the slightly cheaper 'St. Andrews' set with both woods and irons for 3s 6d each per club.

In case the lower price suggested inferior quality the accompanying caption declared that, 'These are first-class clubs, suitable for either experts or beginners. The materials are the same as those used for the best clubs, but, by the introduction of machinery, we are enabled to produce them at the prices stated. Also made in sizes suitable for ladies and youths at the same prices.'

Among the 'other games' included in the catalogue are squash, fives, lacrosse, quoits, bowls, netball, real tennis, polo, ice hockey, table tennis and 'the new game of Whiff-Whaff, or Table Badminton at 10s 6d per set of posts and net, two vellum-covered bats and shuttlecocks. The players are required to provide their own dining-table for both Whiff-Whaff and table tennis, in the latter case the catalogue claiming that, 'It is the revival of a game which was introduced by us about twelve years ago, the improvement in this new game being the discovery of a material which lends itself to the manufacture of what we call a feather-weight ball.'

However, it's quite clear that lawn tennis is absolutely the number one sport for Slazenger and Sons, as it has been throughout the history of the brand in the sports business. The opening pages of the 1910 catalogue emphasise this marketing priority as they highlight the company's four main rackets: 'Demon, Doherty', the new 'Slazenger' and the 'E.G.M.', which is 'made from the instructions of the well-known expert, Mr. E. G. Meers, to whose recognised mechanical knowledge we are indebted for the production of this magnificent racket'. The 'Gore' racket, 'made to the instructions of Mr. A. W. Gore, All England champion in 1902 and 1908,' isn't included in the top four but commands the highest price of 30s, which is applied to only five of the more than thirty frames on offer. The price/volume relationship appears to be a key factor with the 'Demon', which is given by far the most dramatic presentation, available at 15s in 'Ordinary' quality and 21s in the 'Special' version. The introduction to the supporting text for this racket warns that 'The "Demon" racket has the largest sale of any racket, and has induced unprincipled dealers to introduce spurious imitations. We, therefore, beg to caution the public to see that "The Demon" is stamped on every racket.'

But the real strength of their approach to the tennis market is their ability to showcase not only their very popular rackets but also the 'Slazenger' lawn tennis ball, which 'has now been before the public for many years, and adopted without intermission at the All England Championship since 1902' when that supremely prestigious endorsement was wrested from Ayres.

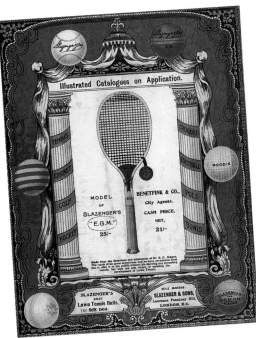

E G Meers was the expert who gave his name to Slazenger's 'EGM' racket, one of their top four frames in 1910, along with 'Demon', 'Doherty' and 'Slazenger'

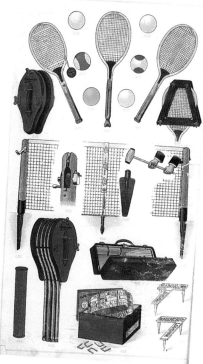

By 1910, the Slazenger tennis line provided all the equipment required to play the game

A 1917 *Sports Trader* ad for the
'World's Championship Ball'

That 1902 switch to Slazenger balls must be regarded as probably the single most important event in the company's history and very much the basis of the brand's strength still evident one hundred years later. It is doubtful if the full and lasting impact of the 1902 decision would have been apparent at the time, but this whole history might well have taken a different course if Ayres had held on to the Wimbledon endorsement they had first secured in 1879.

All of which introduces the name of Archdale Palmer, who joined the company in 1905 and became its sole managing-director until 1927 when Tim Hadingham came to the board as joint-managing-director. He remained on the board until retirement in 1946, which meant that he had provided that vital element of management continuity from the early years of the century, when Ralph and Albert were rapidly building the business, through the testing period following Ralph's sudden death in 1910 and then the difficulties of the first world war, and finally for the nearly thirty years after that through the ups and downs of the 1920s and 1930s and the second war. As he had worked for Ralph and Albert so he subsequently was the senior director when the McMaster twins took the helm after the acquisition of Gradidges in 1931. He was remembered both by 'Buzzer' Hadingham, who would himself become managing-director and then chairman, and by Bill Peters, who joined the company as a filing clerk at Laurence Pountney Hill in 1922, as a gentleman. 'Buzzer' also recalled he was a supreme expert on port and, in other and varied claims to fame, he was a J.P., and an uncle to Raymond Glendinning, the famous BBC sports commentator. More relevantly from the Slazenger standpoint he is also remembered as 'decisive in manner, of first-class business capacity, sanguine but not reckless, with many friends in and out of the City, and a man of the world with no known vices'. He was a bachelor, who lived at Nazing in Essex in a substantial house named 'Rockwood', which, much later, was home to Cliff Richard.

The Slazenger connection with Wimbledon was made three years before Archdale Palmer joined the company. But, crucially, before becoming its managing-director his previous position had been Secretary of the All England Lawn Tennis and Croquet Club. Before the 1902 tournament he had been instrumental in arranging a round robin, signed by a number of the senior players, which stated a preference for the Slazenger ball for use in the championships. Although the Club's committee had been satisfied with the Ayres ball they responded to the players' pressure by agreeing to the switch to Slazenger. However, this was not the end of the matter. In 1905 one of the referees resigned because he believed the balls were the wrong size and, therefore, illegal. The committee were reluctant to lose the benefit of having the balls supplied free of charge and their refusal to change the ball supplier might have ended there except for the fact the referee in question was also a journalist and let it be known that Slazenger had made it a practice to send £100 to the club. Additionally it became known that the company had been contributing to the cost of the Lawn Tennis Association's journal and the whole affair became the subject of wide debate, including suggestions that

Archdale Palmer was exercising too much influence in these matters. Eventually, in 1906, the club took the decision to pay for the balls for the championships but by then Archdale Palmer had resigned and joined the Slazenger board. Although the company had come in for a great deal of criticism during this period, mainly because it was felt in some quarters that they had too strong a hold on the game, particularly in relation to supplying balls at no charge to the major tournaments, they had not been alone in pursuing the endorsement policy as Ayres had operated similar arrangements for the Bournemouth and Eastbourne tournaments.

But the issue re-surfaced at the 1913 annual meeting of the Lawn Tennis Association when Mr. P. W. Rootham told those present that 'representations had been made to the committee of the All England Lawn Tennis Club that the method employed by them of selecting the ball for the championships was bad, but they had practically been ignored'. Mr. Rootham went on to suggest that while the club had stated their selection method was based on asking the players to choose the ball he had grave doubts whether the ball was, in fact, selected in this way. He further alleged that 'a portion' of the committee saw to it that one particular ball was chosen year after year, that a ring had been formed for this purpose and thus a monopoly created. He went on to name two committee members – one of them the father of H. L. Doherty (winner of five men's singles titles) – who owned Slazenger shares and, therefore, stood to benefit in the form of dividends from trading results that would be favourably affected by the ball connection with the championships. This allegation was regarded sufficiently seriously to be placed before an eminent barrister, who, after a formal inquiry, reported to the LTA and the club that while he felt it was wrong in principle for a committee member to be involved in a voting procedure that could be regarded as having a benefit for a company in which he is interested, he was satisfied that 'neither of them had any improper motive in taking part in a vote or were influenced in any way by their holdings of shares in the commercial company owning the ball selected'. He added that he was also satisfied that 'the votes given by the two members in question in no way affected the result arrived at'. Apparently Mr. Rootham declined to attend the inquiry and it was also reported that none of those who did appear before the barrister had any complaint to make about the selection method. Since those early, and slightly shaky years of the relationship between the company and the world's number one tournament, the connection has become immensely strong and is based on much more than simply providing the balls each year, as will be explained later.

This digression into the events surrounding the start of the famous connection with the Wimbledon tournament is justified because it has played such an important part in the company's history. The examination of the 1910 catalogue showed how the number of titles won with Slazenger rackets, and the ball adoption, had become central to the promotional thrust

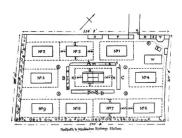

The layout of the Wimbledon courts at the original Worple Road site before the 1922 move to Church Road

Horse-power for the Wimbledon roller in the 1920s – Slazenger and Ayres made boots for the horse to protect the court surface

The style of dress, and the entrance prices, date this queue for Wimbledon as between the wars

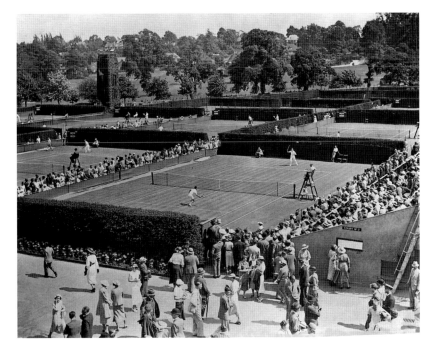

How easy to walk about at Wimbledon in the 1930s

of the business. But 1910 stands out as a landmark year in the overall Dunlop Slazenger story for other reasons as well. It was the year when Ralph died so unexpectedly, when another of the great men of the sports business, William Sykes of Horbury, died, and it was also the first full year of the Dunlop entry into the golf ball market.

Although, in 1910, Archdale Palmer had become a major influence in the conduct of the business, Ralph's early death was a huge blow, and not only for the company. As its first and founding chairman he had been responsible, with Albert, for its early and successful development, and he had also become a major and hugely respected figure in the City of London. The reports of his death noted that he had been born in Lymn, Cheshire – though, in fact his actual birthplace had been Warrington – and went on to record, more accurately, that his name was 'a familiar one wherever lawn tennis is played'. Also that he had been a man of fine physique, keenly interested in athletics of all kinds, a keen sportsman and a good shot, and that he had served for thirty years in the Lancashire Light Infantry, a volunteer regiment, from which he had retired with the rank of captain. His considerable stature in the City had been based on his readiness to devote a great deal of time to public affairs, particularly those related to the City of London Corporation. His name was on the roll of no fewer than eight Livery Companies, he was master of the Needlemakers' Company and in 1909 had been elected to the important position of Sheriff. During his year of office he fulfilled no fewer than 590 public engagements, and when it is noted that he was also Governor of the Royal National Orthopaedic and Christ's Hospital and of the Royal School for Deaf Children, as well as being the chairman of an important and growing business, there has to be the thought that his untimely death could at least in part have been due to trying to do too much at a time when he could just as well have considered retirement.

Despite the severe blow of Ralph's sudden death the successful development of the business was maintained, which was obviously largely due to the skills, energy and continuity of the management team led by Albert and Archdale Palmer. Though not quite so heavily involved in public duties as Ralph had been, Albert had become a prominent member of society, a member of the RAC Club, had been admitted to the Gold and Silver Wyre Drawer's Company and succeeded his brother on the Court of Common Council for the Dowgate Ward, which included Laurence Pountney Hill. Having started the business with Ralph in 1881 he now became its chairman, a position he held until his death in 1940. He was to spend nearly 60 of his 83 years in the business – 60 years of momentous change and many huge challenges – and should be regarded as the principal architect of its success during a period that proved too testing for many of its competitors.

In 1909, at Sandwich, he had married Leila Mary Gully of Theydon Hall, Essex, She was the only daughter of Captain Philip Gully, late of the Cheshire Regiment, and proved to be a most able and supportive partner. She was an accomplished sportswoman, in particular a keen golfer who had represented Sussex and was captain of the Ladies' Parliamentary Golfing Association. She was also an excellent tennis player, narrowly missed international honours at hockey and is believed to have completed the Cresta Run. By now Albert, maybe having noted Ralph's change of birthplace from Warrington to Lymn, had added two Christian names, Egerton and Legh, becoming Albert Egerton Legh Slazenger. Egerton and Legh were two of the richest families in Cheshire at the time.

In 1911, and based on 'the sheer hard work, keen business acumen and grim tenacity' of the brothers during the first thirty years of the company's existence, Albert, who had become its sole owner, set about raising capital for further development. He turned the business into a limited company with the title Slazenger's Ltd. The share capital structure was 100,000 £1 cumulative preference shares and 165,000 £1 ordinary shares with Albert, as vendor, taking one-third of each class of shares as part payment of the purchase consideration. This flotation was presented against the background of a profits record over the previous ten years showing a rise from £26,787 in 1901 to £38,836 in 1910, and Albert was able to announce, at the first shareholders' meeting in April, 1912, that the profit for the year ending December had again risen, to £41,882. A 10% dividend was declared on the ordinary shares and the general reserve fund increased to £15,413. The *Sports Trader* commented that, 'It appears the business of the company has been well maintained in all departments, the demand showing an increase both with regard to the home and export trade.' It can also be assumed that the basis of this success was the company's increasingly dominant position in a tennis market that was benefiting from the increasing popularity of this sport.

By 1914 annual profits had risen to nearly £50,000 but, not surprisingly, the outbreak of war led to a sharp downturn for the next three years. 1914 did, however, bring a very happy event for Albert and

December, 1916

Slazengers Limited *v.* C. Gibbs & Co.

ACTION for LIBEL.

DEAR SIR *or* (MADAM),

I am directed by the Board of this Company to give you a brief summary of the above Action, which was heard in the High Court of Justice, Chancery Division, before Mr. Justice ASTBURY, on November 1st, 1916.

The Defendants wrote a post-card to one of the Company's trading customers, alleging that, being a German firm, it was more than probable the Company would be closed down.

As this was a gross libel and likely to injure the Company's reputation, we instructed our Solicitors to begin an Action against the Defendants to prevent their repeating the same, and on the 14th day of April, 1916, the Company obtained an Order from Mr. Justice NEVILLE restraining the Defendants, until the trial of the Action, from repeating such libellous statements.

In the course of the proceedings it was proved that all the Directors of SLAZENGERS LTD., were British subjects, born of British-born parents, and that the whole of the Staff were British, save one who was a Swiss, and that the Shares, with a very few exceptions, were held by British subjects.

The Action came on for trial before Mr. Justice ASTBURY as above, the Defendants having withdrawn the offensive statements complained of, and their Counsel expressed regret for the Defendants having made them.

Mr. Justice ASTBURY, without calling upon the Company's Counsel to reply to the speech for the defence, held that the statements complained of would be understood by ordinary persons to bear a meaning which was about as defamatory at the present time, and in the present circumstances, as any words could be, and that the statements were defamatory and calculated to injure the Company's business, and that the Company were entitled to have the said Interlocutory Injunction granted by Mr. Justice NEVILLE made perpetual, and he further ordered the Defendants to pay the costs of the action.

I am, SIR (*or* MADAM),

Yours faithfully,

p.p. SLAZENGERS LTD.,

H. J. E. ULLVETT,

Secretary.

LAURENCE POUNTNEY HILL,
LONDON, E.C.

Confirming the Gibbs apology for 'offensive statements' about Slazenger being a German firm

Sam Weaver, a famous salesman for Slazenger and later sales manager for Sykes

Leila with the birth of their only child, Ralph, named after the uncle he never saw. It wasn't such a good year for his other brother, Horatio, who had to endure a harrowing and widely reported prosecution after a serious road accident in Surbiton on Derby Day. He was accused of running over a woman, failing to stop after the accident and driving without a licence. It emerged during the trial that the woman involved, who survived the accident, had been pushed into the road during a quarrel with two men, both the worse for drink, and that Horatio had no chance of avoiding her. He was fined £39, including costs, after pleading guilty to the lesser charges.

Although wartime restrictions forced the company to severely cut back production the very basic price lists published at the time show they continued to offer most of the pre-war range even if supplies to customers were limited. There is evidence of the pressures on production costs in the form of a circular, issued in June, 1918, advising an immediate 10% increase in the price of tennis balls, and a general warning on the front of the price list for the same year stating that, 'As the prices named herein are all liable to revision without notice, orders can only be accepted at prices ruling at time of delivery.'

In common with most businesses at the time 'all sections of the staff shouldered the burden and played their part in the war effort'. More than 10% of the total staff, 125, went on active service, 15, sadly, never to return. Very much not in common with most businesses Slazenger's Limited was attacked by another company in the sports trade – racket gut manufacturers C. Gibbs & Co. of Nottingham – who suggested to one of their customers that as it was more than probable they were a German firm they would be closed down. When Slazenger's solicitors requested withdrawal of this damaging allegation Gibbs's reply was less than placatory as they demanded, 'Will you please say whether there is any just reason why your firm should not be closed down as an alien enemy, and why publicity should not be given.' Following further exchanges Gibbs, while beginning to sound rather less sure of their case, still demanded, 'If not German, will you please say what nationality Slazengers are.'

Enough was enough and the company went to the High Court to request a perpetual injunction to restrain Gibbs from making any further statements of this sort. Big guns were brought to bear at the hearing in the shape of a former Lord Mayor of London and a director of Gamages, both agreeing how damaging such an allegation would be. Archdale Palmer appeared on behalf of the company and was introduced to the court by the judge with the remark, 'If it will help this case any, I can vouch for the fact that Captain Palmer is not a German,' a reference to the fact he had served with the Essex Regiment in the early part of the war before being invalided out. He told the court that all the directors were British born subjects and that out of the firms 1000 employees only one was a foreigner, and he was Swiss. Mr. Justice Astbury ruled that 'to call a person or a firm German at the present time was as defamatory a statement as could possibly be made', and granted the injunction with costs against Gibbs.

The company's already well developed feel for public relations was to be seen in a *Sports Trader* editorial piece, in the same issue which had reported the satisfactory outcome of the libel case, emphasizing the outstanding merits of the company, as one of a number of manufacturers to have established the supremacy of British sporting goods, and, in passing, to observe that 'when we think of the hundreds of thousands of tennis rackets that are made and sold not only in this country, but also in America and all other countries where the game of tennis is known and played, it is a great thing for any one firm to be able to claim that they are the makers of a racket that has had a larger sale than any other racket on the market, either in this country or abroad. The firm who hold that proud position is Messrs. Slazengers Ltd. And the racket is their world famous "Demon".'

Digressing, but only slightly, the next issue of the *Sports Trader*, again reflecting the Slazenger promotional skill, carried a two-page biography of one of their sales representatives, Mr. Sam Weaver, well known throughout the sports trade as 'one of the oldest sporting goods men on the road (he would have been fifty at the time) with a personality, no less than the excellent reputation enjoyed by the house he represents, which makes him a welcome caller throughout the whole length and breadth of his ground'. Sam, who was born in the same year that William Sykes had made his first soccer balls, grew up in Melton Mowbray, the first source of the Melton cloth used to cover tennis balls, and had started his working life in the drapery trade, including a short spell in Peter Robinson's store in London, before becoming an agent for the Prudential and doing

Vive le sport! The branch which Slazenger opened in the French capital controlled the Sporting Club de Paris

so well that 'he was able to invest in a pony and trap in which he drove his rounds'. At the same time the enterprising Sam opened an antiques shop and, based on his own experience of the ponies that pulled his trap, became a horse dealer commanding 'fancy prices' from aristocrats by virtue of his skill in this trade. After a short period selling tyres he found his 'ultimate vocation' with the house of Slazenger, which he represented for some thirty years not only in the UK but also in France, Belgium and Holland. Among the recollections of his career the happiest were of many of the competitors who travelled with him during the earlier days of the sports trade, including both William Sykes senior, and Fred Ayres. 'Many businesses have altered, many changed hands, others have sprung up,' reflected Sam, 'but, thank God, I still ride a winning horse and my people still find me the right goods to carry me to the post.' The magazine wished him well for the future in the certain knowledge he would long uphold 'the best traditions of the "Knights of the Road"'. He was obviously one of the great characters of the early days of the industry. and in the 1920s had become sales director of William Sykes, who he had joined in 1919. Interestingly, he also had a reputation as a poet and was the proud owner of a letter from Queen Alexandra thanking him for a poem on the death of King Edward VII called 'Britain's Sorrow'.

That particular point is mentioned because many years later another Slazenger 'Great', 'Buzzer' Hadingham, published 'Random Rhymes', a delightful collection of poems reflecting thoughts and observations on his fascinating and successful life. Clearly the house of Slazenger has been an inspirational company for those lucky enough to share in its success over the years.

Although the end of war was in sight the *Daily Express* reported in June, 1918 that 'those who delight in the game of tennis have about as much chance of buying a dozen great auk's eggs as of obtaining a dozen tennis balls', and a representative of Slazenger's told the same newspaper that 'even with a quarter of the normal number of workpeople, we can engage only a small percentage in making tennis balls as there are Government inspectors to see that the major part of the work is of national importance – men who would ordinarily make tennis balls are covering electric wires with rubber, which means our customers are strictly rationed'. Nevertheless the company's determination to keep ahead of the competition was reflected by a full-page advertisement in the trade press announcing, 'We have perfected a new composition bowl to be placed on the market as soon as facilities permit.' And despite all these problems the results for 1918 showed a record profit of £57,400 'contributed to by a larger turnover in every branch of the business, but the returns from the waterproof and showerproof department were particularly good'. Apart from covering electric wires with rubber that comment probably referred to the range of bags and holdalls 'made in strong waterproof canvas' for each of the sports covered in the catalogue.

It appears that the sports trade recovered quickly after the war, almost certainly because the general interest in sport of all kinds was growing very rapidly. In 1922 the Wimbledon championships were played for the first time on the much larger Church Road site, and two years later the demand for centre court seats was so great that the ballot system was introduced. An estimated 250,000 tried to see the first Wembley cup final in 1923 and ever since the match has been all-ticket. In the same year the United States won the first Wightman Cup, during a period when crowds were flocking to see the flamboyant and fashion conscious Suzanne Lenglen dominate the women's game. In 1925 a crowd of 70,000 watched the first international rugby match at Murrayfield, in 1927 the United States won the first official Ryder Cup, the following year Don Bradman played his first test match (with his Sykes bat) and in 1929 Fred Perry won a world title – for table tennis.

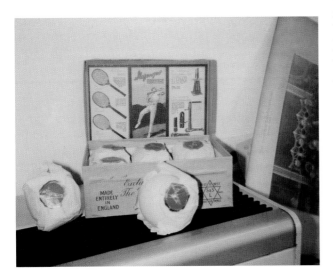

A box of tennis balls in the 1930s, each with its own wrapping

Meanwhile, back at Laurence Pountney Hill, Edward (Tim) Hadingham had joined the company and became a director three years later. Maybe his influence was at work in the revolutionary design of the company's stand at the 1921 British Industries Fair, which was reported as being 'a very distinctive display, the keynote of which was reticence'. Instead of packing the stand with products they used two slender pedestals and a glass showcase to display 'productions which had played their part in adding laurels to the reputation of the firm'. Among the star exhibits was a 'Doherty' racket, 'with which championships of the world had been won seventeen times', a tennis ball used at Wimbledon and the Olympics, the 'Stadium' soccer ball used for the 1920 cup final, the 'G.A.T.' racket used to win the 1920 All-England Badminton Championship, and the hockey ball used for all recent home internationals. The strength of the business was now such that profits were only slightly dented by the disruption caused by the general strike and, in addition to all their successes in other sports, they announced in 1922 that the ten best croquet players in the country were using their 'Corbally' mallet.

In 1923 an incident occurred, which could not be repeated today. A retailer, Charles Riggs of Bishopsgate, London, after being

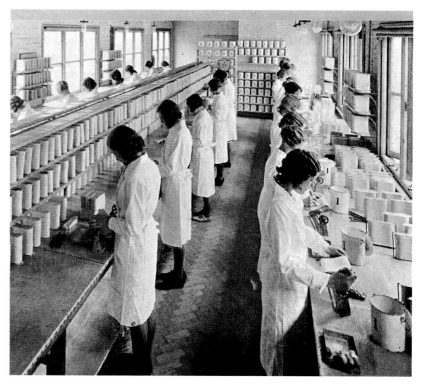

Preparing tennis ball covers for vulcanising at the Woolwich factory in the 1930s

reprimanded by the company, published an apology in the trade press for committing a breach of his agreement not to sell Slazenger rackets 'below certain fixed minimum selling prices'. The company's stand in this matter won support from other retailers, one of whom, in a letter to the press stated that 'the sports trade has been badly clouded by this abominable practice which has spread with such rapidity this last two years; but, out of evil cometh good and we now know we can count on the unwavering support of one of the most important manufacturers ... and to freeze out those manufacturers who only regard us as serfs to be played with, prodded and finally killed, as they may please.'

The company was again in the news in 1927 when what became known as the 'Tennis Ball War' erupted between the LTA and the Tennis Ball Manufacturers. And again the Slazenger relationship with Wimbledon came under scrutiny. The LTA had long held the view that the price of balls to the public was too high and, without consulting the manufacturers, circulated a tender for an 'Official Ball'. This was accompanied by an agreement, to be signed by the successful supplier, which required that the ball should be distributed without any indication who made it and with a commitment that its maximum retail price would be 15s 6d, which compared with a general price for premium balls in the range 18s 6d to 19s 6d. The majority of the manufacturers objected very strongly to what they regarded as an attempt to impose drastic restrictions on the ball business, but retailers, who had for some time been unhappy with the way manufacturers supplied balls direct to clubs and tournaments at favourable prices, expressed interest in the LTA scheme – though they also had reservations about the likely impact on their margins if the 15s 6d price for the LTA-approved ball became the norm for all premium products.

In the event only one manufacturer – John Jaques & Son Ltd – submitted

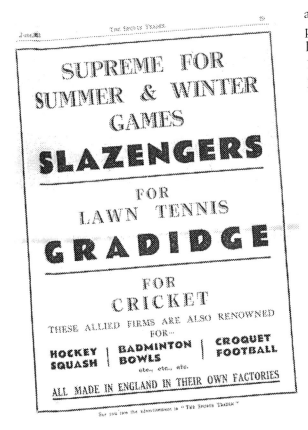

SUPREME FOR
SUMMER & WINTER
GAMES

SLAZENGERS

FOR
LAWN TENNIS

GRADIDGE

FOR
CRICKET

THESE ALLIED FIRMS ARE ALSO RENOWNED
FOR—

| HOCKEY | BADMINTON | CROQUET |
| SQUASH | BOWLS | FOOTBALL |

etc., etc., etc.

ALL MADE IN ENGLAND IN THEIR OWN FACTORIES

The first advertisement after the
merger of Slazengers and Gradidge

Sketch from the Jubilee programme
showing the racket frame finishing
section at the Woolwich factory

a tender to the LTA and they were duly appointed to supply the authorised ball. This immediately prompted speculation that the 'Official Ball' would be adopted for the 1928 Wimbledon championships instead of the Slazenger product. Although the new Jaques ball was used at a number of the main LTA events that year the Wimbledon authorities were quick to point out that its own selection was made by the Joint Committee of Management of the Championships, which consisted of 12 members of the All England Club and 4 representatives of the LTA Council. While the LTA representatives did recommend the use of the new ball, the secretary and manager of the All England Club, Major D. R. Larcombe, announced that the Slazenger stitchless and seamless ball had been chosen on the basis of a series of playing tests carried out with unmarked balls. It was reported at the time that these tests had been instituted to 'ensure that overseas competitors should have no grounds for complaint that they were called upon to use in the championships a ball which was disappointing to them'. The Slazenger connection was maintained.

However the LTA initiative clearly had an impact on ball pricing and marketing policies. In the month prior to the start of the 1928 championships Slazenger advertised 'Two Best Sellers'. The 'Slazenger' stitchless and seamless ball was duly presented as exclusively selected for the 1928 tournament, at 19s 6d per dozen, and it was positioned alongside the brand new 'Demon', 'launched by a successful press campaign and backed up by the organisation and experience of half a century', as a 'lower priced ball having all the characteristics of the best model' and priced at 16s, which justified the claim it was 'unquestionably the world's finest value'. Whether or not the LTA felt that their 'Official Ball' project had been fully justified by the introduction of good quality lower-priced balls is not known but a general truce was apparent when, in time for the start of the 1929 tournament season, they announced that 9 other makes of ball had been added to the authorised and approved list, including specific products from Dunlop, Slazenger, Ayres and Spalding. Today approval by both the LTA and International Tennis Federation (ITF) is achieved by strict adherence to technical and performance criteria and there is continuous and close co-operation between these associations and manufacturers to ensure that ball quality and development is in tune with the demands of the modern game.

By now Tim Hadingham had become joint-managing-director (with Archdale Palmer) and the McMasters had purchased Gradidges. This trio negotiated the Slazenger purchase of Gradidges in 1931, which was Slazenger's Jubilee year and was marked by the publication of a special supplement in the *Sports Dealer*. A key passage in this feature observed that, 'In the past orders flowed in as a matter of course and there was little need to search for work. Now times are changing, the days of relying on reputation have passed and although Slazengers have always been first choice where QUALITY is the supreme test, the question of price must also be considered, particularly in these difficult times.' Those difficulties would not only have reflected the depressed state of the world economy, but also the growing strength of competition for sports equipment business at home and abroad, not least from the expanding Horbury business of William Sykes and the relative newcomer to the market, Dunlop, who by now had begun to extend their range from golf and tennis balls to include tennis rackets. Not surprising that the Jubilee feature reminded the trade that 'Slazenger business does not begin and end with lawn tennis rackets and balls'.

In the shadow of St. Paul's – Slazenger's principal London factory – a 1930s sketch

Describing the business, as it stood in 1931, the Jubilee feature reported that it employed 670 people, of whom 566 were on the manufacturing side. The offices and factories occupied a total of 110,000 square feet in Laurence Pountney, Great Alie Street and the two factories in Woolwich. The Great Alie Street factory, which had been acquired in 1926 and was only a short distance from Laurence Pountney, had been equipped with all the latest machinery for 'economising time and labour', and throughout the company 'every modern labour aiding device has been adopted and that the installation throughout has been on a scale commensurate with the size of the organisation, and specially designed to meet its particular needs'. The longstanding emphasis given to the potential of overseas markets was highlighted by the statement that 'the directors have never accepted the facile belief that first-class goods sell themselves, and, therefore, agencies were established years ago in Australia and Canada to increase sales'. Those agencies had developed to become locally registered manufacturing and marketing operations in both countries and a branch of the parent company had by now been established in Paris, which controlled the Sporting Club de Paris.

The company's concern for its employees is reflected in the account of its welfare department, where 'the well-being of each individual worker is carefully watched and every opportunity is given for playing games at the recreation centre at Eltham'. That facility had been a gift from Albert Slazenger and provided six hard and four grass courts for tennis, a football field and a cricket pitch good enough for first class matches. Albert's generosity had extended beyond the company as, in 1929, he had given a playing field to his home town, Sandwich.

The consistent focus on export business was given further expression in 1935 by the preparation of 'a short summary of the development and present organisation of the House of Slazenger', which was published to mark the appointment of an agent for the USA. This special feature provides further evidence of the company's marketing expertise. Although much of the text is an updated version of the Jubilee supplement the presentation style of line drawings, largely based on previously-used black and white photographs and

The popularity of tennis in the 1930s, and the demand for Slazenger rackets and balls, owed a great deal to Britain's eight times Grand Slam champion, Fred Perry, seen here being carried along the platform of London's Victoria Station on his return from Britain's Davis Cup victory in Paris in 1933

a concise review of the business, put together in a relatively expensive folder with the title 'Slazenger Craftsmanship', exudes quality and would be a credit to any business if produced today. The revised text reports the total number of staff has risen to 825 and refers to the now integrated Gradidge side of the business, in particular the 'unqualified success' of the golf club venture, which is able to boast, only eighteen months after it was launched, that over half the 1935 British Ryder Cup team going to America will be using Gradidge clubs, including the captain, Charles Whitcombe, and his two brothers.

Directly addressing the United States market the closing passage of the brochure voices the confident view that 'there will be no difficulty, with the friendly co-operation of the American sporting goods dealers, in establishing a substantial market for their goods in the USA. They venture to suggest that in 1936 there could be no better slogan for American sports dealers than 'SELL SLAZENGER and SELL MORE!'.

This appointment of an agent was made some forty years after Frank Slazenger had started selling golf clubs from his New York base. His main interest had been the golf potential in the USA but that had been frustrated by the company's inability to provide him with a wound ball once that new and game-improving product had pushed gutta percha balls off the market early in the new century. However, he did not neglect the tennis market and has never previously been given credit for his quite remarkable coup in securing endorsements for the 'Doherty' racket by two of America's greatest early players. They were William Larned, who won the U.S. Open seven times between 1901 and 1911, and Molla Bjursted, who was the U.S. Women's champion for four successive years from 1915 to 1918. In a 1916 advertisement in *American Lawn Tennis* Frank recorded this triumph and gave his address in New York as 12 East 43rd Street. He also revealed his revised name as Frank Legh Slazenger, which was another instance of the family's great respect for the best names in Cheshire society.

Frank Slazenger advertises the 'Stadium' and 'Doherty' rackets in *American Lawn Tennis* in 1916

The very early recognition of the North American potential for both golf and tennis equipment makes the subsequent failure to build a really substantial business in that market all the more disappointing. Although the brand was kept alive in the USA throughout most of the 20th century the scale of sales achieved was very small in relation to the size of the market until the late 1980s and 1990s when the combination of a small tennis operation and a much larger, stand alone golf business supplying premium quality products only to pro shops reached sales in the $50-100 million dollar range and took significant market shares in the ball and clothing sectors.

The comparative lack of progress by the brand in the USA for most of the century contrasted sharply with the much more successful operation across the border in Canada, as well as the other local companies established in Australia, New Zealand and South Africa. One obvious common theme in these other territories was the

Fred Perry (second from left) beside Roper Barrett (centre) with other members of the victorious Davis Cup Team – Raymond Tuckey, 'Bunny' Austin and Pat Hughes – admire the trophy at Wimbledon in 1934.

'Empire' connection and the almost automatic Slazenger brand recognition that went with that. Another, possibly key factor was the fact that the parent company, at some stage, had set up manufacturing units to support these more successful overseas operations. Although encouraging progress was made in the 1970s, mainly on the back of the tennis boom at that time, the brand had not taken root in the USA during the crucial period of major sports expansion following the end of the second world war, and it had no golf presence to sustain the business when tennis lost ground to newly developing sports and fitness activities from the mid-seventies onwards. A definite problem, especially from the 1960s onward, would have been the inability to provide a competitive level of promotional support for the brand in an increasingly media driven market. The notable success of the niche marketed pro golf business in the closing years of the century was driven much more by distribution exclusivity and skilful projection of a brand offering heritage and quality to a market receptive to that approach than it was by a heavy promotional spend that simply wasn't available.

Returning to 1935, it is clear the management team at the time had high hopes for their business in USA and it could have been a very different story if the war had not frustrated their ambitions at a critical early stage. The timing of this fresh assault was excellent. In addition to the early success of the Gradidge clubs, the announcement of a new agent came in the middle of Fred Perry's three successive Wimbledon titles, not to mention his other Grand Slam successes in Australia, France and, in particular, his three US Open wins. The company policy at that time was not to use the names of amateurs in promotional material so the focus was on his racket, the 'All White Slazenger', which 'created such an immense sensation on its first appearance in the hands of leading players on the Centre Court in 1934, and had since been used by the winner of the Championships at Wimbledon (twice), and the Championships of the United States, Australia, France and Belgium and by the majority of leading players in Great Britain and throughout the world'. Comprehensive enough for Slazenger and as this was also the same period when Pat Hughes, who, with Fred Perry, was a member of the all conquering

The Doherty brothers

PORTABLE PUNCHING EQUIPMENT

The 'SLAZENGER'
WALL PLATFORM PUNCHING DRUM

Solid Drum of best heavy plywood. Angle iron supports and wood battens. Folds against the wall when not in use. Absolutely rigid and free from vibration under the hardest usage. The drum of this design is unbreakable and free from warp. The best on the market.

	No.	Code	Price
Platforms only	2856	ZOBYV	50.-

For Punching Balls, see Nos. 2863, 2864 and 2865.

SWIVELS
For Drum and Ceiling Attachments

	No.	Code	Each
Nickel Plated on Iron	2360	ZOJAX	1.6
Nickel Plated on Brass	2361	ZOJEL	3.6
Nickel Plated on Brass with Leather Washer	2362	ZOJKA	3.9
Nickel Plated on Brass with Steel Ball Bearings....	2363	ZOJLE	7.-
The " PRO " Swivel, special design .	2364	ZOJNO	9.-

The 'IMPERIAL'
PORTABLE PUNCHING BALL

Entirely new design. The spring of this Ball is a very powerful and unbreakable one. The base is of solid cast iron and exceptionally heavy, obviating any screws in the floor. The Ball is of Tan sheep, and will stand very hard wear. This Ball will be found to be very fast, and can be safely recommended for Clubs, Institutes, or Private use.

		No.	Code	Price
Complete with Ball	....	2857	ZOBOG	80.-
	Ball only	2835	ZOBUB	16.6
Ditto	Juvenile	2858	ZOBYJ	75.-
	Ball only	2854	ZOCAD	13.6

PUNCHING BALL BLADDERS

Sizes	5	6	7	8	9
No.	2845	2846	2847	2848	2849
Code......	ZOKEM	ZOKLA	ZOKME	ZOKOP	ZOKPO
Per dozen ...	18.6	20.-	22.-	24.6	27.-

59

Everything required for 'portable punching' in the 1939 catalogue

British Davis Cup team from 1933 to 1936 , and was working closely with Dunlop to expand the sales of their new 'Maxply' racket, the foundations were being laid for the post war dominance of the tennis market by these two companies. Nobody in either company at that time would have dreamt that such success would have been shared as subsidiaries of the same parent company.

In 1937 when Tim Hadingham moved to South Africa to set up a tennis ball plant in Durban and develop the local Slazenger business, Michael McMaster became the sole managing-director. He went on to become chairman in 1944 and held that position until his death in 1965. This meant that not only had he, with his brother, crucially brought Gradidges into the Slazenger camp in 1931, but he was also at the heart of the decision making that, in 1942, brought about the purchase of William Sykes, and, in 1958/59, the sale of Slazengers to Dunlop. Clearly his impact on the history of the company was immense.

Four years before Tim Hadingham went to South Africa, his son, Reginald, to become much better known as 'Buzzer', had joined the company's export department at Laurence Pountney Hill to start a career that would finish fifty years later when he retired as non-executive chairman. Much more will emerge about his own remarkable story but it's appropriate to link his introduction to the Slazenger history with a brief explanation of why he was named Reginald, and how Reginald became 'Buzzer'. Reginald was the name chosen by his mother, who had once received a proposal of marriage from a certain Reginald Doherty. That particular Reginald Doherty was to become a tennis immortal, who, between 1897 and 1906, won no less than twelve Wimbledon titles. Four of them were singles and eight doubles, won with his equally famous brother, Laurie. Tragically, Reginald had died in 1910, aged only 38, but when 'Buzzer' was born seven years later he was christened Reginald in his memory. However, the young Reginald Hadingham was quickly to become 'Buzzer' because that was the nearest his brother could get to pronouncing the word 'brother'.

During the second half of the 1930s Slazengers would have been the most prominent sports business in the UK. It also had a flourishing overseas business combining export to a worldwide network of distributors and its own operations in the key 'Empire' countries. The board, which included Albert Slazenger, Archdale Palmer, the McMasters and Tim Hadingham, combined enormous experience of the sports trade with an acute awareness of the increasing importance of skilful promotion, particularly in relation to the leading players and major events. Additionally the Gradidge factor introduced by the McMasters had significantly broadened the appeal of the product line with its emphasis on the increasingly popular sports of golf and cricket as well as the traditionally strong position in tennis.

65

The still separate Gradidge and Slazenger catalogues for 1939 provide a very clear picture of the strength of the product line at that time, and how it was presented to the trade and consumer. The main Gradidge catalogue covered cricket, the racket sports, hockey, fives, football, hockey and lacrosse – with the 60% devoted to cricket featuring Len Hutton and Leslie Ames. The latter was the first of three great Kent and England wicketkeepers, the other two being Godfrey Evans and Alan Knott, to endorse Gradidge and, later, Slazenger bats, pads and gloves. Golf was presented in a separate catalogue, which already would have been able to feature the early successes of the clubs used by Alf Padgham (1936) and Reg Whitcombe (1938) at the British Open and of the choice of Gradidge equipment by half the 1935 Ryder Cup squad.

The headline sports on the first page of the Slazenger catalogue, in that final season before the war, were tennis, badminton, hockey, football and table tennis with an 'Etc.' that embraced croquet, bowls, squash, boxing and lacrosse. Tennis is far and away the main feature, occupying half the pages, and opens with an introduction to the 23 model racket range in the form of a letter from Hollywood written by Fred Perry. He declares that, 'In the last seven years I have used no other rackets than Slazengers and all my major successes have been achieved with their aid.' He goes on to tell the reader that, based on this successful experience with their products, 'I have decided to have an autograph tennis racket made, and since Slazengers make the best in the world, I am writing to ask if you will produce a "Fred Perry" racket for me.' Hardly likely to refuse such a request the autograph racket is duly featured at 75s, which is the same price as the famous 'All White', which is virtually the same product except for minor cosmetic changes. The Fred Perry name also appears on a 'Special' frame for 52s 6d and two Junior models at 21s and 37s 6d. Long-serving brand names like 'Doherty', 'Demon', 'Victory' and 'Queen's' remain in the range. A racket repair service is available to avoid 'the injuries caused to rackets by inexperienced workmen', with a top price of 35s for a complete re-string with the best quality gut. Gut itself is offered in 36 variations with colour options on top of that covering white, red, green, black,

The Fred Perry autograph version of the famous All-White model – his verdict, 'The finest racket ever produced'

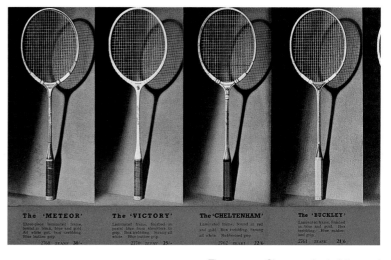

The pre-war Slazenger badminton and squash range

SUNDRIES AND SPECIAL SPORTS GOODS

SPORTSMAN'S SEATS

	No.	Code	Each
"WARWICK," Hammock Seat	2231	VIJON	52/6
"WARWICK," Hammock Seat, Ladies	2232	VIJUP	50/-
"FIELD," Lancewood Stick	2233	VIKAL	30/-
"TOURIST," covered Steel Tube	2234	VIKEN	27/6
"TOURIST," Bronze Steel Tube, Ladies	2235	VIKLA	20/-
"TOURIST," Junior	2236	VIKME	17/6
"CROOK-DE-LUX," Lancewood	2237	VIKOP	20/-
"CROOK-DE-LUX," Steel Tube	2238	VIKPO	20/-
"AIR FLO," Seat Stick	2221	VILEN	45/-
Large Hammock Seat	2222	VILIK	45/-
Hammock Seat, Lancewood, N.P.	2223	VILMA	40/-

	No.	Code	Each
Covered Seat, Lancewood, N.P.	2224	VILNE	25/-
Covered Seat, Beechwood	2225	VILUR	22/6
Seat Adapter .... N.P.			3/6
Spring Clip			1/3
COLONIAL SEAT STICKS			
14" Hammock Seat	2210	VIMEP	25/-
14" Hammock Seat, N.P.	2211	VIMNA	27/6
Brass			
13" Hammock Seat, Wood	2212	VIMOR	21/-
13" Hammock Seat, N.P.	2213	VIMPE	23/6
Brass	2214	VIMRO	16/6
9" Round Shape	2215	VIMUS	15/6
Walking Stick Seat			

LADIES' TENNIS CASE HOLDALL

Specially made in Scratchproof, Stampproof and Waterproof Leather cloth. Fitted to a special frame, cloth lined with inside pockets in lid, sides, and hood pocket with securing straps to hold Tennis Racket. Very light case. Size 29 x 11 x 3 ins. Navy ....677 VERIJ 22/6 Nigger....678 VEKKO 22/6

GOLF UMBRELLAS

	No.	Code	Each
25in., 8 Rib Frame, Stick	2481	VIMVY	8/-
25 in., 8 Rib Steel Frame on Steel Tube	2482	VINAP	9/6
25 in., Double Rib Frame, Stick	2483	VISIR	9/6
25 in., 8 Rib Frame, Stick	2484	VISOB	9/6
27 in., 8 Rib Steel Frame on Steel Tube	2485	VINPA	9/9
27 in., Double Rib Frame, Stick	2486	VISUT	11/-
27 in., 16 Single Rib Frame, Stick, 16 widths	2488	VINSO	12/6
30 in., 8 Rib Frame, Stick	2488	VINVY	9/9
30 in., Double Rib Frame, Stick	2489	VIOCH	12/6
32 in., Double Rib Frame, Stick	2490	VIOFK	15/-
30 in., Double Rib Frame, Stick	219T	VIOHM	16/-
Tartan colour	2192	VIHEN	27/6
24 in., Golf Umbrella Seat Stick			1/- extra
Self Colour Royal			9d. extra
Four widths Royal			

GOLF COATS, WATERPROOF. MEN'S

	No.	Code	Each
Fine Weave Cotton Gaberdine, Egyptian Warp, American Weft, unlined except for Shoulder Lining	2701	ZUDAB	18/6

No. 677

	No.	Code	Each
This Coat made with Leather Shoulders	2702	ZUDEL	20/-
The same material, lined throughout	2705	ZUDKA	22/6
This Coat made with Leather shoulders	2706	ZUDLE	24/-
Fine Weave Cotton Gaberdine, Egyptian Warp, American Weft, lined throughout self material, interlined Shoulders, including top of sleeve. A Triple Texture Coat	2709	ZUDNO	25/6
This Coat made with Leather Shoulders	2710	ZUDOP	27/-
Light-weight Mercerized Cotton Poplin Gaberdine, lined throughout self material	2713	ZUDUP	30/-
This Coat made with Leather Shoulders	2714	ZUECK	31/6
Cotton Gaberdine Waterproof Trousers	2720	ZUFLA	11/6
Light-weight Mercerized Cotton Poplin Gaberdine Trousers	2721	ZUFME	15/-

In addition to this Catalogue, the following publications are issued by Slazengers and Gradidges:

GRADIDGE'S CATALOGUE ...... Cricket, Squash, Hockey, Badminton, Football, Fives, etc. (Summer and Winter).
GRADIDGE'S GOLF CATALOGUE ...... Golf Clubs, Bags, Clothing, etc.
SLAZENGER'S WINTER SPORTS CATALOGUE ...... Skis, Bindings, Sticks, Waxes, Clothing, Ice Hockey Sticks and Equipment.

29

Seats, shooting sticks, umbrellas, a luxury tennis case and waterproof coats plus a plug for ski and ice hockey equipment and Gradidge's summer range

plain orange or orange with dark blue.

The ball section reports that in addition to the continuing adoption for Wimbledon, no less than 112 'officially sanctioned and open tournaments in Great Britain', and 81 'principal overseas championships' used Slazenger balls. A special page features the patented, compressed air tins for balls, which have been designed for 'tennis players in tropical climates, or in countries, the route to which lies through the Tropics', with the assurance that 'players in the remotest parts of the earth can rely on obtaining balls in exactly the same condition as when dispatched from our factory'. The truth of this claim is supported by a letter from 'a prominent British official stationed in an outlying part of the Empire in the tropics', which expresses his delight with the balls supplied in these tins, which have stood up to the climate of a diplomatically omitted country 'than which there is none worse in creation'.

As had been the policy from the very beginning everything required to play tennis in terms of the equipment for the players and to build the court is available and now includes sport hats and visors for men and women, rejoicing in the names 'Tally-Ho' and 'Yoicks', and a small range of tennis shoes, including a 'Fred Perry', specially made to the instructions of the great man, and two leather styles fitted with steel spikes for use on wet grass courts, and 'fitted by a method which prevents them from hurting the feet'. The very best shoe, made of ventilated 'real buck', with a leather 'boodie' sole is offered at 50s.

The size of the croquet range had by now been greatly reduced but the 'Corbally' set of mallets, right at the top of the range, is still presented with the proud claim that 'the open championship has been won twelve times, and the challenge cup has been won eight times with Slazenger's mallets'. Both crown and level green bowls are catered for with a range including the bowls themselves, a set for indoor use, and supported by cases, measures, mats, markers and four styles of leather shoes.

The ten model badminton range includes an 'All White' at the top of the line, the 'Thelma Kingsbury', designed with the help of the all-England champion of 1936, and the long running 'G.A.T.' designed 'under the direction of Sir G. A. Thomas', who writes to tell the company that he likes it immensely and considers it 'admirably adapted for all purposes of the game'. Everything required to set up the court is provided and a full page is devoted to the new 'No. 1 Precision' shuttle, which is the result of 'an entirely new system of manufacture, where the precise methods of modern production have for the first time been applied to the production of shuttles, and instead of the old hit and miss methods, so fatal to accuracy, every shuttle has to undergo scientific tests before being offered for sale'. In particular it is claimed that 'as our glue, sparsely used, is not affected by moist heat, the shuttles do not get sticky in the hand'.

Seven squash rackets are listed with three balls which are interestingly named 'Slazenger', 'Silvertown', and 'Gradidge New Standard'. One racket is offered for the game of rackets with balls 'as used at Queen's, Princes, Woolwich and Camberley'. The nine hockey sticks listed were 'manufactured by expert workmen from finest selected material and used by the leading players for international and county matches', and the eight-strong hockey ball range is supported by a letter from the secretary of the Midland Counties Association declaring that, 'The balls you sent me for last Saturday's match between England and Scotland presented everything that a first class hockey ball should.'

The famous 'Demon' re-appears on the most expensive of the eight soccer balls and referees' whistles are included in the long list of accessories for both soccer and rugby. In the latter case 'Demon' is supported by the 'Boodie', the 'Cannon', which is used by Oxford and Cambridge Universities, and the 'Bing'. Four leading table tennis players, including the 1931 world champion M. Szabados, lend their signatures to the higher quality bats at 3s 6d, which are supported by eighteen other bats from 6d to 3s each, plus six balls, tables priced up to £9 10s, posts, nets, shoes specially designed by A. F. Leibster and no less than 19 different sets of equipment priced from 3s for a pair of cheap bats to 25s for two top quality bats, a dozen balls and the best available posts and net.

The outbreak of war hit the company, like so many others, very hard and the first reported sign of its impact was the reduced level of profit, £27,279, declared for the year ending December 1939. The directors' report mentioned that sales had been adversely affected by very bad weather during the early part of the summer and, more ominously, by 'the unstable international position culminating in the outbreak of war'. This was all the more unfortunate as the business had probably been at its peak during the second half of the 1930s, reaping the rewards of the energy and vision of Ralph and Albert, and, subsequently, of the management skills, especially in marketing, of Archdale Palmer, the McMasters and the Hadinghams. Tennis, the key product sector, had been enjoying enormous worldwide popularity and nowhere more so than in the UK where interest and participation had been driven by Fred Perry's eight Grand Slam titles in only three years, as well as his 45 wins, out of 52 matches, during Great Britain's four-year period of Davis Cup supremacy. Reg Whitcombe had won the 1938 Open with Gradidge clubs,

and, in the same year, Len Hutton had hit the highest score in Test cricket – his 364 against the Australians at the Oval – with his Gradidge bat. And their manufacturing-based businesses in Australia, New Zealand, South Africa and Canada continued to expand.

The first few months of the war did not affect the company too badly. Indeed, the production levels were significantly increased as the Government encouraged export sales to pay for vitally needed imports. However, that period proved to be very much the lull before the storm, which struck the company in 1940. In June of that year Albert Slazenger died, aged 84. The *Sports Trader* acknowledged the passing of 'one of the bulwarks of the sports manufacturing world', noting that he had been at the helm of the business for nearly 60 years, and that following Ralph's death in

TV comes to the Centre Court in 1937

Hand-cutting heavy duty gloves for
army lorry drivers

1911 he had gone daily to his office until only a week before he died. The measure of his wider contributions was also recognised by reference to his work 'for the rapid development of lawn tennis, not only because of the high standards of his products for the game, but because he gave his unlimited and enthusiastic support to the LTA and his financial support to the publication *Lawn Tennis and Badminton*. For all that he would probably have taken as much pleasure from a description of him as 'a man of genial temperament, full of fun and a keen golfer'. What is absolutely clear is that throughout 60 years of momentous change in almost every aspect of life, and certainly within the sports industry, Albert had made sure that the fledgling 'leggings and gaiters' business founded in Manchester had become probably the best-known sports company in the world.

In addition to the death of their inspirational co-founder, the company was now losing numerous members of its staff to the armed forces, including Humphrey McMaster, who, in 1941, enlisted in the Royal Canadian Navy. His distinguished career in this service took him to the rank of Chief of Personnel and was recognised, at the end of the war, by the award of the OBE. The loss of both Albert and Humphrey meant that Michael McMaster, as managing-director, was to carry the main responsibility for taking the company through a very difficult period, but he had the full support of Albert's son, Ralph, who, although the major shareholder, did not wish to become heavily involved in the business. Another departure was 'Buzzer' Hadingham, who was about to switch from being European Sales Manager to army officer, though he did find the time to get married, to Lois, in January of 1940. The expenses accounts for the previous year confirmed his dedication to seeking export business as late as two months before war was declared as he received £5 8s 2d to cover the cost of a visit to Paris.

Although that same ledger was recording monthly payments for firewatching that precaution did not prevent another, and potentially disastrous, crisis occurring in September, 1940, when, during an incendiary raid on London, the main factories at Woolwich, and large product stocks, were severely damaged. The Gradidge factory, also in Woolwich, suffered badly in the same series of raids and this meant the total production capacity of the company had been enormously reduced.

It was obviously extremely important to quickly find alternative capacity, not only to allow resumption of output for the war effort, but also to secure the full recovery of the business once the war was over. Limited tennis ball production was established at the Old Brewery, in Hurstpierpoint, Sussex. Dick Birch, who was later to become a major figure in the Canadian business for the best part of fifty years, remembers being told to go down to Sussex to collect some reconditioned balls so that he, and his fellow officers billeted in London, could relax for a few moments on some tennis courts they had access to in the Regent's Park area. Later in the war another factory was acquired in High Wycombe, where the company's expertise and the local woodworking skills related to the furniture industry combined to produce and repair airframes and wings, probably for the famous, mainly wood-built Mosquito fighter bomber.

However, the most important move was the 1942 acquisition of Sykes and Ayres, which included the former's relatively massive factory and tannery, at least in sports industry terms, in Horbury. There is a suggestion that the idea for this merger grew from a chance conversation, during a train journey, between Michael McMaster and Bill Dunning of Sykes. Whether that was true or not the union of these two companies, particularly in view of the circumstances at the time, made a great deal of sense. Michael appears to have been the prime mover in the negotiations and Bill Dunning was the ideal representative for Sykes. A Quaker, he had been the manufacturing director before becoming managing-director and in that role had played a major role in making the Horbury factory into what must have been one of the most modern and efficient sports equipment plants anywhere in the world, with the capability of producing a huge and diverse range of products.

Horbury's leather skills produce dial sight cases during the second world war

By this time, as described earlier, Horbury was almost entirely engaged in producing a bewildering variety of items for the armed services. The essence of this merger was the marriage of the brand strength and strong financial position of Slazenger, suddenly faced with the loss of most of its production capacity, and the Sykes manufacturing capability, crucially located in a relatively safe part of the country, but with a weaker market position and not having the financial weight to invest sufficiently in further brand and product development. It would have been clear to both parties that once the war was over, and especially when the trend of ever fiercer competition returned, their best chance of future prosperity lay in combining their respective and complementary strengths. It would appear, from what little financial data has been found, that Slazengers Ltd paid £149,270 for William Sykes Ltd, which included the book value of the assets at date of acquisition of £70,730 and a premium of £78,539. These figures were declared in the Slazengers Ltd consolidated balance sheet at year ending 31 December, 1942, which also included a valuation of £45,622 for Slazengers Australia, and £10,688 for the Canadian business. The value of the total 'Group' is shown as £348,500.

Although in the short term Horbury's main task was to continue to deal with the stream of orders from the Ministry of Defence, the management of the new group, which had now become, for the first time, the Slazenger-Sykes-Gradidge-Ayres combination that would feature so strongly in the early post-war promotional material, could begin to at least plan their peacetime strategy. The overall approach was to combine the London based, and mainly Slazenger and Gradidge marketing expertise with the Yorkshire manufacturing strength, which would be reflected in the senior positions on the board chaired by Michael McMaster with Bill Dunning and Humphrey McMaster

Dan Maskell, who won, with his Slazenger racket, the first tournament for professionals staged by the company in 1946

(when he returned from his naval duties in Canada) as the respective production and sales directors. The stage was being set for the emergence of post-war domination of the UK sports market by the newly enlarged Slazenger group and a Dunlop sports division that was recognised by its parent company as a key component within its post war strategy of worldwide diversification and expansion.

'A new era begins' was the theme of the 1946 Slazenger-Sykes-Gradidge-Ayres brochure, which both celebrated the past achievement of the scale and importance of the Horbury war effort, and looked forward to the potential now available from the powerful marketing and manufacturing resources of the 'Famous Four' companies, now to operate as a single force. The pledge was made that, 'We intend worthily to uphold the tradition of British craftsmanship and manufacturing skill in a new age – the age of Reconstruction.' The following paragraph expanded this approach and serves to illuminate both the philosophy of the company and the style of expression, which would not have been out of place in any of their catalogues produced fifty years earlier.

We do not write in any spirit of boastfulness, but we would say that just as the skill of our craftsmen, the discoveries of our research workers and the ability and enthusiasm of our managers were devoted to the national effort in the dark days just passed, so will they be devoted in like manner to the service of the public and the trade both at home and overseas in time of peace. In doing this we shall feel that in no small measure we are helping to foster not only British industry and commerce, but also that worldwide Fellowship of Sport through which so much can be done to promote peace and reconciliation among the nations in the years to come.

This brochure was published in the same year that the reduced tennis ball production in London was transferred to the newly-acquired Barnsley factory, previously occupied by Firth Vickers to produce stainless steel. At the same time the Gradidge factory in Woolwich was also closed, which meant that the company's total production was concentrated in Horbury and Barnsley. This prompted Bill Dunning to tell the *Yorkshire Evening Post* that 'Yorkshire will soon be producing the bulk of the world's sporting equipment in the world's most up-to-date plant'.

In the same report reference was also made to the difficulties Slazenger had

Dan Maskell and Fred Perry opening new tennis courts at the Slazenger sports club at Horbury in 1951

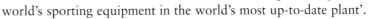

experienced in trying to find alternative accommodation in London for their manufacturing facilities, but it was acknowledged that the move to Yorkshire 'conforms to the policy encouraged by the Board of Trade and the Ministry of Labour'. From the human standpoint the newspaper noted that 'London workers have been given the opportunity of transferring to Yorkshire, but that a number have declined, mainly owing to housing difficulties'. The company did, in fact, build a number of houses in Horbury and, although their ownership has since changed, one of them was occupied for a number of years by Eric Loxton, who is well-known throughout the cricket world as a master bat maker.

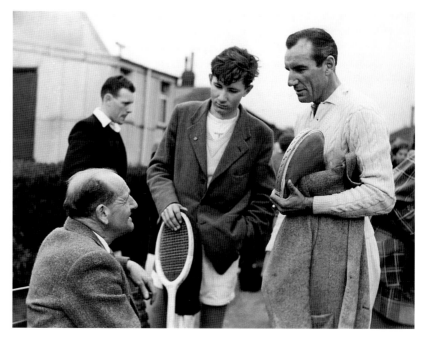

Fred Perry and Michael McMaster, with the Norwegian junior champion, at the 1951 opening of the new courts at Horbury

The total numbers of staff involved during this period of transition were reported as an existing 700 at Horbury and 200 at Barnsley, with an additional 600 required to bring the numbers up to the pre-war standard. 'If the London employees do not come north no difficulty will be felt in recruiting male and female labour locally,' declared an unnamed director of William Sykes.

Not surprisingly Slazenger's trading profits had been severely reduced during the war, dropping from just over £20,000 in 1941 to £14,456 the following year. But by October, 1943 the *Sports Trader* was reporting 'another step forward in recovery' had been announced by the company in the form of a preference dividend, on 30th June that year, which had cleared all arrears. By 1944 the profit figure had recovered to almost £25,000 and at the 1946 AGM Michael McMaster was able to tell shareholders the figure for 1945 was £28,332. Also that the surplus of current assets over liabilities had risen to £169,000.

Against the background of that steadily improving financial position he was also able to announce what was to be the first of many tournament sponsorships, in this case what was described as a 'big money fixture for lawn tennis professionals'. It was, in fact, the first ever major event staged for those professionals, who, as coaches, had not shared the same level of rewards enjoyed both by their touring contemporaries and also by fellow coaches and players in golf and cricket. Staged in Scarborough, a total sum of £1000 was provided, of which £700 was prize money and £300 for the expenses of the entrants. The first winner of the singles title, which had attracted 46 entrants, was Dan Maskell, who received a challenge trophy and 200 guineas. With T. C. Jeffery he also won the doubles, for which there was another trophy, but no money!

The marketing strategy of the business was evolving as post-war demand for sports equipment increased as fast as the availability of materials allowed. The 1949 product range very largely repeated the pre-war pattern of covering a very wide range of activities. Racket sports, cricket and golf were still predominant but the catalogue showed pretty well everything required for archery, basketball, boxing, fives, soccer, rugby, hockey, netball, bowls, table tennis, volleyball, water polo and even leather gauntlets and helmets for motoring. The gauntlets were a reminder of the 300,000 pairs of 'motor transport gloves' supplied to the forces during the war, as were the eight sizes of medicine balls, of which some 25,000 had seen military service. And tucked away at the very end of the catalogue were two rocking horse models wholesaling at £7 10s for the painted version and £9 when 'skin covered'.

The approach to the use of brands at this stage was to have a tennis product front cover showing only Slazenger, both as the corporate name and on all the products illustrated. The back cover, devoted to cricket, also carried the Slazenger name but the Sykes and Gradidge names are clear on the bats and balls with Slazenger just visible on the wicketkeeper's gloves. Every page inside the catalogue is headed Slazenger-Gradidge-Sykes-Ayres but Slazenger is the only brand used in direct association with the individual products listed, specifically the racket range and, for some reason, golf caddy bags.

The star players supporting the premium products are Fred Perry in the tennis section, Bobby Locke for golf clubs (no golf balls at this stage), and, for cricket, an extraordinarily distinguished group: Len Hutton, Don Bradman, Leslie Ames and Godfrey Evans. The water polo balls are linked with the name of an international, Jack Hatfield, and the better quality boxing gloves are linked with Laurie Stevens. The top quality basket ball is 'as used at the Olympic Games', and the 'Zig-Zag' soccer ball is 'as used in the Cup Final'. Special attention is given to South African requirements with a range of bats, pads and wicketkeeper gloves designed for that market. There is a slight nod in the direction of Sykes with just three 'Sykraft' soccer and rugby balls and the 'Sykometer' ball inflator and pressure gauge. Three types of American footballs are listed for the North American NFL market.

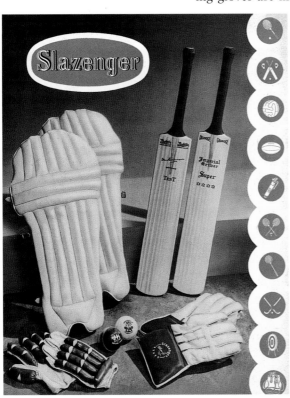

Brand evolution in 1949. Sykes and Gradidge on the bats under a Slazenger heading and both Sykes and Slazenger on the wicket-keeping gloves

The importance of the Sykes/Horbury tannery is quite clear from the huge range of leather products, which account for 20% of total sales now moving above £2 million per annum. Considerable use is still being made of brands that first appeared in the 19th century, like 'Victory', 'Demon', 'Queen's' and 'Meteor'. Many of the wholesale prices quoted are slightly lower than those quoted in pre-war years, except for tennis balls, which have increased from 14s 6d per dozen to 16s 9d. That level of increase also applies to other products, like batting and wicketkeeper gloves, where there is a high rubber content, but the Len Hutton autograph bat, which was priced by Gradidge in 1939 as 45s is now 38s and the three premium tennis rackets are each 5s cheaper, with the 'All White' and Fred Perry autograph strung frames now 70s.

By the time the 1951 winter price list is published, the only brand to appear is Slazenger and even 'Sykraft' has disappeared from the football section. World champion, Richard Bergmann, is endorsing table tennis bats, and Denis Compton's name appears for the first time, but on soccer shin-guards rather than bats.

The 1953 summer catalogue, which is of a much higher quality than earlier post-war issues, is of particular interest. The tennis racket range has a new number one frame, the 'Slazenger I.C.', which carries an individual registration number allowing the purchaser to replace his racket with an exact match. It retails at 147s, which is 7s 6d dearer than both the 'All White' and Fred Perry tournament model. Another new model is the Perry/Maskell Instructional Racket, which has 'actual instructions on the basic strokes of the game printed on it, and also marks on the grip indicting how the racket should be held'. For an extra 1s 6d the customer can buy 'the famous instructional booklet – the Perry/Maskell way to improve your lawn tennis'. The catalogue introduces Padder Tennis, which is played with wooden bats on a court only 39 ft. by 18 ft. and is suitable for any type of level surface. A complete set of posts, net, 4 bats, 3 balls and a rule book retails at 152s. A Padder Tennis Association is formed to promote this new sport, and although it did not take root in the UK it was almost certainly the forerunner of Paddle Tennis, which, today, is very popular in several South American countries, and, thanks to the work of the local Dunlop Slazenger management, has acquired a considerable following in Spain.

Three great brands and three great cricketers – Denis Compton for Slazenger, Don Bradman for Sykes and Len Hutton for Gradidge

A very large archery range is still available, with the very best bows retailing at just over £4 plus an extra 55s per dozen for the strings, the highest quality, 28-inch arrows nearly £3 per dozen, and the targets – complete with target faces and stands – costing well over £17. All these prices include purchase tax then running at 17.5%. The golf section, without any clubs but now all Slazenger branded, is introduced with a full page presentation of the Horbury-made B.51 ball, which was 'first introduced in midsummer, 1952, and the news of its qualities were passed rapidly from one enthusiast to another'. Priced at 42s per dozen it promised the perennial virtues of 'extra distance, controlled flight, greater toughness and paint durability'. The great South African golfer, Bobby Locke, while still endorsing Gradidge clubs, has now allowed his name to be used on a Slazenger golf bag as the lead line in a relatively small accessory range. At the time he was at the height of his powers, winning the British Open in 1949, 1950 and 1952, with Max Faulkner, and his Dunlop equipment, breaking that sequence in 1951.

However, it is the cricket section that reveals the latest stage in the brand policy evolution. Every page of the catalogue is headed Slazenger Tennis, Slazenger Cricket, etc., but in the case of cricket bats each of the premium, autograph models is listed under both the name of the batsman and the com-

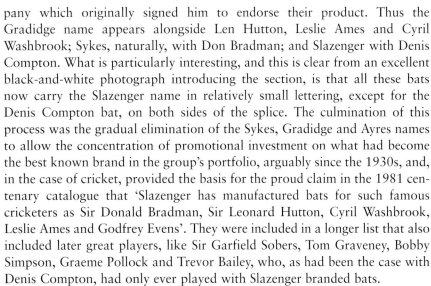

pany which originally signed him to endorse their product. Thus the Gradidge name appears alongside Len Hutton, Leslie Ames and Cyril Washbrook; Sykes, naturally, with Don Bradman; and Slazenger with Denis Compton. What is particularly interesting, and this is clear from an excellent black-and-white photograph introducing the section, is that all these bats now carry the Slazenger name in relatively small lettering, except for the Denis Compton bat, on both sides of the splice. The culmination of this process was the gradual elimination of the Sykes, Gradidge and Ayres names to allow the concentration of promotional investment on what had become the best known brand in the group's portfolio, arguably since the 1930s, and, in the case of cricket, provided the basis for the proud claim in the 1981 centenary catalogue that 'Slazenger has manufactured bats for such famous cricketers as Sir Donald Bradman, Sir Leonard Hutton, Cyril Washbrook, Leslie Ames and Godfrey Evens'. They were included in a longer list that also included later great players, like Sir Garfield Sobers, Tom Graveney, Bobby Simpson, Graeme Pollock and Trevor Bailey, who, as had been the case with Denis Compton, had only ever played with Slazenger branded bats.

The Duke of Edinburgh visits Barnsley in 1957 and is seen below with Michael and Humphrey McMaster

Turning to another aspect of the business – the key area of tennis balls – what was probably the first major investment in the Barnsley plant since it had opened in 1946 was a substantial modernisation programme carried out in 1957. *Harpers Sports and Games* reported in September that year how manual handling operations, largely based on balls being moved around in tea chests, were replaced by a mechanical handling system using a series of hoppers to move the products from the moulding section to the final inspection before they were cloth-covered. This article disclosed that at the time output was running at 10,000 dozen per week, which was only a fraction of the plant's eventual capacity.

As the 1950s drew to a close rumours were circulating that Ralph Slazenger, who had inherited the majority shareholding when his father, Albert, had died in 1940, was interested in selling his controlling stake in the business. For some years he had been living in Ireland and had not been involved in the day-to-day management of the business, which he had been happy to leave primarily to the McMasters, though they had lost the services of Bill Dunning, who had died in 1948. The McMasters were not enthusiastic about the idea of the sale, which they felt would almost certainly mean the company would lose a substantial degree of its independence. However, whatever Ralph's personal consideration at the time it would have been clear that if the business was to continue to grow, in what was becoming an increasingly competitive marketplace, a considerable and sustained level of investment would be required. In particular significant funding would be essential for product development, where the demand was increasing for more and more new products with greater emphasis on the need for technical and performance advantages, and also for promotional activities in relation to both media spend and the sponsorship of both players and events. The company's long-established marketing strength would become increasingly expensive to maintain and it has to be doubtful if Ralph would have been prepared to underwrite such a future.

At that point Ralph's apparent interest in disposing of his holding, and despite the understandably negative attitude of the McMasters to taking that route, would have been bolstered by the steady increase in trading profits, which would have appealed to any potential purchasers. The 1957 gross profit before tax and interest passed £250,000 for the first time, which would have added substance to the rumours of a sale, or, as the *Sports Trader* observed, 'It has been whispered in the trade that a link-up between two of its leading manufacturers was more than likely.' The company itself added to the speculation by asking shareholders not to dispose of their holdings and by intimating that discussions were taking place with a company of 'the highest standing'; which was interested in acquiring the issued Ordinary capital. The *Sports Trader* did its sums based on the current quotation of 8s 6d per share and declared that any bid 'would be in the region of £1 million'.

The trade magazine turned its own estimate of the likely size of any bid for the company into a December 1958 headline – 'The Million Pound Question' – which further speculated that 'the identity of the firm, presumably interested in the sports trade, who could entertain a proposition involving this figure, was not beyond the imagination of most people', and went on to virtually banish all doubts on the subject by reporting that 'Mr. Reay Geddes, managing-director of the Dunlop Rubber Company, had revealed that his company was the interested party'. The need to move quickly to secure this opportunity to bring together the two leading British-based sports brands had been increased by the news that Ralph was in the USA, where he had been talking to Wilsons, one of America's best known and largest sports equipment companies. Therefore, it was not surprising to read in the next issue of the *Sports Trader* that at a Slazenger board meeting held on 2nd December, 1958, the directors had considered an offer from Dunlop based on an exchange of 10 Slazenger ordinary shares of 5s each for 6 Dunlop ordinary stock units of 10s each. The board agreed to recommend the ordinary shareholders to accept this offer, and the February issue of the magazine duly reported that acceptances of the Dunlop offer had been received from holders of over 90% of those shares. One of the reports about these negotiations and their outcome was positioned alongside a small piece, which reflected the strength of Dunlop at that time in terms of a 1958 group profit before tax of £5.5 million, despite the more difficult trading conditions being experienced that year.

This meant that after 77 years the business started by Albert and Ralph in Manchester ceased to be independent and had become part of the worldwide Dunlop empire. That point was emphasized when, almost immediately, the Slazenger business in Australia became part of the local Dunlop organisation, much to the displeasure of its local managing-director, David Blacklock, who, for some years had been its driving force. His proposal to take Slazenger

The *Sports Trader* reports on the 'Million Pound' sale of Slazenger to Dunlop

Greg Norman

Seve Ballesteros

Australia public was turned down and he retired shortly afterwards. However, he might have taken some satisfaction from the 1967 decision by Dunlop in Australia to merge all its sports-related activities under the Slazenger name in order to reflect, at least in that country, the consumer perception that the two brands were respectively industrial and consumer oriented.

Although Slazenger was no longer truly independent, it had been made clear at the time of the Dunlop acquisition that it would continue to operate separately in the marketplace. A Dunlop press release had confirmed that they would be separate entities with the same managements and staff, honouring all existing commitments, agreements and understandings. Furthermore that 'while the productions of Dunlop and Slazenger will still be sold in competition, the two companies will have common aims in so far as the promotion and welfare of sport and the protection of the legitimate trade are concerned'. These assurances would have been well received both within the two companies and also would have gone some way to convince the trade it had nothing to fear from the amalgamation of two of its main suppliers. There was, however, an immediate signal that the pooling of research facilities could be expected to work to the advantage of both users and distributors of the equipment marketed, separately, by the two firms.

Michael McMaster, who continued as chairman, now had a direct reporting line to the Dunlop main board in the person of Frank Smith, who was responsible for the group's consumer-related activities and, happily, had been an earlier and very successful general manager of the sports division. Early proof of the company's continued independence of action, even if such moves would have required main board approval, came with the 1961 initiative in purchasing the Keighley-based Fred Hurtley & Son. This business had been founded in 1925 as a manufacturer of lisle stockings but had become much better know as the leading UK producer of athletic supporters. Its name was changed to Litesome and it began to expand its product line to include a wide variety of clothing for most of the major sports. It is not clear whether or not this particular move sparked an interest in the sports and leisure clothing market, but only a short time would elapse before the Slazenger brand, and its exciting new Panther logo, would become as well known in that sector as it had been for so many years in sports equipment.

The first reference to Slazenger in the *Dunlop Gazette* – Michael McMaster and T. P. Clarke are received as 'visitors' to Waltham Abbey by Jack Morton and Harry Hatfield-Smith

Meanwhile the determination to ensure that the world saw Dunlop Sports and Slazenger as separate and competing organisations is reflected in the approach to the merger by the *Dunlop Gazette*, which, for many years, meticulously recorded all events, major and minor, around the Dunlop world. The acquisition of Slazenger, arguably the most important event in the history of the sports division, was not reported at the time and the first reference to this new member of the group, in May, 1959, was to report, with a picture, the visit of 'the principal executives of Slazengers Ltd., the sports goods manufacturers, to the Waltham Abbey racket factory'. Those principal executives were 'Mr. M. McMaster, chairman and managing-director, and Mr. T. P. Clarke, account-ant', and they are shown in the factory with Jack Morton, who had become the Sports Company's general manager, and Mr. H. Hatfield-Smith, who was the works manager of the racket plant.

It was another three years before the *Gazette* ran a Slazenger feature. In June, 1962 the front cover, which was well known for high-quality photo-graphs, showed racket production at Horbury and the main article in that issue was a detailed description of the range of products still produced at the Yorkshire factories. The *Gazette* reporter was 'fascinated and amazed at the quantity and variety of sports goods made there'. Having reminded his read-ers that 'the Dunlop 65 is the world's best-known golf ball, and that Dunlop tennis rackets and balls are seen wherever tennis is played', he went on to acknowledge that 'Slazengers supply just about everything that could be required for every sport generally known in this country, are considerably the world's largest tennis ball manufacturers, have a very large output of tennis, badminton and squash rackets, are one of the largest makers of golf clubs and make cricket, hockey, archery and table tennis requisites in quantity'. The very large leather goods section (bequeathed by Sykes) was acknowl-edged as 'bringing in a type of manufacture hitherto unfa-miliar to Dunlop', capable of producing 'just about every leather- or fabric-based accessory imaginable for every sport'. The sight of motoring safety-helmets being made at Barnsley convinced the writer that 'the Slazenger range covers practically every kind of outdoor recreation'.

The article, which would have provided its Dunlop readers with a very effective introduction to a Slazenger operation very different from their own sports business, was given consider-able impact by the accompanying photographs of many of the Horbury pro-duction processes. Another *Gazette* feature was its readiness to put names to the faces of the employees it photographed. In this case, and to mention sev-eral of the factory's leading personalities, the action shots included Jack Bedford in the archery department, Rodney Kirkham and Eddie Kenyon assembling tennis posts, Herbert Shaw in the golf ball moulding department, Clifford Spence setting up a stitching machine to make shin-guards, Les Eden at work in the sawmill, Arnold Walker inspecting soccer balls, George Watt checking the loft and lie of a golf club, and the renowned bat-maker Don Ward, finishing an assembled bat. The ladies were represented by Mrs. Joynes and Nora Harrison in the Barnsley tennis ball plant, Mary Hutchin in the golf bag department, Shirley Hinchliffe inspecting safety-helmets and Mrs. Martin putting the padding into boxing gloves. The picture used to introduce the article was a group of six cricket bats from the company's museum, includ-ing two that were by then already nearly 200 years old, the bat used by Gary Sobers to score 365 against Pakistan in 1958, and another autographed by the 1936-37 M.C.C. side in Australia.

It hasn't been surprising to hear differing opinions about how well these two sports businesses combined, not least because of the clear direction they were both given to continue regarding each other as competitors. Slazenger

THE WIMBLEDON CONNECTION

SLAZENGERS'
"DOHERTY"
RACKET

The
"STADIUM" Post

SLAZENGERS, LTD., have supplied the Lawn Tennis Balls and Plant to THE CHAMPIONSHIPS, WIMBLEDON, and the Leading Clubs and Tournaments, for over Twenty Years.

The very first Slazenger advert to appear in the Wimbledon programme

The Slazenger name has been, first and foremost, associated with tennis and at the heart of this focus has been the company's relationship with Wimbledon. The very first Men's champion, Spencer Gore, used an Ayres racket. The Slazenger/Ayres winning streak from 1896 to 1919 was dominated by the Doherty brothers, Laurie and Reginald, Arthur Gore and the Australian, Tony Wilding. Fred Perry was the champion for three years from 1934 to 1936, and, after the second world war, Neale Fraser, Ken Rosewall, Roy Emerson, Manuel Santana and John Newcombe were prominent among the leading men, and Althea Gibson, Margaret Smith, Christine Truman, Betty Stove and Sue Barker among the ladies. In recent years Tim Henman has carried British hopes and played brilliant tennis despite the huge pressure of the nation's expectations. His Slazenger racket was developed by the company's technical staff with his close collaboration.

Ayres balls were selected for the tournament from 1879 to 1901, and the All England Club has chosen Slazenger for every year since, apart from the wartime interruptions. The number of balls supplied for the championships, not unexpectedly, has greatly increased since the fifteen dozen provided for the first tournament in 1877. As the tournament has grown in terms of competitor numbers, prize money and the facilities for both the players and spectators so the number of balls required for the qualifying stages, practice and the championship matches has multiplied many times over. Now nearly 50,000 balls are supplied, every one carefully tested and inspected before leaving the factory. New balls are required after the first seven games – to allow for the warm-up – and then after every nine games. The yellow balls now used replaced the original white balls in 1986 and the 2002 tournament saw the introduction of the 'Ultra Vis' ball with its unique 'Hydroguard' water-resistant cover.

Tony Gathercole checking competitor name cards for the scoreboards in 1972

However, the very special Slazenger relationship with Wimbledon goes a long way beyond delivering those 50,000 balls. Because tennis has always been so important for the company, it invested heavily in sponsoring and supporting many of the UK's major tournaments and set up a tournament department for this purpose. Very few of the thousands that throng the championships every year realise just how much of what they see around the courts has been put in place by this department. A winter visitor to Wimbledon might, for instance, be surprised to see the large open spaces of grass, which, in June, divide into a complex pattern of courts, spectator walkways, temporary stands and marquees.

Indeed, not so many years ago, and before the All England club had increased its staff, more than a dozen Slazenger employees were on duty every Wimbledon fortnight. They were responsible not only for the company's equipment and clothing, but also fulfilling important roles within the total operation. They worked in the Referee's office, helping to make sure each day's programme was completed without delays, had special responsibilities looking after the key matches on the Centre and Number One courts, and were also responsible for the players' transport arrangements.

There is a wonderful (and true!) story that the club secretary once forgot to order the balls and woke up in a panic on the first morning of the tournament. Happily Slazenger had assumed it was 'business as usual' and the balls duly arrived.

However, the company's most important role has always been the work of the equipment staff and this continues to the present day. The task is formidable. With the team also building the court surrounds of the qualifying tournament, held at the Bank of England Club at Roehampton, everything must be absolutely perfect. The preparation for one year starts almost immediately the equipment for the previous year has been dismantled. All the metalwork used to erect the courts – nearly 1400 stakes and rods ranging from 3 to 8 feet – is repainted and the 70,000 square feet of heavy canvas sheeting surrounding the courts, and marking the walkways is repaired or, if necessary, renewed.

It takes around 120 tons of wood, metal and canvas to set up all the courts. This includes 60 nets, 40 pairs of posts, 22 umpire's chairs, 27 hand-operated scoreboards, 2000 yards of stop netting and 3000 yards of polypropolene rope, as well as the stakes, rods and canvas. The team builds the surrounds for the 20 courts required for the main tournament, all with different dimensions and requirements – for instance, in 2001 the Centre Court surrounds had to be adjusted to accommodate a new TV camera. A team of seven men work flat out for six weeks before the first Monday of the championships to get everything ready, and it takes three weeks to take it all down. During the fortnight the Slazenger team is virtually on 24 hour standby to deal with any problems and one or more helpers can always be found in their 'Operations Room' tucked away in a corner behind the private marquees in the southern corner of the grounds.

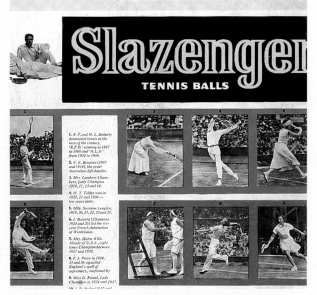

The 1957 Slazenger advert in the tournament programme

The 2001 Slazenger advert. The following year marked the Slazenger Wimbledon centenary

employees, and that by now included a large proportion drawn from the ranks of Ayres, Gradidges and Sykes – especially the latter's Horbury numbers – were properly proud of their long traditions as specialist sports businesses. On the other hand, the Dunlopians were inclined to regard their company as the senior partner, on the basis of the ownership derived from the great strength, at that time, of the parent company, and of their very considerable, mainly product based achievements in the sports world – especially tennis and golf – during a much shorter period. Forty years later it is easy to applaud the decision, at that time, to allow the two businesses to remain as almost entirely separate and independent entities within a generally prosperous and expanding market, and encourage them to develop very different competitive identities in order to maximise the available opportunities.

Although, during the last quarter of the century, circumstances pushed rationalisation for both companies to the top of the agenda, especially for Slazenger, the very different brand perceptions, reinforced in the early years following the 1959 merger, are still valid. More to the point they remain extremely valuable in terms of both consumer perception and the related market targeting.

From the purely Slazenger viewpoint, the record for most of the 25 years following acquisition is of a sturdily independent operation, which added considerable lustre to the brand. The company retained its own board of directors, which included at least one, and sometimes two, Dunlop representatives, one of them always the current general manager of initially the Dunlop Sports Company and, from its formation in 1964, of the International Sports Company. Michael McMaster remained as chairman until his retirement in 1965 – just three years before he died – and he was succeeded by his brother, Humphrey, until he retired in 1975. His death, in 1979, ended the McMaster connection with the Slazenger board, which had begun nearly fifty years earlier, though Humphrey's grandson, Peter, worked in and later managed the sportswear business in the 1970s and 1980s, including a period starting up a similar operation for the Australian company.

The decision to develop the Litesome business was only one of several major Slazenger initiatives after the Dunlop acquisition. In 1962, a company, Slazengers Inc., was set up in the USA as a fresh start in building a significant presence in that market, and in the same year, when the Laurence Pountney Hill offices were demolished to make way for the extension of the Victoria embankment, a new head office, named 'Challenge House', was established in Croydon. It was an entirely Slazenger decision, in 1977, to become distributors of the Puma sports footwear range in the UK, and, in the early 1960s, the hugely significant step was taken to enter the sports clothing market. It's quite clear from the make-up of the later catalogues, especially from the 1970s onwards, that the clothing range assumed greater and greater importance within the total product line. Unquestionably both the range itself, which became very extensive, and the Panther logo, which adorned it, maintained, and possibly increased awareness of the brand, but it is also clear that as the company entered the mid 1970s, and for other reasons to be examined later, the previous strength of the equipment line had declined. In the November, 1979 issue of the *Sportsdesk*, which had succeeded *Panther Press* as the company's newspaper, and which contained Humphrey McMaster's obituary, the content is equally divided between equipment and the combination of Slazenger and Puma clothing and footwear.

Denis Compton and Buzzer
Hadingham examine one of the
famous Sykes 'Zig-Zag' soccer balls.
Dennis endorsed Slazenger
shinguards as well as cricket bats

1962 had been not only the year for what must have been an emotional farewell to the Laurence Pountney Hill building, which had been the head office since 1883, but was also when George Carr became the general manager of the Dunlop Sports Company. He was to play a key role for both companies over the next twelve years and, especially from 1964 when he became the first general manager of the International Sports Company, newly established by Dunlop as the umbrella, or background organisation to 'Operate as the controlling company for all the Dunlop UK interests in sport'. A key responsibility of this new organisation was to maintain 'the emphasis on the individual brand names', an objective certain to receive wholehearted support from the Slazenger board.

While there would never have been any doubt that both Michael and Humphrey McMaster, in their turn, would maintain the essential 'Family' ethos that had characterised the Slazenger style for so many years, it is also very clear that by the early 1960s 'Buzzer' Hadingham, would be the next member of that 'Family' to uphold the Slazenger style and independence.

Buzzer was appointed managing-director in 1973, a post his father had held from 1920 to 1937. Having started at £1 per week, when in 1933 he started in the export department, he had been delighted with the £150 per annum salary that went with his appointment, in 1937, as European sales manager. His fluency in French and German was largely acquired during his training, which involved six month spells working in Paris and Frankfurt. During the time in Germany he had seen one of the early Nazi rallies and also remembers an occasion when, during a walk in the woods near his lodgings, he came across a group of men, no doubt future soldiers, practising arms drill with spades.

Whether or not those early experiences left a deep impression he was commissioned in the Territorial Army, which prepared him for a distinguished military career during the 1939-45 war. He served as a battery commander in the 67th Anti-Tank Regiment during the African and Italian campaigns, winning the Military Cross at Salerno and a bar to it at the Garigliano River crossing. After the war he returned to the export department and became its manager in 1949. He joined the board in 1952, as export director, and became marketing director in 1965. His considerable experience on the export side of the business was the major factor in the company's success in developing overseas markets, though his own assessment was that it was entirely due to the Slazenger tradition of teamwork that had involved everyone from the shop floor to top management.

Nevertheless the fact that under his direction the company's export sales tripled between 1965 and 1970 was recognised by the award of the OBE in the 1971 New Year Honours List. He became managing-director in 1973 and succeeded Humphrey McMaster as chairman in 1976, when Ian Peacock assumed day-to-day executive authority. He finally retired from the position of non-executive chairman in 1983, fifty years after joining the export department at Laurence Pountney Hill. Again, in the tradition established by the directors and senior managers of the company, he had been very active in supporting and leading trade associations and sports promotional bodies. These included the Federation of British Manufacturers of Sports and Games, the European Sports Manufacturers Federation, the Golf Foundation and the Lawn Tennis Foundation, of which he was chairman. He had become a member of the All England Lawn Tennis Club in 1957, was chairman of the Club from 1983 to 1989 and remained a vice-president. In addition to his successes as a businessman, soldier and sports administrator he had, for many years, devoted considerable time and energy to SPARKS, the Sportsman's charity which raises money for research into crippling diseases, and having been its chairman for a number of years became its life president. In retirement, he lived happily with his wife, a few hundred yards from Wimbledon's Centre Court (where else?), and retained not only his energy and enthusiasm for life in general but also a fascinating store of memories, which allowed him to vividly recall his many exciting experiences and the hundreds of sporting 'greats', who had been his friends during a career that included giving rackets to Fred Perry for testing, standing alongside Don Bradman as he signed more than 3000 bats in a day with an old Swan pen at the Horbury factory, signing Denis Compton and Gary Sobers for Slazenger, sending a personal note of support to John McEnroe during Wimbledon, 1984, and playing and working with Ben Hogan, Bobby Locke, Jack Nicklaus, Peter Alliss and Johnny Miller. In one of his poems, published in *Random Rhymes*, in 1980, he muses, 'Don't ever let my time in idleness pass by.' There was very little chance of that!

Although Buzzer was the driving force behind the company during the 1960s and 1970s he would have been the first to acknowledge the support he received from, and the contributions made by what had remained an essentially Slazenger group of people, 'from the shop floor to top management'. When International Sports Company was formed it was acknowledged that the company had brought considerable resources to the Dunlop and Slazenger merger, most notably the multi-product Horbury plant, the newer tennis ball plant at Barnsley, and the sports related strength of the brand. While the production facilities, and also the research and development resources of both companies were co-ordinated and rationalised – for instance all tennis ball production was concentrated at Barnsley and golf ball output at the Dunlop factory at Speke – the original objective to maintain both the appearance and reality of competitiveness between the brands was

Buzzer Hadingham with Gary Sobers, who used Slazenger equipment throughout his playing career and maintained his association with the company when he was later given the responsibility for developing youth sport in the West Indies

Ben Hogan, who was associated with Slazenger for nearly twenty years, is seen here with Michael McMaster and Gerry Craven while inspecting production of Hogan clubs at Horbury

secured by retaining two completely separate sales and marketing departments, supported by different advertising agencies. This meant that regardless of where the products were being made the trade and consumer saw two completely different ranges with Slazenger still covering much the larger number of sports, two markedly different approaches to advertising and promotion, separate tournament sponsorship programmes, and different players endorsing the leading products. In the latter case competition between the two businesses was sufficiently strong to result in several players being enticed from one to the other by a better deal. In what was probably the most significant and far reaching example of a player signing for one brand rather than the other, a last minute decision by the Dunlop main board resulted in John McEnroe's racket carrying the Dunlop 'Flying D' logo instead of the Slazenger Panther. In this case it wasn't a question of Dunlop making a better offer, but of the parent company's board, which owned both brands, deciding that John should be associated with the bigger of the two in terms of worldwide sales. Slazenger had been sufficiently confident they would secure this contract to have designed a range of McEnroe rackets and accessories, and prepared an outline advertising programme. Understandably, at the time, they were hugely disappointed by the board decision and could be excused for having mixed feelings about John's subsequent tremendous success with Dunlop.

The last twenty-five years of Slazenger's existence as a separate operation, albeit wholly owned by Dunlop, proved as dramatic as anything that had gone before and were set against the background of a sports marketplace that was experiencing its greatest upheaval since the explosion of popular interest in outdoor leisure pursuits a hundred years earlier.

For rather more than the first half of that period the company, if anything, enjoyed even more success than during its wholly independent past, which, at least in part, can be attributed to the greater strength of support resources it enjoyed within the Dunlop Group. In fact, within that environment both brands flourished spectacularly enough to be seen as dominant in tennis, and almost equally as strong in golf and cricket. Dunlop or Slazenger rackets won 80 of the 112 men's and women's Grand Slam tennis titles contested between 1960 and 1973, 38 of them going to Slazenger, most of them to Margaret Court, John Newcombe and Ken Rosewall. In the same period Dunlop and Slazenger brands appeared on the balls, clubs or clothing of 13 of the 14 British Open golf champions. Slazenger players at the time included Ben Hogan, Jack Nicklaus, Peter Alliss and Bobby Locke, and, on the cricket pitches of the world, Colin Cowdrey, Gary Sobers, Mike Procter and Alan Knott were among the many using Slazenger bats and gloves.

This period of shared supremacy in their main sports was not sustained during the remaining ten years of the separate Slazenger operation as both companies were forced to confront two main problems. Externally the marketplace was becoming more and more competitive both in terms of overseas based new entrants and their generally more aggressive promotional investment. Internally, the ability to respond to the pattern of this new 'playing field' was restricted by extremely difficult economic and trading conditions in the main UK market, and the inability to keep pace with the rising level of competitors' spending, partly because of the stringent controls on all forms of expenditure throughout the Dunlop Group, which was experiencing the same difficulties, and particularly within its tyre operations. Within the Dunlop-led International Sports Company, possibly for the first time, the difficulty of spreading a restricted level of advertising funds across a multi-brand business operating in a number of increasingly competitive market sectors, was proving a major challenge demanding an allocation of priorities not always to the liking of the Slazenger management.

The original research laboratories and drawing office at the Horbury factory, where both products and manufacturing equipment were designed by the company's technicians

Nevertheless, it is quite clear that throughout the whole of this period and, therefore, during both the good and bad times, the Slazenger management team not only continued to exercise a considerable degree of control over their own destiny, which secured the distinctive style and presence of an apparently still independent brand, but also developed a number of major initiatives, which had an enduring impact on the total Dunlop Slazenger business. The fact that today the brand retains a clearly defined style and prestige, 120 years after it was first launched into the sports trade, owes as much to the marketing expertise deployed during the last 25 years of its operating independence as it does to its much longer and unique heritage. That blend of heritage, and a style highly appropriate to the aspirations of today's sports enthusiasts, provides a powerful platform for the future development of the brand as a quality presence in the sports market.

The separate Slazenger board, always with one or more Dunlop representatives in attendance, held four main meetings each year. Initially Michael McMaster was in the chair, to be succeeded by Humphrey McMaster and, from 1976, by Buzzer Hadingham, who had joined the board, as export director, in 1952. The Slazenger traditions of management continuity and the 'Family' ethos were thus maintained, and were now strengthened by the additional experience and counsel of the Dunlop and ISC representatives, in the latter case first George Carr from 1964 to 1973, and for the following ten years, Findlay Picken. The Slazenger 'continuity' factor was extended in 1976, when Buzzer became chairman and handed over the day-to-day control of the business to Ian Peacock, who had joined the company in 1954, as a sales trainee, and been appointed to the board, as marketing director, in 1973. Ian's experience of and influence on the marketing side of the business was immense, and proved an excellent preparation for his subsequent, high profile appointments as the executive director of the Lawn Tennis Association and, later, chairman of the National Golf Foundation.

It is very clear from the board minutes that while both George Carr and Findlay Picken were consistently supportive of the Slazenger team and their initiatives they also, when they felt it was appropriate, exercised their responsibilities to both challenge those initiatives, and to make the final decisions on key issues in the interests of the entire ISC group of companies. Within this structure the board minutes show that decisions regarding such areas as major player contracts, promotional expenditure that might conflict with other ISC campaigns, key sourcing decisions, the Puma distributorship proposal, investment in the USA business, and capital expenditure; particularly in relation to the major refurbishment of the Challenge House offices and the best way of handling sportswear distribution; all required ISC or, occasionally, Dunlop main board approval. The basic agenda for the board continued to reflect the international scope of the business as the minutes include regular reports on the performance and main issues related to the operating units in USA, France, Canada, New Zealand and South Africa.

Activities in the UK were covered by a general 'Sales' heading with, as appropriate, more detailed reports on the position with the main product groups (golf balls and clubs, tennis balls and rackets). The Litesome and Puma businesses were reported separately, as were special items like the annual reviews of the Wimbledon fortnight, the brand presence at the Open Golf Championship, and the key support functions like manufacturing and supplies.

The evolution of the business from the 1960s to the early 1980s is visible, not only from the board minutes but also from the available catalogues from this period. Additionally there is a very upbeat record covering the twelve years from 1969 when Buzzer Hadingham announced the first issue of the *Slazenger Sports Newspaper*, for distribution to UK and overseas agents. Initially entitled *Panther International* it later became the *Slazenger Sports Desk Newsletter*, which was also distributed to the UK press. The combination of the minutes, which clearly indicate the problems confronting the business as well as its many successes, and of the more success oriented newsletter produced to 'bring together people whose business it is to sell sports equipment all over the world' and to 'keep everyone up to date with what is happening within the company' provides a rich source of archive material. It also allows today's reader to see how fiercely and successfully the Slazenger team fought to maintain the strength of the brand in the face of the mounting pressures that threatened its independent survival within the sports trade.

A more thorough review of the board minutes during the 1970s reveals a number of constant themes, which, when combined with the images of the business as projected by the newsletters, define the most severe of the pressures during this period, and also the most important of the initiatives that buttressed the longer term strength of the brand.

Several of these 'constants' had been present and important throughout all or most of the history of the business. Top of the list would be the huge importance, especially for a tennis-oriented enterprise, of the relationship with Wimbledon. Each year the minutes report the appreciation of the All England Club for the support given during the tournament, in terms of both the quality of the balls supplied and the considerable work to set up the courts, but there was probably a collective gulp at the July, 1974 meeting when it was agreed to pay the price increase, from £50 to £650, for the com-

Slazenger Chairman, Mr Humphrey McMaster, OBE

pany's prized centre court debentures.

There are frequent references to the potential and development of overseas sales, which had been a feature of the business since the 1890s, and within this context the meetings between 1973 and 1978 record the highs and lows of the continuing effort to build a significant presence in the USA market. In the early part of the decade, when the company's strength in tennis had been an ideal match for the boom in that sport, the President of Slazengers Inc., Saul Chavkin, had been successful in taking the annual sales to $7 million, but the subsequent declining interest in the game, and a collapse in ball

and racket prices, plus an inability to provide enough investment to develop an effective bridgehead in the golf sector, virtually removed the brand from the world's largest sports good market until the late 1980s. Ian Peacock, in particular, had argued in 1975 for a major golf effort in the exploding USA market and while it is clear the scale of investment necessary simply wasn't available that inability to take such a strategically important opportunity was a considerable setback, which had long-term implications for the equipment element of the total business.

Ian Peacock offering a helping hand to Jack Nicklaus

At another meeting in 1975 Ian Peacock was making it clear that the company had to realise it was now operating in a buyer's market, and was supported by Humphrey McMaster, by now in his eightieth year, reminding the board that 'it was an essential requirement for goods to be supplied when they were needed and to give the best possible service to the trade in terms of quality and delivery'. This was language that Albert and Ralph Slazenger would have appreciated but it is possible that on this occasion both Ian and Humphrey were addressing themselves primarily to Jack Ellis, the works director of ISC, who was attending that particular meeting. He had a very distinguished, thirty-two year career with the company, both in the UK and South Africa where he had been managing-director, but on this occasion was under pressure because of production and distribution problems, which were holding back sales of both equipment and sportswear. It is clear from the record of subsequent meetings that the service position did improve but difficulties in this area, affecting most product lines, appear to have been a significant problem for a considerable period, and especially during the energy crisis and resultant three day week in 1973/74. As so often happens a period of supply shortage is followed by inventory build-up and although sales in the late 1970s reached the £14-£15 million range – with Litesome contributing an additional £2 million – they were not reaching the annual targets set in the range £18-£20 million.

The combination of the now substantial Litesome clothing operation, the steady growth of the sportswear operation since 1964 and the successful launch of the Puma distributorship in 1978, brought about a major mix change in the total sales by the end of the 1970s, from the previous pattern of mainly equipment to a much higher proportion of the largely fashion oriented clothing and footwear ranges. To further complicate the situation, and this applied with equal force to the Dunlop operations, radical changes were occurring, on a worldwide scale, in the pattern of manufacturing and sourcing golf and tennis equipment and accessories as both existing and new sports companies looked increasingly to the Far East for their supplies. Findlay Picken advised the March, 1978 board that in order to meet low cost competition in the middle price range for equipment products the ISC policy 'would be towards factoring more of these items and rationalising manufacturing to produce only premium products'. At the next meeting, which was to be the last attended by Humphrey McMaster before his retirement, Roy Marsh, who had become chairman of ISC, announced the formation of a new company in Hong Kong, which would have the dual role of sourcing products from the Far East and developing the Group's business in that region. Another, relatively brief minute from the same meeting reported that at the 1978 Open Golf championship 'There was much evidence of the Panther on golf sweaters.' Regrettably, no reference to its visibility on clubs and balls.

Against this background of mounting pressures, and also what was a radical product mix change, an overall rationalisation of the range was taking place in terms of the very wide range of sports the business had supplied for nearly 100 years. A number of the sports no longer covered had relatively small participant bases – archery and boxing are obvious examples – and it was probably an easy decision to drop the limited range of sports footwear, which, in any case, would have clashed with the Puma distributorship from 1977 onwards.

However, what would probably have been the most difficult of these rationalisation decisions was the run down of the original Sykes leather production at Horbury, and, in particular, the 1969 termination of soccer and rugby ball manufacture, just over 100 years after William Sykes had made his first small batch of soccer balls for the local children. A more propitious link with the earliest days of the business was the choice of Horbury-made Slazenger balls for the 1966 World Cup, which was exactly 100 years after William had cut the panels for those very first balls. Soccer balls did make a brief reappearance in the range, and were being sold in the USA as late as the mid 1980s, but they were imported from the Far East.

The 1981 'Centenary' catalogue, which was almost certainly the most expensive ever produced by the company, provides the clearest and most colourful confirmation of this twenty year evolution of both the move from range variety to a focused product line, and also the very considerable emphasis on clothing. In 1981 the key equipment products were shown as racket sports (tennis, badminton and squash), golf and cricket, with smaller ranges for hockey and table tennis. Each of the main ranges is supported by sports luggage, but very few other accessory items. As in the past outstanding players are used to showcase the products – in 1981 Seve Ballesteros for golf and Geoff Boycott for cricket – but just those two compared with the several that would have appeared a few years earlier. There is a rather obvious absence of an equivalent tennis 'Great', who, of course, might have been John McEnroe had he not been signed by Dunlop.

But the most dramatic feature of the catalogue is the pre-eminence given to the sportswear line, which takes up the first third of the pages used in order

SLAZENGER AND
1966 WORLD CUP

When William Sykes was making his first six soccer balls in 1866 he could scarcely have imagined that 100 years later Slazenger balls, made in his Horbury factory, would be chosen for the World Cup. The fact that they were was a tribute to the renowned quality of the balls and to the skills of the employees in the tannery and leather departments of the famous Yorkshire factory. Competition to supply the balls for the 1966 World Cup was intense and FIFA, the governing body controlling the tournament, reported that nearly half those submitted were rejected because they did not meet their stringent specification.

Having been selected the Slazenger balls to be used in the 28 matches of the series were finally measured and checked using four separate scales and templates. Each ball was then initialled by a FIFA official to be handed, sealed, to the referee in charge of each game. Responsibility for getting the balls to the referees was divided between Cyril Smith, who looked after the games played at Wembley and other southern grounds, and George Hartley, who covered the northern grounds like Sunderland, Middlesborough and Sheffield Wednesday.

Dunlop Gazette features Slazenger footballs for 1966 World Cup

Cyril, who worked for both Slazenger and Dunlop Slazenger between 1961 and 1994, including a period in charge of cricket and football promotion and also as manager of the Tournament Department, had been an international standard soccer referee himself so was comfortable when taking the match balls to the world cup referees at their base in a Kensington hotel. For each game the referees were asked to select three from nine of the approved balls, three each in white, orange and yellow. Cyril and George would then take the three chosen balls to the match and would stay 'on duty' to make a half-time check to ensure the ball to be used in the second half was still exactly as specified. This proved a wise precaution as one of the competing goalkeepers,

Jimmy Wilson at the Horbury factory
selecting the 25 leather panels
required to make one World Cup ball

Ken Schofield at Horbury stitching the
panels with the part-stitched ball, still
inside out for this process in front of
him

Photographs courtesy of the *Sunday
Times Illustrated History of Sport*

unhappy with a ball he thought was too hard and bouncy, had been surreptitiously pushing a cocktail stick into the ball's valve to reduce its pressure.

The company's pride in being selected to supply the 1966 balls was communicated by advertising and point of sale material but the balls used in the series didn't show the brand or logo so remained 'anonymous' to the spectators at the matches and to the millions around the world watching on TV. Next time there's yet another TV re-run of Geoff Hurst scoring the final goal remember the orange ball he hits into the German net was made by Slazenger!

to present, most attractively, 100 different styles of clothing for men, women and children, from socks and underwear to tracksuits and sweaters, with more than 200 colour variations, plus the range of sizes offered. In terms of inventory control this would have meant more than one thousand items to select, produce, stock and distribute. So having thoroughly rationalised the equipment range the previous requirement to monitor a very large inventory now had to be applied to the clothing line. Not surprising, therefore, to find that the board minutes in the 1970s contain a number of references to how best to handle this task, and also that it had proved necessary, in 1976, to open a new clothing distribution centre in Batley, Yorkshire. This later housed the sales office and warehouse for what became a much larger Puma distribution operation.

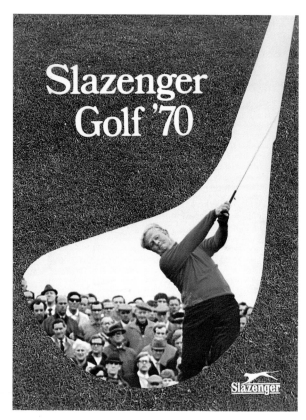

In a sense the combination of using outstanding personalities and sportswear had become the essence of the marketing approach during a period when the importance of sustaining a highly visible brand and marketing profile was becoming a frighteningly expensive element of the cost structure for all sports businesses. And not least because the major competitors, particularly in the key tennis and golf markets, were beginning to invest at unprecedented levels in terms of sponsorship and player contracts.

Jack Nicklaus in full swing on front cover of 1970 golf catalogue

Although by 1981 the use of personalities was restricted to Seve Ballesteros and Geoff Boycott, these two great players were following the tradition of post war relationships with golfers like Ben Hogan, Jack Nicklaus, Peter Alliss and Johnny Miller, cricketers like Denis Compton, Gary Sobers and Colin Cowdrey, and tennis players of the calibre of John Newcombe, Ken Rosewall and Margaret Court. This approach was effective in securing a continuous and persuasive presence for the brand, which, from 1963/64 onwards was given considerably greater visibility by the simultaneous introduction of the sportswear line and the use of the Panther logo, originally designed for that particular product category.

portswear

The extra visibility of the new logo on the clothing line, and particularly on the famous V-neck sweater, was spectacularly increased by the policy of ensuring that Panther emblazoned sportswear was worn not only by the leading players, but also by an astonishing array of celebrities, especially 'Non-Slazenger' sports stars and show business personalities. Winners of

The increasingly glamorous catalogues of the 1970s emphasised the growing importance of the company's extensive range of sportswear

Jacques Kallis

Mark Waugh

PANTHER
THE SLAZENGER SPORTS NEWSPAPER

INTERNATIONAL

September 1970   *Number*

The Panther and you!

This summer the Panther has had tremendous exposure on TV and in the World's Press. At Wimbledon and the Open Championship many leading players were seen wearing our clothing and the commentators too could be seen regularly sporting our distinctive motif.

It's not only sportsmen that are seen in the Panther though, personalities from the stage and screen have also appeared on TV and in magazines in Slazenger clothing. In fact our P.R. file of Panther pictures has been getting so full we thought we would have some fun and make up a montage of a whole bunch of these pictures. Can you put names to all the faces? No prizes for getting them all right we're afraid but to resolve any arguments there is a key with all the names on the back page.

The fact that these personalities appear on TV in the Panther or that their picture appears in the national press is not just an accident. This is achieved by the hard work and application of the Slazenger promotional team, work that is aimed to assure the public becomes aware of the Panther and associates it with Slazengers and the World of Sport.

So we've done **our** bit to promote Panther clothing, now it's up to **you**. Remember the Panther belongs as much to you as it does to Slazengers, for Panther clothing belongs to the Sports Trade and is only sold through your trade, there is *no other* major clothing brand to which this applies, so promote Panther clothing yourselves, stock it in depth, display it in your windows and turn the incredibly successful promotion there's been on the Panther this summer into profits in YOUR shop. Next time you see a Panther on TV remember, the Panther means Slazengers, means the Sports Trade and means profits in your till, so get to it and make the Panther work for all of us.

Spot the famous faces! A 1970 montage of Panther-wearing celebrities

major golf tournaments, contracted for balls or clubs to competitors, were presented with a Slazenger sweater just before receiving their trophies and Peter Alliss recalls the boost given to clothing brands and logos when pro-celebrity golf was launched in 1974. Roy Ullyett, the famous *Daily Express* sports cartoonist, didn't forget to sketch in the Panther when drawing a cartoon of one of the leading tour players in 1972. Included among the famous seen wearing Slazenger sportswear were Muhammad Ali, Ted Heath, Geoff Hurst, Cliff Michelmore, Dickie Henderson, Stanley Baker, Sean Connery, Eric Sykes, Harry Secombe, Jimmy Tarbuck, Bruce Forsyth, Henry Cooper, Joe Bugner and Max Bygraves. The Panther itself, which has become one of the best known sports logos, was conceived and developed by two of the company's advertising agencies, Royds and Childs Greene Associates, and was first registered as a trade mark in 1963. It has been 'modernised' three times since its introduction and in its current form, introduced in 1996, signalled a new beginning for the brand with a stronger design reversing the original direction of the leaping animal. Slazenger can lay a strong claim to creating one of the first sports logos to be so recognizable that the name of the brand was instantly brought to mind without the need to spell it out.

The culmination of this difficult period for the company from the mid 1970s to the early 1980s was the rationalisation of the parent Dunlop company to a largely non-tyre operation, which was still heavily indebted to a consortium of banks. This situation obviously restricted the ability of the retained Dunlop businesses, operating in both the industrial and consumer sectors, to conduct their affairs on anything other than a short term basis.

It was during the relatively short, but dramatic period from the dying months of 1984 to April 1985, which led to BTR (British Thermoplastic and Rubber) acquiring the mainly non-tyre Dunlop businesses that Slazenger ceased to exist as a separately identifiable operation. Within the total reorganisation of Dunlop that then occurred, Dunlop Slazenger Limited was formed as the group to be responsible 'for the sports business, together with all clothing and leisure footwear businesses throughout the world, except South Africa'.

Slazenger had become a brand to be managed, along with Dunlop, Maxfli and Carlton, within the new Dunlop Slazenger business, with its head office at Challenge House in Croydon, which had been the Slazenger headquarters since the move from Laurence Pountney Hill in 1962. A major decision within the early strategic planning for the new sports group was that clothing operations were not regarded as having a viable future. The Litesome business was sold to the Peter Black Company and the Slazenger clothing operation in the UK was licensed to Courtaulds, who had been its main supplier.

So many organisational and management changes took place at this time that the full significance of the Slazenger decision did not receive widespread attention, though its impact would not have been lost on the Slazenger team. In any event, from the consumers' point of view the Panther would still be seen on the licensed clothing range, the brand would continue to feature strongly at Wimbledon and the main equipment products for racket sports, golf and cricket were still available with their own promotional support. But there was no longer a Slazenger 'Champion', nor a separate management team, and as the strategy for Dunlop Slazenger Limited was developed it was decided that the priority emphasis for the golf and tennis ranges should be placed on the Dunlop brands.

However, the Slazenger legacy would provide a major contribution to the development of the new international sports business, and still does today. The brand itself retains a potent image in the sports world and has been successfully re-launched by the Dunlop Slazenger Group in its traditional tennis and cricket strongholds with outstanding players like Tim Henman and a host of English and overseas cricket stars giving the modern Panther enormous worldwide visibility. That visibility has been expanded very substantially by successful licensed clothing operations in many parts of the world, often breaking into new territories for the brand.

The Puma UK footwear distributorship and associated clothing licence for the famous German based brand became a major and separate division within Dunlop Slazenger, which contributed total sales well over £500 million in the ten years before it returned to Puma control in the UK. And, possibly most impressively of all the ongoing Slazenger activities, the combination of the brand imagery mix of heritage and top quality was skilfully used by the David Geoffrey and Associates/ Slazenger Golf USA business, which, financially backed by BTR, was set up in 1986 by former Dunlop managers, David Branon and Geoffrey Gorman. This operation not only contributed over £300 million of new sales over a fifteen year period but also conclusively demonstrated that a high level of targeted marketing expertise, even without massive media spending, was sufficient to establish the significant presence for the brand in the USA North American golf market that had previously been so elusive. In product terms this achievement was based mainly on premium quality balls, sourced from the Japanese plant Dunlop had restarted in the 1950s, and an outstanding clothing line that took

Roy Ullyett, top sports cartoonist of the *Daily Express*, is well known for his involvement in sport of every kind and for his eagle eye that catches the smallest detail of players who make the news.
Recently, in a cartoon of golf's latest colourful character, Formosan Mr. Lu, the Ullyett eye alighted on the Slazenger Panther—the result appeared boldly on the back page of the *Express* and is reproduced on this page

Roy Ullyett, top sports cartoonist for the Daily Express, spots the Panther on the golf course

Prime Minister Edward Heath obviously comfortable in his Panther sweater while rehearsing with the London Symphony Orchestra

This group of overseas Slazenger executives, taken outside Challenge House in Croydon, includes Ron McKenzie (New Zealand), Graham Lovett (Australia), Alan Ross (South Africa), Dick Birch (Canada) and Saul Chavkin (USA) as well as Buzzer Hadingham and Ian Peacock

George Birkin taken shortly after his 100th birthday in 1973

the brand into the 21st century with a style that would have delighted the founding Slazenger brothers as well as their more recent successors, like Buzzer Hadingham and Ian Peacock. They were quick to recognise both the quality of the product line and the marketing skills involved as a worthy revival of the principles that had been consistently fostered throughout the history of the business Ralph and Albert had established in 1881.

Throughout its history an obvious feature and strength of the Slazenger group of companies was its personality as a people oriented organisation. Its image as a 'family business' went way beyond the leadership thread provided, during a 100 year span, by the Slazengers, Hadinghams and McMasters to include several generations of families involved throughout, like the Wycherleys, and also the many individuals who spent all their working lives with one or more of the 'Famous Four'.

Short of providing a complete roll call of the many outstanding people who were part of the effort that propelled the name of Slazenger into sports history a glance at the company's newsletters, published between 1969 and the early 1980s, affords a glimpse of just a few of those who Buzzer Hadingham would have had in mind when he talked about 'the Slazenger tradition of teamwork that involved everyone from shop floor to top management'.

In 1973 the *Panther* newspaper recorded the 100th birthday of the company's oldest pensioner, George Burkin, who had spent 58 years in the sports trade. He had joined F. H. Ayres in 1888, making billiard tables and cricket bats, including some used by W. G. Grace. For the first six years he was paid 2s per week, which was then increased to 5s. He remained with Ayres, at their Aldersgate Street factory, until they were taken over by William Sykes in 1940, and then, despite being nearly 70, moved to their Horbury factory, where he retired in 1946, aged 73. One of his sons also worked for the company, at Croydon, but even their combined years of service didn't match the record of the Skull family. Jack Skull, who retired at Croydon in 1971, after 49 years service had followed his father and grandfather into the business and they notched up a total of no less then 124 years with the company.

Another with 49 years service was Bill Peters, who had joined the company in 1922 as a filing clerk in the Laurence Pountney Hill office and retired as depot manager at Croydon. He had clear memories of Albert, Frank and Horatio Slazenger, the latter as manager of the leather section in the 1920s that produced spats for gentlemen and gaiters for ladies, which recalls the 1890 Post Office directory that included 'legging and gaiter manufacturer' among the activities of Slazenger & Sons, newly arrived from Manchester. One of those pictured at Bill's retirement presentation was George Norton, who had also started at Laurence Pountney Hill, in 1928, as a junior in the secretarial department, earned a considerable reputation, fulfilling a host of important 'behind the scenes' responsibilities, won many friends among both colleagues and leading Slazenger golf and tennis stars, and, as company secretary, wrote an invaluable history of the company in 1981 to mark its centenary year.

Peter Alliss, who was one of those stars and remembers George, not least because of his tiring daily commute from Essex to Croydon, also recalls his many discussions at Horbury with the company's golf club makers, 'Kings in their own right'. Possibly the best known of those 'Kings' was John Reid, who had nearly 50 years experience of making clubs, most of them with Slazenger. As manager of the club department at Horbury in the 1970s, he and his assistant, Tom Gamble, were responsible for a 70 strong work force, most of them with 15 years experience and many of them with more than 25 years. Peter Alliss also remembered Ian Mitchell as a 'larger than life figure', who, during the 1960s and 1970s, was widely known as the company's golf manager

'A firm of sportsmen and a sporting firm' was how Albert Bowler described the company. He was well qualified to make such a judgement having spent 50 years in the company, mainly on the sales side, before retiring in 1980 as home sales manager, though he continued to be part of the support team Slazenger provided for the Wimbledon Championships where he had worked for some years as right-hand man to the referee. His counterpart on the export side, Bob Boomer, travelled the world for the company for more than 40 years of his 50 plus years service and as export sales director was largely responsible for overseas sales accounting for more than half the total turnover in the early 1970s. Renowned for his sense of humour and speaking ability he travelled well over a million miles in extending the company's distribution network to virtually every country in the world. The nearest 'overseas' market was France where the Dupont family, father Marcel and son Jean Louis, managed the Slazenger company from their Paris office for nearly 70 years.

Both the Duponts were international sportsmen, Marcel at tennis and Real Tennis, Jean Louis at amateur golf. As were John Barrett and Mickey Stewart, the latter combining his cricket career with Surrey and England with his product and promotions activities in relation to the cricket and football ranges. John Barrett's appearances at Wimbledon in the early 1950s coincided with those of Czeslaw ('Spike') Spychala towards the end of the latter's playing career before becoming the company's tournament representative. Both represented their countries in the Davis Cup, in Spike's case for his native Poland before the war. Winner of numerous important tournaments in the UK his service to the game was recognised in 1972 when he received the Lawn Tennis Writers' Association annual award to people considered to have made an outstanding contribution to British tennis. And the final name in this too short list is that of Rob McCowen, whose fluency in French, German and Spanish proved invaluable when he followed in the footsteps of Buzzer and Bob Boomer as export sales director, and, subsequently, when he added to the ties between the company and Wimbledon by becoming the All England Club's marketing director and the driving force behind its highly successful merchandising programme.

Names of some of the world's greatest sportsmen, especially tennis players, golfers and cricketers, who were associated with Slazenger read like a hundred year 'Hall of Fame' and it's quite clear that the relationships between the company and many of these 'greats' were extremely close and enduring. This was very much due to the fact that Slazenger was widely recognised as a company that, for many years, had been largely staffed by people who were genuinely enthusiastic about sport – many of them talented participants – and who understood the pressures on the 'stars', pressures that were steadily

Roland Baum, manager of bat production at Horbury, hands a signature bat to Colin Cowdrey, watched by George Carr, Mickey Stewart and Jack Ellis

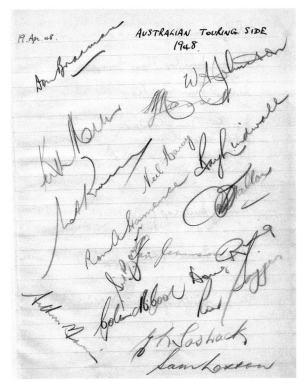

One of the many 'priceless' pages from the Laurence Pountney Hill office visitors' book. This one carries the signatures of the 1948 Australian cricket tourists to the UK, including Don Bradman, Lindsey Hassett, Ray Lindwall, Keith Miller and Neil Harvey

increased as spectator numbers were hugely increased by media exposure and the sums of money involved grew ever greater.

Confirmation of the relationship between the company and the players can be found in a remarkable visitors' book that was kept at the Laurence Pountney offices for a number of years before the move to Croydon. It would appear, from reading the signatures in that book, that a steady stream of either individual players, or complete teams touring the UK, felt they should call on Slazengers while they were in London. The very first page, dated April 1948, sets the tone with the signatures of that year's Australian cricket tourists, including Don Bradman, Keith Miller, Bill Johnson, Neil Harvey, Ray Lindwall, Colin McCool, Don Tallon, Doug Ring, Ian Johnson and Arthur Morris. Many of those names appear again, when the 1953 and 1956 teams are in the UK, and they are joined by others from South Africa, New Zealand, India and the West Indies. In the latter case their 1948 team heading for India 'dropped in' and the list of names is headed by Everton Weekes and Clyde Walcott. Other cricketing callers include Denis Compton, Godfrey Evans and the Bedsers, with virtually identical signatures. Golf is represented by, among others, Bobby Locke, Gary Player, Bob Charles, Bernard and Geoff Hunt and Norman von Nida, tennis by such as Fred Perry, Jack Kramer, Don Budge, 'Pancho' Segura and Mervyn Rose, table tennis by Richard Bergmann and even athletics by the great New Zealander, Peter Snell. Add to that the USA Wightman Cup team, the India and Pakistan Davis Cup squads, the Argentine Olympic hockey team, the Swedish Junior Tennis team, the 1957/58 Wallabies rugby team and the South African Universities hockey team and the impression is that of locker room in the City of London for the world's best amateurs and professionals.

Many of the signatures in this extraordinary visitors' book are those of the company's overseas agents and distributors, who provided the cutting edge for all the hard work by the export teams that had been despatched around the world, not only by Slazenger but also by Ayres, Sykes and Gradidge, for so many years, certainly since the last decade of the 19th century.

They played a major part in building up export sales that were regularly more than half the company's total turnover. For many of them the relationship with the company went way beyond the purely commercial aspect as, over the years, they built strong personal connections with members of the UK management. Testimony to the very special link that existed between supplier and distributor can be found in a 1985 letter from Rob McCowen, which lists 'the articles of Slazenger history' then held in the Croydon office. Sadly, most of the items mentioned are no longer to be found in the company but, hopefully, somebody, somewhere is taking good care of them because they were well earned. The list is below and reflects the esteem in which the name of Slazenger was held across a broad spectrum. It also provides a fitting, final flavour for this remarkable story – as far as it goes, because there are surely many more chapters to be written.

- The Turisport Oscar presented in 1981 to 'The most outstanding sports company in Spain that year in terms of product, service, promotion and advertising'.
- The Santiago Medal presented in 1982 by the Tennis Association of Santiago 'To commemorate 50 years of association between Slazengers and the Association'.
- A beautiful reindeer skin presented in 1981 by the Berner Company of Finland as a tribute to mark the Slazenger centenary.
- The Cleo Award presented by New York advertisers for the creative interpretation in the 'Pea Pod' tennis ball campaign.
- A chandelier presented in 1981 by the Lawn Tennis Association to mark the company's centenary.
- A pottery bowl presented by the Rye Tennis Club as a centenary gift and to acknowledge the club's long-standing relationship with the company, which had included the sponsorship of an important annual tournament.
- A silver junk presented by Jock Mackie, who had worked for the company for 30 years before building up his own distributorship in Hong Kong – Robertson Wilson – which was immensely successful with the Slazenger brand.
- A Japanese warrior helmet presented in 1981 by the Far East distributor, Jardines, to mark their successful, 20-year relationship with the company.
- A 4ft. sword, with Slazenger embossed on the hilt, presented by Wilkinsons, to acknowledge the relationship between the company and their subsidiary, the True Temper golf shaft company.
- A bust of Albert Slazenger, one of the founding brothers of the company.
- A 1981 letter from the Prime Minister, Mrs. Margaret Thatcher, to congratulate the company on its centenary.

DUNLOP

1909 TO 1918

ORIGINS OF SPORTS BUSINESS AND ITS EARLY YEARS WITH ONLY GOLF BALLS

John Boyd Dunlop, whose face appeared in Dunlop advertisements for many years after he severed all links with the company

The early history of the Dunlop sports business is very different from that of the Slazenger companies. It's very likely that when in 1909 the first trickle of golf balls emerged from the Manor Mills tyre factory in Birmingham neither of the Slazenger brothers, nor Messrs. Sykes, Gradidge and Ayres, would have been too worried about this new entrant to the sports trade. Nor, for that matter, would such news have bothered established golf ball makers like Spalding, Wright & Ditson, Haskell and the India Rubber and Gutta Percha Company (later to become British Goodrich and ultimately BTR). The latter produced the formidable 'Silvertown' and 'Silver King' balls close to the Slazenger and Gradidge factories in Woolwich. In fact, since Dunlop initially asked their tyre salesmen to handle these new products, they first appeared in garages and tyre depots so would not have been very visible in the sports trade.

It's not unreasonable to assume that the Dunlop management in the years before the first world war were mainly focused on building their successful tyre business, so the infant golf ball production, at least initially, would have seemed an interesting sideline. On the other hand, and as their early catalogues show during this period, Slazenger, Sykes, Gradidge and Ayres were paying little or no attention to the relatively small golf market and were much more interested in building their presence in racket sports, cricket, croquet and winter sports like rugby, soccer and hockey, all of which offered much larger sales opportunities at that time.

And, of course, all the Slazenger companies were independent, self-sufficient operations, pillars of the sports trade, and even the youngest of them, Slazenger, had already been in business for nearly thirty years. Ayres, indeed, were just about to celebrate the centenary of their beginnings as furniture and indoor games manufacturers in Clerkenwell, and it was forty years since William Sykes had made his first soccer balls in Horbury.

Possibly the most fundamental difference between Dunlop and the Slazenger businesses, and this was largely maintained during the fifty years leading to the Dunlop acquisition of Slazenger in 1959, was the core technology of the two operations. With the major exception of the Slazenger tennis balls produced first at Woolwich and, later, at Barnsley, the Slazenger companies built their activities primarily on the manual skills required to produce high-quality products from leather and wood. On the other hand the birth and growth of the total Dunlop enterprise was rooted in the ability to develop mainly rubber-based products and to design increasingly sophisticated and much more mechanical methods of production.

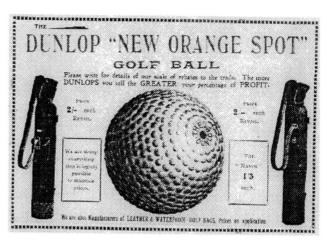

A 1909 advertisement for the 'Orange Spot' ball and golf bags

This approach sat comfortably with their powerful resources in the R & D and production engineering functions as applied not only to tyres but also an ever widening range of consumer and industrial products. As Dunlop, from the 1920s onwards, broadened its sports equipment line to include items like rackets and golf clubs, it generally acquired smaller companies already skilled in these areas, while the Slazenger acquisition of Gradidge, Sykes and Ayres created a large group of companies with similar manufacturing skills. All of them for instance, from very early stages in their existence, had made rackets, cricket bats, hockey sticks, croquet equipment and large ranges of leather goods like boxing gloves, all sorts of leather balls, batting and wicket-keeper gloves plus many types of sports bags.

While it's almost certain that Ayres and Sykes purchased their tennis and golf balls from small, specialist ball makers, Slazenger did make what proved to be a crucial and very courageous investment decision to produce their own tennis balls but they, too, probably bought in their early 'guttie' golf balls, which disappeared from their catalogues soon after the introduction of the wound Haskell balls at the end of the 19th century. They didn't get back into the golf ball sector until 1951, and there are those that still argue that they didn't have a really competitive ball to offer until they started to draw from Dunlop production at Speke early in the 1960s.

Within this context it is also appropriate to note that it's most unlikely Dunlop would have turned their attention to golf balls in 1908/9 had that product not been transformed, in manufacturing terms, by the advent of the Haskell ball into an item that the company's technical and production skills could first of all handle in an environment like Manor Mills and, subsequently, build into a significant part of the total business.

All the Slazenger factories made only sports and leisure goods, and all of their companies were owned and managed by individuals who spent all or most of their working lives in the sports trade. Their salesmen called only on sports distributors and retailers, they were already very experienced in using major events, like Wimbledon and cup finals, and the leading players to promote their brands and products, and could have been excused for thinking that the Dunlop venture into golf balls was unlikely to ever develop into any sort of competitive

The intricate core of the wound golf ball that revolutionised production methods in the late 19th century

THE WINNERS OF 5 NATIONAL CHAMPIONSHIPS
USED

DUNLOP GOLF BALLS

OBTAINABLE FROM ALL PROFESSIONAL AND SPORTS DEALERS

DUNLOP BALLS
HAVE WORLD-
WIDE FAME.

Dunlop Golf Ball
in Japan.

Copy of letter received by our Depot Manager at Kobe, Japan.

38, Lakayamatadori,
3, Chome, Kobe,
August 18th, 1909.

Sir,
I just find that I have quite omitted to send a report on the two "Dunlop" Golf Balls. I am pleased to say they are excellent balls, and I won my match against the best of the Hongkong Team with the aid of them.
I might add truthfully, that I have not yet played with a better ball.

Dunlop 'Orange Spot,' 2/-. 'Dunlop Junior,' 2/-. Manor Ball, 1/3.

NOTE.—A white of ball is offered as "Junior" and "Orange Spot" when purchasing one one.

DUNLOP RUBBER CO. Ltd., Manor Mills, Aston, BIRMINGHAM.

Early international fame – golf ball success in Japan

threat to their powerful positions in the trade, let alone signal the birth of an organisation that, fifty years later, would own them. That final amalgamation, in 1959, of the 'Famous Four' Slazenger companies with the sports division of the giant tyre company would have been completely unthinkable in 1909, and for many years in the future, not least because it would be 1927 before Dunlop first signalled its long-term commitment to its sports business by registering the Dunlop Sports Company Limited.

The hectic early days of the company, as it established itself as a major international player in the rapidly developing automotive and tyre industries, deserve mention as the business then created provided the foundation for what was to become one of the most famous British companies marketing a huge range of industrial and consumer products in virtually every country in the world. It also established an exceptionally strong level of brand recognition, obviously for tyres and other transport related items but also for what was to become one of the best known and most widely used ranges of sports equipment, particularly for tennis and golf enthusiasts. The Dunlop Rubber Company was formed, in Dublin, in November 1889 with capital of £25,000. Its first title was the Pneumatic Tyre and Booth's Cycle Agency, later to be abbreviated to the Pneumatic Tyre Company, then the Dunlop Pneumatic Tyre Company, and, in 1900, the Dunlop Rubber Company.

The original purpose of the new company was to manufacture and sell the pneumatic cycle tyre patented in 1888 by John Boyd Dunlop, a Scottish-born veterinary surgeon. Mr. Dunlop was a director of the new company but, for reasons which are not exactly clear, resigned from the board in 1894 and the company's subsequent development was the work of Victorian entrepreneurs, who had been quick to see the potential of their new product, first as a means of revolutionizing bicycle riding, and, very soon afterwards, as a vital component in the explosive development of the automobile. None other than Henry Ford observed – on a plaque at the Ford headquarters in Dearborn, commemorating the achievement of John Boyd Dunlop – 'The inventor of the pneumatic tyre made the automobile possible'. Remarkably, although that inventor had left the company so soon after it was founded, his bearded face became its trademark and was revered in a number of West African countries, where it was taken to be the features of Jesus Christ. That interpretation did not apply in Japan but the local Dunlop company continued to use this highly distinctive mark on its golf ball packaging right through to the end of the 20th century.

An early indication of what was to become a major characteristic of the business, the international expansion of its activities, very soon gathered pace. By 1893 selling companies had been set up in Germany and France, in the same year the first cycle tyre factory opened in Australia, and, a year later, tyre manufacturing was licensed in Canada. In the same year (1909) that saw the first production of golf balls in the UK, Dunlop opened its first tyre factory in Japan, in Kobe. It's tempting to think that this event inspired a *Golf Illustrated* advert at the end of that year headed 'Dunlop Golf Ball in Japan', which showed a Japanese golfer launching a drive, and which printed a letter, under a Kobe address, to the local Dunlop depot manager informing him the writer was pleased to say that he had never yet played with a better ball than Dunlop, and that he had won his match against the best of the Hong Kong team with the aid of them. In less than a year from the start of production at Manor Mills, as the advert states, 'Dunlop balls have worldwide fame.' Kobe, inciden-

The front of the Manor Mills factory where Dunlop golf balls were first made in 1909

tally, was a very appropriate location for this early focus on golf activities as it was there, in 1903, that the first Japanese golf course (nine holes) was built by British residents, who are believed to have played with a solid gutta per-cha ball.

Meanwhile the headquarters of the company had transferred from Dublin to Coventry, where car tyre production started in 1900, and in 1902 – the first year Slazenger tennis balls appeared at Wimbledon – a larger factory was acquired at Aston Cross in Birmingham to cope with the rapidly increasing demand from the motor industry. At the same time cycle tyre production was established at the nearby Manor Mills. This was to become the first site for the manufacture of Dunlop golf balls.

Although the early golf ball production was on a small scale it is interesting to note that this additional activity within the Manor Mills plant was one of the very first signs of diversification away from tyres and the motor trade, although it's also true that at the time the connection wasn't difficult to make as golf, as a recreation, was largely confined to those with the means to own a motor car. Even twelve years later a Dunlop Rubber Company advertisement extolled the combined delights of golfing and motoring – 'The spring in the turf is making the Dunlop balls sit up and you're getting an extra 15 yards off the tee. The life and joy of it! 18 holes and then home in the car with its sturdy, service-giving Dunlop tyres, as the sun sinks down and the chill of the evening comes on.' Even more to the point another 1920s message, which appeared on the cover of *On the Road* (a pictorial road plan) encouraged the reader to 'play Dunlop, fit Dunlop and be satisfied'

The first golf ball department at the Manor Mills factory

because 'on the links and on the road Dunlop stands for supremacy'.

So it's not surprising to find that while the sports business remained within the Dunlop family of companies, its fortunes and misfortunes were signif-

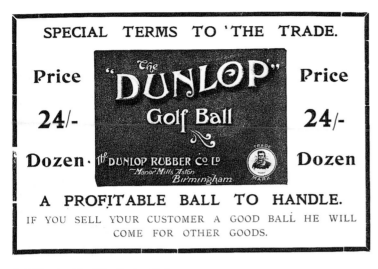

SPECIAL TERMS TO 'THE TRADE.

Price
24/-
Dozen·

"DUNLOP"
Golf Ball

The DUNLOP RUBBER CO LD
Manor Mills Aston
Birmingham

Price
24/-
Dozen

A PROFITABLE BALL TO HANDLE.

IF YOU SELL YOUR CUSTOMER A GOOD BALL HE WILL COME FOR OTHER GOODS.

A 1908 advert for 'The Dunlop Golf Ball' – possibly purchased from a small producer before Manor Mills production started up

icantly influenced by the ups and downs of the core tyre operation. This would have been the case during the very early years at Manor Mills and, later, at Fort Dunlop, and especially in 1921, when, due to a combination of financial mismanagement and slowness to react to the increasingly fierce, post war competition from North American tyre giants like Goodyear and Firestone, the Dunlop board reported a loss of £8.3 million – close to £300 million at today's values. This low point in the early Dunlop history led to the introduction of a new board, which included, most notably, Sir George Beharrell and Sir Eric Geddes, who were to be the architects of the recovery that took the company to a position of enormous, worldwide strength. They were also powerful advocates of the policy of broadening the product base of the restructured company, which would be the trigger for the development of the sports business, as well as many other non-tyre activities.

The first, major thrust to diversify the Dunlop product line took place in the 1920s, and after the new board had been put in place. That period saw the start of new businesses based either on the company's own technological innovation, like Dunlopillo, or on existing activities that had been started by other pioneering rubber companies. In the latter case this included the establishment of product divisions for general rubber goods, clothing and footwear, all of which were subsequently successfully developed under the Dunlop flag.

The sports business was to feature very strongly in the diversification policy pursued in the 1920s, but, uniquely, the embryo golf ball operation, established in 1909, was the first, albeit at the time, small scale and tentative step to make and sell a product not directly linked to the transport sector. The initial use of the tyre sales and distribution organisation to get the balls to the golfer was a further sign that, at that stage, the idea of developing a dedicated marketing approach to a new sector had not yet taken root.

The unknown author of a 1937 *History of Dunlop* has written that 'in the year 1910 it was rumoured amongst the trade that the Dunlop Rubber Company intended to manufacture golf balls'. He went on to observe that this news had caused some surprise because 'the golf ball business at that time showed some of the less encouraging aspects of the fashion trades in that one make might suddenly spring into prominence only to fall from favour with equal rapidity and for no very clear reason'. The latter comment is still valid nearly 100 years later, but there is some confusion about the starting date for golf balls. Although a Dunlop employee, based at Fort Dunlop, should have known the correct date the *Sports Trader* magazine carried an advertisement for 'The Dunlop Golf Ball' as early as 1907 supported by the claim, 'as used by the leading players', and repeated it in April, 1908 with an offer of 'special terms to the trade' and the prom-

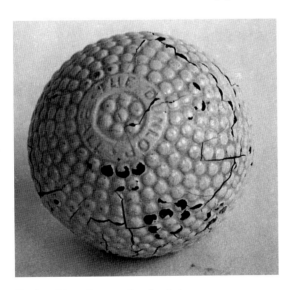

The bramble pattern used on the first Dunlop ball

ise that 'if you sell your customer a good ball he will come for other goods'. The following month a reduction in the trade price was announced to allow an increased margin against the 2s 0d per ball retail price and an additional ball, 'The Manor', was offered with a retail price of 1s 3d and a guarantee it would last for 18 holes.

Only a month later the *Sports Trader* magazine carried an open letter from Dunlop, at Manor Mills, Salford Street, Aston, Birmingham, informing 'dealers in golf balls' that as they felt very strongly on the question of price cutting they would be prepared to stop supplying any customer found guilty of such a practice, not least because they were 'fully alive to the necessity of protecting the trade from experience we have had in other branches of our business'. Basically the same message was publicised in December of that year with the hope that 'the Trade will support the company that has done something more tangible than the giving of promises and fair words'. It's certainly possible that the balls first offered by Dunlop, at least during this first year or so when their advertisements were as much devoted to the problems of price cutting as they were to product performance, were purchased from one of the many small-scale ball manufacturers then in existence. It may be more than just a coincidence that one of their warnings to dealers on this subject shared a full page in the trade magazine with another advertisement sending out exactly the same message, which was placed by Golf Balls Limited of West Lodge Wharf, Hammersmith, London, and which featured their 'Black Star' at the same price as the Dunlop ball with the claim it was 'the longest driving ball ever made'. The *Sports Trader* had fully approved of the company's stance on the price-cutting issue and under the heading 'Virtue Unrewarded' chastised those professionals who had given Dunlop 'the pride of place' in deciding who to kick on this subject. The article went on to assure them that 'they can feel easy in their minds about the Dunlop company as to sell a few dozen extra balls is not a matter of life or death to their finances, as, to use an expressive phrase, they have money to burn'.

A very definite change in the promotional approach is evident in early 1909. Instead of simply describing a 'Dunlop Ball', and talking as much about price-cutting as products, both *Sports Trade* and *Golf Illustrated* began to carry much more attractive and descriptive adverts which feature the 'Orange Spot' and 'Junior' balls, both with the then popular, raised bramble pattern (so called because it closely resembled the appearance of a wild blackberry). Writing in *The Curious History of the Golf Ball* the notable golf ball historian, John Stuart Martin, records that at this time 'Dunlop joined the rubber-core parade', but is dismissive of these early offerings as being 'only so-so and long since forgotten'.

However, the Dunlop sales and marketing departments, almost certainly still 100% staffed by tyre personnel, were, not surprisingly, much more upbeat about their new products. In particular the 'Junior' was featured as being 'the sensation of the 1909 Open Golf Championship' and, according to every professional who tried it, 'the longest driving ball he has ever struck'. Between them these two balls won five of the main amateur and profession-

An Orange Spot ad gets the feminine touch in 1909

A 1909 *Sports Trader* report on the Dunlop Challenge Cup for Scottish professionals

Phew-w-w-w !

they're a couple of beauties and no mistake !

DUNLOP'S LATEST.

"Heavy Dunlop" - (Large Size) - Blue Spot.
"Heavy Junior" - (Small Size) - Blue Spot.

REMARKABLE SUCCESS OF THE NEW DUNLOP BALLS

69 St. Andrews Old Course—Andrew Kirkaldy, Dec. 12. Score certified by Captain Roland Hay, 6th R.B.   **69** C. H. MAYO, BURHILL LAST WEEK.

"*Heavy Junior*" *was used in each case.*
EXPERTS' OPINIONS OF THE NEW HEAVY BALLS.

H. B. Simpson (Professional, Fairhaven).
"I find the 'Heavy Juniors' very good indeed—they fly very well."

W. E. Reid (Professional, Banstead Downs).
"I find the 'Heavy Junior' a very good ball."

A. Matthews (Professional, Rhyl).
"I have given the balls 'Heavy Dunlop' and 'Heavy Junior' a good trial, and I think they are both splendid balls. The 'Heavy Junior' has a nice sound when you hit it."

C. H. Mayo (Professional, Burhill).
"The 'Heavy Dunlop' is the best large size ball I have ever had the pleasure of playing with."

Major Lacon Ashland Wise.
"I like the 'Heavy Junior' very much—it seems a good ball all round."

W. Gray, Junr., Esq. (Glasgow).
"The 'Heavy Junior' goes sweetly off the driver, and putts and pitches very reliably."

Ready for Delivery.
Price 2/- each.

DUNLOP RUBBER CO., LTD., MANOR MILLS, ASTON, BIRMINGHAM.
British-made Dunlop tyres lead in popularity and length of service.

The John Boyd Dunlop figure in the background doesn't look too happy about his 'couple of beauties' in this 1910 Christmas advert

Possibly the first Dunlop sports gift – a porcelain matchbox holder combining an Orange Spot ball with a Dunlop tyre

al tournaments in 1909. No doubt encouraged by these early successes the golf team announced their first tournament sponsorship that autumn when they offered the Dunlop Challenge Cup for competition amongst Scottish professionals to be played over the Dodhead Links at Burntisland with total prize money of £25 and a 26-inch-high solid silver trophy.

Although not so sophisticated as later post-war advertising, but certainly upbeat, one of the most memorable of the early trade press insertions, appearing in the Christmas, 1910 issue of *Golf Illustrated* was headed 'they're a couple of beauties and no mistake'. It pictured two balls as babes in the arms of a distinctly forbidding nanny while a clearly distracted John Boyd Dunlop figure, in a dressing gown, hovers nervously in the background. The balls featured were the 'Heavy Dunlop' and 'Heavy Junior' and evidence was provided of their remarkable qualities by reports of rounds of 69 posted at St. Andrews Old Course and Burhill that month by Andrew Kirkaldy and C. H. Mayo respectively. True to then current policy the last line of copy reminded the reader that 'British-made Dunlop tyres lead in popularity and length of service'.

Whether or not the very first golf balls carrying the Dunlop brand were bought from another manufacturer remains open to question but first-hand evidence is available about the start of production at the Manor Mills plant. In 1959 the *Birmingham Mail* recorded the retirement of Jack Smart of 63 Kempson Road, Castle Bromwich, who was then the only known survivor of the team that started up that first production line. He had joined the company in 1908, aged 14, at the Aston Cross factory, and moved to the new golf ball department at Manor Mills the following year. Taking the evidence of the Dunlop advertising at that time, especially the early 1909 announcement of the launch of the 'Orange Spot', and Jack Smart's recollections of his first year with the company, it seems reasonable to work on the basis that the first golf ball line was built in 1908 and went into production either at the end of that year, or very early in 1909. Jack, who for the last 20 years of his career had been in charge of tyre examination at Fort Dunlop, remembered that the first golf ball department had been staffed by a manager, one man, three women and himself. His job, which paid 6s 8d per week, was to make the gutta percha outer cases for the balls, which had a solid rubber centre. The output, at the start of 1909, was 144 balls per day, which compares with something like a quarter of a million per day in 2003. Early quality control involved bouncing the balls on a concrete floor and making a judgement from the sound they made.

Although the initial output was so small it's clear, not least from the evidence of the immediate and sustained advertising programme, that whoever had made the decision to make the balls alongside the cycle tyres was convinced of the potential for the new venture. What was then so significant for the new Dunlop ball operation, and what would have contrasted so sharply with the activities of the many smaller manufacturers then servicing the growing market, was the scale of the resources available to develop the business. The six 'pioneers' of that first production line were literally surrounded by the experienced rubber technologists, engineers and production managers of the tyre operation, and, perhaps even more importantly in those early days, were able to take advantage of the relatively sophisticated marketing and distribution operations that had already established the Dunlop brand, albeit for tyres, throughout the United Kingdom. The downside of that approach was the negative reaction of the 'legitimate' sports trade, and also of the golf professionals, who, perhaps fortunately for Dunlop, had not yet established well organised trade associations. The upside was that the tyre related route to the market was bound to catch the attention of the relatively better off motoring class, which provided the golfing majority in the years before the first world war. That post war advertisement extolling the virtues of '18 holes and then home in the car with its sturdy, service-giving Dunlop tyres' aptly sums up the company's early marketing style.

Evidence of the progress made before the outbreak of war comes from two sources, and confirms the benefits of the resources available, especially on the technical and production side. Included in the 1920 Dunlop publication entitled *The Development of a Great Industry*, which was intended 'as a souvenir of the Dunlop Rubber Company's gigantic and successful effort to cope with the universal demand which it created', are photographs showing the main offices in London, the Far East plantations, the 'gigantic' Lancashire cotton mills, Fort Dunlop under construction, and the factories at Aston Cross, Manor Mills and Coventry. Virtually everything in this book depicts buildings and machinery utilised for tyre manufacture but among the Manor Mills illustrations is a picture of 'one of the golf ball shops'. The very large and lavishly equipped department shown – one of several – is in marked contrast to the sight that would have met Jack Smart's young eyes when he first entered the golf ball 'room' only a few years earlier.

The other endorsement of Dunlop progress comes from the same John Stuart Martin, who was so disparaging about the very first Dunlop balls, but who acknowledged that by 1912 their balls 'were better'. Even the Dunlop historian, whatever the adverts might have claimed, hadn't been too excited by the 'Orange Spot', which he described as having 'little apparent difference with other balls of the period' and its orange spot at the two poles being no more than a 'common means of identification or branding'. By the time the company was ready to have a stand at the trade exhibition at the 1912 Open Championship at Muirfield the original 'Orange Spot' and 'Junior' balls, both of which had bramble covers, had given way to a new range starting with the 'Nimble Shilling', retailing at, no surprise, 1s, the slightly more

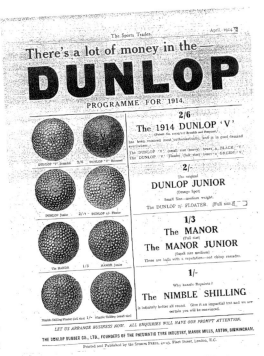

The full Dunlop range in a 1914 advertisement, mainly bramble covers but the 'V' also available with recessed pattern

The trade show at the 1912 Muirfield Open and probably the first ever Dunlop golf exhibit

Typical of the early Dunlop adverts to combine praise for both tyres and golf balls

The vacuum process 'V' ball is number one in this 1913 advertisement

expensive (1s 3d) 'Manor' in standard and small sizes, the basic 'Dunlop' now offered as a 'Floater' in standard size, as 'Medium' (the original 'Junior') and 'Heavy', all of these with bramble markings. But in addition to these the company launched the 'V' Floater, which the *Sports Trader* deemed worthy of 'more than a passing notice'. Having tested it they declared it 'an ideal ball for most courses under present conditions – it flies well, has a fine run after the carry, goes off quickly from an iron club, and putts well and truly on the green'. A strong enough recommendation that would be well received today, but of more significance was the revelation that the 'V' stood for vacuum as the new ball was made by a patented vacuum process which 'by extracting all air from the ball during the operation of moulding, renders it more homogeneous, the shell and the core becoming practically one mass, not only making splitting and loosening of the shell impossible, but resulting in the production of the most perfectly spherical ball yet made, which retains its shape and is the most durable ever produced'. The company also claimed that the new method of construction, in particular the combination of a thin, highly resilient cover, with a tightly wound core, 'enables each class of player to get full value for his shot'. On top of all that the 'V' was the first Dunlop ball with both a bramble (raised) and recessed (dimpled) cover pattern.

Evidence that marketing skills were also being applied to the improving technical performance of the golf ball operation is provided by the special packaging for the new 'V' balls. Each ball was packed in a small canvas bag and, instead of the cardboard box then in general use, a strong metal box was used for the dozen pack. As many as 25-30 years later these 'V' boxes were still to be found in pros workshops, being used as handy containers for nails, tees and small accessories.

Underpinning this improving presentational approach was the higher level of technical expertise to be expected from the Dunlop organisation, and which would be one of its main strengths, in all product sectors, for many years in the future. By this time scientific methods were being widely introduced into golf ball manufacture with Spalding in the USA and The India Rubber and Gutta Percha Company in Woolwich leading the way by introducing increasingly sophisticated constructions and cover patterns. A major part of this evolution had been the recognition of the value and importance of research, especially by the larger producers, which by now included the expanding Dunlop operation at Manor Mills. Attention was being given to ballistics, or the study of projectiles, and the effect that varying weights, sizes, cover markings and coats of paint had on the length and direction of the flight of the ball were being carefully examined. As it was obvious that no golfer, however skilful, could make two successive drives in exactly the same way, the importance of eliminating the variables of the human factor had now become apparent. It was at this stage, certainly in the Dunlop laboratories, that the first, crude form of a machine was developed which would strike ball after ball on the same spot and with the same strength. The much more sophisticated and complex test equipment subsequently developed, right to the present day, follows the principles of those very early driving machines.

By now the Dunlop balls were being endorsed by Arnaud Massy, who had used them in 1911 to win the French Open and to come second in the British Open. They were also being widely praised by UK club professionals, like A. F. Kettley, the pro at the Edgware club, who told the company that their latest 'Junior' was the best ball they'd ever made because 'against the wind it is perfect in flight and travels quick and straight'. And, already, the first sign of the eventual international reach of the Dunlop golf ball was to be seen in a 1911 advertisement, which advised that the Dunlop Tire & Rubber Goods Co. in Toronto was now selling the balls.

Not content with that, and the 'phenomenal success' of the 1913 range, the *Sports Trader* for October, 1914 reported that Dunlop had just placed on the market 'a new ball which is sufficiently far ahead of the favourite "V" as to entirely supersede the last'. At that time it was anticipated that golf's ruling bodies would standardise the weight of balls and the company had decided to introduce improved versions of the 'V' at the expected weights of 29 and 31 dwt., as the Dunlop '29' and '31', with a new recessed cover pattern, very much closer to modern dimple designs, and a completely revised internal construction designed to allow increased length off the tee and greater control around the green. Even though the new ball was a 'half-crowner' (2s 6d) in the shops it was generally well received. John Stuart Martin thought well of it and the Dunlop historian records that 'a well known professional, later to become Open Champion, when bouncing a '31' on the edge of Prestwick station platform to listen to the click, declared to a Dunlop official, 'That's it! You've got it!'

Having made sufficient progress in just five years to be numbered among the front rank of ball makers, the Dunlop golf team would

A 1909 advert linking the 'Junior' to that year's Open

A 1911 endorsement by the famous French golfer, Arnaud Massy. A mixture of stud and bramble cover patterns

The '31' ball with its new recessed pattern

have been devastated by the outbreak of war in 1914, but, like their counterparts in Slazenger and Sykes, had no alternative to switching their priorities to supporting the military effort. As mentioned before, the War Office had requested a limited supply of balls for the off duty moments of army and Royal Flying Corps officers, and it was the '29' and '31' balls that were chosen to boost morale in this way.

The frustration at Manor Mills was confirmed by a company spokesman, Mr. T. W. Niblett, who told a trade press reporter, early in 1915, that 'the company was selling more balls than at this time last year' and that this increase was due to the popularity of the new '29' and '31'.

Mr. Niblett's frustration would have been shared by all those who had contributed to the remarkably rapid development of the ball business from those very tentative beginnings, in 1909, with one manager, four adults and a boy, to its very strong presence in the market just six years later. Apart from a very brief flirtation with the accessory market, in the shape of leather and waterproof golf bags, the consistent priority had been to build, and noticeably improve, the ball range. This approach was supported and made achievable by the development of what, at the time, would have been the most up-to-date production plant in the UK.

The war years stopped this momentum, not least in terms of ruling out all investment in new and replacement plant at Manor Mills. This meant that the same '29' and '31' balls, launched at the end of 1914, were still the basis of the range when business began to return to normal in 1919. So in the space of 10 years, despite being relative latecomers to the sports market in general, and to golf balls in particular, and with at least 4 years lost to the different wartime priorities, Dunlop had laid a solid foundation of product excellence and forceful promotion that would, in the 20 years between the wars, become what was probably the most successful ever international sports equipment business.

THEY DO KEEP BOBBING UP!

HERE is another big Tournament won with a Dunlop ball. We couldn't wish for anything nicer than Mr. Ian McMunro's remarks and his opinion must carry weight!

"*The Links Hotel,*
St. Andrews.

I just wish to thank you again for giving me the Dunlop 29's to play in the tournament here.

They are absolutely *the* ball on the market just now.

With kindest regards,
Yours sincerely,
IAN McMUNRO."

1919 TO 1939

BETWEEN THE WARS EXPANSION WITH A WIDER RANGE

Even before the end of the war Dunlop was confidently telling the trade that 'we've got things so fixed we can deliver'. To be more accurate these words were shown as being spoken by the newly introduced 'Dunlop Caddie', who was to feature for some years in much of the golf advertising. Frequently with a cigarette dangling from his mouth or hand he wore a flat cap, jacket and baggy trousers, and always had a scarf knotted at his throat. He had with him a small, tubular bag, which usually held no more than three or four clubs, and his facial expression was generally neutral no matter how exciting the news he was bringing.

For a while there wasn't a great deal of excitement to convey and the advertising, in the absence of any new products, was mainly devoted to listing tournament wins. There was probably more excitement, within the company, and of a wholly unwelcome nature, about the mounting financial problems brought about by a combination of excess forward buying of rubber and cotton, an expensive start-up tyre operation in the USA, quality problems with a new, non-skid tyre, and the first signs of the recession.

However, in 1919, a very significant step was taken for the future of the sports business when Dunlop obtained the services of thirty-five-year-old Albert Edward Penfold, described by John Stuart Martin, when writing about him fifty years later, as the individual 'who would do more to, and for, British golf balls than any Englishman before or since'. Penfold, who was regarded as a master of chemical analysis and innovation, had learned his trade at the Silvertown factory of the India Rubber & Gutta Percha Co., and had been responsible for the development of the famous 'Silver King' wound ball with its renowned 'mesh' cover pattern, which he had patented. That particular patent had been assigned to his employer but he had retained his patent for a 'lattice' design and was soon introducing it to the Dunlop range. The impact on Dunlop of this acknowledged ball expert was to be enormous and, before long, would extend beyond golf balls.

Penfold would only stay with Dunlop for eight years before moving on to the North British Rubber Company and, later, to found his own famous ball-making company. However, in that relatively short period he would play an absolutely crucial role in securing the company's position in the front rank of golf ball producers, and then turn his attention to successfully establishing tennis ball manufacture at Fort Dunlop. Sadly, his career was cut short in 1941 when he was drowned off the Irish coast when the ship bringing him back to the UK from a war mission to the USA was torpedoed.

The first new ball to be added to the range after the war was the 'Magnum', which was described as large size/medium weight and specially

The famous Dunlop Caddie in an advert for the lattice cover '162' ball introduced after the war'

Golf and Mr. Dunlop

MR. DUNLOP not only made *motoring* possible by producing the pneumatic tyre, and motor-cycling and cycling pleasurable by his discovery, but he is largely responsible for the growth of the Royal and Ancient Game of Golf, and for the breezy, healthful hours it brings to an ever-increasing Army of Golfers.

The Car, the Motor-cycle, yes! even the unpretentious bicycle, recently returned to respectability, have made possible the refreshment of a friendly round, which without them would be impossible, for most Golf Courses are beyond easy walking distance of all save persistent pedestrians.

Moreover, the birth of the pneumatic tyre is delightfully linked to ball games. Noticing a boy filling a rubber bag with air to put into a football, a thinker began to ponder the effect of such a rubber air-filled bag inside a bicycle tyre. The result of his thinking brought about Dunlop tyres.

Not content with providing the most comfortable means for taking Golf lovers to their game, the inventor's modern house has a " bonny " taste in Golf Balls, and the eyes of many a keen golfer light up when the rendings of paper wrappings disclose the favourite.

Thus does Mr. Dunlop gather to himself fresh laurels, and the descendants of the veteran tyre inventor keep " a good name ever green " *and on greens.*

Tyres and balls together again in the 1919 edition of the annual Dunlop guide for motorists

The Penfold lattice design

designed for 'soft courses'. It was, unfortunately, given the same name the company had first used for the non-skid tyre, which suffered severe quality problems, and was quickly superseded, as the number one ball in the range, by the '162'. This designation reflected the 1920 decision by the Rules of Golf Committee to standardise balls at 1.62 inches diameter and 1.62 ounces in weight. Launched with only recessed marking it was soon to appear with the Penfold designed 'lattice' cover pattern, which was described as being unique because its markings were 'symmetrical over the surface of the ball so that it provides that perfect balance necessary for accurate and sustained flight'.

At the same time, and again probably a Penfold innovation, a system of colouring the name 'Dunlop' on the balls was introduced to indicate the 'necessary distinguishing marks between the various weights and sizes now listed'. The 1921 range of balls offered 3 sizes, 3 weights and 2 cover patterns, and, for the first time, were guaranteed to conform with the limitations laid down by both the Rules of Golf Committee and the United States Golf Association. The 'Dunlop Caddie' announced to potential golf professional and athletic outfitter customers that it was impossible to have too many Dunlop balls in stock as 'the demand is phenomenal'. The same 'Caddie' was used on an advertisement, late in 1921, to 'whisper' to the trade 'Sh – something new and good is coming along', which heralded the launch of the 'lattice' pattern balls. An American professional, who employed 'the mercury test' to check whether the balls he selected for important matches had their centre of gravity in the centre, was reported as saying that the Dunlop balls showed a higher percentage of accuracy than any he had ever put to trial. At the start of 1922 the company proudly announced that the lattice marked balls were 'creating something of a sensation – the demand is of the snowball order and every ball sold is of itself a selling agent'.

At this point, and through 1922 and 1923, the golf ball activity becomes almost feverish. The 'lattice' cover was obviously enormously successful and the use of three different Birmingham addresses for the golf ball department in that period – Manor Mills, Kingsbury Road in Tyburn and Easy Row, Broad Street – suggests the order handling staff resources had to regularly find larger office space. In addition to deploying his 'lattice' patent, Penfold refined the core, threads, winding and cover composition of the '162', which led, in May 1922, to the launch of a completely new ball, the 'Maxfli' (derived from maximum flight). At first only small quantities were available because, probably due to the company's continuing financial difficulties, funds were not immediately forthcoming to purchase the additional plant required to expand the output. Despite the initial retail price of 3s 6d – easily the highest in the UK at the time – demand far outstripped supply.

The momentum created by the success of the 'Maxfli' is obvious from the combination of the advertisements and editorial material in the trade press. The printing on the ball is blue so it quickly becomes the 'Blue Maxfli', and it becomes the first ball to be numbered (the balls in each dozen box contain three sets numbered 1, 2 and 3 and one set is unmarked) to overcome the problem of 'lifting' to determine ownership. An early 1923 advertisement claims it has become 'The World's Best Ball', which is given considerable

November, 1921.   THE GOLF TRADER.   5

Sh—

SOMETHING NEW—
AND GOOD—
IS COMING ALONG!

DUNLOP GOLF BALLS   STOCKED BY ALL GOLF PROFESSIONALS. AND ATHLETIC OUTFITTERS

Say you saw the Advertisement in "THE GOLF TRADER"

A 1921 *Golf Trader* advert previewing the launch of the lattice pattern balls

credibility when it's used by A. G. Havers to win the 1923 Open at Troon, despite the worst weather ever experienced for the Championship. The *Golf Trader* reports that in the qualifying rounds no fewer then 322 out of a total 412 competitors play 'Maxfli' and that the ball took the first three places in the Long Driving Championship at Sandwich in the same month (the winning drive was 290 yards). During Open week Charles Whitcombe used the ball to set two course records at Troon, and great praise was given to the 'controllability' of the ball in the appalling weather that week. 'Maxfli' was also being used to win numerous other important events that year, including the USA Amateur Championship, the Welsh and Dutch Open championships and, in the UK, both the Boys and Girls Open titles – 28 out of 32 of the competitors in the Boys and all the Girls used the new Dunlop ball.

For the first time advertisements show a Golf Ball Sales Department, which is now located at what was then a nearly completed Fort Dunlop site, and the 'Caddie' has been replaced by a wasp-like 'Maxfli' character complete with driver, felt cap, an oversize pair of golf shoes, a pair of gloves more suitable for a motor-bike than a golf course, and a distinctly mischievous facial expression. As 1923 drew to a close a *Golf Trader* advert, which resurrected a portrait of the bearded John Boyd Dunlop, reminded readers that 'the most successful ball is the easiest to sell' and that 'supreme merit and consistent advertising have created a phenomenal demand for Dunlop golf balls, which are the easiest to sell, satisfy every player and carry a generous and assured profit'. The last point might have been queried by the trade, which found the price of the 'Maxfli' was now 2s 6d, though the company was quick to point out this reduction had been made possible by 'improved methods of production and enlarged output'.

Probably the main reason for the increased output was the 1923 transfer of the ball plant from its first home at Manor Mills to Fort Dunlop, where it would have been possible to plan a highly efficient layout in the much larger space available. And to put the icing on the cake for the sports operation, and for the rest of the company, the new board was now in place to begin the task of reshaping Dunlop.

The new directors, and especially Sir Eric Geddes, with their vision for Dunlop of a company with many more products to offer than tyres and wheels, must have been impressed by what had been achieved in the golf market with no more than a relatively small range of balls, albeit, as was already a basic Dunlop characteristic and strength, balls of steadily improving quality and performance. The rapid progress from the obscurity of the Manor Mills golf 'room' to the modern and efficient plant at Fort Dunlop, which credibly claimed to be turning out the 'World's best ball' must have caught the attention of the new board. And it's also likely that the obvious energy and ball-making expertise of Albert Penfold ensured that the opportunity to expand the sports operation was not overlooked in the 1920s enthusiasm for diversification that saw the Dunlop brand applied in new areas like footwear, clothing, belting and hose. The difference, at the time, between those sectors and sports was that the latter was already firmly established within the company while

The first advertisement to report Dunlop balls comply with the requirements of the game's governing bodies.

The Maxfli dominates the 1923 Open and is used by the champion, A. G. Havers. A smiling Maxfli character stands on top of one of the new lattice pattern balls

Fort Dunlop in the 1920s – home of
the Maxfli

Core winding department at Fort
Dunlop

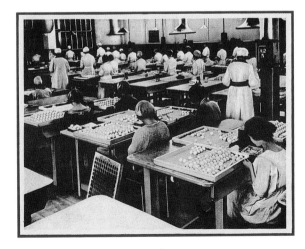

Painting Maxfli balls

most of the others were entered by the acquisition route.

Having galvanised the golf operation, which would now go from strength to strength, Penfold turned his attention to tennis balls where, again, there would have been immense on-site support at Fort Dunlop from the company's technical and engineering resources.

Maybe Slazenger, Sykes and the rest of the competition still weren't too concerned about those 'tyre boys', who were inclined to use the motor trade as a large part of their distribution network. However, the undoubted and international success of the 'Maxfli' was to be followed by an assault on their presence in the tennis market and, this time, wholly based on using the legitimate sports distribution arrangements.

The first priority for Penfold and the sports team was to develop the right product. Interviewed at the beginning of 1925 by *The India Rubber Journal* he revealed that when the directors of the company had suggested the manufacture of tennis balls his initial thinking had been influenced by his view that 'The troubles which players have with the ball are as nothing compared with the troubles of the manufacturers.' His main point was that the production process then generally in use was incapable of making balls to anything like a reasonable specification, and that this resulted in manufacturers having to guess how big a ball to make to allow for an unknown storage period when, because the rubber used was not airtight, inevitable deflation could mean balls would not meet the required size standard. He emphasised this view – and it's impossible to know whether or not he was exaggerating to make his point – that any manufacturer with 30,000 balls in stock might end up scrapping half of them, and 'owing to the varying ratio of deflation in each ball it is practically impossible to issue even half a dozen balls which are uniform in play'.

The Penfold solution, at least partly based on his golf ball experience, was to make the core from two thin shells of gutta percha joined together like a ping-pong ball. In order to make sure this sphere retained its shape he used gas to create the internal tension that had previously relied on air introduced through a needle inserted in a less than airtight soft India-rubber plug. The gas was produced by 'placing certain chemicals and a few spots of water within the two shells before they were sealed together'. The next step was to completely enclose the hollow gutta percha sphere in two pieces of very thin and soft rubber sheet and vulcanise the ball at 300° Fahrenheit. This had the effect of making the outside rubber covering elastic and, at the same time, the chemical action of the gas-forming process produced the necessary inflation pressure. The moulded spheres were then plunged into ice cold water provided by a newly installed refrigeration plant capable of producing four tons of ice per day. By careful adjustment of temperatures it was possible to control the gas content of the core to manipulate the size of the ball to meet performance requirements. The covering process was carried out by existing methods but Penfold claimed that the adhesion between cover and core was significantly improved by the internal gas pressure forcing the core against the inside of the cover. And a bonus from this new process, claimed Penfold, was that 'for the first time since tennis balls were made, standards of compression and bounce for all balls can now be established with scientific exactitude instead of the previous situation where differences in bounce have been so great there has been no uniformity at all in the products offered to the user'. To illustrate this point, and based on work with the compression testing machine that had been developed for testing golf balls, he told the *Journal* that 'balls at present used varied from, say 90 to over 200' but the new Dunlop production process meant that 'each ball which we are turning out answers an exact test of hardness'. He looked forward to meeting any standard that the Lawn Tennis Association would lay down and concluded the interview with the powerful claim that 'the player will now be able to get tennis balls every one of which will be scientifically accurate and consistent in play, so enhancing his confidence in his game'.

A 1926 advert for the Blue Maxfli with lattice and recessed covers and showing the numbers on each ball

Anyone reading the report of this interview would have assumed that everything was going according to plan with the tennis ball project. However, the Fort Dunlop historian records that initially 'manufacturing changes caused difficulties, which retarded progress', which could well have been due to the revolutionary nature of the Penfold process. Nevertheless, by 1926 the ball was sufficiently well established to have been adopted for one-third of the open tournaments in the UK, and in 1929 for Dunlop to be included in the Lawn Tennis Association's relatively short list of approved makers of their 'Official Ball'.

Sir Eric Geddes, who would have been one of those directors urging Albert Penfold to start producing tennis balls, felt the launch of this new product was sufficiently important to be a highlight in his Chairman's address to the 1925 Annual General Meeting. He had christened it 'the only ball with an inner tube', which provided a strong clue to the main activity of his company. The *Dunlop Newsletter*, which described itself as 'a little journal issued every now and again in the interests of Dunlop sales and those who promote them', and which, in theory at least, was only for 'the use of Dunlop Officials', briefly turned its attention away from tyres and wheels to report in its December, 1925 issue that 'the introduction of the Dunlop lawn tennis ball this year has undoubtedly proved an epoch-making event in the history of the sports trade' and that its special construction 'has, at one swoop, made all other tennis balls on the market out of date'. Not to be diverted too long from its normal preoccupation with tyres it picked up Sir Eric's remark about the ball with the inner tube to observe that 'this factor alone brings the ball into the same category as the goods which are the mainstay of our business, name-

Albert Penfold pictured in the tennis ball department

Sir Eric Geddes

ly Dunlop tyres'.

The same issue of the *Newsletter* carried the announcement, also of sufficient importance to have been made by Sir Eric, 'For the marketing of the tennis ball we have deemed it necessary to ally ourselves with a firm of more experience in tennis tournament organisation and the handling of sports goods. Your board has therefore acquired an interest in the well-known firm of sports manufacturers, Messrs. F. A. Davis, Ltd., who will be the sole distributors in this country for this our new venture – the Dunlop Tennis ball.' Three Dunlop representatives – the company's managing-director, Sir George Beharrell, Mr. L. V. Kenward and Albert Penfold – joined the Davis board, and it was this step, involving as it did the recognition of the importance of becoming part of the sports trade, that can be said to have marked the arrival of Dunlop as a force to be reckoned with in that industry.

The chairman of F. A. Davis was a well-known tennis player, A. H. Riseley, who had introduced the company's best-known product, the 'Riseley Hexagon' tennis racket, which had been extremely popular for more than 20 years. His brother, Frank Riseley, had been runner-up in the Wimbledon men's singles – using a Slazenger racket – in 1903, 1904 and 1905, losing on each occasion to Laurence Doherty and his Slazenger racket, but had two men's doubles titles to his name in 1902 and 1906, when he and his partner, S. H. Smith, had beaten the Doherty brothers. In fact Riseley and Smith were the only partnership to interrupt Doherty doubles wins between 1897 and 1906. The Davis company had been founded in 1903 and when Dunlop acquired an interest in the business its offices and factory were located in Brooke's Market, Holborn, behind the massive Prudential offices. This building was eventually to be re-named Rubber House and became the London office for the Dunlop Footwear and General Rubber Goods Divisions following the departure of the sports business to Essex in 1929. Like the Slazenger factory in Woolwich it was to be destroyed by German bombs in 1941.

Nowadays it seems strange to think of a factory situated in the heart of London but in the 1920s life in the Davis factory was rather different. There was no machinery as everything was made by hand and so it was far less noisy. The clamour and clatter of the nearby Leather Lane street market provided another type of noise but even that was overcome by the singing that went on every day in the factory. Bob Slack, who went on to become a senior supervisor at the Waltham Abbey plant, worked as a young man for F. A. Davis and remembered the singing. He also recalled the old fashioned benches, the rows of pegs, gluepots and clamps and watched and learned from men who had years of experience behind them in making each stage of a tennis racket frame themselves.

At the time of the merger with Dunlop, the Davis range included a large number of rackets for tennis, badminton and squash, tennis balls, court equipment, croquet sets, bowls, hockey sticks and balls, footballs and sports shoes. Their reputation, according to the *Newsletter* was for 'producing goods of exceptional quality at moderate prices', which obviously made them very suitable partners for Dunlop, and it was noted, with satisfaction, 'They

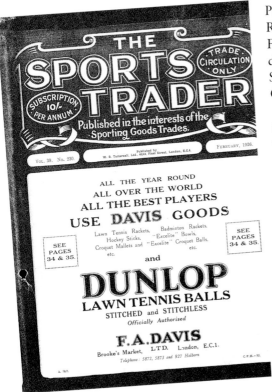

1926 Davis advert including Dunlop tennis balls

agreed without demur to the discontinuance entirely of the Davis balls they had previously manufactured because of the supreme excellence of the Dunlop ball, and that they naturally became interested in putting a first-class article on the market, and in placing the whole of their resources throughout the sports trade of the world at our disposal.'

For their part the Dunlop management let it be known they did not expect their tyre sales force to sell Davis products and the new tennis balls, but they did wish them to discuss sports goods generally whenever the opportunity occurred. Early in 1926 the front cover of the *Sports Trader* promoted the new partnership by claiming that 'all the best players' use the Davis range of equipment and Dunlop stitched and seamless tennis balls, obtainable from Brooke's Market. This might have confused the trade because the latest 'Maxfli' advertisements showed the Golf Ball Sales Department had moved from Fort Dunlop to Albany Street, London, N.W.1. The separation between golf and tennis sales offices would continue for some time but the first signs were appearing of a co-ordinated sports operation, in particular as Dunlop-appointed managers started to have more influence in the Brooke's Market offices.

For the next two years Davis continued to market equipment under their own name, together with Dunlop tennis balls, as is shown in a 1926 photograph of a display stand at the Haymarket Stores in London. In addition to the Holborn premises they had smaller factories in Wandsworth, where they made bowls, and at Loughton in Essex, where they prepared racket frames for finishing at Brooke's Market. However, the success and steady expansion of the Davis/Dunlop combination led, in 1928, to the search for larger premises, preferably in the London area but outside the centre, which had now become very expensive. This coincided with the approach by two gentlemen, Mr. Hopwood and Mr.

1928 Davis advert – no reference to Dunlop who made their Argus golf balls and Matchpoint tennis balls

In 1929 the St. James's House office advertises Dunlop tennis balls

A 1926 shot of Dunlop tennis balls on a Davis stand at the Haymarket stores

March, 1929   THE SPORTS TRADER.   11

Two Best Sellers!

'ARGUS'
TENNIS RACKETS
and
'ARGUS MATCHPOINT
TENNIS BALLS

THE Argus Sports Company's range of Sports Goods comprises many improved models. Particular attention is drawn to the famous 'Argus' Racket (from which this Company derives its name) and its perfect ally the 'Argus Matchpoint' Tennis Ball.

Argus Sports goods will be nationally advertised this season—be ready for the increased demand.

THE
'ARGUS'
MATCHPOINT
TENNIS BALL
has now been reduced in price from
15/6 to 15/- per doz.
RETAIL.
14/6 to 14/- per doz.
to Clubs.
The Trade price has also been reduced. Full particulars on application.

THE ARGUS SPORTS
CO. LTD.
Formerly
F. A. DAVIS LTD.,
BROOKE'S MARKET, BROOKE
ST., HOLBORN, E.C.1.

The Argus Sports Company's Rackets are made in the following models:

L.H.K.
ARGUS.
REVERA.
RISELEY.
HEXAGON.
CARLTON.
PIONEER.
DRYAD.
VIKING.
TRIUMPH.
SIVAD.
LEADER.
YORK.

Write for Trade Terms and full particulars.

Say you saw the advertisement in "THE SPORTS TRADER."

Davis change their trading name to Argus and still based in Brooke's Market

56   THE SPORTS TRADER.   January, 1930

DUNLOP RACKETS FOR 1930.

At the present time, when we as a nation are straining every nerve to popularise British goods throughout the world, and when our national leaders are urging us to employ British labour in our factories, it is well to consider the value of British goods.

Scientific research covering a considerable period has proved that the soil and climatic conditions of England produce the finest ash for tennis rackets, with the result that even in the United States of America, France, and Germany, we find manufacturers purchasing our frames, so that they can offer the general public the finest quality materials and workmanship.

The craftsmen employed in the manufacture of British sports goods are unequalled the world over. They have raised their art to such a standard of perfection, that both dealers and players know that a British made racket will hold its own, on all courts throughout the world.

Whilst the quality of the British racket is indisputable, the price is necessarily higher than the inferior makes of foreign goods, but dealers and players who sell and use British rackets, find that the length of service is greatly enhanced—thus the eventual cost is considerably reduced.

This is a point of particular interest to dealers, who would only sell those goods which they can recommend to their customers with complete confidence.

The Dunlop Sports Company when they entered the field of sports goods manufacture two years ago, determined to supplement their already famous golf and tennis balls with other sports goods, which would not only bear the hall mark of "British," but enable players to purchase high grade sporting equipment at moderate prices.

During the year 1929 this has been evidenced by the fact that the Dunlop golf ball has been reduced from 30/- per dozen to 24/- per dozen, and the Dunlop tennis ball, from 16/6 per dozen to 14/6 per dozen, and we understand that in the Dunlop range of rackets for 1930, the Company is able to offer a high grade racket at the extremely moderate price of 55/-.

It is interesting to note that whilst the retail prices of Dunlop goods have been reduced, the same high standard of quality is strictly maintained. In addition, we understand that the Dunlop Company's policy is to stand solidly behind the dealer and fight consistently for fair play, and loyal trading methods. It is in fact almost a slogan in the trade that Dunlops never let the dealer down.

Their range of rackets for 1930 will comprise three models: the Dunlop "de Luxe," the Dunlop "Natural," and the Dunlop "Popular."

The Dunlop "de Luxe" model is an achievement of modern scientific research and workmanship, and combines the very best that skill and craftsmanship can produce. The whole racket is British from end to end, and

Dunlop de Luxe.   Dunlop Natural.

1930 and the Dunlop range widens to include tennis rackets

Goodrich, who owned a small firm of sports goods manufacturers, Gardner Brothers, which was located on the banks of the River Lea at Waltham Abbey, fifteen miles north-east of London. Negotiations between the parties resulted in Dunlop taking a financial interest in Gardners, and it was agreed that in addition to continuing to make their own rackets they would also produce them for Dunlop and Davis.

This was a particularly significant point in the history of the Dunlop sports business as it marked the company's first major venture into the equipment sector. It was also decided to end the Davis/Dunlop link in marketing terms though the two companies were still operating from Brooke's Market at that time and were supplying each other with products – Davis sold Dunlop-made tennis balls and Dunlop took hockey sticks from Davis. To emphasise this change in the relationship, the name of the Davis business was changed to the Argus Sports Company. The Dunlop evolution into being a racket manufacturer was completed in 1929 when the company announced it had assumed control of Gardners and that this move 'provides yet another example of its continual growth, and, incidentally, allows Dunlop to claim to be the actual manufacturers of its rackets'. The *Sports Trader*, in its December 1928 issue, reported the launch of the first racket to carry the Dunlop name as 'a matter of widespread interest to the trade when a firm such as Dunlop announce they are introducing a new tennis racket'. Their verdict on the new product was that 'although these rackets are produced with the same care as if they were destined for first flight tournament use, they will be put on the market at a price that is strictly moderate, and that will provide the retailer with a substantial profit'. The retail prices of these first rackets were in the range 16s 6d to 50s. At a senior management dinner, held at the Café Royal in November of that year, with Sir Eric Geddes in the chair, one of his fellow directors, referring to the 'forthcoming introduction of the Dunlop tennis racket', described it as 'a first-rate product, which would appeal not only to the crack player, but would enable a 'rabbit' to develop into a 'hare'.

The acquisition of Gardners accelerated the departure from Brooke's Market. First to go was the manufacturing section, which went to Waltham Abbey with part of the offices, the warehouse and the despatch department. Shortly afterwards the general management, advertising and tournament departments were transferred to the Dunlop offices in St. James's Street and the accounts to Waltham Abbey. Advertisements for tennis products now carried the St. James's address while the golf ball sales department continued to operate from the Albany Street site, which was, for many years, the company's main tyre depot in central London.

At the time of the original 1926 agreement with F. A. Davis, the Dunlop directors involved had been Sir George Beharrell, Mr. L. V. Kenward and Albert Penfold, and only the latter was wholly concerned with sports business as its principal technical manager. During the process of considerably expanding the scope of the business, and establishing both the London offices and the Waltham Abbey factory, both Sir George and Mr. Kenward would retain their main board level involvement with the business but Albert Penfold would, in 1927, move on. That was the same year that saw the registration of Dunlop Sports Company Ltd on November 21st at 32, Osnaburgh Street, London, N.W.1 (in effect, the office entrance address for the Albany Street depot). That particular event, in itself, confirmed the stated intention to develop a significant sports business but, of more importance in terms of executing that policy, was the arrival on the scene of a number of experienced senior managers, who would shape the destiny of the new subsidiary company until after the second world war. In Slazenger terms it was rather like having Albert himself, Archdale Palmer and Tim Hadingham all joining the business at the same time, though, in contrast, the new Dunlop managers were mainly drawn from outside the sports trade. It didn't take them very long to become not only the driving forces behind the Dunlop sports venture, but also respected industry leaders, thus establishing a pattern that would be maintained throughout the company's history.

A 1931 advert includes Footwear Division's tennis shoes for the first time

The first to be considered was, indeed, another 'Albert'. Albert Burden, OBE, generally known as 'A.E.B.', who was born in the same year as the first Wimbledon Championships (1877), had started his working life, aged 17, as a clerk for London County Council. His career, initially as an accountant, had taken him to senior positions in the transport industry and, during the war, to Chief Commissioner rank for the British Red Cross, with responsibilities in the Mediterranean area. When the war ended he held a senior post in the Egyptian civil service before returning to the UK in 1926 to become company secretary of F. A. Davis. He was quickly snapped up by Dunlop to run the offices at Brooke's Market and St. James's and became sales manager of the company in 1935. Immediately after the war he was appointed director and general manager and held that appointment until his retirement in 1950. His contributions to the sports industry included membership, for 23 years, of the Council of the Federation of British Manufacturers of Sports and Games, a six-year presidency of the Sports Manufacturers Federation, a fourteen-year chairmanship of the Lawn Tennis Ball Convention, and chairman of the Golf Ball Manufacturers Conference. Bill Evans, whose own, invaluable history of the Dunlop sports business covered the fifty years up to 1978, remembers 'A.E.B.' as 'a shrewd man with a good business brain, radiating personality and authority, who had seen the company grow to success through its many trials and tribulations'. Not least of those trials would have been a Dunlop main board decision in 1932 to change the status of the sports operation to that of a 'Division', rather than as a separate company, almost certainly for financial reporting purposes. Happily it was restored to being a separate company in 1946.

A key figure, from 1929 onwards, was Guy Proctor, who joined the company at the time of the move to Waltham Abbey, and was responsible for the development of that factory – originally a builder's yard – from the relatively small scale Gardner Brothers operation to what became one of the largest,

Albert Burden

Guy Proctor, the driving force in the development of Waltham Abbey

Sammy Ball pictured here in his Fort Dunlop days

and certainly the best known, of racket plants in the world. He had a technical background, had trained at Manchester Technical School and started his career in the bleaching and dyeing industry before joining a subsidiary of the Charles Macintosh company, which was taken over by Dunlop in 1924. His achievements, as a director of the Sports Company and general manager of Waltham Abbey, played a huge part in taking the business to the front rank of racket manufacture. He was also remembered when he retired in 1952, as reported in the *Dunlop Gazette* at the time, for his 'shrewd judgement, sound advice and scrupulously fair attitude when dealing with people, and for his great interest in the social and sports activities at Waltham Abbey', which, as the company's various internal magazines show, were famously varied and strongly supported by virtually all personnel on that site. Cyril Bradford, who joined the company in the packing and despatch department at Waltham Abbey in 1932, aged 16, remembered Guy Proctor with enormous respect as a manager who was completely in control of his factory. And that in spite of the fact he was sacked by him in 1934 for being half an hour late, though that didn't deter him from returning to the plant two years later with a weekly wage of 17s 6d compared with the 12s he had been paid when he first joined. Sadly, Cyril died, aged 84, towards the end of 2000.

The third member of what Bill Evans called 'the triumvirate that during nearly thirty years steered the company through the shoals and currents of very difficult seas indeed, and when more than once it seemed as if it might founder with all hands' was a Birmingham born physicist, S. G. (Sammy) Ball, whose Dunlop career spanned 46 years from 1919 to 1965. That retirement year of 1965 was particularly appropriate for the man, known by many as 'Mr. Golf', who was responsible for developing one of the most famous and successful golf balls ever produced, the 'Dunlop 65'. Sammy Ball had originally joined the company from Birmingham University and, after an initial period in the physical research laboratory at what would have then been a brand new Fort Dunlop, spent five years at the Dunlop Japan plant in Kobe as technical manager. At that time he would have been working on the tyre side of the Japanese business as its golf ball sales were based on imports from Fort Dunlop. On his return from Japan in 1928 he was appointed technical manager of the golf ball operation, which had been so successfully built up by Albert Penfold before his departure in 1927. The point has already been made that Penfold had transformed the prospects of the golf venture when he arrived in 1919, particularly with the development of the 'Maxfli'. What was then equally important was the arrival of a successor who was immediately capable of taking the company to new levels of technical and performance achievement. It was also fortunate that Sammy was very familiar with the golf ball processes because Albert Penfold took all his records and specifications with him and it was necessary to re-write them all again. This may explain the existence, today, of very detailed descriptions of every stage in the production of both golf and tennis balls at Fort Dunlop, each step accompanied on the facing page by a photograph of the particular action described.

As the technically trained Guy Proctor had had an immense impact on the Waltham Abbey plant, so Sammy Ball was to be hugely influential on golf ball production at Fort Dunlop during the period before the second world war and for the twenty years after it, when the operation was transferred to the Speke factory on the outskirts of Liverpool. Although for some years he combined his responsibility for Speke golf ball production with the management, on that site, of the newly established belting and precision components operations, and of the central laboratory, it was his work on golf ball development that won international respect. He was among the first to apply scientific methods to golf ball manufacture and led the way in exploring the importance of precision engineering in relation to the aerodynamic characteristics derived from the design and manufacture of dimples. In addition to working closely with many of the leading professionals his sympathies for the average golfer led him to experiment with radioactive balls that could be found with Geiger counters, to test balls with scents that proved irresistible to tracker dogs, and even to make balls with a metal filling that could be picked up by mine detectors. There's no record of what the Royal and Ancient thought of these ideas!

While these three professional and long serving managers provided the core leadership during the formative years of the Sports Company, there was a fourth figure, of a very different kind, who also played an important and charismatic part in promoting the newly established business, especially the tennis range, albeit for a much shorter period. This was the Honourable F. M. B. Fisher, who had originally been associated with the Davis Company but became the first Dunlop director responsible for the sports operations until his retirement in 1934. He negotiated the purchase of the Gardner Bros business and their Waltham Abbey factory, which took Dunlop into racket manufacturing, and is credited with devising the name 'Maxply' for the world famous racket developed at that factory before its launch in 1932. 'F.M.B.' was a New Zealander described by Teddy Tinling in his book *Sixty Years in Tennis*, as 'big, fat and jovial, with a broad face, a strong handshake, and a slap on the back for most people, who came from a well-known New Zealand sporting family but had adopted an authentic English manner'.

Tinling also detected that behind the joviality there would be no holds barred in any business argument. The courtesy title of 'Honourable' derived from his membership of the New Zealand government as Minister of Marine.

That he brought a number of important and unique attributes to the business is quite clear from an article he wrote towards the end of 1933 for the *Dunlop Newsletter*. Entitled 'Tennis' it describes his lifelong passion for an involvement with the game he had begun to play 'as a kid, very well back in the Victorian era' winning his first open tournament in 1896 and, at the time of writing, the most recent in 1933. He was

F. M. B. Fisher, carrying the holdall, pictured entering the Cannes Tennis Club with Bonar Law and his daughter

undoubtedly an accomplished player, who had competed at major tournaments, including Wimbledon, was on familiar terms with many of the leading players and was a keen student of the game and its history. The article mentioned, very proudly, that he had 'enjoyed the privilege of partnering the great Laurence Doherty in what was his final appearance on a tennis court – at Queen's Club in 1916'.

More importantly, as Bill Evans acknowledges, he travelled extensively in Central Europe and began to build up export business for the company, espe-

WAR OF RIVAL BALL MAKERS.

"INTRIGUES."

A great lawn tennis ball war is now raging between the leading manufacturers.

The battle front extends from South Africa to the Riviera and throughout England. The reverberations...

"L'AFFAIRE CANNES."

THE TRUTH ABOUT A RIVIERA TENNIS DUEL.

The Riviera tennis ball comedy is now at an end. Mlle. Suzanne Lenglen and Miss Helen Wills, according to a message received in London, have both entered for the Singles in the Carlton tournament which opens at Cannes to-morrow. Here, after several delays alleged to have been occasioned by the tennis ball controversy, the two should meet for the first time in the South of France.

The beginning of the present tennis ball "affaire" really dates back to last autumn, when Mlle. Lenglen tried a stitchless gas-filled ball with a smooth cloth in a friendly game at the Royal Botanic Gardens, when she partnered M. Brugnon against M. Mishu and Colonel Mayes.

Since then a duel has been waged merrily between this smooth ball and a new grooved ball used at Nice at the beginning of the month. Lenglen ... Hel...

LENGLEN-WILLS MATCH NOT IN SIGHT.

BALL DIFFICULTY.

PARIS, Thursday, Feb. 4.

The French papers are beginning to express in no uncertain language their astonishment that nothing has as yet been settled for a meeting between Mlle. Lenglen and Miss Helen Wills.

A well-known French tennis player, writing in the "Auto," ... that t... is gre...

LAWN TENNIS BALL WAR.

PLAYERS "DICTATING TO THE AUTHORITIES."

A PROTEST.

Mr. H. G. Reddy, editor of "The Sports Dealer," makes the following statement:—

The great agitation which has been disturbing the lawn tennis world seems to me to have been based on a very unsound principle. As I see it, the main di... ly arises f... the fact...

The Lenglen/Wills match makes the headlines

cially in Germany and Austria. His widespread connections not only with tennis players and administrators, but also in the leading social circles at that time were put to good use in promoting the revolutionary new Dunlop tennis balls launched in 1926. The ability to blend his social influence with the commercial interest of what Teddy Tinling described as 'one of Europe's most progressive sporting goods manufacturers' was very evident during the events surrounding the famous 1926 match in Cannes between the two great lady champions of that era, Suzanne Lenglen and Helen Wills. 'F.M.B.' and Mlle. Lenglen were both close friends with the noted English socialite, Lady Wavertree, herself a great tennis enthusiast, and a regular winter visitor, with 'F.M.B.', to the Riviera, where it appears that the Dunlop brand and products, despite being relatively new on the tennis scene, were then enjoying great prominence at a number of local tournaments.

The Lenglen–Wills match was the final of the singles tournament at the Carlton Club and attracted not only enormous international press coverage but also such a large crowd that the normal 2000 spectator capacity of the main court was doubled by the addition of a temporary stand built just for this game. Tinling, who was present on this famous occasion, recalled that 'an ovation greeted F. M. B. Fisher when he walked on to the court solemnly carrying three boxes of six Dunlop tennis balls as piously as any acolyte approaching an altar'. Lenglen won what was a very exciting match 6-3, 8-6 but the press interest in the event was divided between the importance of this clash between the two great players and what was described in one newspaper as 'L'Affaire Cannes' and which prompted a headline in another declaring 'The Riviera – a hot bed of intrigue'. The object of all this attention was made clear in the piece that followed the latter, which included a statement by a director of Slazengers Ltd to the effect that 'it is perfectly true that certain players are refusing to take part in tournaments unless the brand of lawn tennis ball which they prefer is being used, and early and drastic action by the Lawn Tennis Association with regard to certain incidents may be looked for'. The editor of the *Sports Dealer* was sufficiently exercised by these goings on to seek a wider than usual audience for his views by writing to the *Daily Express* to declare, 'As a quite impartial observer both from the point of view of the game itself and also from the manufacturing side, no lawn tennis player, whatever his or her prominence, has any right to dictate to the authorities under whose jurisdiction tournament or champion matches may be played as to the type of ball to be used.'

So far as the Cannes final was concerned the choice had been between the newly introduced, gas-filled Dunlop ball with a smooth cover developed by Penfold, and a competitor's new grooved ball. It is reported that both Mlle. Lenglen and Miss Wills preferred the new Dunlop ball, which probably didn't startle the enterprising 'F.M.B.' too much and allowed him to make his grand entrance as the 'pious acolyte' clearly suppressing any tendency to exhibit what would have been a well justified sense of triumph in pulling off this considerable coup for his progressive company.

What was almost certainly another notable coup for 'F.M.B.' was the appearance of an article in the 1926 edition of *The Dunlop Book* (a hugely impressive annual publication of immense detail providing 'A concise guide to the British Isles') by his friend, Mlle Lenglen. Alongside an advertisement by F. A. Davis for their range of equipment and Dunlop tennis balls – 'The perfection of modern scientific production' – the great French champion contributed 'An incisive article on Tennis', which would serve today as an outstanding guide on how best to approach the game. It probably wasn't a coincidence that among her many insightful comments was the opinion that 'Today the tennis ball is standardised and has reached a very high degree of perfection – thus the old-time errors so often attributable to the balls no longer exist and the burden of accuracy is being forced more and more on to the player'.

'F.M.B.', at least in the tennis world, had introduced a vivid, new element to the process of building a Dunlop presence in the sports market. It's unlikely that while the Slazenger team probably hadn't paid much attention to the Dunlop golf ball business, not least because golf still hadn't attracted their serious attention, they would, by the late 1920s be looking hard at this headline-making invasion of their tennis preserve, and especially at their tournament sponsorship base in the UK. Not many years later, and after Dunlop had begun to advertise their ball connection with a number of events, including a four year run (1928-31) of supplying balls to the Challenge round of the Davis Cup, the two companies formally agreed not to poach each other's tournament business. Among the Slazenger directors watching the Dunlop progress, Archdale Palmer would certainly have recognised 'F.M.B.'s tennis credentials as it's very likely they would have met on tennis courts, as competitors, around the turn of the century. The younger 'F.M.B.', who had not been shy of reciting his tennis pedigree, including during the Victorian era, and Archdale Palmer, who had been a regular entrant for the men's singles at Wimbledon during the 1890s, would have been contemporaries as leading players.

The extended look at 'F.M.B.', in terms of both his eight years as director of the Dunlop business and his obvious capability to promote the company at the highest levels in the tennis sector it had only just entered, serves to emphasize the considerable transformation in its fortunes at the time. Between the mid 1920s and the early 1930s the foundations were laid for its eventual powerful position in the market, not only in the UK but around the world. And, as would be expected from an organisation with an immense technical and manufacturing strength, the exuberance of the 'F.M.B.' approach was underpinned by a continuing bedrock of product innovation and improvement. Bill Evans felt that this period saw the company 'getting a foothold in the sports trade, when there must have been many times when it was touch and go and the Board might seriously consider withdrawing'. He went on to describe the remaining years before the start of the second world war as 'years of consolidation' and though it was clear by then that Dunlop had come to stay he believed that the parent company had taken the view that because 'the Sports Company was not profitable it could only be looked upon as a convenient and attractive vehicle for advertising the Dunlop name'. He wasn't the only person to express that view, and there were undoubtedly periods in the history of the business when its results did not directly contribute to the Group's bottom line, but it's also true that there were long periods,

A signed photograph of Suzanne Lenglen is the heading for an article she wrote for *The Dunlop Book* in the 1920s

especially after the war and during BTR's ownership, when it was a very profitable operation as well as continuing to attract very favourable attention to the brand.

The flurry of activity from 1924 onwards that characterised the development of Dunlop as a sports brand, and which had initially been inspired by the parent company's determination to diversify its activities, established a significant new presence in the market in a remarkably short time. What had been a small and purely golf ball operation, with a somewhat murky reputation for using a tyre sales and distribution network to boost its sales, had become, quite suddenly, a legitimate sports equipment force covering both golf and tennis. No longer a 'sideline' activity, it was being driven by a combination of a newly recruited and experienced group of professional managers covering the key functions, a technical resource capable of applying a new look at such as racket manufacture as well as at rubber based products, and, with the unique benefit of the 'F.M.B.' combination of influence and promotional skills, was in a position to mount an assault on trade and public awareness of Dunlop as a new and exciting sports brand. And all of this against the background of rapidly growing interest, all round the world, in both watching and playing the major sports, especially tennis and golf. Much of that interest was at least partly fuelled by the matching growth in public and private transport, which greatly simplified access both to previously remote golf courses and the main sporting arenas like Wimbledon and Wembley. That connection between sports and transport was never lost on those promoting the Dunlop brand as was quite clear in a PR release to the trade press in 1930, which, having extolled the virtues of the new racket range for that year, and mentioned the company's foresight in using sports goods to assist in the development of trade throughout 'our Empire', closed by reminding the reader that 'The Dunlop Company are the pioneers of the British tyre, which is unequalled in the world of motoring, and their whole policy in entering the sports trade in such an enthusiastic and consistent manner is to give high quality British goods at prices to suit every pocket.'

The business had been very prominent in the areas of advertising and sales promotion well before 'F.M.B.' had arrived on the scene, as has been seen from the number of advertisements and editorial pieces in the trade press. The link between motoring and sports was very apparent for a number of years but as the sports business developed its own presence in what was a very different market it was allowed increasingly to project a separate existence. Bill Evans recalls that Charles Griffin was responsible for sales promotion at that time and was still involved after the war as an issue of the *Dunlop Digest* in 1946 carries his picture as the editor of *Dunlop Golf News*, published for the first time that year.

Whether it was Charles Griffin or his directors, the sales promotion function had plenty of product ammunition to work with. In 1926 a very expensive *Book of the Maxfli* was published, with excellent pictures of the still new and immaculate golf ball unit at Fort Dunlop illustrating how the balls were made, plus a formidable barrage of recommendations from leading professionals – including major tournament winners like A. G. Havers (1923 Open), earlier Open winners Alex Herd and J. H. Taylor and the Whitcombe brothers – on the excellence of the ball, and an impressively long list of tournament wins during 1923/25, which included numerous professional and amateur open championships not only in the UK but also in eighteen overseas countries. Pride of place was given to Havers 1923 Open win but only slightly less important to the image of the 'Maxfli' was the emphasis given to four successive victories in *The Field* Long Driving Championship. The company's technical focus was represented by a photograph of the 'mechanical driving machine for furnishing comparative data', which 'is the envy of everyone who sees it – its accuracy is almost heart-breaking but it does provide a comparison of results that would be utterly impossible if the human element were allowed to enter into the test'.

Possibly the first 'working' golf ball stand at Birmingham Brighter Homes Exhibition in 1927

Confirmation of the growing importance of the sports operation is provided, from the mid 1920s onwards, by the increasing exposure given to its development and successes in the company's in house magazines previously virtually 100% preoccupied with tyre and transport related matters. These include regular shots of the sports stand at the annual British Industries Fair, at the Birmingham 'Brighter Homes Fair' in 1927 and of a 1930 display at Selfridges's, which included several Fort Dunlop ladies making golf balls.

Both the *Dunlop Newsletter* and the trade press carried a detailed report, early in 1928, of the introduction of a dating scheme for tennis balls. This item was covered shortly after the announcement of the formation of the Dunlop Sports Company with a sales policy 'framed on a basis which gives maximum support to the dealer'. The company's spokesman told the reporter that 'they had decided to assist dealers by the adoption of what is termed a dating scheme because it had been realised that, being a perishable article, no tennis ball will retain its properties indefinitely'. Dunlop had recognised this 'militated against the retailer because if he sells the ball long after the date of manufacture he is in danger of selling an unsatisfactory article, not because of any defect in manufacture, but simply because the age of the ball is such that its playing properties have deteriorated'. The company's solution to that problem, which would have been regarded as a major step forward at the time, was to 'authorise all sports dealers that they are at liberty to return for exchange any boxes of stitchless balls on the expiration of a date marked on the box, and up to a period of seven days from that date, provided the seal on the box is not broken'. Such returns were replaced free of charge, which allowed the retailer to make sure that he sold only balls fit for the court, and the *Newsletter*, addressing itself to all Dunlop salesmen, encouraged them to use the scheme to 'foster the prosperity of this side of our business'.

MECHANICAL DRIVING MACHINE FOR
FURNISHING COMPARATIVE DATA.

An early shot of the first mechanical driving machine

In the same year a trade press advertisement announced that France had chosen the Dunlop tennis ball for their defence of the Davis Cup, and another that hockey sticks and tennis rackets had been added to the range. Early in

Shaun Pollock

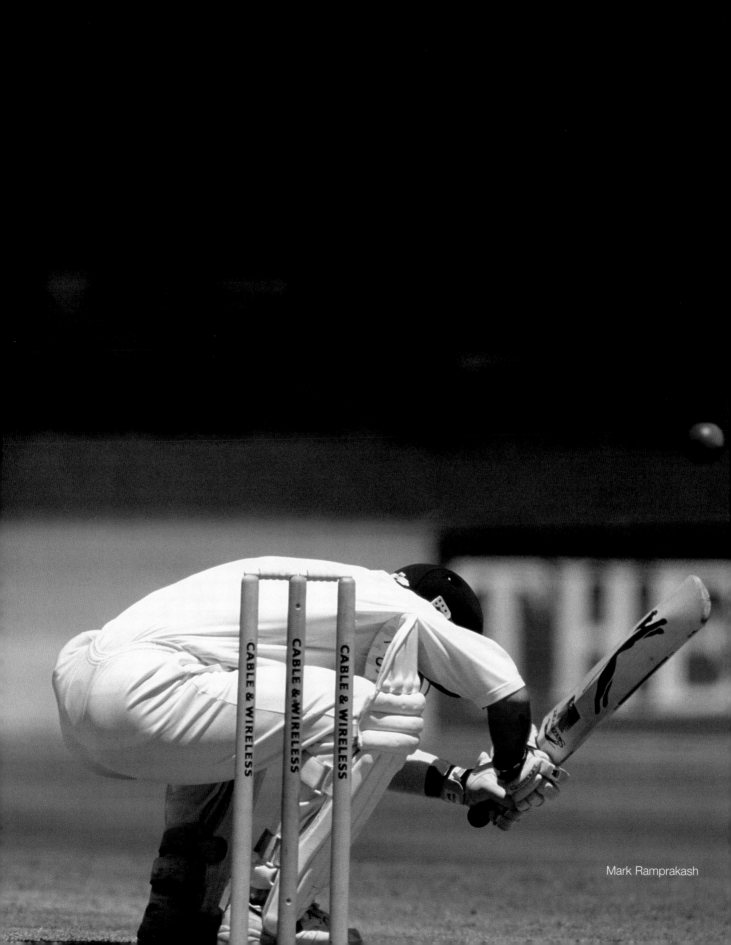

Mark Ramprakash

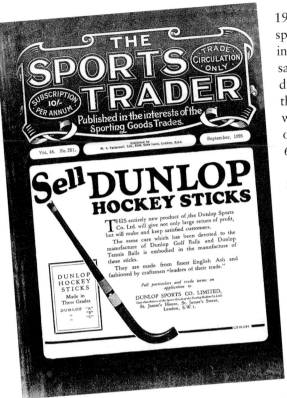

A 1926 advert for hockey sticks, made for Dunlop by F. A. Davis

1929 visitors to the British Industries Fair were able to see 'a spectacular new machine actually used at Fort Dunlop for testing balls and also the gut and frames of tennis rackets all at the same time ... the electrically-driven racket moving at 40mph drives balls in rapid sequence against two boards off which they rebound to a chamber immediately above the racket where a mechanically timed device releases them to be struck once more by the racket, which they leave at a velocity of 60mph'.

The gathering momentum of the business is reflected by the number of significant events that occurred as the 1920s gave way to the 1930s. At Fort Dunlop Sammy Ball was beginning to develop the new ball that would become the '65', and at Waltham Abbey the 1931 racket range featured a new premium product, the '31', named to mark the year of its introduction, and which retailed at 80s. It was supported by the 'Dunlop De Luxe', with a choice of red or blue bindings, at 75s, the 'Argus' and the ever popular 'Riseley Hexagon', both the latter two recalling the link with the Davis company. In the middle of the price range was the new 'Courtier' at 60s and the 'Popular' at 55s, and additional styles took the prices as low as 16s 6d. It was becoming clear from the descriptions of these frames that considerable attention was now being given to their cosmetics in terms of the selection of woods, bindings and colours. Experience in this aspect of racket production would bear spectacular and long lasting fruit only a year later when the 'Maxply' was launched.

Overall range expansion was now evident in trade press advertising. Although the golf operation continued to focus on the increasingly successful Fort Dunlop-made balls, the Sports Company's product portfolio now included squash rackets and balls, complete sets of badminton equipment, seven hockey sticks from 10s to 22s 6d, sports shoes from the Footwear Division's factory at Walton, Liverpool – though the *Sports Trader* believed it was run by the Sports Company – and the expanding range of tennis rackets and balls. A number of the rackets were using newly-developed synthetic stringing (a mixture of rubber and silk that wasn't entirely successful) and an increasing proportion of the racket production was being strung mechanically by equipment developed by Fort Dunlop engineers. Other benefits of the parent company's capability to apply its engineering and technical skills to the manufacture of sports equipment included the single lever racket-press developed from a design patented by a member of the Flowers brewing family, and a revolutionary all-steel tennis-net post designed by a naval officer in such a way that it was the first to overcome the tendency to lean inwards as the net tension was increased.

The *Sports Trader* report on the manufacture of Dunlop sports shoes made much of the company's 'courageous battle in the interests of an English industry that is meeting intense and unnecessary foreign competition' and noted that the manufacturing processes at the Walton factory were 'considerably more modern that those in effect in any other country'. Also that textile technologists at the giant Dunlop cotton mills in Rochdale had developed 'special flexible cotton fabric' for the uppers of the sports shoes. This recurrent theme of the strength of Dunlop technology was also emphasised by the company's chairman, Sir Eric Geddes, in a 1931 booklet entitled *Mass Production*, which had warned that 'if our manufacturers cannot be equipped with the full armour of mass production our export trade must pass from us'. The ever vigilant *Sports Trader* noted with delight that Sir Eric had singled out an exception to his argument in relation to the sports trade where he had acknowledged that 'the peculiar nature of the products which necessitate a degree of manual skill and craft which the cleverest machine cannot produce'. This line of thinking is in interesting contrast to what his engineers were actually doing at the time as they diligently sought increasingly mechanised and more efficient ways of making rackets, strings, presses, hockey sticks and sports shoes. In the case of tennis shoes, even as early as 1931, forty operations were required to produce one pair but the final assembly time had been reduced to eight minutes.

Shortly before the publication of *Mass Production* a large party of sports trade distributors and retailers had visited Fort Dunlop, at the invitation of F. M. B. Fisher, to view the tennis and golf ball manufacturing operations. The all day schedule allowed the visitors to look in detail at the separate production departments, the numerous testing and quality control processes, the packing and despatch area and even the 'facilities for soccer, rugger, hockey and tennis enthusiasts, the shooting range and a bowling green for the less energetic'. As is still the case the party was particularly taken with the tests to check the balls would perform to specification. In the case of the tennis section the balls 'were dropped from a given height at a controlled temperature (68° Centigrade) into a long wooden box divided into two compartments and if a ball did not bounce sufficiently well it fell into the first of the two compartments'. Even more interesting to the visitors was the golf ball tester installed in the sports field facing the newly constructed main office building. The demonstration of this mechanical device involved balls being 'driven about 250 yards, 210 of the 250 being travelled before landing'. American as well as English balls were used and it was noted there was a marked difference in their flight – 'the angle of elevation of the American type was distinctly greater than that of the English, but incidentally the distance covered amounted to approximately the same'.

While the test procedures were probably of most interest to the visitors they were clearly very impressed by everything they were shown during what must have been a five or six hour tour of what had by now become a very large site and very much the flagship factory for the whole Dunlop organisation, especially the tyre operation. They were particularly intrigued by the combination of machine and manual processes required to produce the finished balls, in the latter case exemplified by the dexterity of the girls applying the felt covers of the tennis ball to its core, and by the hand painting (three coats) of each golf ball. They were told that 'up to the present no machine has been devised which would take the place of the old method of treatment by hand', and that notion of meticulous attention to detail had been as well received as their guide's assur-

A party of sports trade distributors and retailers visiting the golf and tennis ball production lines at Fort Dunlop in 1929

When production first started at Fort Dunlop many of the workers travelled from Aston Cross by canal barge

ance that the girls working with 'amazing rapidity' to cover golf ball cores with rubber tape were only going at their usual speed rather than accelerating to impress the visitors. The party were quite clear that 'the standard attained by the Dunlop Sports Company is the result of years of experimenting and hard work on the part of the highly skilled staff employed at Fort Dunlop, and the articles produced all go to prove that the best materials only are relied upon to keep up the name acquired through giving honest value for money'. This striking testimony to what was a relatively recent venture for the company – the ball plants at Fort Dunlop were still less than ten years old – reflected the obvious strength of the total business, clearly so evident at the giant Birmingham complex, and was reinforced by the final comment in the report, which unequivocally declared, 'It can be safely said that using anything produced by this well organised firm is no speculation.'

As might be expected a sports trade press report about a visit to an increasingly important ball manufacturer (and advertiser) would be favourable so it's interesting to have a different perspective on the Fort Dunlop scene. This is provided by an account of what it was like to work in the golf department there in the mid to late 1920s. The source of this record is Mrs. Daisy Blake, who had first worked in the golf ball section at the Manor Mills plant before its transfer to Fort Dunlop in 1923 and remembered that when she, and many of her colleagues, started in the new location they had travelled there from Aston Cross by canal barge, not least because the dilapidated, pre-war buses then operating had a tendency to topple over when fully loaded. She continued to work at 'The Fort' until her marriage in 1932, a step that, in those days, meant that her employment was automatically ended. Daisy, who was clearly a remarkable young woman, and who was a member of the sports and social club rifle section, was interviewed by a member of the Dunlop Archive Project. This was created in the late 1970s to pull together as much of the company's history as could be found but was wound up a few years later as a victim of cost reduction programmes.

Her wages in 1924 were £2 5s. per week (her male colleagues earned around £1 more) but she was quick to point out that 'mind you, Dunlop did pay a little above the average'. Although there was no sick pay there was no unhappiness amongst the employees and an excellent relationship existed with management. If anyone had a complaint about working conditions it would be quickly and amicably sorted out with the departmental manager, or with the help of the Fort Dunlop Works Council if there was no immediate agreement. This atmosphere would have been expected in an environment where the managers joined in all the social occasions, including regular outings to Blackpool, which required two train loads to accommodate all those wishing to make the trip. Daisy, who transferred from golf balls to tennis balls, felt the latter had more prestige because it was an entirely new section – compared with the older golf ball operation that had come from Manor

Mills – and she recalled that everyone in it 'was rather nice, really, nice girls with very few men working there and only on the big machines'. And those machines, she remembered, 'were never silent and there was no wasted time whatsoever in those days. No such thing as stopping – if you went to the toilet you went and you came back and no such thing as doing your face up or stopping for anything like that'. She was very clear about the condition of the factory at the time:

Daisy Blake

> Well everything was clean. It was a new factory so that everything was clean and as up to date as possible. There were no showers or baths or anything of that sort but there were wash basins and the toilets were nice and clean, there was always a lady in the ladies room and there was always a man in the gents to keep it clean and tidy. Above all it was essential that both golf and tennis had got to be scrupulously clean. It would make it a reject immediately if there was any speck of dust on the painting or even on the cover itself.

Asked if she remembered Mr. Penfold, who had so transformed the company's golf ball technology, and started up the tennis ball operation she was again clear about how things had been.

General view golf ball department

> He didn't interfere at all with the work. He just saw that the job was being done right. He had nothing to do with the work only to see that they were doing the job right. And he had a secretary and she also worked in close cooperation and she was also walking about to see that everything – he was a perfectionist in other words. If he didn't like something he'd got the power to stop the girls doing what they were doing and altering the whole thing at once. He'd got that power.

And when asked about the atmosphere in the factory – because she had originally grown up in the countryside – she remembered not only the change she had then found but also how different it had since become.

> Oh, the change was tremendous. But you could go into an office with 15- and 16-year olds today and hear more bad language, more filth than you ever heard in that factory. And in golf and tennis balls, believe me, the girls were ladies. If you heard a bad word you immediately reported it and you could get the sack if it was a real bad word. There was no such thing as a four-letter word in those days. You would have been thrown off the grounds immediately. Believe me, they were really nice girls. But you could always smell the rubber and when you came home if you sat in front of the fire you could smell the rubber until you changed your clothes and had a bath.

General view hand building section/golf

Daisy would have been there when, in 1931, the Prince of Wales paid his second visit to Fort Dunlop,

FORT DUNLOP GOLF AND TENNIS BALL MANUFACTURE IN THE 1920s AND 1930s

Smearing golf ball cores with gutta percha

Weighing and measuring golf balls

Hand painting golf balls. Note scraper on left hand side to remove surplus paint

Filling centre bags with paste

A pyramid of new golf balls

Golf ball wrapping machine

Individually wrapped golf balls being packed in boxes

FORT DUNLOP GOLF AND TENNIS BALL MANUFACTURE IN THE 1920s AND 1930s

General view of tennis ball department

Weighing and crushing chemicals for tennis balls

Tennis ball moulding presses

Fitting tennis ball covers to cores by hand

Measuring the roundness of tennis balls. Note the Davis box in background

Soldering the lids on tennis ball tins

The mechanical driving machine on the Fort Dunlop sports field

THE NEW DUNLOP
'SIXTY-FIVE'
GOLF BALL

65 launch in 1934

Henry Cotton

which he had first seen in 1923, and showed particular interest in the 'keenness of inspection of stages in the manufacture of golf balls'. Among those covering that visit was a *Daily Herald* reporter, who was mightily impressed by what he described as 'one of the greatest factories in the world, hard not to regard as a complete city'. As he entered the site he had seen golf balls being tested and then 'tennis balls travelling at Tilden speed against wooden walls' alongside the test equipment for the tyres to be used on Captain (Malcolm) Campbell's racing cars.

While this succession of visitors marvelled at the quality and quantities of the balls being produced in the UK, Dunlop engineers were installing golf ball plants alongside the tyre lines in Buffalo and Kobe, which reflected the company's early recognition that the USA and Japan would become the two largest markets in the world for golf equipment. That would have been easy enough in the case of the USA, where the game had been growing rapidly since the turn of the century, but it displayed a great deal more foresight and enterprise to invest in what was still a relatively immature Japanese market. The influence of F. M. B. Fisher was again evident in relation to this international manufacturing, and marketing expansion as he had been the driving force in setting up the USA sports sales operation in 1929, and in securing the services of one of America's greatest tennis players, Vincent (Vinnie) Richards as its first chief executive, a position he held until his premature death in 1959. He had first met 'F.M.B.' in 1923, at Wimbledon, where he had won the men's doubles title in 1924 and been runner-up in 1926.

Taking the twenty years from 1919 to 1939, which can be seen as the period when the company was establishing itself in the sports trade, it's appropriate rather than convenient to see that the first ten years were largely devoted to creating a structure and the necessary resources required to make the next ten years so phenomenally successful. By 1929 what had been a one-dimensional, small scale golf ball business, with very limited clout in the trade and minimal consumer awareness restricted to golfers with motor cars, had become a very different animal. The combined efforts of key managers like Penfold, Sammy Ball, Burden and Proctor, plus the acute and widely influential promotional skills of F. M. B. Fisher, had developed a much wider-based equipment presence based not only on the increasingly efficient and modern plants at Fort Dunlop and Waltham Abbey but also on the beginnings of an overseas network of ball supply sources, which was quite unique. The Buffalo and Kobe openings at the start of the 1930s were quickly followed, in 1932, by a golf ball plant in Australia and there had also been continuous upgrading of the tennis ball units in Germany (Hanau) and France (Montlucon).

Throughout the 1920s the product policy had been one of innovation and improvement, especially in terms of value and performance. This was exemplified, in particular, by Penfold's 'Maxfli' golf ball, and by the increasing respect, so evident in trade press reporting, of the technically advanced range of tennis rackets. In the case of the 'Maxfli', which had propelled the company into the top rank of international ball producers, its refinement and development, pursued by Sammy Ball, paved the way for what was to become, arguably, the most famous of all golf products, the '65'. Henry Cotton's involvement in this project had been signalled as early as 1930 when his name, and also those of his brother, L. T. Cotton, and Reg Whitcombe, appeared as tournament winners in an advertisement for a new ball introduced that year. Sammy Ball had been given the task of producing a ball superior to any other in the market, and which would give the first-class golfer the increased length and accuracy he had always sought (and still does). Months of research and experiment led to radical alterations in every stage of construction of new processes. Large numbers of prototype balls were used in tournaments during late 1933 and into 1934 giving results even better than expected, but none more so than Cotton's crowning achievement in winning the 1934 Open when his historic second round of 65 on the Sandwich course provided the name for the new ball. Triumph was followed by a degree of embarrassment as thousands of 'average' golfers clamoured for supplies of the sensational new ball, convinced they could match the startling distances and accuracy achieved by the new champion. But, as described by the company's in house historian, 'because the cover was less resistant to cutting than the 'Maxfli' – in order to achieve greater length and crispness – which was not a problem with first-class players, it was bound to mark severely when mis-hit by less expert golfers'. Sammy Ball, writing in the *Dunlop Newsletter*, acknowledged that the new ball was designed primarily for leading amateurs and professionals but was quick to point out that 'in introducing this new ball the claims of golfers other than the experts have not been ignored. Their need for a ball having a maximum length of flight is equally great, but of equal importance is the need for a ball which will withstand occasional mis-hit shots'. So, for those players, 'who not infrequently top their shots', the company offered an improved 'Dunlop' ball, in both recessed and latticed cover markings, and, more importantly, with greater durability.

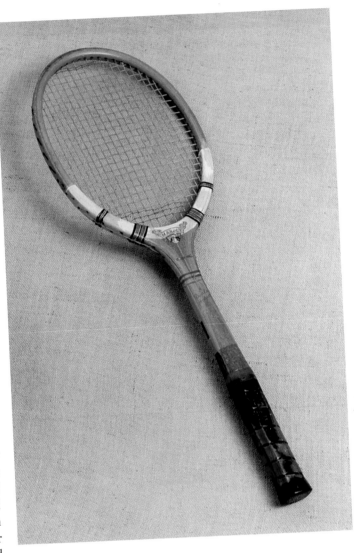

One of the first Maxply rackets launched in 1932

While the technical team at Fort Dunlop were working towards the introduction of the '65', another group, at Waltham Abbey, were creating a revolutionary new form of racket frame construction, which led to the 1932 launch of the 'Maxply'. The *Sports Trader* had been very impressed by the quality and scope of the 1931 range mentioned previously, which it described as giving 'both the best value at reasonable cost' and 'models suitable to many degrees of playability'. The *Dunlop Newsletter*, increasingly alert to the growing reputation of the sports business, had picked up this theme with its own advertisement, which proudly advised company personnel that not only had 42 players at the 1931 Wimbledon championships used Dunlop rackets, but also that three of the titles at the Italian Open that year had been won with Dunlop. In an issue that was otherwise exclusively devoted to reporting tyre matters it observed that 'Dunlop tennis rackets are rapidly achieving the

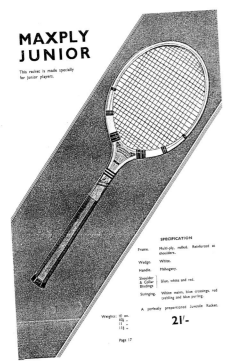

MAXPLY

Code Word: "ZABMA"

This unique model marks the most striking advance in racket construction of modern times.

Multi-ply frame, manufactured from the finest woods, specially selected for lightness, strength and rigidity. Made under a special process and bent without steaming—thus retaining all the natural life and resiliency of the wood cells.

The centre section running through the wedge binds the hoop of the frame to the handle, and gives that "touch of life," greater speed and accuracy so essential to modern play.

Used by Members of the BRITISH DAVIS CUP TEAM

The racket which became world famous in a season

Strung to Tournament tension

75/-

Complete with Best Leather Grip

Specification

Frame.	9-ply. Rolled and reinforced at shoulders.
Wedge.	Specially constructed with centre section connecting head of racket to handle.
Handle.	Mahogany.
Shoulder & Collar Bindings	Red, white and black.
Stringing.	Finest selected English natural gut. All white. Red trebling and box purling.

Weight : 13 ozs. ... Code Word : ZEBYX
" 13½ " " " " ZECAS
" 14 " " " " ZECET

JUNIOR MODEL—see Page 16

Page Seven

The Maxply featured for the first time in the 1933 price list

MAXPLY JUNIOR

This racket is made specially for junior players.

SPECIFICATION

Frame.	Multi-ply, rolled. Reinforced at shoulders.
Wedge.	White.
Handle.	Mahogany.
Shoulder & Collar Bindings	Blue, white and red.
Stringing.	White mains, blue crossings, red trebling and blue purling.

A perfectly proportioned Juvenile Racket.

21/-

Weights: 10 oz.
10½ "
11 "
11½ "

Page 17

The Junior Maxply in the 1936 price list

popularity they deserve'. All of this before the 'Maxply' had been added to the line.

When this famous racket was launched, in 1932, any reviewer could have been excused for not perceiving this was the beginning of a fifty-year product success story, without precedent and never to be repeated, but the *Sports Trader* did acknowledge that the company's 'remarkable advance in racket production during the past year is exemplified by the introduction of the "Maxply", with a nine-ply bent frame without steaming and thereby retaining the natural resiliency of the wood cells making it light, strong and rigid'. The cold bent laminated frame of multi-ply construction used in the new racket replaced the solid, steam bent ash stick skilfully bent by craftsmen from the log to follow the grain, which had been the main method used for many years.

The origin of the new racket can be traced back to early 1931, when the company's sales representative in the Midlands, Harold Dicken, saw a multi-laminated frame that had been imported from America. Thinking there could be a future for this new type of construction Harold reported what he had seen to Albert Burden, who was quick to pass the information to Guy Proctor at the Waltham Abbey factory. It was known that these new frames were being produced by the Kent Company in the USA and as tests carried out on samples were very promising it was decided Guy Proctor should visit the Kent factory and investigate their manufacturing process. He returned with an agreement that they would supply their new frames to Dunlop in the form of rough 'bends', which would be shaped, finished, polished and strung at Waltham Abbey.

It became evident fairly soon that although the new frames lived up to their reputation for appearance and warp-free qualities, they also had a number of serious defects. The timber used in their construction quickly developed weakness which resulted in softening at the shoulders of the frame. The result was close to catastrophic as large numbers of failed rackets poured into the service department for replacement and it became obvious that something would have to be done or this promising new method of manufacture would be abandoned.

Something was done and quickly. Waltham Abbey began to make their own frames. The early efforts were little better than the Kent version but after testing various combinations of timbers a construction was developed that remained largely unchanged throughout the life of the racket. The eventual build-up of the distinctive veneers used in the frame used hickory, ash, a strip of hide (later replaced by Leatheroid), beech, ash, beech and ash originally glued together with skin or animal glue, which was later replaced by urea resin glues developed by the aircraft industry during the second world war. A further, and fundamental design feature was the shape of the frame. The traditional round head shape was too large for the new construction as it allowed excessive movement at the shoulders leading to softening and breakage. A revised shape was introduced with smaller bow and straighter shoulders, which had the desired effect of preventing warping and premature weakening at the shoulders. Originally the new frame was almost entirely hand-made but over the years the number of machine operations used increased to the point where production was virtually 100% machine-made, ensuring much greater uniformity.

Guy Proctor was obviously in charge of the whole process of developing the new racket but important members of the team assisting him were the works manager at the time, Harry Hatfield-Smith, the maintenance foreman and carpenter, Mr. Jest, who made the first moulds for the new frames, Bert Bowtle, the production foreman, Charles Selby, who was an expert on stringing, and the supervisor of the polishing and transfer section, Daisy Chaplin, who would have been very much involved in designing the cosmetics for the new racket which remained so instantly recognisable all over the world for so many years.

Daisy Chaplin, a member of the team that designed the first Maxply, receives her long service award from George Vaughan in 1953

When it was first introduced the new racket retailed at 65s (72s 6d for the Tournament version) and led a 14 model range, which included the '31' introduced the previous year, the long-running 'Riseley Hexagon' and Blue, Red and Green Flash models. These latter designations later became equally well known, and for many years, as differing qualities of tennis shoes.

The following year (1933) – when Buzzer Hadingham was starting his Slazenger career in the export department, and Bunny Austin was startling the crowds at Wimbledon as the first man to wear shorts at the tournament – the new racket was credited with being used by members of the Great Britain Davis Cup team and, another first, was being sold complete with a 'Best Leather Grip', which replaced the previous scored wooden handles (though players often added their own rubber, tape or leather grips after purchase). 'Not for nothing,' said the price list, 'has Dunlop developed the largest and most modern tennis factory in the British Empire.' And although this list was produced by the sports business it maintained the overall Dunlop theme with the claim that 'Dunlop tennis rackets are rapidly achieving a pride of place in the world of sports equivalent to that which the Dunlop name has enjoyed for so long in the motoring world'. The *Newsletter* celebrated Britain's Davis Cup triumph over the French in Paris by mentioning Dunlop balls had been used and that this success was strong evidence to support the company's belief that what mattered in product terms was 'performance not price'.

The range of Rackets produced caters for every tennis player, from the "rabbit" to the Wimbledon champion, and models are sold at prices to suit all purses.

Apart from Bunny Austin, another member of the victorious British team was Fred Perry's doubles partner, Pat Hughes, who had joined the F. A. Davis company in 1926 and was to play a vital part for Dunlop in introducing the 'Maxply' to his fellow leading players – to such effect that it was to become the dominant frame internationally for many years.

Machine stringing introduced to Waltham Abbey

As the press had been drawn to the 'complete city' of Fort Dunlop so they also went to see what one national newspaper described, in the 1930s, as the 'largest racket works in Europe', which, by virtue of its size, was providing ample proof of the enormous growth of the popularity of tennis. The visiting journalist, who concentrated on the newly introduced multi-ply frames, noted the number of employees at Waltham Abbey had risen to 200, and that they were producing around 2500 frames each week and 500 racket presses each day. He was particularly impressed by the six girls applying four coats of cellulose to finish the frames and who, by Act of Parliament, were required to drink half a pint of milk each day. It is doubtful if that procedure would have been acceptable to today's Health and Safety Inspectorate.

Even before the new rackets had taken Dunlop to the number one position at Wimbledon, and before the '65' had been immortalised by Henry Cotton's 1934 triumph at Sandwich, the *Dunlop Gazette*, addressing itself to company personnel, ran a feature in June, 1933 to celebrate the growth and success of the 'infant' sports division, though, as the editor was quick to point out, 'it is important to have in mind that the infant is of the lusty type, highly developed, and developing, a member of the Dunlop family deserving of the greatest respect'. The following extracts from the article give a flavour of both the pride in the success of the 'infant' and also of the contemporary literary style.

Of course the foundation of it all was the golf ball, with which it may be said that the Dunlop Company took the world by storm. The unqualified success achieved in this direction lured the directors on to deal with the sister-sphere, the tennis ball. This led to an immense amount of experimentation, which ultimately succeeded in enabling the Company to produce, at great cost, a tennis ball that fell far below the standard sought. This result, without doubt, was of immense value to all concerned. Firstly, because having made a ball of the sort indicated, it was incumbent on all concerned that Dunlop should now make the best (thereby, incidentally, deriving some benefit from the capital already expended); secondly, it was obvious the Dunlop personnel are not the kind to suffer under a sense of defeat for long.

If space permitted, much might be said of the rapid growth of the Sports Division and the means by which this was accomplished. It will be of more vital interest to our readers to know where we are and how much further we are going. The answer to the first is not difficult. We are in the happy position of being the premier sports business in the world outside the USA. The answer to the second question can only be that we are going as far as our ability and energy, combined with our standard of quality, will take us. We are confident that we shall attain to heights which, in the beginning, were not even dreamed of. This confidence is not bred out of the imagination; it is based upon incontrovertible evidence which accumulates from day to day. It has its origin in the ability and determination of our manufacturing experts to make our products outstanding in quality, durability and finish. At Fort Dunlop we have the brains, and the money to ensure that we make not only what is good, but better than that of any competitor. There is probably no sports business in the world which has, or ever has had, the resources which we have behind us.

Readers are so well accustomed to reading and hearing of Dunlop successes that probably they take many of them for granted. Players of Dunlop golf balls and tennis balls, and users of our tennis rackets, are often, we think, disposed to regard their perfection somewhat as a matter of course. Contact with our technical staff, however, soon gets rid of the illusion that the production of sports goods to the Dunlop standard is a simple and straightforward matter. Specifications that must be adhered to strictly and uniformly necessitate a high degree of accuracy at every stage. Tests of all materials to be used in construction are part of a rigid practice, and all operations in manufacture have to be delicately precise if the product is to have the ideal char-

acteristics and yet conform to requirements in all other respects. Striving for improvement is continual, and the activities of the Research section of the division provide quite a 'story' by themselves.

The effect of the combination of the resources available to the business, and its ambition to reach heights 'not dreamed of' was now becoming clearer. The author of the *Gazette* article, who had insisted on remaining anonymous to emphasize that the achievement of his colleagues had always been based on a dedicated team ethic, would have been delighted by the stream of successes recorded in the years remaining before the start of the 1939-45 war. Henry Cotton's historic 1934 win was the first of five successive Open championships for the '65'. Alf Perry followed Cotton at Muirfield in 1935, Alf Padgham was next at Hoylake in 1936, Cotton won again, at Carnoustie, in 1937, and Reg Whitcombe was victorious in 1938 when the championship returned to Sandwich. And both Padgham and Whitcombe used the new clubs being produced by Gradidges at Woolwich. Sir George Beharrell, the parent company's managing-director, proudly announced, at the annual dinner for the directors, that the '65' was not only winning literally hundreds of individual titles around the world, but also that 'for the first time on record the members of an international golf team played with one make of ball'. He was referring to the 1935 Great Britain Ryder Cup team, which had lost 9-3 to the United States, and hastened to add that 'the lack of success of the team was certainly not due to the ball played'. In the same year the '65' made its first appearance in Japan.

While Dunlop golf balls were becoming overwhelmingly dominant on European courses, and rapidly increasing their presence in the main overseas markets, the tennis ball business continued to grow steadily. By the mid 1930s Dunlop balls were being selected for 133 of the 255 tournaments played in Great Britain and Ireland (Slazenger would have accounted for most of the rest), and for 53 National and major championship events around the world. In 1935 the new 'Fort' ball was launched with its 'Duronap' cover, which had a deep, tough nap replacing the previous smooth Melton cloth. Only a year later an improved version appeared with an even deeper nap with 'sufficient toughness to make the ball crisp and con-

Golf ball development from the original Feathery and gutta percha balls to the Dunlop lattice pattern, original Maxfli, '65' and DDH of the 1980s

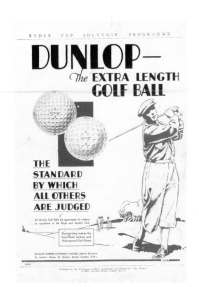

trollable'. 'Crisp' appears to have been a much prized characteristic for both tennis and golf balls at that time. The work to produce 'Duronap' would undoubtedly have been carried out with Wm. Playne & Co. Ltd. of Minchinhampton, Gloucestershire, who, as long established woollen cloth makers, had specialised in producing the special fabric required for the best quality tennis balls, and who would be suppliers to both Slazenger and Dunlop for many years. At the time their verdict on Dunlop was that 'in dealing with the company it is not sufficient to suppose that the best is good enough as something better is always being searched for'.

In the same year (1935) Waltham Abbey introduced the 'Maxply Fort' racket as its premium product. It was priced at 75s, which compared with 67s 6d for the 'Maxply Tournament' and 57s 6d for the standard 'Maxply'. Reading the price list specifications it's difficult to spot major differences between the three models – apart from cosmetic variations – but the 'Fort' stringing was of 'finest selected English natural gut' rather than simply the 'selected gut' used for the other two. The range that year also included the 'Queen Mary', to celebrate the launch of the famous Cunard liner, which sailed with a large showcase in its shopping arcade packed with Dunlop sports and footwear products. Every mattress on the new ship was made of Dunlopillo, as were, for the first time, the cushion insoles in the better quality tennis shoes. Dunlopillo had been invented five years earlier in the same Fort Dunlop technical department that had worked so successfully to produce the new generation of golf and tennis balls.

Rather bluntly Pat Hughes reported to the *Dunlop Newsletter* that the 1936 Wimbledon was 'undoubtedly one of the dullest on record'. He complained that not only was the weather bad but also that 'the results went too much according to the book'. Nevertheless, his Davis Cup partner, Fred Perry, would have pleased Slazenger with his third successive men's singles title and the American, Helen Jacobs, playing with a 'Maxply', won the ladies' singles at the fifth attempt. She had enjoyed more success at the US Open, winning four straight titles from 1932 to 1935. Hughes modestly omitted to mention he had won the doubles title, with C. R. D. Tuckey, but triumphantly reported that no fewer than 84 of the competitors had used the 'Maxply', which was the highest number up to then, represented 30% of the total entry and was considerably more than any other manufacturer. Finally, he added that 'Dunlop shoes were also much in evidence' and 'figured most prominently on the centre court on Finals day'.

The mid 1930s can be regarded as the first 'golden era' for the Dunlop and Slazenger businesses in terms of the number of leading players using their equipment and also the successes being achieved in major events, especially in the UK. It would be interesting to imagine the promotional impact that could be extracted by today's advertising agency from the sequence of Dunlop Open golf wins from 1934 onwards, Fred Perry's three Wimbledon titles – not to mention his other five open wins in the US, France and Australia – Helen Jacobs's four Open wins, the first Open successes for Gradidge golf clubs and the spectacular run scoring feats of Sykes and Gradidge players like Bradman and Hutton.

1936 was the first year when the Fort Dunlop golf and tennis ball departments both produced more than 250,000 dozen balls. Add to that around 80-90,000 rackets from Waltham Abbey, and the steadily increasing sales of a broadening range of accessories – not least over 100,000 racket presses at 2s

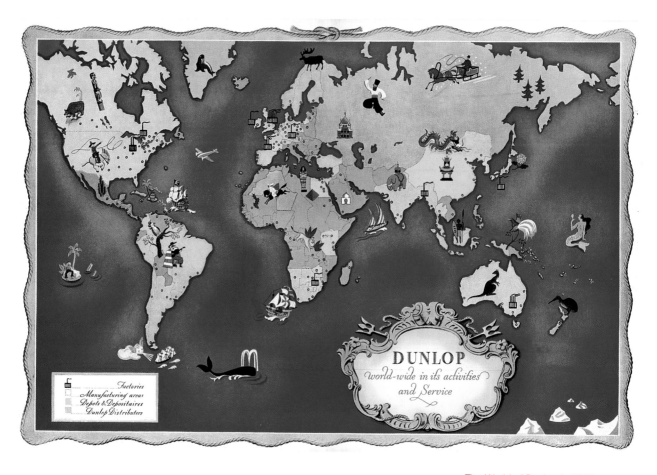

The World of Dunlop in 1938

6d each – and it can be estimated that total sales had moved well past the £500,000 per annum mark, which would be worth around £15 million today.

In the same year William Sykes completed the transfer of their Horbury production to the huge Albion Mill, which would eventually become the largest single factory for the combined Dunlop and Slazenger businesses. Both this move and the record ball output at Fort Dunlop reflected the still rising demand for virtually all types of sports equipment, especially, and fortunately for the Dunlop and Slazenger companies, for tennis, cricket and golf. Fred Perry's heroics, both as the leading singles player in the mid 1930s and also as the leader of Britain's successful Davis Cup team, had done wonders for tennis in the UK, and the new level of interest in the game he had done so much to stimulate would have been a factor in attracting the TV cameras to Wimbledon for the first time in 1937. The viewers would have seen Donald Budge winning the first of his two men's singles titles by beating Gottfried Van Cramm, who was making his third appearance in the final – with a Maxply.

However, it wasn't all that easy for sport businesses as Albert Burden reported to his senior management colleagues in Dunlop. Drawing on his long experience in 'many spheres of work' he expressed the view that 'there is considerably more variety in the sports trade than in marketing any other products'. Among the concerns he identified were 'the vagaries of climate and weather, which provide many problems' and he quoted specific difficulties in this context like the rackets 'which stand up well in England but may develop unexpected defects in extremes of humid heat or dry cold, and the sheep gut used to string the most expensive rackets being susceptible to sudden changes in temperature, which if it does not break under contraction can seriously warp the frame'. His anxieties about varying weather conditions even included the difference between those prevailing in Scotland and the North of England and those experienced in the South – 'our goods, which are of an extremely susceptible nature, have to stand up to entirely different conditions in the North as compared with the South, for instance the tennis ball which is ideal on a dry, hot day will certainly be very heavy and sluggish on a wet court'. Another problem was deterioration of stored products. 'Even under the best conditions golf balls can become yellow, tennis balls are always losing compression and becoming smaller, while rackets lose their tension'. And to cap it all, 'players themselves constitute a third problem as they have numerous fads and fancies which are very often quite absurd'. He was particularly exercised about those tennis players 'who say the Dunlop ball gives them tennis elbow'.

He goes on to declare his worries about the chaotic state of the distribution arrangements for sports goods involving professionals, golf club secretaries, sports dealers – mostly comprising 'ironmongers, saddlers, stationers, cycle agents, radio dealers and village general stores' – departmental stores like Harrods and Selfridge's, tennis club groundsmen, school shops, wholesalers and shippers. And then there are special terms for tennis leagues, for tennis clubs staging tournaments and prominent tennis players, who were obliged to return their rackets for repair before they were re-sold as used tournament rackets. He lamented the lack of any manufacturers' association to deal with golf balls but was appreciative of the work done by the Federation of Sports Goods Manufacturers, which dealt with all other sports products, and of the Lawn Tennis Ball Convention. Apart from these trade organisations 'the ruling bodies governing each game must be taken into consideration, their ideas to be cultivated and their possible reaction to any variations in manufacture or marketing to be thought of'. On top of all that, the work necessary to secure ball adoptions for tennis tournaments, and to organise the work related to the numerous golf events 'makes almost a business of its own'.

In case anyone was in any doubt about his 'bed of nails' he closed with the hope that 'although these remarks are restricted to a great extent, they may give some indication of the many-sidedness of our business and show that its aspects and problems are quite out of proportion to the volume of its turnover'. There's no doubt Albert Burden was an absolutely key figure in the development of the Dunlop sports business, and it's also clear that he became one of the industry's most influential leaders, so it's not too far fetched to imagine that his tale of woe could have been constructed, as some of his successors might acknowledge, to convince his Dunlop peers, with their responsibilities for such as tyres, wheels, flooring, rubber goods, plimsolls and Wellingtons and mattresses, that running the sports business was nothing like as glamorous and exciting as they might imagine.

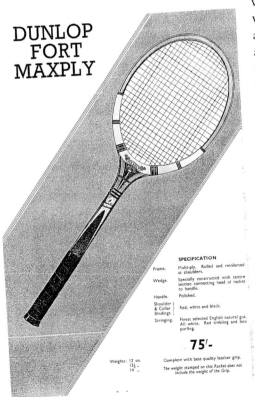

DUNLOP FORT MAXPLY

SPECIFICATION

Frame. Multi-ply. Rolled and reinforced at shoulders.

Wedge. Specially constructed with centre section connecting head of racket to handle.

Handle. Polished.

Shoulder & Collar Bindings. Red, white and black.

Stringing. Finest selected English natural gut. All white. Red trebling and box purling.

75/-

Complete with best quality leather grip.

The weight stamped on this Racket does not include the weight of the Grip.

Weights: 13 oz. 13½ „ 14 „

The 1937 price list features the Dunlop Fort Maxply, not the Maxply Fort

There was, however, a new and larger problem for the business. Reporting on 1936 results the managing-director, Sir George Beharrell, told the annual meeting of senior managers that the Sports Group turnover had dropped compared with the previous year not only because of the bad weather that had spoiled Wimbledon but also because of 'the necessity of manufacturing tennis balls in a number of territories hitherto drawing their supplies from the UK'. This was probably the first time there had been any reference to what would prove to be a conundrum for the business over many years. Unlike the company's main competitors in the golf and tennis ball sectors, who generally chose to operate one very large production unit serving all territories, the Dunlop policy of establishing ball manufacture in many of its overseas tyre plants meant that its total output was broken down to a number of smaller operations, at times as many as eight or nine for both golf and tennis balls. There were obvious benefits in this approach, in terms of the ability to customise production and distribution to meet specific local requirements, but there were potential downsides in relation to maintaining uniform quality standards around the world, and also the cost implications of not only having to operate several low volume units but also, and more significantly, not being able to maximise the efficiency benefits of the total volume involved. This was a manufacturing policy developed on the back of a tyre-based approach to international marketing, which identified cost benefits for its overseas operations from the multi-product factories in Europe, North America, South Africa and Asia Pacific. Today both golf and tennis ball production is mainly concentrated in one high volume plant for each product.

One of the speakers to follow Sir George's review of 1936 was Mr. F. A. Szarvasy, who had played a major role in the re-financing of the company in the early 1920s. He reported on a much more sinister event than the international production complexities of tennis balls. He said he had recently had 'the privilege of having interviews with both Signor Mussolini and Herr Hitler', which had emphasised, to him, that the world was divided into hostile camps, at the root of which were economic causes and their social consequences. The two dictators had told him, 'We will not suffer our people to starve to oblige anyone,' which he was clear meant, 'If you do not enable us to acquire all we require to live, we will fight for it.' That fighting was to begin within a matter of months of that meeting at London's Café Royal, which was to suffer the same fate in the 'blitz' as the offices in Brooke's Market and the Slazenger and Gradidge factories in Woolwich.

Exactly a year later Sir George is again reviewing the company's results by product division and is able to report that, while tennis ball sales have again suffered because of overseas manufacture, the total turnover has increased. This improvement is largely due to record golf ball and racket sales, in the latter case with the Maxply again the dominant frame at Wimbledon. His final comment is that 'in this division we have broken new ground with our dartboard', which reflected a marketing decision to add to the range 'an attractive product having a high potential sales value and, in particular, one

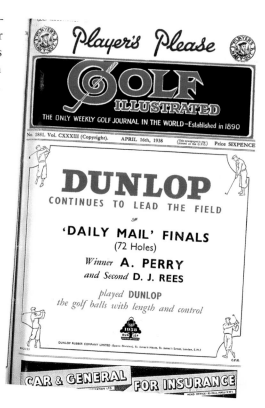

In 1938, one of the many *Golf Illustrated* adverts reporting Dunlop successes

Steffi Graf

Tim Henman

The sports product page from a
Dunlop brochure illustrates the extent
of the 1939 range

which would keep Dunlop sports equipment permanently
before the public during the winter months when the main
tennis business was naturally quiet'. The emphasis on only
tennis being quiet during the winter, rather than golf and
tennis, points to the fact that, initially, dartboards were produced at Waltham Abbey and is a reminder that there was
still something of 'separate states' about the organisation
with ball production still sitting alongside tyres at Fort
Dunlop and virtually everything else being produced and/or
distributed from Waltham Abbey.

Writing in the *Dunlop Digest* shortly after the end of the
war the then general sales manager of the division, D. S.
Robinson, saw 1938-39 as 'the zenith of Dunlop achievements to that date' in the sports world. He believed there was
general acknowledgement of the company's supremacy
among equipment manufacturers, especially with rackets and
golf and tennis balls. While admitting there were no reliable
statistics available he was confident 'that half the golf balls
sold in Great Britain are Dunlop' and was able to recite the
overwhelming dominance of the '65' as the ball used by the
winners of the Open and the main amateur championships
during the years leading up to the outbreak of war.
Interestingly he also referred to the six out of seven pre-war
winners of the Dunlop Southport Professional Tournament,
calling them 'master golfers'. The first Dunlop Masters
Tournament was staged in that same year. Turning to tennis balls Mr.
Robinson explains that while Dunlop is 'predominant where free choice of
the player is allowed there are very good reasons (which do not cast discred-
it on the Dunlop ball) for the fact that the Wimbledon Championships con-
fine themselves to a competitive ball'.

As Mr. Robinson had claimed, the progress of the business from 1909 to
1939 had been remarkable. Among sports equipment manufacturers, and
largely because of the worldwide strength of the parent company, it had
developed a unique international reach, which had resulted in a very strong
presence being established for Dunlop as a sports brand in all those countries
where racket sports and golf had been growing so rapidly.

By 1939 the product range was probably more diverse than either it ever
had been or would be again. The only obvious gap was the absence of any
golf clubs, which closely mirrored the situation that existed with the
Slazenger companies until the 1935 introduction of the Woolwich-made
Gradidge clubs. The 1939 Dunlop golf ball line was based on four main balls:
the '65', 'Maxfli', 'Warwick' and 'Blue Flash', with the dimple patterned covers now much more evident than the older, latticed design. All the balls were
available in the 1.62inch/1.62oz. size but one of the 'Maxfli' balls (Blue
Dunlop) was also listed in 1.68/1.62. The tennis ball range was even smaller
with just the 'Fort', 'Dunlop', 'Warwick' and low price 'Service'. The 'Fort'
was described as 'the world's best ball' and the 'Dunlop' for those 'who find
the Fort a little out of their reach'. In typical Dunlop fashion 'Warwick'
appeared as both a tennis and a golf ball, and also as the name for the
Footwear Division's number one selling industrial Wellington.

The racket range was rather more extensive, headed by 16 tennis frames.

Again, a 'Warwick'; appears, in the value category with the Red and Blue 'Dragonfly' models – the 'Dragonfly' name had originally been used by Gardner Bros. before they, and their Waltham Abbey factory were acquired by Dunlop – 'Matchpoint', 'Blue Wing' and a mid-price selection using names much favoured by the Footwear Division – Blue, Red, White and Green Flash. A 'Blue Flash Tournament' model was the low end of the premium section, which also featured 'Standard' and 'Tournament' versions of the 'Maxply' with the 'Fort Maxply', still retailing at 75s, as the 'flagship' model.

The badminton enthusiast could choose from eight rackets, for the most part using the same names as the tennis line except the 'Goblin' and the 'Nimble', the latter being a throwback to the 'Nimble Shilling' golf ball that first appeared in 1912. Four qualities of shuttle were available and also a complete set of equipment for four players. Six squash rackets were listed including two 'Dragonfly' models and another 'Nimble', and all these rackets were supported by three types of the very successful presses, head covers, gut reviver and a range of Oxford style canvas shoes specifically designed for each of the three racket sports. The uppers were now made of Dunlop 'Ventiflex' canvas, which was 'porous yet wet-resisting, allowing the foot to breathe, reducing perspiration', the insock was 'impregnated with antiseptic, which deodorises and disinfects the shoe', and the 'self-ventilating Dunlopillo cushion insole' was 'porous, springy, wonderfully comfortable, adds liveliness to footwork, protects against shock and keeps feet cool'.

Hockey players could buy sticks, balls and canvas boots, and the total range also included rubber medicine balls, composition cricket balls, the newly introduced dartboards and 'Golfstacle', which was described, rather optimistically, as the original miniature golf game and was supplied, complete with a book of rules, balls and the obstacles, including hoops, rings, tunnel, bridge and tray. Putters made by John Letters could also be supplied. This 'ideal garden putting game' could have been taken straight out of one of the Ayres or Slazenger catalogues of the 1890s. And to complete the 1939 range the catalogue devotes four pages to five types of all metal tennis posts, including the De Luxe model designed 'to overcome unsightly leaning', and all of them 'specially designed to meet the requirements of the best tennis court makers in the country'.

All of which was suddenly less important as Germany marched into Poland and all parts of the huge Dunlop empire set about applying its skills and manufacturing capacity to supporting the war effort. The company was particularly vulnerable to the likely effect of hostilities on its rubber supply but by virtue of its purchasing skills, technical resources, an outstanding ability to innovate and sheer ingenuity it made an enormous contribution to the eventual victory. From the decision to launch its own carrier pigeon service to secure internal communications in the UK to such inventions as the Run-Flat tyre, new types of sand tyres, rubber decoy tanks and guns, mass production of barrage balloons, and the Pneumatic Wave Controller used on D-day, Dunlop definitely went to war with great effect. And continuing to do what it had done for many years the company, during the period 1939-45, produced more than 50 million car and cycle tyres, 1 million tank tyres and 750,000 tank wheels, 6 million pairs of rubber boots, thousands of 'revolutionary' straw dartboards for service messes and Sir Winston Churchill's mattress. James McMilllan, in his book *The Dunlop Story*, writes 'the years 1939-45 were, in truth, Dunlop's finest hour'.

1939 TO 1958

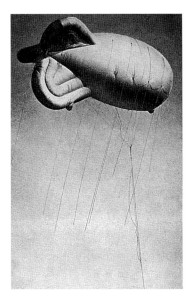

From sporting goods to balloons

WARTIME FRUSTRATION AND POST WAR REBUILDING

The 1939-45 war may well have been 'Dunlop's finest hour'. Sir Ronald Storrs, the distinguished author of *Dunlop in War and Peace*, commented that 'the company's service to the Kingdom, the Empire, the Allies and to the cause of freedom is historically significant as showing what the Western world could achieve in the heyday of capitalism'. And he was very sure that the company's ability to transform a great peacetime industry into an organisation meeting the needs of war 'with daily and nightly destruction raining upon it from the heavens' was mainly due to the 'brains, character and endurance of all ranks in this great public service'.

The impact of worldwide war on the sports business was immense. The golf and tennis ball plants in Germany, France and Japan were to be lost to enemy occupation and subsequent destruction by allied bombers. A much reduced level of ball production continued at Fort Dunlop in the early days of the war – mainly for export and currency purposes – but stopped entirely in 1941 as all available space was required to increase tyre production. The factory was hit repeatedly by both high explosive and incendiary bombs during the 1940-42 raids on Birmingham and Coventry, and a number of employees were killed or injured. In 1975 two boxes of '65s' were discovered, which had been made in 1941, and although there had been some deterioration in the materials used in their construction they were still playable. They would have been among the last balls made before both ball plants were dismantled and stored on the site only to be very badly damaged in one of the 1942 raids. Balls would never again be made at 'The Fort'. Had production continued there, or anywhere else, an added complication would have been the shortage of natural rubber, which became acute after the Japanese occupation of Malaya in 1942. This led to the Ministry of Supply first of all cancelling licences for the manufacture of tennis balls and, later, prohibiting the use of rubber, balata and gutta percha for the manufacture or recovering of golf balls.

The situation at Waltham Abbey was very different. For a while it seemed about as far removed from the war effort as could be imagined. During the period of the 'phoney war', in 1939/40, life continued much as before but with the emphasis, as requested by the Government, on producing its rackets and other products for the export market. The only reminders of hostilities were the disappearance of familiar faces to the forces and the many export orders which had to be made three or four times to replace goods lost at sea.

But Dunkirk changed all that. While the sports business did continue to 'tick over' right through the war – by virtue of living off its very large pre-war inventories – Albert Burden and Guy Proctor increasingly turned their attention to a rapidly growing volume of war work. Instead of rackets, presses, tennis posts and hockey sticks, the production schedules called for barrage balloon fins, gas valves, snatch clips (peg-like safety devices for balloons), ballast release fuses, clog soles, valve hoods, turret hoods and life belts. No doubt individual works managers, responsible for production geared to the war effort, were not encouraged to talk to each other but Guy Proctor and his opposite number at the Sykes factory in Horbury, Bill Dunning, would have been experiencing very similar challenges at that time.

Balloon fins

The fins for barrage balloons were among the first of the wartime products to be made. These were required for the mobile balloons used by ships in convoy and had to be produced very quickly because of the shipping losses which began to increase after Dunkirk. The balloons flew at the end of a thin steel cable run out from a winch on the deck and each had three fins acting as stabilisers. As soon as the fins were ready waiting R.A.F. lorries rushed them to the docks so they could be used to protect convoys heading for the Middle East.

Fort Dunlop and Waltham Abbey worked together to produce the small balloons that were used to carry propaganda leaflets into occupied Europe. 'The Fort' made the balloons and Waltham Abbey the vital ballast release fuses which released the leaflets when, according to wind calculations, this 'secret weapon' had reached its target.

By 1941 the factory was under maximum pressure. Machines were running 24 hours a day, seven days a week putting everyone under strain. Salesmen were called in to act as inspectors and planners, housewives were recruited for morning and afternoon shifts and cars collected girls from outlying villages to increase the workforce. There were countless air raid warnings, particularly in September 1940, and a spotter scheme was worked out to stop everyone racing to the shelters time and time again, which allowed production to continue almost normally. Towards the end of the war the spotters watched, in blissful ignorance, as only the second V1 flying bomb to be launched on the London area spectacularly blazed its way right over the factory. Through all of that the factory escaped damage until one of the last of the much more powerful V2 rockets fell within a hundred yards of the site lifting roofs, shattering glass and causing some of the structure to sag. Miraculously, only one person was slightly injured.

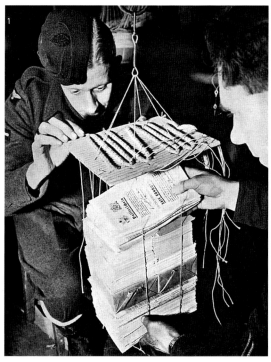

Release fuses

At least one sports product was manufactured throughout the war. The dartboards, which had been introduced just before war started, were judged to be valuable for morale, particularly for the forces, and official approval was given to continue their manufacture. However, this presented the company with another challenge because the original design had been made from rushes imported from China and Japan. Considerable experiment was required to

Waltham Abbey from the air with the River Lea flowing past it

find a substitute for this traditional material and the eventual solution, which produced a far superior board, was to use wheat and straw compressed by a process developed on site, which provided a density greater than spruce, and which could be cut and glued like wood. So much like wood, in fact, that the company received an official query as to how, without a licence, they had obtained the timber being used in their dartboards. The Waltham Abbey process involved the use of hydraulic pressure to reduce the straw to one-fifteenth of its original volume, each board requiring 60,000 two-inch lengths running from one surface to the other. A pressure of sixteen tons was applied to secure the four circumference strips of mild steel to the board and to make sure the Dunlop board was simply the best, a test machine was constructed to fire dart points into boards at the rate of 72,000 per hour. Most competitor boards were destroyed within a few minutes, none outlasted the Dunlop product. Some years after the war this unique dartboard operation was transferred to a small factory at nearby Great Chesterford, which also became the location for the manufacture of table tennis bats and tables.

An interesting footnote to the account of events during the 1939-45 war harks back to the instructions from the War Office, during the first world war, that Dunlop golf ball production should continue on a limited basis to ensure that army and Royal Flying Corps officers could relax during their off-duty hours by playing golf. The golf ball link relates to an incident in Shanghai when the invading Japanese seized all the godowns and warehouses owned by British companies and sealed them up. When the Dunlop godown was inspected it was noticed that one of the Japanese officers took a great interest in the small remaining stock of '65' balls. It emerged that he, like many of his countrymen, was an enthusiastic golfer and, apparently, agreed with the view that off-duty officers should be allowed to relax on the golf course. The Dunlop godown was left unsealed!

In some ways the period immediately after the surrender of the Axis powers was more difficult for the Sports Company than it had been during the six years of the war. The priority for all parts of Dunlop had been to support the war effort, which had meant that while Fort Dunlop ball production had stopped completely the sports production capability at Waltham Abbey had been maintained though intensely focused on meeting orders for the Ministry of Defence. The return to peacetime would quickly bring renewed demand for sports goods of all kinds and the first priority for the team of Burden, Proctor and Ball was to recondition the company's manufacturing equipment, especially the ball production lines that had been damaged during wartime storage. It was also necessary to find a new home for ball manufacture as it had been decided that Fort Dunlop should be exclusively engaged with expanded tyre production.

On top of that there were major problems with both the supply of raw materials and Government restrictions on the distribution of finished products. At first it was only permissible to manufacture the balls from a synthetic material (GR-S) with a small percentage of natural rubber. This meant it proved impossible to make either a golf or tennis ball with an acceptable level of performance and none were ever distributed in the home market. Waltham

This much straw made one dartboard

Abbey, although not faced with the same extreme position regarding its materials, had difficulty in finding both the selection and quality previously available and it became apparent there would be a delay before pre-war quality standards would be achievable. When a trickle of balls did become available, the Board of Trade instructed that 43% of tennis balls and 36% of golf balls were to be exported and 29% and 9% of tennis and golf respectively must be reserved for the services.

The most important event in 1945 for the recovering Sports business was the announcement that Dunlop had leased the huge airframe factory at Speke, on the outskirts of Liverpool, 'as a preparation for the rehabilitation of many products which have been compulsorily abandoned, or severely restricted by emergency regulations' and, as stated by Sir George Beharrell, to meet 'a considerable demand for the Company's varied products to be expected during the post war years'.

The Speke plant, built in 1937 for the production of heavy bombers, occupied a site of 101 acres and had a total floor space of nearly 1.5 million square feet. At the peak of wartime output nearly 10,000 had worked there and Dunlop would eventually employ close to 7000. Preliminary work on converting the factory from making bombers to producing Dunlop products started in mid 1945 and it was only a matter of months before tyres, Wellington boots, bicycle saddles and tennis ball cores were becoming available.

The first complete tennis ball was produced in February, 1946, followed by golf balls in May. In a remarkably short time the giant plant had become probably the best example of the Dunlop multi-product approach to manufacturing with the main tyre operation supported by the golf and tennis ball units, the main production operation for the Footwear Division and the location for the company's UK production of conveyor belting. Later experience, combined with the need to identify the true profitability of more clearly defined and separated product divisions, would raise questions about the cost implications of manufacturing relatively low unit price items, like tennis balls and canvas footwear, in the type of high cost environment required to operate the much more sophisticated equipment needed to produce tyres. Debates about the allocation of overheads in such circumstances would last for some years – not only at Speke but around the Dunlop world – and only went away for the Sports Company, at least in relation to manufacturing costs, when its product line was drawn entirely from a combination of sports only factories and bought in items purchased by its own buying departments.

PROGRESS AT SPEKE
A Year's Accomplishment

No. 6. Vol. II.   OCTOBER, 1946

Aerial picture of Speke factory in 1945

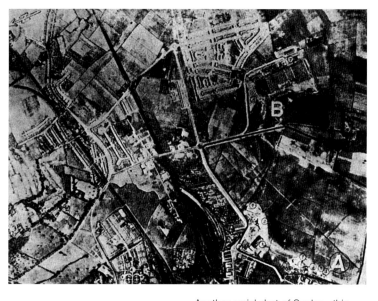

Another aerial shot of Speke – this time taken by the Luftwaffe during the war – A pinpoints the airport and B the factory

A new van for the Sports Company in 1947

Victor Barna still dynamic in 1962

Victor Barna pictured more than 20 years earlier at the English Open championships – he is in the centre of the shot with Fred Perry on his right'

So, despite the shortages and restrictions, and the need to rebuild production capacity both at Waltham Abbey and, from zero, at Speke, the Sports Company was just about back in business. A 1946 advertisement in the *Sports Trader and Exporter* claimed that 'Dunlop quality is as good as ever', and the chairman reported to shareholders that 'several of the firm's products have been prominently featured in important tennis and golf events'. Close to Fort Dunlop the parent company opened a large, modern Research and Development Centre, which would have an important part to play in providing the Sports Company with a stream of new and improved products. One of the scientists working at the new Research Centre was Bob Haines, who, in 1959, would be recruited to the Sports technical staff at Speke by none other than Sammy Ball, and would eventually follow in the tradition of both Sammy and Albert Penfold by piloting the development of revolutionary and award winning new golf and tennis products. To set the seal on the first full year at Speke the plant was visited by both the Lord Mayor of Liverpool and the City's Roman Catholic Archbishop, and they may well have shared the view of the reporter from the local newspaper who had noted enough golf balls were now being made 'to make a clubman's tongue hang out', and enough tennis balls 'to gladden the heart of many a true enthusiast'.

What would certainly have gladdened the heart of all tennis enthusiasts in 1946 was the resumption of what Pat Hughes described as an 'austerity Wimbledon' though he conceded that 'at least the courts were up to par'. The singles champions that year were Yvon Petra and Pauline Betz, which, despite Hughes's hope that Great Britain players would soon be able to offer stiffer opposition, rather set the tone of overseas domination of the finals for the next fifty plus years. The '65' balls, despite the impression given to the reporter visiting Speke, were in desperately short supply but Max Faulkner used them successfully in the Dunlop Southport Tournament, as did Bobby Locke, whose wins in this year included the only ever joint first place, with James Adams, at the inaugural Dunlop Masters event held at Stoneham, near Southampton, with entries limited to 'winners of major events'.

Another significant event in 1946 was the arrival of arguably the world's greatest ever table tennis player, the Hungarian-born Victor Barna. His combination of supreme skill as a player and outstanding abilities in product development and marketing took the company from nowhere in the table tennis market to a dominant position with bats, balls and tables for nearly thirty years. His life-long involvement with the game had brought him into contact with two other Dunlop Slazenger 'greats', Fred Perry and Ann Haydon Jones, who were champions both on the table and on the court. Victor was a charismatic and hugely admired figure well remembered by those who worked alongside him, especially by Bill Evans and also, mainly on the export side of the business, by Bert Allam.

Bert had joined the company in 1937 and achieved considerable distinction in developing overseas sales before retiring as export director in the late 1970s. His career was interrupted between 1939 and 1946 when he achieved a very different sort of distinction as an RAF bomber pilot. He has also been a rich source of information about the company's history, especially during the post war years, and maintains a very active link with many of his contemporaries. For some years he has organised a twice yearly luncheon reunion for a number of former colleagues, which always takes place in one of the several pub restaurants in the shadow of Allington House, or at least the relatively new building bearing that name that has replaced the original structure that was the company's very well known headquarters for nearly thirty years. Bert has particularly strong memories of the problems in the early post war years when it was so difficult to generate any sort of viable sales volume because of the material shortages and the initially slow process of rebuilding ball production at Speke. In the latter case there was a period when the weekly production forecast of no more than 2000 dozen sometimes didn't reach 200, which was one of the reasons for giving customers A, B and C allocation categories, which entitled them to receive shipments of 5, 3 and 2 dozen balls respectively. At that time he was also frustrated by having to quote his overseas customers 10 month delivery delays for rackets.

Final inspection at Waltham Abbey in 1956

However, things did slowly improve and under the headline 'Golf Ball Headquarters is on the upswing again' the *Daily Mail* reported in 1947 that 'the men and women at Speke are striving against the inevitable shortages to lessen the world's present famine in tyres and golf, tennis and squash balls'. 'This place,' continued the report, 'has an inspiring thoroughness and efficiency.' The 'thoroughness', by this time, included the provision of a barber's shop and a billiards room and work would have been well advanced on a very large sports field, opposite the factory, that would, for many years, be the setting for a wide range of activities including locally famous annual galas and flower shows. An echo of Daisy Blake's experiences at Fort Dunlop nearly thirty years previously comes through in the reported words of Joyce Mitchell and Greta Williamson, who were applying 'with cheerful artistry' the several coats of paint required for golf balls. They told the man from the *Mail* it was 'nice work'.

The emphasis at this time on the importance of exports, mainly to secure foreign currency to pay for much needed imports of food, petrol and raw materials, was a major factor in starving UK customers of their '65s' and 'Fort' tennis balls. The *Dunlop Digest* made this point vividly to employees by showing the import purchasing value of key products. One tyre would buy 46 dozen eggs, a pair of rubber boots, 18lbs of meat and, rather amazingly, just one golf ball at 2s each (maybe they meant one dozen) would be worth 11 dozen eggs, 9 loaves of bread, 3lbs of meat and 1¾lbs of butter.

During this obviously stressful period for the senior management the ques-

Frank Smith

tion of appointing a successor to Albert Burden, who was 70 in 1947, became more urgent. The first likely candidate was D. S. Robinson, who was general sales manager in 1945/46, but was transferred to South Africa as sales director for the local company. He was followed by R. C. (Bob) Hiam, who was also with the Division for only a short period before beginning an outstandingly successful career in the Tyre Division. His successor, yet again for a very short period, was Donald Hawkins, who took over the company's Plantations operations before becoming a main board director. Then an internal candidate, the chief accountant, Oscar Walker, was appointed but, as Bill Evans recorded, 'assumed his new position with enthusiasm but unfortunately soon died in harness'.

So in less then five years four possible new general managers had come and gone. It was now 1950 and the then 73-year-old Albert Burden retired with considerable applause from his own company and the sports trade for his commitment to and achievements for both during a turbulent quarter of a century. At this critical moment, with the business still struggling to survive on its inadequate production output, one of the parent Dunlop Company's best known and most widely experienced executives, Frank Smith, became the general sales manager of the Sports Division. Remembered better by many as F. H. Smith, he had joined the company during the first world war as a 14-year-old junior clerk in the main London tyre depot. During the next 30 years he held increasingly important posts, mainly in Tyre Division and at the parent company's London head office, before his move to the Sports Division, which had by then moved its own main office to 19/20 New Bond Street, a building it shared with Dunlopillo Division.

Bill Evans believed that 'Mr. Smith can be said to have established the Sports Company as a major business with forward ideas and a determination to succeed in the trade'. As Pat Hughes had been doing for some years in building the rackets business, Frank Smith travelled extensively to spend time with overseas agents and distributors, and he also worked closely with the production teams at Waltham Abbey and Speke to co-ordinate the marketing and manufacturing resources of the business. It's important to remember that up to this point the overall responsibility for all the Group's UK factories lay with the main board's production director and it wasn't until 1957 that the Sports business, previously only a selling and distribution organisation, was given responsibility for running its manufacturing units at Speke, Waltham Abbey and Great Chesterford, which was by then turning out dartboards and the table tennis range. Frank left the Sports Company in 1958 – a year in which it made a profit of £20,000 – to become general manager of the Semtex flooring business, later added Dunlopillo to his responsibilities and, from 1962 until his retirement four years later, was group general manager for all the Dunlop consumer products businesses. There's no doubt that in his eight years at the helm of the business he not only ensured its identification within the Group as a separate and valuable entity, but also took it to a position of sufficient strength both within Dunlop and the sports market to make possible the 1959 acquisition of Slazenger. Albert Burden's legacy of a solid sales and administration organisation strong enough to survive the 1930s recession and the difficulties caused by the war, which had persisted right through to his retirement, was the basis for Frank Smith, the archetypal Dunlop manager with strong connections throughout the parent company, to develop what would become the dominant UK sports equipment business for the next 50 years.

The first signs of the future dominance of the Dunlop name in the UK sports scene were appearing as Albert Burden was preparing to hand over to a successor. Henry Cotton played the '65' to win his third Open in 1948 and Bobby Locke (1949, 1950 and 1952) and Max Faulkner (1951) would use the same ball to win the next four in a row, Bobby Locke setting a new low score of 279 in 1950. In fact only Ben Hogan in 1953 (with a Slazenger ball) deprived Frank Smith and the '65' of a ten year clean sweep of the Open as both Bobby Locke and Peter Thomson were four times winners between 1949 and 1958. Peter Thomson's 1955 win made history as it was the first time the champion took a four figure cheque (£1000) and it was also the first time the event was shown on live TV.

This sort of success was not confined to the golf course. The early 1950s also saw the start of the extraordinary sequence of Maxply tournament wins that would dominate Grand Slam tennis championships around the world for nearly 25 years. And it became almost a stranglehold on the major titles when the Slazenger winners were added from 1959 onwards. This pattern first emerged in 1954 when Jaroslav Drobny was the first ever winner of the Wimbledon men's title to use a Maxply, and it would be 20 years before that particular final would be contested without either a Dunlop or Slazenger racket on view.

Drobny and his Maxply in action at Wimbledon in 1954

Not all that long before the start of that sequence, in 1948, sports equipment manufacturers were still having to cope with the fall out from the war. This included the impact on tennis ball sales of an almost prohibitive level of purchase tax, which the International Lawn Tennis Federation considered was 'choking lawn tennis' and led them to encourage their International Ball Committee to seriously study an amendment to the rules of the game, which would allow the use of an uncovered rubber ball with a single stipulation that it would be necessary to have 'a uniform outer surface'. While this change would have allowed balls to be made without the heavily taxed outer cloth, it was recognised that the flight of a smooth ball would be erratic. It was proposed that this disadvantage could be overcome by having a pattern stamped on the outer surface, not unlike the dimple pattern approach to improving the flight of golf balls. Slazenger certainly experimented with a grooved ball as early as 1947, and both Dunlop and Slazenger were among five manufacturers to offer a Lawn Tennis Association approved all-rubber ball in 1953, which had what can be best described as a lattice pattern 'deemed to be especially practical for schools and practice'.

This work on uncovered balls reflected the efforts at the time to rebuild sports goods revenues still held back by shortages right through the supply chain, and the relatively high, tax inflated retail prices. A premium quality Maxply racket was likely to cost at least one week's wages for aspiring young players and one golf ball would retail around 2s, roughly equivalent

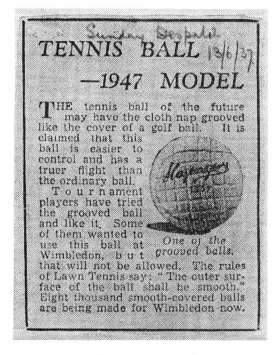

Slazenger grooved ball

The Chairman, Lord Baillieu, accompanied by David Collett, Dunlop director, with Harry Hatfield-Smith and Bill Evans during a 1957 visit to Waltham Abbey

to £4 today. This was if you could find one, which went some way to explaining the fact that the golf ball department at Speke was surrounded by a wire cage intended to discourage 'smugglers' from trying to earn some extra shillings on the 'black market'. No wonder the company instituted the allocation category 'rationing scheme' so clearly remembered by Bert Allam.

However, amidst all these difficulties Frank Smith was paying as much attention to the longer term strength of the business as he was to dealing with the immediate problem of trying to meet the growing consumer demand for 'luxury' products, which, if anything, would have been exacerbated by the string of major golf and tennis tournament successes highlighting the performance qualities of the Maxply and '65'. Although, in the early 1950s, the manufacturing side of the business was still controlled by the parent company – for instance the sports technical and development team at Speke reported to the general works manager on that site, and the works manager at Waltham Abbey to Fort Dunlop – it's clear these resources were being increasingly directed towards meeting market requirements and to keeping ahead of the rapidly developing product strength of major competitors – like Spalding, Wilson, Penfold, Acushnet and the Pennsylvania Athletic Products Division of General Tire (later as Penn to be mainly a major tennis ball producer but then also making golf balls). Denis Osborne, who started as a development assistant at Speke in 1951, remembers that he was initially told to concentrate on sports products within a department responsible for developing all non-tyre products and that remained the structure until the 1957 decision to make the Sports Company a self-contained operation. At that time the Liverpool plant, with Sammy Ball as the manager, was producing shuttlecocks, medicine balls and the pimpled rubber for Victor Barna's table tennis bats – but only squash balls survived for any length of time with the main golf and tennis ball activity.

Both at Speke and at Waltham Abbey, which had the advantage from a development standpoint of being 100% focused on sports products, the emphasis throughout the 1950s would have been on combining the availability of better performing products with the pressing need to increase the efficiency and capacity of the production processes. Although the 'wide open spaces' provided at Speke had allowed the planning of ideal layouts, the equipment brought from Fort Dunlop was old and difficult to maintain after years of inactivity and some damage. So, having made sure the balls were secure from contamination by the carbon black powder used in mixing tyre compounds, the first priority was to refine and simplify the processes originally drawn up in the 1920s, when both golf and tennis balls started up at Fort Dunlop, and, at the same time, make sure that Denis Osborne and his colleagues were continuously looking for better performing and more durable products. From a Sports Company perspective it was very fortunate that it was their own Sammy Ball who was responsible for the overall development

George Vaughan

function at Speke, as well as the production of the sports range.

At Waltham Abbey change was more radical. The principal architects of what was nothing less than a revolution in racket manufacture were Guy Proctor, who had steadily developed the plant since his arrival there in 1929, and George Vaughan, who had transferred to Waltham Abbey from Fort Dunlop in 1935 and been appointed technical manager in 1944. When Guy retired in 1952 George succeeded him as works manager and continued the programme of modernisation and expansion until, in 1955, he became works manager of the newly opened Semtex flooring plant at Brynmawr. An element of continuity, from much earlier days of racket making, was provided by one of the best remembered 'characters' at Waltham Abbey, Harry Hatfield-Smith. He started his working life in 1910, as an apprentice racket maker, was working for the F. A. Davis company when it became part of Dunlop in 1926, and had been one of the team involved in the development of the first Maxply racket in 1931. Another key figure in the transformation of the factory was Len Rennocks, who had joined the company in 1945 as senior draughtsman, became chief engineer and was appointed works manager in 1961, a post he held until the plant closed in 1979.

The old method and...

In 1955 Dunlop published a booklet entitled *An Achievement in Production*, which recorded the modernisation of the Waltham Abbey plant. The foreword introduced 'a story of craftsmanship and production – a story with a moral for the 1950s' and went on to summarise the scale and importance of what had been achieved:

> A long established industry, built up largely on hand working, has been able greatly to increase output and to develop a thriving export business – an asset to the country as a whole. This has been done by bringing to bear new techniques and machines, either specially devised or adapted from other industries, on a particular problem. That problem was the manufacture of tennis rackets. The factory where a fresh solution has been worked out is the Dunlop factory at Waltham Abbey. The men who have carried the work through are Dunlop staff and workers, trained in the traditions of the greater Dunlop organisation. The policy followed has been a double one – to examine every stage in the process of manufacture with a view to simplification and increased efficiency, but to take no step until experiment has proved its value to the product. A tennis racket may be thought of as a minor product, but it is one which is used, and will be praised or criticised, all over the world. From a national point of view it is a product to which a great deal of prestige is attached – for good or bad. What has been accomplished by Dunlop at Waltham Abbey is of special interest to factory managers and business people faced with the never ending task of modernisation. But it has interest also for all who believe that, in the tightening competition of the post-war world, only the application of brains and effort and capital through new techniques can ensure that our country holds its own. No great claims are made for the tennis racket as an article of world importance, nor for a factory of 400 people as a vital element in our national economy. But a good tennis racket at a good price can be a symbol of

...the new method of spraying lacquer onto racket frames

high quality, and a sample of Britain's capacity to produce the goods the world wants at a competitive rate. And the ability of management and men in a comparatively small factory to co-operate in modernising their processes, cutting out waste and improving both the product and the method of production is an example in miniature of changes which we, in Britain, are called upon to make throughout our whole industrial life. It is not that the old ways were bad, but that they are no longer good enough.

This philosophy, expressed in this style nearly fifty years ago, certainly represented the overall Dunlop approach at that time to the modernisation of its worldwide business. It also has strong echoes of the sentiments expressed in relation to sports goods manufacture by both Dunlop and Slazenger companies on many occasions during the first half of the 20th century. Both had consistently given high priority to the competitive importance of innovation and quality and to the need to regularly modernise to achieve those objectives. And both, from their earliest beginnings, had understood that while they should relate their 'Britishness' to both fostering in house pride and also as being indicative of an automatically high standard of quality that element of their business would be a powerful factor in developing their overseas operations, especially in the 'Empire' countries. Although it's indisputable that, less than 25 years later, the Waltham Abbey plant and its main products no longer exist, the scale and importance of that particular modernisation achievement was huge. Racket manufacture was taken to a level of increased quality and efficiency that did allow the company to dominate the market for another 20 years, and, in that time, to provide sufficient and enduring strength for the brand to ensure it maintains a powerful presence in the 21st century.

To be more specific about what was done at Waltham Abbey, literally every process required to produce a racket was radically changed and modernised in the sense that the most up-to-date manufacturing techniques and equipment – several adapted from other industries – were brought to bear on

The pleasantly rural Great Chesterford factory

a process that had seen very little change for fifty years, except for the notable introduction of laminated frames in the 1930s. Essentially the team led by Guy Proctor and George Vaughan changed racket manufacture from what had remained largely a handicraft to flow-line production. Several of those who worked at Waltham Abbey at the time credit George Vaughan as being the driving force of the change so he was able to depart to Semtex in 1955 with the satisfaction of knowing that a revolutionary job had been well done. The most important changes involved new ways of making the laminated frames, the introduction of new glues and a high frequency gluing process to improve lamination, mechanisation of the drilling of the holes in the frames to carry the strings (the hand drilling rate of 9 rackets per hour was increased to a machine rate of 100), a completely new method of polishing and decorating the frames, and a new approach to stringing which included the introduction of a new synthetic gut, 'Durolastek'. One of the most dramatic effects of the modernisation process was the impact of using an electrostatic-based spraying system for applying the finishing coat of lacquer to the decorated frame. The one gallon of lacquer required to spray 105 frames when using the previous hand spraying system was now sufficient for 710 frames.

The main benefits for the customer of all this work could be seen in the improved quality of the rackets and a retail price increase, compared with pre-war, of only 60% (from 75s to 120s before purchase tax), which compared with a reduction of 70% in the value of money during the same period. In volume terms the annual output of tennis, squash and badminton rackets had been increased from 115,000 in the best pre-war year to nearly 300,000, of which more than half were exported. On top of this the production of Barna table tennis bats reached 50,000 a year, before the move to Great Chesterford, and racket presses were running close to 200,000. The modernisation process continued over the next 15 years and by the early 1970s, boosted by the explosion in the squash market, total racket production reached close to 1 million. The peak level for the combined Waltham Abbey and Horbury output at that time was 1.3 million.

Even before the increase in sales of both tennis and squash equipment the post war expansion of the UK business was considerable. In addition to the racket expansion sales of golf balls, by 1955, had more than doubled from the highest pre-war figure to 650,000 dozen. The only downturn at that stage was a small drop in tennis ball sales to 200,000 dozen, due mainly to the loss of pre-war central European markets and the build up of the Group's overseas production. Eventually worldwide production of Dunlop Slazenger tennis balls would pass the 5 million dozen mark.

Important events, both inside the business and also in the world at large, came thick and fast during Frank Smith's eight years as general manager. Quite early on the 1951 Festival of Britain celebrated many of the achievements of Britain's post-war recovery and among the thirty Dunlop contributions to the South Bank exhibition were several displays of sports equipment and footwear. The next major national celebration was the coronation in 1953 and, in 1957, the same year of the famous visit by the Duke of Edinburgh to Horbury and Barnsley, another royal event saw the Queen Mother visiting Speke. Her day there included lengthy stops in the tennis and golf ball departments where she was received by Sammy Ball, Denis Osborne and George Mallett (golf ball production manager), and was told by Mrs. Halligan, in the golf ball core winding section, that her new and improved winding machine was much quieter and easier to operate. The 'cold war' was still the major issue in international affairs but it didn't stop a party of Russian sports journalists visiting Waltham Abbey to marvel at the world's most up-to-date racket plant.

In addition to the Dunlop stranglehold on the Open Golf Championship during the 1950s the early Maxply major tennis wins by Drobny (Wimbledon

Sports and Footwear exhibition at the 1951 Festival of Britain

Peter Thomson chats with John Letters outside the Hillington factory

The Sports Company's famous
Allington House headquarters

and French Open) and by Angela Mortimer at the French in 1955 were the prelude to the unforgettable power game of Lew Hoad – first mentioned in the *Gazette* as 'Lewis Hoad, a racket stringer at the Sydney branch of Dunlop Australia' and possessing, according to Drobny, 'the best service at Wimbledon in 1956/57'. Between 1955 and 1960, led by Lew Hoad, Ken Rosewall, Neale Fraser, Margaret Smith, Angela Mortimer, Althea Gibson, Maria Bueno and Christine Truman, Dunlop and Slazenger players won 22 Grand Slam titles.

In 1954 the crucial decision was taken to enter the golf club market with a Peter Thomson club, which was sold under the Dunlop brand and supplied by the well-known Glasgow-based company, John Letters Ltd. John Letters, a golfer himself, had started making clubs in 1918 on the first floor of a building in the centre of Glasgow. Later his five sons joined him in developing the business, which became a limited company in 1936. During the war John Letters's two daughters kept the business going, mainly by renovating used clubs. After the war, and boosted by the rapidly increasing demand for clubs, the business went from strength to strength, building a particularly good reputation for irons. In 1948 manufacture moved to Thornliebank and in 1953 to a modern factory on the Hillington industrial estate. The success of the ini-

Great news for tennis players in 1957
adverts

tial, offtake relationship between the companies encouraged Dunlop to purchase Letters in 1957, which provided the opportunity to build a more complete presence in the golf market both in the UK and overseas. In the case of the increasingly important Japanese market a team from Letters would, in 1964, introduce golf club manufacture to the Kobe factory to put alongside the golf ball line that had been re-started in 1957 with the help of a UK technical team directed by Sammy Ball.

In the same year as the launch of the Peter Thomson club line (1954) the Sports Company head office moved from New Bond Street to Allington House, directly opposite Victoria Station. This particular building, replaced some years ago by a modern office block, was, for nearly 30 years, synonymous with the Sports Company and, after so many previous locations in Birmingham and London, became almost the equivalent of the Slazenger head office at Laurence Pountney Hill, some three miles to the east. It would later become the first headquarters of the International Sports Company.

With a new head office, Waltham Abbey in the final stage of its modernisation programme, Speke steadily improving the quality and volume of its ball output and, with the worldwide successes of Maxply and '65', Frank Smith could fairly claim the business had become a major international force. The icing on the cake would have been the 1957 decision to give him responsibility for his own technical and manufacturing resources, which could well reflect the strength and experience of a management team that included longserving executives like Pat Hughes and Sammy Ball – both widely regarded as, respectively, 'Mr. Tennis' and 'Mr. Golf'. Additionally, another very experienced Dunlop sales executive, Jack Morton, who had been a regional manager for the Footwear Division, joined the team as sales manager in 1956. This appointment allowed Frank Smith more time to concentrate on the future strategy of the business before his move to Semtex in 1958 and at this point Jack Morton succeeded him at Allington House as general manager. Ralph Sammells, who Frank had 'spotted' as manager of the South African sports business, followed Jack as the company's sales manager but moved to a finance company in 1959 to be succeeded by I. A. (Bunny) Thorpe.

Jack Morton

Confirmation of the importance of the Maxply and '65' as the foundations of the business for so many years, and especially during its rapid expansion during the 1950s and 1960s, can be seen in the 1956 price list. The golf ball line is built around the 'Warwick' – 'outstandingly the first favourite where high playing qualities are required at a moderate price', and, of course, the '65' – 'the world's most successful ball used by the winners of the greater majority of leading events', which would have included 12 of the 16 British Opens since its introduction in 1934. Peter Thomson is pictured alongside an impressive list of 1955 successes, which included 16 national Open titles and 19 amateur championships in seven countries, 5 of them ladies events. The 'Warwick' brand also appeared as a tennis ball with its value connotation – 'made for tennis players who require a good ball at a low price' – and with newly incorporated nylon fibres to provide improved quality and durability. The description of the 'Fort' ball wasn't short on superlatives as this was the product that 'offers tennis enthusiasts longer first class playing life than ever before in the history of the game' with extra wear and damp-resistance provided by the 'Terylene' and 'Nylon' fibres in its deep nap cover. The supporting list of tournament adoptions is as impressive as the golf ball successes including 26 national or international championships in 19 countries and 17

Electronic machine installed at Speke
to measure tennis ball rebound

You'll never know
how well you play...
until you play with a

Dunlop
GUARANTEED*
TENNIS RACKET

ask your sports dealer for

Dunlop *–it's the finest!*

THE STRINGING, TOO, IF IT'S 'DL'

Remember . . . there is a special rebate for
Dunlop employees

A typical racket advertisement in the late 1950s

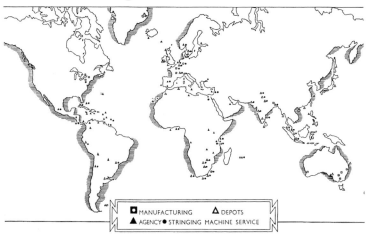

Dunlop SPORTS GOODS

□ MANUFACTURING   △ DEPOTS
▲ AGENCY ● STRINGING MACHINE SERVICE

Dunlop Sports worldwide in 1956

Davis Cup matches.

Five versions of the Maxply appear in the tennis racket range, including a 'contemporary' version listed as the 'Gold Star' and offering 'an alternative to those who prefer the modern trend in design'. That was probably optimistic in view of the general and longstanding preference for the traditional, mainly red and white cosmetics. Supporting models included familiar names like 'Warwick', 'Blue Flash', 'Gold Wing', 'Matchpoint' and 'Pioneer', which was first mentioned in a 1931 *Sports Trader* review of the range. The badminton range of five frames (all with names used for tennis models) included a steel shafted 'Fort Maxply', which carried the promise that the new shaft would be 'firmly connected to the head and handle'. Also a choice of four shuttles, including, intriguingly, the 'Plastic Carlton' produced by the company of that name, founded in 1949, which would be acquired by International Sports Company in 1968. The range was completed by squash rackets and balls – not at this stage as important a sport as badminton – the Barna range of bats, balls and tables, the Great Chesterford dartboards, a Speke-made moulded-rubber practice football and medicine ball and Dunlopillo-based gymnasium mats. The back cover of the export list for this year reminded customers that this was a worldwide organisation and that 'in every country of the world possessing normal trading channels there is a part of the organisation making and marketing Dunlop sports goods – in each of the five continents Dunlop factories make Dunlop sports goods of the same high standard and quality as those sold by the British sports dealer – and over 50% of the products made at Speke and Waltham Abbey are sold in overseas markets'.

This, then, was the shape of the business that Frank Smith handed over to Jack Morton in 1958, but the later stages of this history will describe how and when this pattern of a UK-based manufacturing strength changed virtually 100%. By 2002, apart from their major golf ball plant in USA, the vast majority of Dunlop (and Slazenger) products were either manufactured in, or bought from the Far East. That upheaval, which was shared by most of the company's main competitors, would be encouraged by the arrival of revolutionary new materials and manufacturing processes and further assisted by the simultaneous and extraordinary improvement in the speed and capability of communications. In the UK it would bring about the end of well over 100 years of manufacture of a wide range of sports goods and not one of the eight factories operated by Dunlop and Slazenger would survive this process.

1959 TO 1983

MERGER WITH SLAZENGER TO FORM INTERNATIONAL SPORTS COMPANY BUT DUNLOP PARENT RUNS INTO PROBLEMS

Three men – Albert Burden, F. M. B. Fisher and Frank Smith – in their different ways contributed to the establishment and development of the company during the first fifty years of its existence. For the next twenty-five years the responsibility for what had been achieved, and for developing it further, would pass to three more – Jack Morton (1958-62), George Carr (1962-72) and Findlay Picken (1973-84). Jack Morton and George Carr, with their mainly sales backgrounds, would have the benefit of a period of general and considerable growth for the business, but Findlay Picken, an accountant, would have to deal with the combined effects of sharply increased competition, especially in the rackets sector, and of the difficulties, mainly financial, encountered by the parent Dunlop Company during the years that led up to the disposal of most of its tyre operations, and shortly after, the acquisition by BTR.

The 'Flying D' lands in 1960 to give Dunlop a new image

All three of these general managers were long service Dunlop men, whose careers included experience in other parts of the Group. Like Frank Smith they had strong connections throughout the company and were highly regarded at main board level. Despite all of that, and this would apply mainly to Findlay Picken, the Sports Company in the late 1970s/early 1980s, would find itself, like most other divisions in the Group, the victim of general problems that would severely restrict the management's ability to defend the dominant position that had been constructed during the preceding seventy years. Both the need for this defence and the declining ability of the parent to support it would coincide with a competitive situation characterised by a mixture of established companies, like Wilson and Spalding, being acquired by 'wealthy' new owners, and relative newcomers, like Prince, Head and Adidas, combining new technologies and substantial promotional investment to rapidly build strong market presences. Even the strongest part of the Dunlop business, the core tennis and golf ball operations, would feel the beginnings of new pressure for similar reasons, though the impact in these areas would not be so severe until the late 1980s and onwards, and after BTR had acquired ownership.

The rationalisation of UK production, which would start in the late 1970s with the closure of Speke and Waltham Abbey, was an outcome of not only

THE DUNLOP GAZETTE

APRIL 1967

Dunlop and Barna so visible in the table tennis world

the factors already mentioned but also the development of new technologies and lower cost sources in the Far East. Both Dunlop and Slazenger had been aware, for many years, that relatively small scale and poorly organised racket producers in India and Pakistan could supply low cost rackets of poor quality, and Dunlop Footwear, since before the war, had battled in their UK market against large quantities of Asian manufactured cheap canvas and rubber footwear. In the case of the Sports company, Bill Evans visited Pakistan and India in 1959 to assess the potential for bringing in an improved quality of racket for the lower end of the price range, and Dunlop Footwear, during the second half of the 1950s, had laid the groundwork for importing plimsolls and sports shoes from Hong Kong. Bill Evans's exploratory studies would lead to further work, in Japan, China and especially Taiwan, and, ultimately, during Findlay Picken's period in charge, to the establishment of a Hong Kong-based purchasing operation. Over the same period the imported proportion of the total Dunlop Footwear business would rise to 75%.

The scale and eventual pace of these changes would have been difficult to imagine in 1958 and Jack Morton could not have been expected to have them in the forefront of his mind when he received the trade press at Speke in June of that year, only a few months after he had taken over from Frank Smith. 'A Dunlop golf ball is sold every two seconds throughout 365 days of the year' he told the assembled journalists, which would amount to some 1.3 million dozen per annum. The bulk of them would have been produced at Speke and he was probably including the relatively smaller quantities being produced at the time in the USA (in the Buffalo tyre plant), Australia and the newly re-started unit in Kobe. He went on to impress upon them that, contrary to the general opinion that the Sports Company was a small offshoot of a very large tyre group, it was in fact 'a limited company within the Dunlop organisation with a turnover counted not in tens of thousands, or even hundreds of thousands, but in millions'. At that time the figure was probably close to £3 million. He went on to highlight the absolute independence of the business, in particular that it was responsible for all its buying, product development and manufacture, all of which had been part of the 1957 decision to identify the separateness of the business within the group. And, in terms of marketplace success, he talked about the huge success of the newly introduced Peter Thomson clubs, which were being 'rationed' for sale only through golf professionals, the fact that the Maxply was being used by the majority of top-line world class players, the success of Victor Barna's table tennis range and the huge influence he had throughout the game, the difficulty in meeting the rapidly increasing worldwide demand for squash balls, and the fact that the company 'factored in a large way sports footwear manufactured by their associate company at Speke'. That last comment could have been expected from a former Dunlop Footwear sales executive, speaking only a couple of hundred yards from the tennis shoe production lines, but the relationship between the two operations wasn't always as comfortable, or constructive, as suggested to the press on that occasion. In later years a radically altered marketplace would expose the fact that the two businesses, for reasons both could defend, had very different footwear objectives. Partly because of that, and also because of the general shortage of investment funds, the Dunlop brand of sports footwear, once even more dominant than Maxply rackets on the world's tennis courts, would virtually disappear from that scene.

Jack Morton was at the helm of the Sports Company for a much shorter period than any of his three predecessors, or of the two general managers that followed him. The leadership of Burden, Fisher and Frank Smith covered the more than thirty years from the 1926 formation of the original selling operation in Holborn, and George Carr and Findlay Picken would pilot the business from 1962 to 1984. But the 'Morton years' at Allington House were very eventful and included major developments for both the company and sport in general. His later success in rapidly developing the relatively new Semtex flooring business only served to emphasise the forceful reputation he had established during both his earlier career with the Footwear Division and his very important four years in the Sports Company.

Bobby Wilson, Mike Sangster and Alan Mills with their Davis Cup captain, John Barrett in 1961 – both Alan Mills and Bobby Wilson were Dunlop employees at the time

As the still rather austere 1950s gave way to the more affluent and exciting 1960s public interest in nearly all forms of sport grew enormously with a very intense focus on the new breed of young stars. Suddenly nearly every household in Europe and North America could afford a television set and share in what the *Sunday Times* called 'the golden dawn of the superstar'. The post-war domination of the British Open by Bobby Locke and Peter Thomson was broken by a wave of outstanding younger players, like Gary Player and, especially, Arnold Palmer. When Palmer's phenomenal 'army' of supporters on both sides of the Atlantic cheered not only his majors wins between 1958 and 1964, but also his exciting skills and charismatic style, it was their acclaim that signalled that golf had been 'catapulted into a million pound business'.

In 1959 two 19-year-olds, who would dominate their respective sports for years ahead, announced their arrival on the world's tennis courts and golf courses. The unseeded Rod Laver reached his first Wimbledon final, losing to Alex Olmedo, and Jack Nicklaus won his first important event, the US Amateur Championship. John Barrett believes that but for the hiatus surrounding the introduction of professional tennis Laver, 'arguably the greatest singles player of all time', could have won nine successive Wimbledon titles from 1961 onwards, and Peter Alliss, assessing the Jack Nicklaus career that had started in the late 1950s, simply states in his book, *Golf Heroes*, that 'he is the man with the most remarkable record in the world of golf'. And 1961 was an outstanding year for British tennis with four men, Bobby Wilson, Billy Knight, Mike Sangster and Roger Taylor, reaching the last 16 of the Wimbledon singles, and Angela Mortimer and Christine Truman contesting the first all British Women's final since 1914. Angela Mortimer won her third Grand Slam title in this very close, three set battle with the 1959 French Open winner. In the world of cricket huge crowds were drawn to a series of exciting test matches involving some of the greatest ever players, like Worrell, Sobers, Benaud, Lindwall, Trueman, Statham, May and Graveney, and the

Angela Mortimer receiving a silver salver from Jack Morton and Pat Hughes to mark her Wimbledon success in 1961

Coles wins with '65'!

Neil Coles' great round of 65 to win the Ballantine Tournament at Wentworth was played with the American-size Dunlop '65', and recalls the historic round at Sandwich in 1934 which gave this famous ball its name.

Coles' win rounded off a magnificent Dunlop '65' season when no less than 14 major tournaments were won.

Amateur Championship
English Amateur Championship
Artisan Championship
Boys Championship
Girls British Open Championship
Dunlop Masters Tournament
News of the World (P.G.A. Championships)
Esso Golden Tournament
'Yorkshire Evening News' Tournament
Cox Moore Tournament
Hammonds Carling Jubilee
Ballantine Tournament
Gor-ray Assistants Championship
Coombe Hill Assistants

YOU'LL DO BETTER WITH

Neil Coles in action at the 1961
Ballantine Tournament at Wentworth
with 1.68 size '65'

Dunlop chairman, Sir Edward
Beharrell, opens the Westminster golf
ball plant in 1960

Gillette sponsorship of one day games was about to attract even greater interest.

Against this background of general sporting excitement and expansion of interest, especially for golf and tennis, Jack Morton and his team were not only steadily consolidating the company's position but also giving a great deal of thought to the future development of their marketplace – which wasn't entirely problem free. Jack, himself, was a very visible general manager. Naturally at home with customers he also took a prominent role in presenting the company's products and policies to the press. Looking beyond the immediate evidence of increasing participation in the major sports, he warned a group of journalists visiting Speke in 1959 that 'the trouble with golf balls is that we shall soon have nowhere to use them if links continue to go to the builders' and that 'unless local authorities get a move on with municipal courses in the next few years we will arrive at the stage where too many golfers are chasing too few courses and finding the queuing extremely frustrating'. The number of golfers had grown by about 30% since the early 1950s without any increase in the number of courses and Jack felt this required action rather than just observation. He initiated a research programme in London and the Home Counties, involving club secretaries, professionals and local government officials, designed to more accurately define the scale of this problem and to find ways and means of dealing with it. This included promoting the then new idea of spreading the load on course capacities by making more use of them in mid week, and to impress upon those with ability to take action to provide more facilities for week-end players in the more congested areas.

Meanwhile Pat Hughes was expressing his concern about the dangers confronting lawn tennis. Writing in the *Guardian* in 1960, not only as a former international player and the company's tennis manager, but also as the manager of Jack Kramer's European tour, he declared that the game's governing bodies 'must regard the 1950s as the most disastrous decade in the history of the game'. He was particularly concerned that the best players had turned professional, that this had resulted in reduced interest in the game and that the amateurs were now 'running around the world playing for whatever money they can get', which was being paid 'over the counter' rather than discreetly as in the past. He was deeply depressed by this situation but, more positively, did then predict the arrival of open tournaments, which would lead to tennis finally becoming like the other professional games attracting big crowds with prize money comparable with that offered to golfers. He was quite clear that the future of the game was professional because 'you cannot expect people to reach the required standards while working in a bank'.

Because of his Dunlop connection, Pat Hughes's views were also seen as representing the views of the equipment manufacturers, who, in the golf sector, were also paying close attention to another major issue that was highlighted in 1960. This was the debate about the relative merits of the UK's 1.62" diameter ball and the larger 1.68" ball, which had been approved in the USA since 1931. Although it would be another eight years before the larger ball was approved by the PGA in the UK, it made its first tournament appearance at the 1960 Ballantine event held at Wentworth.

This debate would not have been on the agenda later that year when Sir Edward Beharrell, chairman of the parent Dunlop Company, opened the new Westminster plant in South Carolina, which housed the 1.68" ball production transferred from the North American company's Buffalo factory. This American connection may have had something to do with the decision to hold the inaugural dinner to honour the first fifteen winners of the Dunlop Masters tournament. This event was very much an echo of the tradition established by the Augusta National Club for its champions, and extended to the presentation of special 'Masters blazers' to those attending. However, they definitely took them home with them, which was in contrast to the Augusta Masters blazers always remaining in that famous clubhouse.

Ten winners of the Dunlop Masters, in their special blazers, at a 1960 dinner in their honour

Increased emphasis was given to the Dunlop Masters the following year. Following a review of the company's policy towards sponsorship of golf events it was decided to discontinue the separate tournament which had been staged for club professionals since 1929. It was felt that because the British tournament calendar had become so well supported, Dunlop resources would, in future, be concentrated on developing the Masters in the UK and by promoting two new events in France and Germany. These would involve collaboration with the local Dunlop companies, and were designed to support both the development of the game in those countries and also the interests of the professionals, many of them from the UK, who were playing such an important part in that process.

And going way beyond Europe it's clear from the growing number of reports in the *Dunlop Gazette* at that time that the company had recognised that the marketing of sports equipment was increasingly becoming a global operation. This was another development accelerated by the huge interest in the activities of the 'superstars', whose successes around the world, often clearly associated with prominently displayed 'Maxply rackets and '65' balls', were getting more and more exposure in the press and on TV.

Waltham Abbey veterans 1963, Bill Bowman, George Tinkler and Cyril Bradford receive their long service awards from George Carr. Also in the picture Len Rennocks and Bill Evans

Items related to the rapidly expanding sports operations in Japan were becoming more frequent. The British Ambassador to that country is pictured inspecting the golf ball department at the Kobe factory, which Sammy Ball had just re-visited for the first time since the end of the war and described as 'like a miniature Speke'. The newly appointed Japanese production manager, for both golf and tennis balls, Takeshi Kuzuoka, had travelled in the opposite direction for a three-month training stint in the UK spent mainly at Speke, where he found time to exercise with the Judo Club, and a party of his fellow countrymen, representing Japanese sports manufac-

Pat Hughes welcomes Jaroslav Drobny to the Dunlop tennis team in 1961 25 years after their first meeting at the Czechoslovakian championships in Prague

Bert Allam with David Sealey before his USA visit in 1961

turers, are shown at Waltham Abbey. A special feature recorded the history of the Australian Dunlop company, which had been founded in 1899 and had started tennis ball production as early as 1908, with golf balls following in 1932. In 1959 Victor Barna went on a month-long tour of West Africa to promote both table tennis and the company, and in 1961 Jaroslav Drobny joined the company as assistant to Pat Hughes. Alun Morgan, who was the technical manager at Waltham Abbey, joined Bill Evans in the expanding project to assess the viability of importing rackets from India and the Far East, and they would both eventually have the difficult task of balancing total production between the UK plants and these new sources.

A particularly interesting report was provided by export manager, Bert Allam, which first of all emphasised the fact that the business was exporting more than half its output to 150 different overseas markets and also that Dunlop sports goods were being manufactured in nine other countries. His main subject was his 1961 visit to North America where he combined discussions with the Buffalo and Westminster based local Dunlop sports operation and direct selling calls in other parts of the USA. A key item on the agenda for his discussions with the local management was the co-ordination of racket production based on Waltham Abbey supplying frames finished to the completed woodwork stage only, which would leave the USA plant to do its own finishing operations. The philosophy of regarding North America principally as an export market to be serviced from the UK, rather than what could have been regarded as the most important part of a business to be managed on a worldwide basis, persisted until well into the 1980s, and was applied to other important overseas territories, notably Europe, South Africa and Australia. It was, of course based on the overall Dunlop approach to the management of its huge international operations, which, naturally enough, was primarily focused on the tyre market. However, with the benefit of hindsight and a later recognition that the most successful international sports businesses (including virtually all the company's main competitors) were managed on a global basis, it is at least interesting to speculate what might have been, especially in the USA, if the Dunlop and Slazenger businesses had been able to take that same organisational route some twenty years earlier than they did – possibly coincidental with the 1964 formation of the International Sports Corporation, which only went part of the way towards that structure. The other side of that particular debate was the local advantage of giving ball manufacturers in many of these territories the benefit of an interim, if not longer term tariff protection.

One of Bert Allam's objectives, during his 1961 American visit, was to look for distributors for fishing reels. This was in part related to the company's arrangement to distribute the high quality products made by the well-known manufacturer, Young's, but could also have been prompted by the 1960 acquisition of the Sealey fishing tackle business, which was a market leader for fish hooks. Fish hooks had been made all over the world for hundreds of years but it took the Great Fire of London and a recurrence of the Black Death plague in the 17th century to drive a number of leading hook-makers from the capital to Redditch, where the availability of iron ore and forest charcoal for smelting had allowed the development of the skills related to wire-drawing and needle-making, obviously ideal for the manufacture of fish hooks. In 1895, Edgar Sealey, employed by one of the firms making hooks, built a factory in the garden of his large Victorian house, and started on his own. A family business was established, with sons joining their father as the enterprise grew, and in 1920 fishing rods were added to the range. Although Sealeys would part company with Dunlop in 1969, because it was then thought the 'fit' wasn't quite right, the acquisition was prompted by an interest in diversification and the belief that Sealeys would benefit from an association with the resources of the larger company. A longer-lasting acquisition was a member of the family, David Sealey, who stayed with Dunlop to become marketing director of the Sports Company.

Unquestionably the major event for the Sports Company during Jack Morton's stewardship was the acquisition of Slazenger. This was completed in February, 1959 following the discussions between the parent Dunlop company and Ralph Slazenger, which had started during the autumn of 1958. The Slazenger perspective of the sale of their company is dealt with in the history of that business and was mainly driven by Ralph Slazenger's wish to dispose of his majority holding at a time when it was seen as both growing and profitable, though probably not sufficiently so to adequately finance further growth. Reay Geddes, who was then managing-director of Dunlop and had been its director responsible for sales, would have been quick to appreciate the importance of bringing the Slazenger operation into the Dunlop family. Firstly, it would remove the danger of the brand's considerable strength in key markets, like the UK, France, Canada, Australia and South Africa, falling into the hands of a competitor. That was recognised as a definite possibility based on the knowledge that Ralph had been talking to Wilson Sporting Goods, and, more positively, the acquisition would combine the two leading sports equipment manufacturing brands in the UK and those key overseas territories to create one of the strongest operations in the world in this field, albeit outside the massive USA market.

It's clear that Reay Gedddes and the Dunlop board moved quickly and decisively to secure Slazenger. However, they were also quick to assure the customers of both companies, and their employees, that the two businesses would continue to operate independently of one another, indeed as determined competitors. Jack Morton certainly accepted that approach and continued to concentrate on his Dunlop responsibilities as both he and Michael McMaster, as chairman of Slazenger, reported direct to the Dunlop main board.

For instance, Slazenger were not required to adopt the famous 'Flying D' symbol, which Dunlop introduced in 1960. Research had shown that the consumer perception of the company, while recognising its virtues of reliability, quality and stability, did not extend as much as had been hoped to rather more exciting attributes like courage, liveliness and technical leadership. The new symbol was selected from a range of designs to provide the focus for a completely new advertising campaign designed to tell the world that Dunlop was a worldwide, forward looking and very vigorous organisation. Of equal importance the new symbol became a unifying promotional logo across all

A 1961 advertisement for the Edgar Sealey fishing tackle company – starring Jack Sealey

George Carr and Michael Bonnallack in good form at a Golf Foundation presentation

George Carr on air

Arnold Palmer signs for Dunlop in 1964. George Carr and Mrs. Palmer both looking delighted

products, divisions and territories largely replacing the many and varied styles previously used to present and print the word 'Dunlop'. The 'Flying D' has become one of the best known of company logos and in surviving the break-up of the Group is still prominently visible around the world despite the present multi-ownership of the brand.

In 1962 Rod Laver, using his Maxply racket, won his first Grand Slam, and George Carr succeeded Jack Morton as general manager of Dunlop Sports Company. Among the senior managers in the Group the opportunity to manage the sports business was a widely-held ambition and George Carr acknowledged his delight at being offered the post. He would also have been encouraged by the fact that the Group's sports operations, which had been rather slowly, as well as carefully, built up over the previous fifty years, had been given an enormous boost by the Slazenger acquisition. Add to that the fact that at this juncture the parent Dunlop company was, as described by James McMillan in his *Dunlop Story*, 'truly sitting pretty: an establishment concern with a proven record of achievement and a constant technological itch to improve itself' and it's not difficult to understand why the application of George's considerable management skills and feel for the business resulted in a period of notable success that can be measured in terms of both increased presence and financial results.

When, in 1962, George was summoned to Reay Geddes's office in Dunlop House he imagined it would be to confirm his widely anticipated appointment as general manager of Dunlopillo. Instead he was delighted to find that he was to exchange his Rochdale office for Allington House, and that his immediate future lay with rackets and clubs rather than beds and pillows.

He certainly brought much more than the positives of excitement and enthusiasm to this new challenge and to the ten years he would be in charge at Allington House. Bill Evans has written that 'he had very firm ideas on how the company should be run and under his guidance it prospered with turnover and profitability rising each year'. He remembers his considerable energy and ability and credits him and Tony Carter, his marketing director from 1963 to 1972, with 'the consolidation of the company's position in the trade both at home and overseas'.

George, who was born in Canada of English parents, was 50 when he moved to Allington House. He had joined Dunlop in 1930 as a postal clerk in the Cambridge Street factory in Manchester. Before the war he moved to the relatively new Dunlopillo Division and was one of its first four salesmen. Returning to the division after the war, he remained on the sales side, including a spell in the export department, becoming general sales manager and, later, assistant general manager. During the 1950s and early 1960s the sporting skills he had shown in his youth, especially in rugby and cricket, prepared him for his 'other career' with the BBC. Working mainly in the Northern Region he first joined Kenneth Wolstenholme's 'Sports Special' as the rugby union reporter covering senior club, county and international matches from famous grounds like Waterloo, Sale and Twickenham. When the region started a new Saturday evening winter sports programme, 'Sport Spotlight', George introduced the whole broadcast. For a number of years he was also one of the team reporting on the Isle of Man Tourist Trophy and Grand Prix motorcycle races. While contributing sports features to 'Children's Hour', he met his wife, Gwen, better known to millions of children and their mothers as 'Auntie Gwen', and who was then the programme's organiser for North Region. Gwen, who had trained as an economist, later became very active in local council work after the couple had moved from Lancashire to Surrey. She also used her training and experience, especially in the media world, to provide a guiding influence to many of the sometimes temperamental or nervous sports stars contracted to the company while George was general manager.

Roberto de Vicenzo shares his delight at winning the 1967 Open with George Carr and golf manager, Eric Hays

In the tradition established both by Albert Burden for Dunlop, and by the Slazenger management for many years, George gave freely of his time to outside, mainly industry-related activities. Or, as *Golf Illustrated* put it when reporting his retirement, 'outside office hours he officiated on numerous committees for the furtherance of sport'. These included the Golf Ball Manufacturers Association, the British Sports Council, the Golf Foundation, the British Professional Golf Association, and as President of the Federation of British Manufacturers of Sports and Games. He certainly deserved the title bestowed on him of Dunlop's 'Mr. Sport' during the decade when his lifelong love of all forms of sport was so effectively combined with his management of the business he led through its most successful period up to that time. However, enthusiasm isn't everything and apparently his rugby and cricket prowess didn't extend to his skill on the golf course. Several of his colleagues have recalled that on the occasion of a pro-am tournament when he was paired with Roberto de Vicenzo, the 1967 Open Champion, that great player, reflecting on George's performance, observed that it was fortunate that he had his own golf ball factory.

In fact, before he retired in 1972 he would have two factories. Then the brand new, purpose-built Normanton plant, located in the same triangle south of Leeds as Horbury and Barnsley, would add significantly to the company's production capacity. The decision to make that major investment could well have been influenced by the view that if anything the growth rate of sport in general, and golf in particular, as a multi-million dollar business had accelerated throughout George Carr's ten years at Allington House. This was certainly true in the case of the sports where Dunlop (and Slazenger) were most heavily involved, which covered not only golf but also tennis, squash and cricket.

Rod Laver and Pat Hughes discussing the Maxply at Allington House in 1965

When Rod Laver won his first Grand Slam, in 1962, the Wimbledon presentation was made by Her Majesty the Queen, which remains only the second occasion since the end of the war when the sovereign has handed the famous trophies to the champion. The prizes that day were miniatures of the Challenge Cup and the Renshaw Cup. On that occasion they were not accompanied by a cheque but when, as a professional, he won his next Wimbledon title, in his second Grand Slam year of 1968, the cups were accompanied by a cheque for £2,000. That wasn't an inconsiderable sum at the time but by the time George retired four years later it had more than doubled, and would reach five figures shortly after. In 2002 first round losers received over £9,000.

Bretton Priestley and Tony Carter 'talking squash' with Jonah Barrington, Peter Stokes and David Brazier

On the golf course, in 1963, Arnold Palmer, who George would sign in the same year to play Dunlop clubs in Europe, became the first player to win $100,000 on the US tour, but only seven years later Jack Nicklaus was the first to $1 million. And during this period British golf was electrified by having its own champion in Tony Jacklin (a '65' player) who followed up his British Open victory at Royal Lytham in 1969 with his 1970 triumph in the US Open and was a member of the 1969 Ryder Cup team that drew 16-16 with the USA at Royal Birkdale.

Cricket was given a huge boost by the expansion of the one day game, including the introduction of the Sunday League in 1969, with its 2 p.m. start because of the Sunday Observance Act, and by the agreement to allow the counties to sign one foreign player. During the second half of the 1960s squash began to rapidly increase its popularity, which was further boosted by the commercial development of the previously very limited number of courts available for the thousands of new players. Spectator and TV access to the game was significantly improved by the 1971 introduction of glass walls. Dunlop, driven by its squash manager, Bretton Priestley, was heavily involved in the development of the game and enjoyed a close association with the six times Open Champion, Jonah Barrington. The effect on squash racket production at Waltham Abbey was to increase the weekly output from 300 to 3000.

The biggest sporting event in the UK during this period was the 1966 Soccer World Cup, which featured Slazenger balls, but was only one of the many occasions which contributed to the enormous visibility then enjoyed by the Dunlop and Slazenger brands. '65' golf balls were consistently dominant in European golf tournaments, but it was Wimbledon that provided the strongest evidence of the company's strength at that time. In addition to the ever present Slazenger balls, Dunlop sports shoes, with the 'Green Flash' continuing to be the choice of the majority of the competitors, and Dunlop and Slazenger rackets maintained their 23-year run of appearing in every men's final since 1951. During George Carr's ten years they were in the hands of the winner eight times and on seven occasions were used by both finalists. Overall more than 60% of the total competitors each year were using the rackets made either at Waltham Abbey or Horbury, and, almost inevitably, this resulted in players using the company's rackets accumulating more than 50 Grand Slam singles titles between 1962 and 1972.

This powerful factor of brand visibility, generally associated with leading players appearing in the major events around the world in a range of sports, but especially golf and tennis, was consolidating a dominant presence in the UK and also increasing the Dunlop and Slazenger strength in the majority of their overseas markets. However, what was more important at this

The 'massed brands' of ISC on the front cover of a 1969 brochure

stage in securing, and growing from that position was the attention now required to making sure that the perceived potential from combining the resources of the two previously separate companies was fully developed. It was to be George Carr's priority responsibility to make this happen and, at the same time, keep in mind that the Dunlop board had asked him 'to keep an eye on Slazenger' rather than completely absorb it within the Dunlop environment.

For many years within Dunlop there had been a perception that the sports business was primarily a glamorous PR activity not over-burdened with the need to be particularly profitable. Whether or not that was true – and the reputations of Messrs. Burden, Frank Smith and Jack Morton don't

Albert Johnson, who retired from the Horbury factory in 1966 after spending 54 years making tennis rackets

fit comfortably with that assessment – the structure of the Dunlop accounts tended to obscure the real profitability, or otherwise, of all the individual product divisions. However, George Carr was quite clear on this subject. What today would be regarded as his 'mission statement' was his stated determination to make sure that the Sports Company, and later International Sports Company were profitable and would be run as businesses, and not mainly as promotional vehicles for the Dunlop brand.

The formation of International Sports Company (ISC) on 1st January, 1964 after a year's preparatory work driven mainly by Frank Smith and George Carr, was not only one of the key moments in the history of Dunlop Slazenger but also gave George, its director and general manager, the structure that allowed him both to maximise the combined resources of the two companies and, at the same time to apply his profit-based approach to their future deployment and development.

The philosophy of ISC's structure, which was to be regarded within the Dunlop Group as confidential, was that it was purely a 'background' organisation and that the outside world would continue to see the marketing emphasis being placed on the individual brand names. This focus on brands, or 'famous names' as described in ISC's marketing department, was sensibly not seen as leading to automatic success, not least because their maturity wouldn't have an altogether obvious association with an organisation in the forefront of progress, but it was believed that 'in sport they represent established tradition and customer acceptance'. The histories and achievements of Ayres, Sykes, Gradidge and F. A. Davis were mentioned to substantiate the element of tradition within the new organisation but it was immediately made clear they had no place, as operating units, in this structure. Having recalled the history that, in the case of Ayres, reached as far back as Waterloo, the more immediate importance of what ISC represented was described as a group that 'embodies all the latest raw material, production and design knowledge, stemming from an international research and development organisation with its products contributing in a very marked way to the development of international sport, which is such a feature of the world today'. The strength of its steadily expanding export operation was seen as highly relevant to that claim and the platform for future success was based on the group's 'combination of long tradition and ultra-modern technical development, probably unique in the world of sports goods manufacture'.

Both Dunlop Sports Company and Slazenger maintained their separate head offices and marketing operations, as did Letters, Sealey and Litesome. The real consolidation and effectiveness of the ISC concept revolved around the rationalisation of the manufacturing, development and other main support functions. The bulk of production was concentrated in four main plants. Within the giant tyre plant at Speke, ISC now occupied a virtually self-sufficient $2^{1}/4$-acre area devoted entirely to all the golf balls sold by Dunlop and Slazenger, and the $1^{3}/4$-acre Barnsley plant produced all the tennis balls for the group. In both cases significantly different specifications were used for the two brands. The 5-acre site at Waltham Abbey continued as a source for Dunlop rackets and strings with the Maxply still very much the lead product, while the much larger $9^{1}/2$-acre site at Horbury, as it had done throughout its Sykes and Slazenger history, turned out a very wide range of mainly Slazenger branded wood and leather products for cricket, tennis, golf and hockey plus a range of larger balls for soccer, basketball netball and volleyballs, punch balls, medicine balls, table tennis bats and the archery range bequeathed by Ayres but by now branded Slazenger.

The smaller, specialist factories producing Dunlop golf clubs (Letters in Glasgow), fishing hooks and rods (Sealeys in Redditch) and sportswear (Litesome in Keighley) continued as before and were joined in 1968 by a

Metal badminton rackets at Carlton's Saffron Walden plant

company that would outlive them all as part of the Dunlop Slazenger group – indeed the brand is still very much alive in the 21st century – Carlton.

Bill Carlton, a brilliant production engineer employed by the Ford Motor Company and a keen badminton player, decided to form his own company to make precision engineering products. He had also decided to develop his own idea of a one-shot injection moulded plastic shuttlecock, which he believed would be an attractive alternative to the traditional, and much more expensive product made from a framework of natural feathers. After the successful completion of the development process, sales and production increased steadily over the next ten years from the company's first factory in Hornchurch, which didn't have any space for further expansion. In 1960 a new factory was built at Saffron Walden and a wider range of products introduced, including a revolutionary steel shafted badminton racket, which offered advantages over the conventional wooden product and, again, proved very popular.

By 1968 annual production included 11 million shuttlecocks and 100,000 rackets and the company's success had caught the attention of George Carr, who had not only noted the in-roads being made into the badminton market but was also concerned that Carlton's next move, based on their engineering expertise and success with steel shafts, could be into the tennis and squash sectors. His concern was fully justified by the first appearance of metal rackets at Wimbledon in 1969, when they were used by nearly fifty competitors but, by that time, accompanied by his finance director, Tom Clarke, he had been to Saffron Walden to negotiate the purchase of the business. The deal was done there and then, in

Bill Carlton's office, and the cheque, for £100,000, handed over. Bill, himself, retired shortly afterwards from active involvement in the business but Carlton has continued to play a major role in the ISC and Dunlop Slazenger story, not only as the main badminton brand but also as a rich source of innovative engineering development, which was to prove immensely valuable across the whole group. And, in a completely different vein, management of the largely stand-alone Carlton business was an important element in developing the careers of several key ISC managers, notably Peter Wycherley, Ray Houghton, Roy Sherwin and Gordon Baird.

The Carlton engineering resource was a significant addition to ISC's Group Technical Development Department, originally established at Speke by Denis Osborne and later led by Bob Haines from Barnsley with golf ball development continuing at Speke. This particular group function did fulfil a genuinely international role with a liaison officer at Speke controlling a worldwide flow of technical information between not only ISC's own plants but also with all the other Dunlop Group factories with sports manufacturing operations. The other main ISC group functions were based at Horbury and covered manufacturing, productivity, personnel, purchasing, engineering development, distribution and a central export department.

The ISC board, with George as director and general manager, was a compact but strong mix of skills and experience. The finance director, Tom Clarke, and works director, Jack Ellis, were both from Slazenger, as was 'Buzzer' Hadingham, the marketing director for Slazenger. The team was completed by Tony Carter, as the Dunlop marketing director. George and 'Buzzer' brought considerable experience of senior management and marketing, including export, Jack Ellis had been the Slazenger managing-director in South Africa before returning to run Horbury. Tony Carter, who had trained as an accountant after military service with the Commandos and 2nd Parachute Brigade, joined Dunlop in 1951 and spent eight years in Malaya as chief accountant of Dunlop Malayan Estates before returning to London as P.A. to Donald Hawkins, then the main board director responsible for the consumer product companies. He moved to the Sports Company in 1963 to take part in the planning of ISC and would later follow the path taken by previous senior Sports Company Managers – Frank Smith, Jack Morton and George Vaughan – to join Semtex in 1973, as marketing director.

When it was formed in 1964 the total sales of the ISC group companies were just under £7 million, which included export business of £2.6 million and sales of £1 million by the overseas Slazenger companies. The operating profit was just over £400,000. By the time George Carr retired at the end of 1972 total sales had more than doubled to over £16 million, export sales had risen to nearly £6 million and sales by the overseas companies had passed the £4 million mark. Operating profit had risen even more rapidly to well over £2 million, which would have been at least in part due to an impressive productivity record, which showed an increase of only 13% in the numbers employed in the group (from 3,000 to 3,400) generating a sales increase of 128%. Sales had been boosted by the acquisition of Carlton, but had to absorb the loss of golf ball sales due to the opening of plants in South Africa in 1965 and New Zealand a year later. Also the 1969 sale of the Sealeys fishing tackle business.

These results clearly indicate the scale of ISC's success during this period. However, it has been interesting to learn from one of its directors that the first title chosen for the new structure was 'International Sports Corporation', which reflected the initial thinking that it would indeed be the 'truly international operation' that it would later claim it had become. The fact that it was prevented from having the worldwide responsibility for the management of all the sports operations within the Dunlop Group was mainly due to the unwillingness, at that critical moment, of the main overseas subsidiary companies to lose the local control of what they regarded as their own sports divisions. The largest of these companies were operating their own tennis and golf ball plants and managed their local sales and distribution operations, which would have handled a high proportion of the UK-made products included in ISC's export sales, notably the racket range, golf clubs and many accessory lines.

There's absolutely no doubt good relationships existed between ISC and these overseas companies, especially in the area of technical exchange and co-operation, but the decision-making responsibility for the key investments in their sports operations remained with the territory management, subject only to the approval of the London-based Overseas Division, and not to that of ISC. Within the framework of this structure, funding decisions were made to set up a number of the low volume ball plants around the world, servicing tiny, local markets, which contributed to the reduction of the off-take from the UK highlighted in the ISC brochure. It could also, and did create situations where limited availability of funds in a major overseas market, like the USA, understandably forced local management to prioritise their investment towards their key, tyre plants. And, perhaps not surprisingly in these circumstances, another factor within this approach to international marketing was ISC's determination to be the only sports business with an export department. It's easy to understand that George Carr and his board would have been anxious not to allow further inroads into their UK output figures, but it did mean that distributors in markets like Bermuda, the Caribbean and South America were obliged to buy their golf

ISC's Bob Haines is in the centre of this 1965 picture of the combined technical teams from the Speke, Barnsley and Horbury factories

and tennis balls only from the UK, and not from the much closer sources in the USA. And neither Germany nor France, both with substantial tennis ball plants, could ship product to any other European country.

The same territorial restriction applied to the expanding sports division of Dunlop Japan and while it was perfectly sensible to ensure that all these separate operations weren't competing against each other in world markets, the benefit of hindsight provides the opportunity to wonder just how much stronger the Dunlop and Slazenger brands could have become on the worldwide sports stage if, in 1964, ISC had been given the authority to truly 'rule the world' by co-ordinating and directing all the considerable sports resources then available within the Dunlop Group. In this context it's also worth remembering that not only the ISC board, but also a large number of its managers had accumulated very many years of experience in the sports equipment market both in the UK and in virtually every country where racket sports, golf, cricket, table tennis, hockey, soccer, rugby and all the other games the company supplied had been growing so rapidly since the war. That was only rarely the situation in terms of management direction in the sports divisions of the Group's overseas and mainly tyre operations.

Maybe it would be best to note the comment on this subject in an extract from a Strategy Review carried out by the parent Dunlop company in 1983 when it was reviewing its options in relation to the extreme difficulties then being experienced in the European tyre operations. In a section devoted to an analysis of the company's overall strengths and weaknesses, and under the heading 'Structure', it was indicated that one problem had been that 'conflict between geographical and product management has sometimes inhibited progress'. Less than two years later, and as part of the restructuring programme carried out by Sir Michael Edwardes, ISC was superseded by Dunlop Slazenger Limited as the organisation responsible for all sports operations throughout the world.

Putting aside, at least for the moment, the 'what might have been' debate about the longer term implications of ISC's 'international' remit being only partially implemented in 1964, as the earlier analysis of its results have shown, George Carr and his team fashioned a much stronger and more efficient sports business. It became one of the largest divisions within the Dunlop Group, outside the core tyre business, and certainly put paid to the notion that selling golf and tennis products provided more pleasure than profit.

At this stage the emphasis on the large portfolio of brands, which was enlarged by Dunlop becoming the distributor of the Fred Perry range of golf and tennis clothing and by Slazenger in Canada acquiring the Raymond Lanctot ski equipment business, was a much more appropriate approach to the market than it would later become. Apart from the key factor that Dunlop and Slazenger should continue to be seen as competitors for mainly golf and racket business, the other main ISC brands – Carlton, Sealey, Litesome and Letters – were product and market specific. In promotional terms this policy, at that time, was both affordable and effective but it would come under severe pressure from the late 1970s onwards when even the reduced number of main brands – Dunlop, Slazenger and Maxfli – had to combat the impact of massively increased competitor spending with a level of funding probably only adequate to properly support just one of those brands.

The Dunlop product policy continued to be firmly anchored on the huge strengths of the Maxply brand across the range of tennis, squash and badminton rackets, and on the '65' golf ball, in both cases by now the flagship products for more than 30 years. Of course, both had been regularly upgraded and re-launched on the back of the consistent strength and excellence of the Dunlop technical and development resources at Speke and Waltham Abbey, and now enhanced by ISC's central development operation at Horbury.

Appropriately 1965 was the year chosen to launch the latest, Mark V version of the '65', which would have been Sammy Ball's last project as it was also his retirement date, 46 years after joining the company at Fort Dunlop. Under the headline 'Dunlop Sports Company introduces latest edition of the world's most famous golf ball' the *Dunlop Gazette* listed the main features of this wound product as its new cover material of TPI (Transpolyisoprene), a synthetic balata supplied by a special plant at Fort Dunlop, the introduction of polyurethane paint to give a longer last-

Sammy Ball in 1965, the year he retired after 46 years with the company

Bob Letters with the Dunlop Japan team he helped to start production of Maxfli golf clubs in Kobe in 1965

Jimmy Connors

John McEnroe

ing whiteness to the cover and the first use of 'Polypower' thread in the winding process. The life of the TPI cover would be shortened by the 1967 introduction of Dupont's synthetic thermoplastic resin, later to be named 'Surlyn' and first used on Ram balls.

The range of golf clubs had been steadily developed in conjunction with the Letters brothers and was powerfully endorsed by Peter Thomson, Bob Charles, Arnold Palmer, Roberto de Vicenzo, Tony Jacklin – the rising star signed by Dunlop before his British and US Open triumphs – and, for the ladies clubs, Jessie Valentine. The same issue of the *Gazette* that featured the new '65' carried an article about Bob Letters's eight week stay in Japan to set up club production in Kobe though the accompanying photograph betrayed less than 100% brand co-ordination by showing that the new lines would be branded 'Maxfli' in Japan. Throughout this period Maxfli was also the lead brand in the USA, mainly because production from Buffalo and Westminster was entirely in the larger, 1.68" ball, while the '65' continued at Speke only in the 1.62" size.

The main change in the total ISC product line during the 1960s and early 1970s was not in the equipment sector. A 1971 feature in the *Gazette* observed that 'we live in an increasingly clothes-conscious age' and that a particular manifestation of this trend to dress more stylishly was the urge to have special clothing for sporting activities. Sports shoe manufacturers, like Adidas, were in the early days of the design revolution that would mean the end of the dominance enjoyed by the 'Green Flash' in the tennis market and that whole process would be hugely accelerated by Nike and Reebok from the early 1970s onwards. 'Serious games players are now expected to dress the part' said the *Gazette* and was pleased to report that the forward-looking ISC was very conscious of these changes. Slazenger had led the way from the early 1960s with an initial emphasis on golf, represented most visibly by the panther badged sweater, and later expanding the line across racket sports and casual wear and so comprehensively it included a 'socklet with a bobble to prevent it slipping inside the tennis shoe allowing the wearer to sunburn right down to the shoe-line'. Dunlop distributed the mainly tennis range of Fred Perry clothing, which was worn by two-thirds of the competitors at the 1970 Wimbledon championships, and Litesome,

Left to right George Carr, Vaughn Clay, Dick Birch and Paul MacDonald review North American operations

the only one of the three clothing operations to manufacture their products, also offered a wide range but with an emphasis on football and pioneering development work on tracksuits.

During this period Dunlop Footwear, with its traditional strength in the supply of protective and industrial footwear, sports shoes and slippers through the shoe trade distribution network of wholesalers and multiples, quite deliberately broadened its product line away from what was becoming an increasingly overcrowded sports sector about to begin the process of developing direct supply lines to specialist retailers. The relatively new brands that would become so dominant, notably Adidas, Puma, Nike and Reebok, were apparently able to invest much more heavily than Dunlop in promoting their new products, especially in securing player endorsements. This was a key consideration in shaping what proved to be the Footwear company's consistently profitable approach at this time based mainly on using its existing shoe trade connections more effectively.

As the 1960s gave way to the 1970s all the outward signs for ISC were very positive. Not only were the long-established lead products for the main brands still dominant in many world markets, and being used by a very high proportion of the leading international players, but also public demand had driven sales and profits steadily upwards. The apparel ranges had substantially widened the total product line and the 1972 addition of 'Swingball', a tennis practice game franchised from South Africa, would very quickly add another £3 million to annual sales.

A consistently successful element of the business was the growth of export sales. The histories of both Dunlop and the Slazenger companies has shown that from their very earliest beginnings they had been quick to recognise the potential that existed for sales of sports equipment in most overseas countries. Undaunted by the prospect of the long and difficult journeys then involved they used a combination of agents, distributors and, when the market was large enough, their own locally established operations – often with manufacturing facilities – to build a formidable worldwide sales and distribution network.

The North American example of this approach combined a mainly Slazenger-led business in Canada, which had its origins in the Toronto-based company established by Henry Sykes immediately after the end of the first world war, and the mainly Dunlop sports operations in USA, which had been initially established with ball production in the Buffalo tyre plant and were subsequently developed, from the 1960s onwards, from two custom-built plants in South Carolina and Georgia. During this period the Canadian Slazenger business was also responsible for distribution in the USA, which operated from Philadelphia. In 1967 this combination of the ISC-managed Slazenger business, Dunlop Tire and Rubber's Sports Division and the efforts of the UK-based Dunlop and Slazenger export sales teams achieved, as reported by the *Dunlop Gazette*, 'A record year for Dunlop Sports Group in North America'. That headline didn't acknowledge the considerable Slazenger contribution to that result but George Carr's comments did include a reference to that brand as well as to the growth of UK-made tennis and golf equipment, the increase of soccer sales in the wake of the 1966 World Cup, the range expansion provided by Sealeys fishing tackle and Lanctot ski equipment and the sales growth of the locally made golf balls, including the 1.68" Maxfli which had become 'the equal top seller in the US market'. At the American Sports Trade Exhibition that year, the local management, which included a vice-president (Vaughn Clay), an assistant vice-president (Paul MacDonald) and a Canadian president (Dick Birch) were joined by 'six top British sales executives'.

Notwithstanding these organisational considerations, ISC was the main force behind the growth of export sales, or 'Exporting Sport' as the *Gazette* reported in 1969 when reviewing the 'sunrise to sunset' spread of the company's sports products around the world, including 'to the remotest specks on the map'. Proper tribute was paid in this article to not only the efforts of

The presentation ceremony at Horbury for the 1971 Queen's Award

much travelled senior managers like George Carr, Tony Carter and 'Buzzer' Hadingham but also to the perpetually-travelling export sales managers like Bert Allam for Dunlop, Bob Boomer for Slazenger and Len Thompson for Dunlop Foorwear. Mention was also made of the tireless work of Victor Barna, still promoting both table tennis and Dunlop, and another leading table tennis exponent, Mickey Thornhill, who had represented England fifty times in international matches, and had become the Dunlop assistant export manager.

Official recognition of these export achievements, always such an important factor within the total UK economy, as well as for ISC, came in 1971. The New Year's Honours List included the award of the OBE to 'Buzzer' Hadingham 'For services to export'. He had been the driving force behind his company's overseas business virtually since joining the export department at Laurence Pountney Hill in 1933 and since 1949, when he was appointed export manager, had increased sales from £500,000 to nearly £3 million – which accounted for nearly half the total Slazenger turnover.

This award for an outstanding individual achievement was followed later in the same year by ISC receiving The Queen's Award to Industry, which was 'Cognisant of the outstanding achievements as manifested in the furtherance and increase of the Export Trade of Our United Kingdom of Great Britain and Northern Ireland, our Channel Islands and Our Island of Man'. The main ceremony took place at Horbury in April when Brigadier K. Hargreaves, the Lord Lieutenant of the West Riding of Yorkshire, handed the award to George Carr in the presence of a number of distinguished guests, including representatives of the Golf Foundation and Lawn Tennis Federation, the representative of the Dunlop main board – Dan Flunder, and the golf professionals – Peter Alliss and Jessie Valentine, who, for a number of years, had been closely associated with Slazenger and Dunlop respectively. In his acceptance speech George Carr acknowledged that this very special occasion was not only a reflection of recent successes but also recognised the company's consistent achievements in this highly competitive market. He was also able to report that 1971 exports were running 14% higher than the previous year when they had reached a record £5 million. While Horbury was the scene of the main, and very splendid award ceremony, George made sure that everybody in the business shared in this notable success by touring the country to show the award to employees at Keighley (Litesome), Saffron

George Carr, with ISC employees at Horbury, flourishes the Queen's Award

Walden (Carlton), Glasgow (Letters), the two head offices at Croydon and Allington House and the main factories at Barnsley, Speke and Waltham Abbey.

The following year ISC won a further major award when it received

Dunlop's own Baillieu Trophy (named after the former chairman, Lord Baillieu), which was given to a division or department within the worldwide group to have shown 'Exceptional endeavour in promoting and improving the competitiveness of the company'. Unquestionably this was further recognition of the company's outstanding export record and George Carr, when receiving the trophy from Sir Reay Geddes, would have been the first to acknowledge all 3000 ISC employees could share in this success. They, in turn, would have been quick to salute the leadership of the man who chose business rather than sports broadcasting as his career, and who was to retire at the end of that year.

At the same time that ISC was enjoying these tangible rewards for its successes its management was aware of signs that more difficult days lay ahead. However, it's doubtful if anyone could have foreseen the extent of the changes and pressures that would confront the business during the next ten years. George Carr, himself, had been quick to see that the development of steel racket fames was a potential threat to the dominance of Maxply. That had been a major factor in his pursuit of Carlton but had not stopped him from predicting, as early as 1967, that wooden rackets in general would face a severe threat from new technologies. By the time he retired proof positive of this trend had become highly visible at the major tennis tournaments. Nearly 100 competitors at the 1971 and 1972 Wimbledon championships were using steel frames and 1973 saw the first handful of graphite rackets. The fact that wooden rackets still accounted for 80% of those used that year – and 78% of those were Dunlop or Slazenger – could well have encouraged a complacency that would be rudely shaken and all too quickly.

However, it's also very clear that ISC were aware of the rapidly developing racket manufacturing capability in the Far East, which, for some time, had been seen as a potential source for cheaper frames unlikely to seriously threaten the UK capacity at Horbury and Waltham Abbey. The original team from Waltham Abbey of Bill Evans and Alun Morgan, which had initially looked at India and Pakistan racket production, had, by the mid 1960s, moved on to also look at Japan, and especially Taiwan, and had been expanded to include a North American representation of Tony Wells for Dunlop and Dick Birch and Saul Chavkin for Slazenger. ISC's own steel frames first appeared in 1970, at mid price points, and three years later the 'Slazenger Plus' with Accles & Pollock steel and used by Mark Cox, came very close to establishing an extremely strong market position. However, the belief that in the long run wooden fames would prevail encouraged substantial investment well into the 1970s to improve the efficiency of the traditional production methods at both plants. In the same year (1973) that saw the first moulded carbon fibre frames the *Dunlop News* (successor to the *Dunlop Gazette*) report on the arrival of an 'Austrian Giant at Waltham Abbey' described the installation of a 40 feet long and 20 feet wide sanding machine that would take over the work of the 12 men who had been sanding wooden frames. The new machine was designed to eliminate the variations that occurred in what had been an unpleasantly dirty and sometimes dangerous hand process and would produce a much improved product at 300 frames per hour.

A more immediate and dramatic change had hit the world of golf balls. In 1967 an American, Jim Bartsch, issued a patent for a one-piece ball, which, itself, only achieved limited success, but its technology paved the way for the two-piece ball, first sold by Spalding in 1971, and which, when combined

A special window display at Dunlop House in St. James's to celebrate Tony Jacklin's victories at the 1969 Open and 1970 US Open

ELIZABETH THE SECOND,

by the Grace of God of the United Kingdom of Great Britain and Northern Ireland and of Our other

Realms and Territories Queen Defender of the Faith, to

INTERNATIONAL SPORTS COMPANY LIMITED

Greeting !

We being cognisant of the outstanding achievements of the said body as manifested in the further-

ance and increase of the Export Trade of Our United Kingdom of Great Britain and Northern Ireland,

Our Channel Islands and Our Island of Man and being desirous of showing Our Royal Favour do

hereby confer upon it

THE QUEEN'S AWARD TO INDUSTRY

for a period of five years from the twenty-first day of April 1971 until the twentieth day of April 1976

and do hereby give permission for the authorised flag of the said Award to be flown during that

time by the said body and for the device thereof to be displayed upon letters and communications of

the said body and upon its packages and goods and in other ways in the manner authorised by Our

Warrant of the thirtieth day of November 1965 as amended by Our Warrant of the twenty-ninth

day of March 1971.

And We do further hereby authorise the said body during the five years of the currency of this Our

Award further to use and display in like manner the flags and devices of any former such Awards by

it received.

Given at Our Court at St. James's under Our Royal Sign Manual this twenty-first day of April in the

year of Our Lord 1971 in the Twentieth year of Our Reign.

By the Sovereign's Command

The citation for the Queen's Award, signed by Edward Heath

with DuPont's Surlyn cover, would account for 80% of all balls made. At the start of this revolutionary period, when the balata-covered three-piece ball was still predominant, ISC's production at Speke had been steadily increasing to 25,000 dozen per week, but even then had been insufficient to meet demand. Deteriorating industrial relations at the Merseyside plant worked against further investment there, which led to the 1972 opening of the custom built Normanton factory, which was able to add another 15,000 dozen to ISC's UK output. In the same year both plants switched to the Surlyn cover but this coincided with the virtually immediate impact of this much more durable material on total market demand. It's possible to see some similarity in this situation with the introduction of radial tyres in the 1950s, which was to have such damaging consequences to the world's tyre makers, including Dunlop, but the long term effect on ball sales was much less damaging because golf continued to attract more and more players for most of the next thirty years.

However, the immediate impact on ISC's golf ball production in the UK was dramatic. The zero stock position quickly changed to one of surplus capacity – but this clearly didn't deter the Overseas Division of the Dunlop Group sanctioning new ball plants in South Africa and Malaysia. Among the many problems that would confront George Carr's successor, Findlay Picken, two of the most difficult would be how to deal with this sudden swing from shortage to surplus golf ball production, and, as already seen, the consequences of the decline in sales of wooden rackets that would gather momentum from the mid 1970s.

The latter years of George Carr's time at the helm of ISC saw the departure of several senior managers, who had played key roles in the development of the Dunlop sports business from the very earliest days. Three of them, Sammy Ball, Pat Hughes and Victor Barna, were also internationally known and respected as individuals who had made very significant contributions to the development of the different sports that had attracted most of their attention and enthusiasm. Sammy, who developed and regularly improved the legendary '65', had been the driving force behind the company's rise to golf ball leadership for nearly forty years prior to his retirement in 1965 and his contribution to the overall development of ball technology – mainly for golf but for most other games requiring a 'round object' – is frequently acknowledged by sports historians. As Sammy Ball had been at the heart of the company's golf business, so Pat Hughes, who retired in 1968, had, during almost exactly the same forty years, taken the fledgling racket business from near obscurity to a dominant international position, and, in the process, made Maxply the most famous racket ever produced. As a player he had been supreme on the doubles court and it seemed appropriate that his successor as Dunlop tennis manager was Bob Howe, an Australian who was also regarded as one of the world's very best exponents of doubles play, and who maintained an active connection with the company well into the 21st century.

A sudden loss, in 1972, was the death of Victor Barna while on one of his frequent overseas tours – on this occasion to South America. It's impossible to find any other leading international sportsman more closely identified with the game he had chosen. As a player he is recorded in the *Oxford Companion to Sports and Games* as 'The greatest of all, but he is equally well remembered for his achievements in popularising table tennis all over the world, and, by his Dunlop contemporaries, for his rare combination of outstanding product development and marketing skills'.

Pat Hughes would have been the first to salute another individual, Charles Selby, who retired in 1967 as the production superintendent at Waltham Abbey, having been involved in racket manufacturing for 46 years. He had seen the evolution of the Essex plant from the days when individual craftsmen made each racket from start to finish, and had been one of the small team, which included Pat Hughes, that had created the original Maxply design. Another key member of ISC's production management team, George Mallett, had also died suddenly in 1968. As the Sports Company's production manager at Speke when Dunlop took over the factory in 1946, he played a major role in re-establishing golf and tennis ball manufacturing during the difficult period immediately after the war and went on, as works manager, to work closely with Sammy Ball and Denis Osborne to expand the early trickle of balls to the levels of output that underpinned the company's post-war growth and success. Like Denis he had also contributed to the development of technical co-operation with the Overseas Division's ball factories, including an important visit in 1956 to the USA and Canada, which, apart from identifying numerous areas for mutually beneficial action, was remarkable for the fact that he was allowed to closely inspect Penn's tennis ball production line in Pittsburg and Spalding's golf ball operation in Canada. In the case of Penn – and this makes even more remarkable reading nearly fifty years later – he reported that he advised them how to significantly reduce the melton cloth waste figures, and they, in turn, were happy to give him valuable pointers on how to improve the control of direct and indirect labour costs. At that time Penn, who also made Wilson's balls, had a 57% share of the 600,000 dozen per annum USA market so it's possible they felt they could be helpful to their visitor from the UK, who was representing a competitor with only a 9% share. His report also mentions that Buffalo's annual golf ball output at the time of 500,000 dozen represented a 17% market share, which the local management felt could be increased by a full point if the Speke-made American-size ball could be 'produced with the requisite hard feel or click' demanded by USA golfers.

So, in 1972, George Carr followed these distinguished and long-serving members of the Dunlop sports team as he started what proved to be a very happy and extremely active retirement shared with an equally active wife, who has been very helpful in providing valuable archive material about the successful and eventful 'Carr years'. It's absolutely no reflection on George himself, nor on his successor, Findlay Picken, that his departure signalled the start of what proved to be the most turbulent and difficult period for the

1972 and George Carr receives the
Baillieu Trophy from Sir Reay Geddes

Dunlop Slazenger business since its early beginnings one hundred years previously.

When, in 1973, Findlay Picken succeeded George Carr as General Manager of ISC the company that had been set up ten years previously to co-ordinate at least part of the Dunlop Group's sports interests would have another ten years of life. It would be superseded by the enlarged Dunlop Slazenger organisation, which would, at last, mean that all the sports businesses still owned by the Group would operate on that 'truly international basis'.

At the start of this second decade in the history of ISC, it is doubtful if anyone in the business, or, for that matter, anywhere else in the sports equipment industry, could have imagined the speed and scale of the changes to come. This would be particularly true in relation to the technological advances that would have an enormous impact on so many key products, some of which had been largely unchanged in technical terms for fifty years or more. Possibly the most striking example was the demise of the wooden racket, which, in 1973, was still hardly challenged but within little more than ten years would virtually disappear. For ISC, and later, briefly for Dunlop Slazenger, there would be the additional and crucial factor of the fall-out from the decline in the fortunes of the parent Dunlop company. And for all industries worldwide there would be the enormous difficulties caused by rocketing oil prices and spiralling inflation – with the UK also having to cope with a testing period that included deteriorating industrial relations and a three day working week.

Bearing in mind that ISC was a wholly-owned subsidiary of Dunlop Limited, it's obvious that the fortunes of the parent, in good and bad times, would directly affect its sports operation. The evolution from a tiny golf ball plant in the corner of a Birmingham tyre factory to the Dunlop Slazenger 'giant' of the sports equipment world would not have been possible without the financial, technical and management resources of a group that by the start of the 1970s, and as it entered a Union with Pirelli, was the 39th largest company in the world outside the USA, operating 130 factories in 22 countries and employing well over 100,000 people – of whom 56,000 were located in the UK. Again, in little more than ten years those employee numbers would be halved and by 1985 most of Dunlop would be split between Sumitomo Rubber Industries tyre-making and BTR's control of the rest. Both the new owners would retain the name of the company founded nearly a hundred years earlier and, as James McMillan noted in *The Dunlop Story*, 'both groups have high admiration for the name Dunlop – for millions it has a magic ring'.

Into what would become this maelstrom of change for ISC, both in the marketplace and for its owner, stepped Findlay Picken, at the age of 42. Like his post-war predecessors, Frank Smith, Jack Morton and George Carr, he had gained his considerable management experience with Dunlop. A Scot and an accountant, Findlay had joined the Dunlop-owned India Tyres at Inchinnan in 1955. He returned to that company four years later as chief accountant after overseas appointments in South Africa and Singapore, and, back in the UK, with Bintex (part of the Dunlopillo division based in Harrogate) and at the Hose division. After three years at Inchinnan there were shorter spells working with Campbell Fraser (later to become manag-

Findlay Picken

ing-director and then Chairman of Dunlop) and at Stanford University in California before, in 1964, moving to the Metalastik division in Leicester, again as chief accountant. Metalastik was a well-known engineering business specialising in the highly complicated process of bonding rubber to metal, which had a multitude of industrial uses but was an especially important element of the component supply sector for the motor industry. His final appointment before moving to ISC was as general manager of National Tyre Service, another wholly-owned subsidiary, which was the Group's retail and distribution chain with over 400 outlets. He would return to National Tyre Service after leaving ISC in 1984 and remain as its managing-director during periods of subsequent ownership by Michelin and Continental Tyre. As a low handicap golfer he was never likely to be on the receiving end of any comments similar to Roberto de Vicenzo's observation about George Carr being fortunate to have his own golf ball factory, and it was very appropriate that after retiring from National Tyre he became chairman of the Golf Foundation, which has an excellent record of development work for the game in the UK, especially in providing encouragement for young players. To add a final Dunlop Slazenger touch his successor in that position was Ian Peacock, the former marketing director and chief executive of Slazenger.

Anne Rhymer and Susan Parr with their Barnsley colleague Royce Pridgeon at Hartwell to help the tennis ball start-up

Findlay would need all his training and experience of both UK and overseas operations to steer ISC through the 1970s and early 1980s. Like his predecessors he would have the benefit of widespread, senior level contacts throughout the Group and, despite the mounting difficulties confronting them, he was able to count on the consistent respect and support of the Dunlop main board. That support would prove absolutely vital in one particular area of the business and was ultimately of enormous value to the later development of the business during the period of BTR ownership. James McMillan has identified that despite the mainly tyre-related financial nightmare that had such a negative and restrictive effect on the whole of the Group, the company's research and development teams, both centrally and in the individual product divisions, continued to receive as much top level backing as was possible. In the case of ISC this would result in the development of hugely important, award-winning and radically new rackets and golf balls that would ensure the legacy of the '65' and Maxply years would not be lost.

The first year (1973) for the new general manager wasn't very different from what had gone before, though it would close with David Sealey succeeding Tony Carter as the Dunlop marketing director. Overseas Division opened their new golf ball factory in South Africa and two young ladies from the Barnsley factory – Ann Rhymer and Susan Parr – went with technical manger, Royce Pridgeon, to the USA company's plant at Hartwell in Georgia to help start up a tennis ball production line. At Wimbledon that year 151 competitors used Dunlop rackets and another 84 chose Slazenger, a combined 62% of the total entry. However, for the first time the steel frames that had accounted for around 18% of the total since 1969 were joined by just 11 composite frames. The Dunlop and Slazenger dominance at Wimbledon during most of the 1960s was maintained into the early 1970s by John Newcombe's wins in 1970 and 1971 and by Evonne Goolagong's success in

Swingers

'A couple of beauties' again, this time giving a boost to the 1973 launch of Swingball

1971. Jan Kodes won the 1973 men's title in an event seriously disrupted by a boycott by the Association of Tennis Professionals but the other three Grand Slams were taken for Slazenger by John Newcombe (Australian and US) and for Maxply by Ilie Nastase (French Open). The Slazenger Panther was very prominent on Tom Weiskopf's sweater as he won the Open at Troon and the same brand was on Colin Cowdrey's bat as he scored his 100th century.

Confirmation that in 1973 it was still very much 'business as usual' for ISC is provided by a number of reports in *Dunlop News*. These included the installation of the sanding machine at Waltham Abbey, and a successful press visit to the golf ball operation at Speke, with the emphasis there on 'the actual making of the Dunlop balls', the test 'gun' checking durability and performance, and new, fully-automated wrapping machines operating at 4000 balls per hour. There were also accounts of the progress being made to build up production at the new Normanton plant, 'which brought to eight the number of golf ball plants scattered around the world', two photo-shoots of the very photogenic young ladies from Barnsley sent to show their Hartwell counterparts how to put covers on tennis balls, and another showing a couple of bikini clad girls demonstrating how to play Swingball.

As the year drew to a close the newspaper showed the two leading ladies of the English Badminton world, Gillian Gilks and Margaret Beck, visiting Allington House, and the company's golf manger, Richard Brown, preparing for the 28th Masters tournament at the increasingly popular St. Pierre venue, near Chepstow. The most significant items of sports news appeared in the November issue, which reported that ISC's export sales for the first nine months of 1973 had increased by 20% over the previous year to hit a record £6.1 million. Findlay Picken commented that the main growth had come from Europe and North America and that the principal factor driving up the figures was the growing popularity of tennis.

This mix of news items would have been very similar to the pattern established for most years since the war, which would have consistently featured reports on new investments to improve the performance, quality and quantity of a product line that hadn't changed significantly during that same period. The newspaper regularly carried the adverts being used to promote the range – in 1973 the theme was 'Sport is our Game' – and, in the pre-Christmas issue encouraged employees to include 'Maxply' rackets, 'Fort' tennis balls, 'Maxply Fort' table tennis bats, 'Maxpower' golf clubs, '65' golf balls and 'Green Flash' tennis shoes when shopping for presents. Most of those products, apart from the war years, could have been on the Christmas list for nearly forty years.

A more ominous note also appears in the 1973 issues with headlines like

David Sealey and Billie Woodgates of Fred Perry Sportswear with badminton stars, Gillian Gilks and Margaret Beck, at Allington House in 1973

'Pirelli – what went wrong?' and 'Half year results – warning on profits'. A combination of adverse economic factors at home and abroad – raw material shortages and higher prices, high interest rates and disappointing trading results in major territories – were combining with the pressures related to the union with Pirelli and industrial disputes in some UK operations to distract attention from the very positive reaction that greeted the launch of the revolutionary run flat Denovo tyre. By the end of the year the *News* had temporarily shrunk to just four pages as a result of the fuel crisis and resultant three-day working week.

That Dunlop commitment to technical excellence, so well typified by the Denovo tyre, would eventually serve ISC very well, but an argument can be made that there were occasions when important, and sometimes groundbreaking, new ideas did not translate quickly enough into products ready for the marketplace. The process of making regular improvements to established premium products, like the 'Maxply', '65' and Slazenger's 'Challenge' racket had, before and after the war, been sufficient to maintain the strong Dunlop and Slazenger positions in the market, but it would not prevent serious damage to that position when new and existing competitors proved quicker to exploit radically new technologies. A crucially important factor with many of the new competitors in the racket sector was the fact they made early decisions to buy in their new products from outside suppliers, usually located in the Far East, which allowed them to concentrate their financial resources on promotional activities rather than either investment in the new manufacturing techniques, or the costly process of rationalising existing facilities. This scenario would bring enormous pressure to bear on the Dunlop and Slazenger racket ranges as ISC's finite resources were stretched to pay for promotion, new manufacturing equipment and, eventually, a rationalisation process that led to plant closure.

A 1973 advertisement for the Maxply squash racket featuring Geoff Hunt

Bearing in mind the combination of the growth of racket sports during the 1960s and 1970s, their increasing exposure on television, and ISC's commanding position at that time in terms of the number of leading players using their frames, this sector, arguably, provided the company's most effective element of brand visibility. The fact that, up to this point, a promotional benefit of this kind had been achieved at a relatively low cost meant that the changing environment from the mid 1970s onwards would create the basic vulnerability that significantly weakened the dominance the company had earned and enjoyed for some forty years.

In 1969 the German Dunlop company had bought the Erbacher Hammer company, located in Bavaria, which had started manufacturing skis in 1924. The connection between a ski manufacturer and a revolution in racket technology is not immediately obvious but it was to prove crucial. In the 1960s not only Erbacher, but several other, and larger ski manufacturers had begun to produce plastic skis and had steadily developed the use of advanced plastic materials for this market. When the ski market was particularly hard hit by the fall in demand following the oil crisis in 1973-74, several of the leading manufacturers decided to diversify by applying their expertise to the cre-

The new golf ball plant at Normanton shortly after its 1972 opening

ation of tennis rackets, which, although more expensive, were lighter and superior to conventional frames. Erbacher would add rackets to their range but larger companies like Rossignol, Fischer, Head and Donnay would be joined by newcomers like Prince, with their racket head 35% larger than the old type, to swell the 11 frames that first appeared at Wimbledon in 1973 to over 100 by the end of the decade. In the huge USA market it took Prince only three years to reach a one-third market share with frames designed in North America, made in Taiwan and supported by a powerful and innovative promotional approach, combining large scale player endorsement with an intense focus on the grass root participants via the clubs and professional coaches.

During this period tennis ball technology was focused on improvements, rather than radical changes, and these included a colour change from mainly white to yellow and improved cover durability. In contrast golf balls were going through a period of very considerable development mainly designed, as usual, to improve player performance. This process, which had been initially sparked by the durability improvement afforded by the introduction of Surlyn covers in the late 1960s, had moved on to marry the new cover material to two-piece balls, and a new focus on the relationship between the aerodynamics of dimple patterns and the critical factors of distance and control.

All these revolutionary changes, being brought to bear on a sports industry that had little recent experience of managing radically new technology, took place within a relatively short period, mainly between 1968 and 1975. And it would be wrong to imagine that ISC felt it was so 'locked in' to its existing production methods that the serious implications of change could not be contemplated. George Carr's earlier move to acquire Carlton had been driven by his recognition that steel racket frames could be a major threat to wood. He had also taken on board his first-hand assessment of a very early, and then imperfect form of injection-moulded frames, which he had seen during a visit to the USA to predict that the dominance of traditional frames in general, and Maxply in particular, would be seriously threatened.

Very soon after taking over ISC, Findlay Picken, very impressed by the extra yardage of the Uniroyal 'Plus Six' ball, with its hexagon dimple pattern, was asking Bob Haines to look at an alternative to the pattern that had been used on the '65', virtually unchanged since the ball was introduced in 1934. And by the end of 1975 Slazenger's Ian Peacock was calling for a low-cost production route to give ISC a highly competitive moulded racket.

Both these initiatives would lead to ISC having outstanding new products but there would be several years' delay between concept and delivery. In fact although the development team responded very quickly to the identification of these requirements it would be 1980 before a distinctively new golf ball and the injection-moulded racket were available to the public. In the case of the new racket the nature of the development work required was so revolutionary that it is not surprising that it took four years to complete the project but it did mean that during this period the company's longstanding market leadership position, based on 'Maxply' and 'Challenge', was significantly weakened.

Whether or not ISC moved quickly enough on all fronts during the period from the mid 1970s to the early 1980s to adapt to the changes in its trading environment remains a topic for lively debate amongst those who were involved at the time in both the Dunlop and Slazenger operations, which, in marketing terms, remained separate and competitive. What is certain is that despite worldwide economic problems, the pace of technology change and the special pressures within the parent Dunlop Group, ISC not only did change, but also remained sufficiently strong to provide a platform for a remarkable regeneration in the 1980s.

On the manufacturing side there was an increasing commitment to product development based on technical excellence and the beginnings of a rationalisation of the manufacturing capacity. The latter factor acknowledged that while it still made sense to invest what had become restricted funds in the development and manufacture of relatively 'hi-tech' products, e.g. golf balls and injection-moulded frames, increasing use should be made of outside suppliers to source less complex and 'fashion oriented' items. In 1978 Findlay recruited Laurie Roberts from Woolworths to establish a purchasing operation in Hong Kong to expand the range and volume of products to be drawn from the Far East. On the marketing side a number of fringe products, like archery, table tennis and a re-launched Dunlop 'Masters' darts line, would be dropped. More significantly there was no mistaking the shift from equipment to clothing and footwear for the Slazenger organisation, which was significantly expanded by the 1977 decision it should also handle Puma footwear and apparel in the UK. And, although it wasn't implemented until late in 1984, Findlay and the ISC team had become advocates for the introduction of that 'truly international' management of the worldwide Dunlop sports operation.

Anyone scanning the pages of the *Dunlop News* during this period cannot fail to see that ISC's activities, and obviously its successes, were probably the most heavily reported after tyre-related subjects, and provided a consistent, upbeat note in contrast to some of the more serious issues covered. The successes of other divisions were also featured but the stream of news items about what was happening in the sports and leisure market reflected the assessment in the 1983 Strategy Review that 'This is the main diversified market in which the Group sells direct to the consumer market, **and a good deal of the Company's public image turns on these products**'. This factor would later be recognised by BTR, who consistently featured Dunlop Slazenger success stories in their annual reports and corporate advertising.

The front page report in the April 1978 issue of the *Dunlop News*, under the headline 'Boost for Sports R & D', serves to illustrate ISC's focus on technology and the support this priority received from the Dunlop Group. This

The Maxpower golf club at work and play in 1970 – hitting a '65' at 100 mph and below in more relaxed mood

The new Dunlop Maxpower 2.

Not just a beautiful shape.

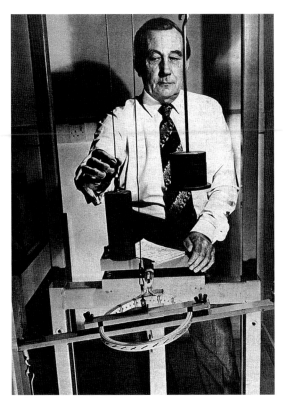

A tennis racket undergoes a flexibility test at the new ISC research centre at Horbury opened in 1978

article would have delighted William Sykes because it described the opening of a £300,000 research and development centre at the Horbury factory he had taken over in 1936 to expand his rapidly expanding production. Roy Marsh, who had been appointed chairman of ISC in 1977, told the guests that 'since 1973 the sports development budget has increased five times and by concentrating the activities in a specially designed building we can maximise the effectiveness of the research and development effort'. Sir Campbell Fraser, who performed the opening ceremony, emphasised the importance of the sports business, which, he said, 'accounted for 10% of the Group's activities around the world and was expected to grow'. The Mayor and chief executive of Wakefield Metropolitan District Council was among those present to hear Sir Campbell add that 'the company had recognised it was essential to have a facility to introduce new products more quickly into the marketplace' and that 'the new facility will work closely with the Central Research Centre and with the company's research operations in USA and Japan'.

The new Horbury centre became the focal point for the two most important product development projects: the post '65' evolution of the golf ball and the injection-moulded racket. The complete stories behind both these critically important products would fill two more books but the following summary accounts of how they were translated from original ideas to award winning realities will show how a combination of ingenuity, determination and good fortune propelled them and ISC into a much more successful period in the 1980s than would have been the case without them.

An appropriate starting point for the story of the DDH golf ball is an article, by an American club professional, Richard Jewell, in a 1981 issue of *Golf Illustrated*. Having reminded his readers that throughout the 1970s ball manufacturers had been placing increasing emphasis on developing new dimple shapes and patterns to optimise aerodynamic performance, he observed that 'the latest and most significant of these has been the Dunlop DDH'.

The press release sent to Richard Jewell referred to 'an extensive five-year research programme' that had led to the development of the new ball. However, Bob Haines, who was the manager of the research and development operation during this period, dates the start of work on the DDH, or dodecahedron – meaning a ball with a geometric configuration of 12 pentagons – from 1974. It was on a Friday evening that year that Bob first saw this design when it was sketched on the back of a beer mat while he and a mathematician friend, Peter Reynolds, were having a drink in the saloon bar of the Cranworth Arms in Rotherham. Very conscious of the growing use of completely new dimple patterns to improve ball (and player) performance, including not only the Uniroyal hexagon spotted by Findlay but also Titleist's icosahedron and Wilson's octahedron, Bob set to work to explore the potential of the pattern sketched by Peter, which is one of geometry's oldest designs.

Work on this revolutionary new design progressed quickly enough to allow Bob Haines and his co-inventor and colleague, Mike Shaw, to apply for a UK patent in 1975 and to file the USA application a year later. As the development work continued one of the UK's leading professionals, Neil Coles, started testing prototype balls in 1977 and by 1980 was being widely reported in the golfing columns of the national press as he took the lead in a tour event in the North of England. The *Yorkshire Post* reported that he was using 'a new type of golf ball which has added 20 yards to his tee shot' and the *Daily Telegraph* described the 'experimental new DDH ball with its erratic dimple pattern', which the player had hit more than 300 yards from the tee on at least two occasions.

Although Bob and his team were convinced of the likely potential for the DDH, especially in view of the increasing consumer interest in and respect for the new generation of dimple patterns, ISC had continued to rely on the '65' as its lead ball. This was reflected by another re-launch in 1975 for 'The new, the unsurpassable Dunlop "65"', which was also used as an opportunity to let the press see the progress being made at the Normanton plant to put it 'amongst the most modern and efficient in the world'. It was also pointed out that the updated and improved production process the visitors were seeing in Normanton had been installed at Speke and in a number of overseas factories, including Australia, South Africa, USA and Japan. So far as the ball was concerned the approach taken by David Sealey and Bob Haines was to first of all stress that although it remained 'unaltered in fundamental structure' it had been significantly improved by the introduction of 'an exceptionally tough cover, unique to Dunlop and called "Polydur"' and by an improved painting system and the introduction of a new and bolder style of lettering. Reference was made to the fact that 1975 saw the 41st 'birthday' of the '65', forever linked with Henry Cotton's record round at the 1934 Open, and also to the fact that an announcement would shortly be made about the opening of a new golf ball plant (Malaysia), which would bring the worldwide total to eleven.

Work on the DDH dimple wasn't sufficiently advanced to be used on the latest '65', nor was the new design used when, in 1977, Normanton was again the setting for the launch of 'a new high performance golf ball, the "Maxfli", to meet the requirements of the most discerning golfers'. The key feature of this new product was the return to a balata cover, which was the basis of the claim that its qualities of feel and control would have special appeal for experienced players. It may also have been the trigger to encourage the revival of the 'Maxfli' brand in the UK, and which certainly inspired the press office to issue a release extolling the virtues of 'A rare species of insect, classified as Maxfli, thought extinct in the 1920s but now reported to be proliferating throughout Britain, especially on or near golf courses where specimens can be seen exhibited in glass cases and available at 75p each'.

Slazenger was not forgotten in terms of new golf balls. The first two-piece ball produced at Speke, in 1976, was the 1.62 'Slazenger Plus', and the following year saw the launch of 'The new B51', a wound ball, produced in both 1.62 and 1.68 form, and promoted as 'The greatest invention since the golf ball'. And in the USA the locally managed Dunlop Sports Corporation, also responding to the emphasis on more sophisticated dimple patterns, produced the balata-covered 'XLT-15' with smaller and deeper dimples, and the two-piece 'Silver Maxfli' with wider and shallower dimples for higher flight.

Neither of these new Greenville-made balls used radically new dimple pat-

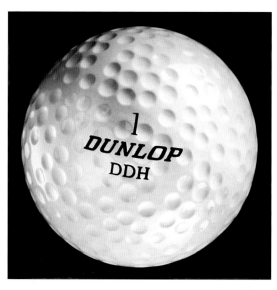

The DDH dimple pattern in close-up

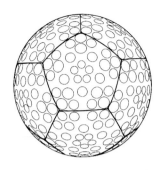

The DDH dimple pattern is based around the twelve pentagonal sides of a dodecahedron

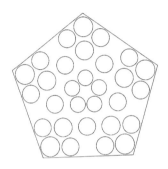

Detail of the DDH dimple layout. This pattern is repeated on each of the twelve faces

The Maxfli DDH approach in USA

terns, nor did they transform the fortunes of a business that had been suffering badly in the golf market as a result of serious quality problems with 'out of round' balls. During the 1979 visit to the UK that company's newly appointed president, Dean Cassell, was shown a sample of the DDH with its strikingly different appearance and was quick to see it as an opportunity to start re-building the Dunlop presence in the USA market. Cassell, and his vice-president for marketing, David Branon, developed a powerful promotional story and launch campaign, which linked the special merits of the 360 dimple dodecahedron pattern to the importance of aerodynamics to show that the link between these two factors developed by ISC's intensive research programme had resulted in 'An idea becoming a high-performance fact'. More to the point they were able to demonstrate they were offering not only 'Golf's most innovative product' but a ball that was demonstrably longer and more accurate than most of its main competitors.

Backed by the endorsement of several leading American players, including the winner of the 1977 US Open, Hubert Green, and Fuzzy Zoeller, who had won the 1979 Masters, the ball was launched in the USA in 1980 and was so successful that throughout the following year it was necessary to run the Westminster plant on a three shift, seven day basis in order to meet demand. Fuzzy Zoeller was quoted as saying 'Somebody's got to be kidding' when he first saw the new ball but went on to declare that 'It's amazing how far you can pump the DDH out there and you feel like you've always got a handle on it'.

True to local tradition the USA company decided to name the ball 'Maxfli DDH', while back in the UK the ISC marketing team, alerted by American enthusiasm to the potential of the product that had been evolving at Horbury for five years, decided on 'Dunlop DDH' for their 1981 launch, with the new ball as the 'flagship' of a completely revised range. This also included a 'relegated' but upgraded '65' as the number two product and was completed by a two-piece 'Silver Max' and the 'Dunlop Maxfli Pro Special', which provided 'Anglo-American' branding for the Normanton-made balata ball.

As the original 'Maxfli' era had given way in 1934 to nearly fifty years with improving versions of the '65' so the DDH took over the lead role in 1981. Although, in turn, it was succeeded as number one by a much faster stream of new developments, it remained in the range into the 21st century branded either 'Maxfli' or Dunlop. Particularly important were the two-piece 'DDH Marathon' launched in the UK in 1982 (Normanton's first two-piece 1.68 ball), and the 'Maxfli DDH 500', launched by the UK in 1987, with the dimple count increased from 360 to 500. And following its introduction to the Japanese market in 1982 the DDH brand became, and remained, a major feature in the Japanese Dunlop range of not only balls but also clubs and accessories.

The importance of the DDH should be measured by far more than the many millions of dozens sold all around the world. As a brand, or sub brand, it provided a highly effective worldwide unifying factor for ISC and, later, Dunlop Slazenger marketing with the mark being used in identical form both by those companies that remained with Dunlop ownership and those, like Dunlop Japan, that were transferred to new owners. As a revolutionary and highly distinctive new design it pushed the company back into the forefront of ball manufacturers, where it has remained ever since. And it was a major factor in preventing the demise of the USA sports business.

It was, therefore, no more than appropriate, and a source of considerable pride, when in April, 1982, Bob Haines, on behalf of the company and Mike Shaw, accepted the Design Council Award from the Duke of Edinburgh 'To mark the selection of the Dunlop DDH golf ball for its excellence in design and in recognition of an outstanding product from British Industry'.

As the DDH ball had given a fresh impetus to ISC and to the Dunlop brand in the golf market, so the injection-moulded racket, with almost exactly the same timing, provided an enormously important boost to the company's position in the worldwide tennis business. And, probably even more significantly, it did so at the moment the Maxply, 'after 50 glorious years', was finally giving way to technological change. In terms of recognition for the technical skills and innovative thinking required to develop this radically new racket, it received even wider acclaim, winning a whole series of major awards.

Ian Peacock's earlier call for a more competitive production method to combat the threatened inroads of the steel and composite frames was repeated in 1977 by ISC's operations director, Peter Wycherley. At a meeting in Horbury he briefed Bob Haines 'To come up with a tennis racket based on a new technology which would give Dunlop a lead on the competitors using very cheap labour'. This was a critical factor because it was ISC's intention to manufacture the new racket in the UK, rather than purchase it from abroad. That made it essential to devise a completely new process with a much lower labour content than the more labour intensive moulding techniques already expanding so rapidly in Taiwan where labour costs were much lower. It was also seen as important, especially from a marketing perspective, to develop a racket that would be demonstrably different and superior when compared with the new wave of compression-moulded graphite frames, which were all very similar in appearance and performance apart from the cosmetics used to identify their different brands.

Against the background of the crucial decision to find a new production route, Bob Haines set up a brainstorming session in January, 1978. He assembled a team that included members of his own R & D department at Horbury, a representative of the Dunlop Central Research Division in Birmingham, and Frank Popplewell, who was the technical director of Carlton in Saffron Walden. Frank had considerable experience of the injection-moulding techniques Carlton had been using for mainly non-sports products. As Bob recalls he also had a remarkable capacity for finding ingenious ways around apparently intractable problems. Described in a case study on how the racket was designed and developed as 'a practical instinctive engineer' Frank would be a key figure in translating the idea of using injection-moulding into the fact of a high performance racket.

Nevertheless, this was a risky approach because, despite many attempts, nobody had ever succeeded in making a satisfactory racket with this process. However, having decided it would be necessary to construct a hollow-section

We make 24 tennis rackets including the Maxply Fort.
We also make 4 types of tennis balls and a variety of clothing and accessories. We're Dunlop Sports. And we specialise in winning. **DUNLOP** We specialise in winning.

'We specialise in winning' advertisement from the 1970s

The award winning injection moulded rackets – on the left the 150G and on the right the 200G with its larger head size

Martina Navratilova

Aranxtha Sanchez-Vicario

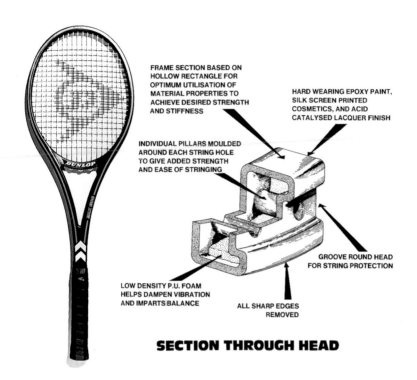

FRAME SECTION BASED ON HOLLOW RECTANGLE FOR OPTIMUM UTILISATION OF MATERIAL PROPERTIES TO ACHIEVE DESIRED STRENGTH AND STIFFNESS

HARD WEARING EPOXY PAINT, SILK SCREEN PRINTED COSMETICS, AND ACID CATALYSED LACQUER FINISH

INDIVIDUAL PILLARS MOULDED AROUND EACH STRING HOLE TO GIVE ADDED STRENGTH AND EASE OF STRINGING

GROOVE ROUND HEAD FOR STRING PROTECTION

LOW DENSITY P.U. FOAM HELPS DAMPEN VIBRATION AND IMPARTS BALANCE

ALL SHARP EDGES REMOVED

SECTION THROUGH HEAD

The construction of the injection moulded rackets

frame in order to match the weight of existing rackets, one of the first tasks was to decide on a core that would first of all withstand molten plastic, and then be melted out of the moulded plastic frame without damaging it. Within two weeks Frank produced a carbon-fibre reinforced nylon hollow test piece using a fusible core, and the team were sufficiently confident they had a viable design to file the first patents in April, 1978. Using prototype moulds made in-house, the first ever injection-moulded hollow-framed rackets were ready for evaluation four months later.

The initial reaction from ISC's marketing staff was not 100% enthusiastic. They fully understood the significance of the technical breakthrough but were not happy with what they felt was too bulky a profile for the new frame. However, encouraged by positive comments by the former British Davis Cup player, David Lloyd, and determined to build up more play test data, the Horbury team invested £5,000 for short-run tooling to produce enough pre-production rackets to allow much more intensive testing. Three of these prototype rackets, by now known as the 150G, were given to the three-man team of the Northern Club in Manchester, which promptly won the National Club Knock Out Competition to record the first competitive success for the new racket.

Full scale production of the 150G started at Horbury in November, 1980. Although it received excellent coverage from both the technical and sporting press, the sales figures were slow to pick up, largely because of the trend to larger head sizes that had been accelerated by the growing popularity of the compression-moulded frames. Nothing demonstrated this more clearly than the breakdown of the rackets used at the 1981 Wimbledon tournament when, for the first time, the number of wooden frames (139) was overtaken by the new generation of plastic models (202) with metal (64) making up the balance. In only five years (1977-81) the proportion of wooden rackets used by the total entry had fallen from 68% to 35%, and that decline continued to virtually zero by the mid 1980s. Furthermore, and to underline the point about the size of the racket, 30% of those at the 1981 championships had the increasingly popular large heads.

At this point it should be acknowledged that the several references to the types and makes of rackets used at Wimbledon between 1968 and the early 1980s, which saw the transition from 100% wooden frames to virtually all graphite or steel, have been based on a meticulous record, by manufacturer and type of material used, compiled by the Dunlop tennis manager at this time, Bob Howe.

Undeterred by the problem with the larger heads Bob Haines and his team re-designed their new process to produce the mid size 200G, which was launched in 1982, and became one of the best-known rackets ever produced, and, for Dunlop second only in popularity and numbers sold to the Maxply. Unquestionably a major factor in its success was its link with John McEnroe, who as a junior player and before he signed with another maunufacturer, had been introduced to Dunlop rackets by Bob Howe. Then, early in 1981 he contracted to play the 'Maxply Fort' and three months later used it when winning the first of his three

Findlay Picken and Peter Wycherley welcoming John McEnroe to Dunlop in 1981

Wimbledon singles titles. He continued to play with the standard head size wood frame, including a specially designed 'Maxply McEnroe', until, in 1983, when looking for relief from a painful shoulder condition, he tried the 200G belonging to his brother, Patrick. The switch was made from one to the other during the Tournament of Champions in Dallas. Not only was he successful on that occasion but went on to win 13 of the 15 tournaments he entered the following year. And a bonus for John (and Dunlop) was that he not only found the pain in his shoulder had eased but he also increased the range of his ground strokes without any sacrifice in control. James Hartbridge, the author of *Please Play On*, a biography of John McEnroe, quotes John as saying, after the Dallas win, 'If I can keep on improving like the way I have since I picked this new racquet up I might end up using it forever'. Not only did he continue to use the 200G for most of the rest of his time on the professional tour, but his close association with Dunlop has been renewed by his current endorsement of the company's new range of rackets (including a brand new 200G) and tennis balls.

The original, worldwide impact of John McEnroe joining forces with Dunlop was immense and his subsequent sustained run of successes with the 200G was a key factor in propelling sales from 5000 in 1982 to 300,000 in 1985. Later, Steffi Graf would also achieve enormous success with the same racket and keep the 200G in the tennis headlines until well into the 1990s. A memorable occasion for all concerned took place in November, 1988 when Steffi, having that year won the Grand Slam and Olympic Gold, presented the one millionth injection-moulded racket to the 1977 Wimbledon champion, Virginia Wade.

The collection of prestigious awards given to the racket added considerable lustre to its, and the company's reputation. In 1981 the original 150G received the Design Council Award. The following year, at the Design

John McEnroe and the Maxply McEnroe – a 1983 USA advertisement

1981 and Findlay Picken receives the Design Council Award for the 150G racket from the Duke of Edinburgh

A rare shot of Rod Laver in the changing room — with Dunlop

McEnroe and Maxply make the headline after John beats Bjorn Borg to win the 1981 Wimbledon title

Engineering Show, the 200G received an award for 'Excellence in Engineering', followed by the Willis Faber Award from the Institution of Mechanical Engineers for 'Improving Manufacturing Effectiveness'. Finally, in 1985, Bob Haines, on behalf of his team and the company, received the Queen's Award for Technological Achievement, which was presented at Horbury by the Lord Lieutenant of Yorkshire, Lord Ingrow.

Among the many awards and compliments received for this ground-breaking and hugely successful racket, two very different ones are worthy of special note. James McMillan, again writing in *The Dunlop Story*, commented 'As an example of a superb technical and marketing riposte to the challenge of change, the development of the 200G should be an inspiration and comfort to British industry'. And nearer to the heat of battle in the world's major tournaments, Martina Navratilova, having borrowed Carling Bassett's 200G, used it with great success – but without payment – during 1987 and 1988, which included her 1987 Wimbledon singles victory. To avoid offending her official racket sponsor the 200G's cosmetics were heavily blacked out and the string stencilling was restricted to her personal 'MN' markings.

During the second half of the 1970s and into the early 1980s both the DDH, and to a much greater extent, the 150G and 200G rackets were examples of the benefits derived from the overall Dunlop determination to continue investing in technically advanced, high performance products. Despite the disappointing Group results during much of this period, this approach was applied across the whole company, which, to again quote a James McMillan view, showed that 'Dunlop's abiding strength, its sheer technological skill and inventiveness, remained unimpaired in the non-tyre side of the business, which would flourish more strongly than ever under the more sinewy management of BTR'. That verdict would certainly apply to the sports operations.

For Findlay and his team managing ISC through these years would have been a roller-coaster ride mixing both successes and setbacks, which made the headlines not only in the company newspaper but also in the national, local and sports trade press. It is also clear that although ISC's operations could not be insulated from the pressures affecting the parent Group the public and trade perception of the ISC businesses and brands would have remained very positive despite these problems. Despite the fact competition in all their main market sectors was intensifying at the time when ISC's funds for promotional spending were very restricted, the level of interest in the powerful stories behind the development of the new golf balls and rackets was such they commanded priceless columns of editorial attention around the world.

In the case of John McEnroe this was especially so not only when he first signed with Dunlop, but during the following years as journalists reported not only his many tournament victories, and occasionally controversial behaviour, but also, and more importantly for the business, an immense amount of detail about the rackets he had chosen and helped to design. A glance at what the company's PR agency in the USA called 'A national blitz of exposure' reveals such gems as 'McEnroe's kick has helped blow Dunlop out of doldrums' (a reference to the fate of a racket famously mangled on the centre court), 'Dunlop hopes to bounce back in the tennis market', 'McEnroe boots Firm's sales', 'McEnroe's temperament hasn't hurt racket firm', 'Dunlop's $3 million McEnroe gamble begins to pay off', and, to sum it all up, 'McEnroe good for Dunlop'.

However, John wasn't the only ISC tennis star to keep Dunlop's 'Flying D' and Slazenger's Panther in the news between 1975 and 1983. On top of John's six wins there were eleven other Grand Slam title winners for ISC. These included Virginia Wade, Evonne Goolagong/Cawley and Ilie Nastase for Dunlop, and John Newcombe, Guillermo Vilas, Manuel Orantes and Sue Barker for Slazenger.

Sir Campbell Fraser presents a gold brooch in the shape of a Maxply racket to Virginia Wade in honour of her 1977 Wimbledon victory

Amongst the most memorable of these tennis successes was Virginia Wade's 1977 Wimbledon win in what the *Sunday Times* reported as 'A glorious summer, the Queen was celebrating her Jubilee and Wimbledon was staging its centenary. To crown it all Virginia Wade won the singles title'. In his book, 'Sixty Years in Tennis', Teddy Tinling described her as both 'an exceptional athlete' and as having 'the only really good serve we can record in 100 years of women's tennis in England'. Virginia had switched from her first racket, a Slazenger All White Challenge, to a Maxply in her early teens and had been delighted with her first 'big deal' from Dunlop, which was a couple of free rackets. She would later play with the 200G but used a Maxply to win her three Grand Slam titles – the 1968 US Open, the 1972 Australian Open and the centenary Wimbledon. Among her abiding memories of that famous occasion are the championship winning forehand return from Betty Stove's serve to the left court, and, as she left the centre court, of a blind girl called Mary, who had for years been one of her most ardent supporters, asking 'Ginny, is it really true? Please tell me its true!' It was, and, in the words of the BBC's commentator that day, Max Robertson, 'Virginia has grasped the title she thought would never be hers'.

On the golf course leading players associated with the company (several of them only using Dunlop and Slazenger equipment in Europe) were winning 13 majors between 1976 and 1983, amongst them Johnny Miller and Jack Nicklaus for Slazenger, David Graham and Fuzzy Zoeller for Dunlop, and Seve Ballesteros, who used Slazenger clubs and Dunlop balls. And, in 1981, Dunlop signed Bernhard Langer to use both balls and clubs.

Geoff Boycott signed for Slazenger in 1978, just one year after scoring his 100th century, and was joined the following year by Mike Procter, the Gloucestershire and South African star. And a combined Dunlop Sports Company and Dunlop Footwear initiative resulted

FOR SPEED AND BALL CONTROL
Dunlop Rapido
ITALIAN STYLE FOOTBALL BOOTS

RAPIDO BOOT. In crush calf with red lining. Made on a much flatter last than previously used. Black leather sole with nylon studs with separate nylon washers and continental thread. Free set of rubber studs also given away with each pair. £5.5.0.
RAPIDO POPULAR BOOT. Also made on the flat last. Black sole and studs of nylon continental type. £3.19.11
RAPIDO BLUE FLASH BOOT. With black one-piece moulded rubber studded sole, blue tongue and trimmings. £2.19.6.
Ask your rebate representative for full details

Dunlop Sports Company Ltd., Allington House, 136-142 Victoria St., London, S.W.1.
Published by Dunlop Rubber Co. Ltd., Birmingham—Printed by Burman, Cooper & Co. Ltd., Birmingham 5.

Souness, Brooking and Charlton endorse Dunlop soccer boots

TYRE BLOCKADE MEANS

SPEKE STAYS CLOSED

Sports Co to run down racket plant

Dunlop News in 1979 reports the double blow for ISC

in a redoubtable trio – Bobby Charlton, Trevor Brooking and Graeme Souness – endorsing soccer boots. Darts had remained in the Dunlop range until the early 1980s and were endorsed by the world number three, Tony Brown.

In 1978, after an eighteen month programme of construction and equipment installation, a new tennis ball plant was opened in the Philippines. This was a joint venture project with the Australian Dunlop company, which required a low cost source for its home market in order to compete more effectively with Far East imports. The Anglo-Australian project and management teams, led by ISC's Martin Price and Denis Obsorne, who would be the first president of the local company, and the Australians, Alan Michie and John Briscoe, successfully established the target annual production of 600,000 dozen. However, it is unlikely they would have foreseen the day, twenty-five years later, when on a much larger site only a few hundred yards from the original factory, output would be running at several millions of dozens. This plant, located in the Bataan Export Zone, is now the main source for all Dunlop and Slazenger tennis balls, which reflects the original premise that the skills of the local workforce would be capable of meeting all the necessary high quality standards across all markets, including the USA and Europe.

As one new door was opening – in the Philippines – so, sadly others were closing. Findlay obviously knew what was about to happen but the contents of the February, 1979 issue of *Dunlop News* would have made sombre reading for him and all Dunlop employees, but especially for those working in Tyres and Sports. A major rationalisation programme for the UK Tyre Division meant the closure of the Speke factory, as well as redundancies in other plants. It was also announced that the world famous Waltham Abbey racket factory would be run down during the following year with production being transferred to Horbury.

This was a heavy double blow for ISC. The problem confronting the golf ball operation at Speke was that it was entirely dependent on the tyre services for supplies of steam, water and power. It was explained to the work force that no final decision had been taken about the future of golf ball production and that discussions would continue, including with the Government, about the possible options. They included setting up the necessary services at Speke, or relocating the production equipment to another site, possibly nearby. Convinced the only option ever seriously considered was transfer to Normanton, the Transport and General Workers Union argued strongly against that move on the basis the plant should remain on Merseyside to service what they considered would be a viable long term operation. However, that solution called for Government implementing import controls and tariffs on what the Union recognised were lower cost foreign balls. Not unexpectedly that form of protection was not forthcoming and ISC consolidated its UK golf ball production at Normanton in July, 1979, thus ending 34 years of sports production at Speke.

At Waltham Abbey the employees were told the main reason for closure

Charles Selby and Len Rennocks with the very last Maxply made at Waltham Abbey

was that ISC now had excess production capacity due to the rise of imports from the Far East, principally Taiwan. Also that the generally poor economic situation had depressed the sales of sports goods for sometime and, most damaging of all, that 'The development of non-wooden rackets had provided a serious challenge to the traditionally manufactured product'. It was explained that attempts had been made to maintain viable operations at both Horbury and Waltham Abbey by reducing the level of activity on both sites, but that this had resulted in serious losses which could not be sustained in the face of the certainty there would be no reversal in the trend of competitive imports.

Concentration of racket production at Horbury, with its much wider range of products at that time, was seen as the best way of safeguarding the future of the business as a whole and that process was completed before the end of the year. This meant that, apart from the continuing Carlton badminton operation at Saffron Walden, ISC's UK manufacturing would be concentrated in the Sykes/Slazenger strongholds of Barnsley and Horbury, plus the nearby, and expanded golf ball plant at Normanton. The final years of Maxply production would be in Yorkshire and the world's best-known racket factory at Waltham Abbey would be closed after more than fifty years of producing the highest quality frames for tennis, squash and badminton.

The closing years of the decade had also seen a number of changes among senior members of the ISC and Dunlop management teams. Jack Ellis, who retired in 1977 as ISC's works director, would have regretted the Dunlop plant closures as much as anyone but it was very much his work in developing the Horbury plant after the 1964 formation of ISC that made it feasible to concentrate so much of the company's production there. One of the many who remembered Jack with great affection and respect was Peter Wycherley, who had reported to him for several years as operations director. In 1980 he became general manager of ISC when he took over from Ronald Lowe, who had joined the company from Gola Sports in 1978. Others to depart during this period were Neil Roberton, who retired in 1977 as sales secretary after 47 years with Dunlop, and Maurice Seward, the Sports Company's advertising manager for 15 years, who, in 1978, moved to the parent company's central advertising department. He was succeeded by Richard Braddon, who went on to become a key figure on the golf side of the business for nearly 20 years, and was one of a new generation taking up key positions in a 1978 reorganisation. Among them were John Crump (racket sports), Richard Brown (golf equipment and accessories) and Roy Sherwin (commercial manager). Roy, in particular, would fill a number of important posts during the next 20 years, including running the French Slazenger business and management of the Carlton operation.

Findlay Picken and ISC trade marks head a 1982 *Dunlop News* article on the importance of Europe. The five marks are for Dunlop, Slazenger, Letters, Litesome and Carlton

The reason Roy Sherwin's later responsibilities in France were restricted to Slazenger was due to the parent company's decision, in 1982, to terminate all Dunlop operations in that country. This was brought about by mounting losses, mainly in the tyre manufacturing and selling operations, which accounted for the bulk of the business. Ownership of Dunlop France, and all the company's

1979 advertisements for the Maxply
Fort featuring Virginia Wade (with the
frying pan) and Evonne Cawley (on
the banjo)

trade marks in that country were then acquired (for 1 franc) by Sumitomo Rubber Industries, who had become the majority partner in Dunlop Japan in 1978, and went on, in 1983, to also purchase the bulk of the remaining Dunlop tyre operations around the world. They would run the Dunlop sports business in France until the mid 1990s, a situation which created a number of issues between them and the European operations controlled by Dunlop Slazenger from 1984 onwards.

A more positive note for ISC at this time was the 1982 opening of a new distribution centre at Wakefield, which was the purpose-built replacement for several warehouses previously used, most of them attached to the factories, plus an overflow site in Leeds. It also provided a more efficient method of dealing with the increasing volume of factored products mainly purchased from Far East suppliers. This became the fifth ISC site in South Yorkshire and remains the only one in operation today. A less happy event was a decision forced on Findlay to put an end to the annual Dunlop Masters golf tournament. The cost of staging it, which was largely met by the other Dunlop divisions using it for customer entertaining, had risen steadily and the final blow was Tyre division's withdrawal of support. The 1982 event, at St. Pierre, was the last and ended an unbroken run of 37 years.

Possibly the most significant event in 1982, and one that would prove very important during the period leading up to and after the BTR acquisition of the remaining Dunlop businesses, was the decision to appoint a new Director, Consumer Group, who would be responsible to the main board for ISC, Dunlop Footwear and Dunlopillo. The individual selected for this task was Alan Finden-Crofts, who was recruited from the Norcros company, and took up his appointment in October. In view of the 'wind of change' that was about to sweep throughout the whole of Dunlop – and that would become even more apparent after the BTR takeover – ISC and Dunlop footwear, which would be joined with the sports business – were fortunate that the board had chosen an individual who proved more than equal to the task of redefining the shape and objectives of the consumer businesses during this critical phase. He also had the necessary credentials and experience to cope with the considerable pressures created by the urgent restructuring programme pushed through, 'with furious speed', by Sir Michael Edwardes prior to BTR's arrival.

Most important of all he was able to firmly and successfully establish the operational reality of that 'truly international sports business' that had previously existed only as a loose relationship between ISC and the various overseas sports operations, which was characterised more by liaison and co-operation than by any defined structure which provided for either shared responsibility or accountability as a single enterprise. He would move on in 1987, but by then the Dunlop Slazenger International Limited he had put in place was essentially the operation that would reach sales of nearly £300 million worldwide and be the subject of the management buy out from BTR in 1996.

However, in 1982, Findlay Picken, contributing an article to a *Dunlop News* series about the implications of the UK's closer trading relationships with Europe, continued to reflect the mainly UK-based nature of ISC's operations, describing Europe as the company's 'power base'. His analysis made it clear that ISC regarded the combination of its business in the UK and sales to the other Dunlop sports operations in Europe as a springboard from which to attack the USA and Far East markets, which accounted for well over half the world demand for golf and tennis products. In the case of golf it would be nearer three-quarters of the total. It's not unreasonable to imagine that Findlay, and George Carr before him, both very much internationalists, would have been frustrated by the fact that their European power base had not been able to direct its own assault on that enormous USA market, rather than operate mainly through the relatively small scale local operation. Indeed there are those that believe that the correct strategy for creating a really powerful, international Dunlop sports presence would have been to locate it in and direct it from the USA as a separate organisation within the Group reporting to the main board. That would have been at odds with the parent company's longstanding organisational philosophy, but completely in line with general practice in the international sports trade.

The other international sports trade 'power base', at least during the last thirty years, has been Japan. It's interesting to note that successive Dunlop and Sumitomo managements of the Kobe-based sports business, for many years leaning heavily on considerable technical support from the UK, recognised the potential of the enormous local golf market (second only to the USA in annual sales since the 1970s) and were able to develop a mainly golf-oriented operation that was eventually larger than Dunlop Slazenger International. Trade mark agreements prevented it selling Dunlop branded products outside Japan, and it did remain almost completely integrated within the structure of what was mainly a tyre business, but its highly profitable growth justified sustained and substantial investment in not only R & D, but also advanced manufacturing processes and a consistently high level of promotion.

'Better late than never', and possibly too late to achieve the full potential of the Dunlop Slazenger heritage, Alan Finden-Crofts would be given the opportunity to play 'catch-up' in the USA, and would see the start of an overdue expansion in that market for Dunlop, Slazenger and Maxfli, which only served to confirm 'what might have been'.

For the first two years of his Dunlop career, Alan Finden-Crofts was responsible for the £300 million sales by what had been identified as the Consumer Group, of which ISC accounted for £100 million. In the 1983 Dunlop Strategy Review a figure of £150 million was shown as the total for the 'Sports & Leisure' category, which included a number of unspecified 'other leisure products', in particular for the DIY market. More detailed figures for 1982, obtained from Dunlop finance records, confirm that sales for the UK-based sports business were close to £100 million and this still included the overseas Slazenger companies, £2 million tennis ball sales from the Philippines plant and export sales of £18 million. More than 50% of the latter were to sports divisions operated by overseas Dunlop companies. In addition a further £45 million sales are shown for operations outside ISC's control in USA, Germany, France, Malaysia, South Africa and New Zealand. Finden-Crofts was told that ISC in the UK was just about breaking even, but that losses of more than £3 million were being incurred in the overseas operations, mainly in the USA.

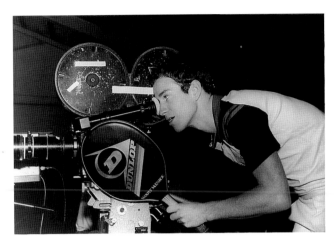

McEnroe filming and...

The following extracts from the Dunlop Annual Report for 1983 summarise much of what was happening with the company's sports businesses during this period:

The UK sports operations experienced highly competitive trading conditions in both home and export markets. The rapid trend away from wooden tennis rackets led to wholesale clearance sales by international manufacturers which seriously affected margins, and a UK operating loss was recorded. However, the company is well to the fore in the new mid-head size racket range which is spearheaded by the patented Max 200G carbon fibre model. In golf, sales of the unique two piece DDH Marathon ball are rising rapidly.

The DDH golf ball and mid-head rackets also gained increasing acceptance in North America. The new products and a broadened distribution base in the USA contributed to a substantial reduction of operating loss in a static demand situation. In Continental Europe, the trading situation was similar to the UK with strong pressure on margins. As a result, both the French and German operations reported lower profits. Elsewhere, the growth of imports continued to put pressure on local manufacture. Accordingly, rationalisation took place in New Zealand (closure of the Slazenger operation) where profits were lower. Increasing demand for Far Eastern sourced products led to further significant improvements in the trading results achieved by the Philippines tennis ball operation and the Hong Kong trading company.

This snapshot of the business, which was the last review of the ISC structure established in 1964, reflects several of the main problems then confronting it. However, it also highlights those key product successes, which had allowed it to continue to project a sufficiently strong image to provide a platform for a future improvement. That improvement would be secured by a management style very different from anything previously applied to the Dunlop and Slazenger companies.

... Lew Hoad the cricketer

THE DUNLOP MASTERS GOLF TOURNAMENT

As Wimbledon has been so important to Slazenger, in emphasising their commitment to tennis in general and to that great championship in particular, so the Dunlop Masters golf tournament, for nearly 40 years, was the annual 'big event' for the Dunlop Sports Company.

First played in 1946, at the Stoneham course, entry to the event was limited to 50 players, most of them qualifying by winning an important UK or overseas title, or as members of the British, and later, European Ryder Cup team. The quality of the competitors meant that it probably ranked second only to the Open in Europe and, in its latter years, regularly attracted total crowds of 20,000 to 30,000.

During its 37 year history the tournament visited 20 different courses around the UK, mainly in England and Wales. Nine of the last twelve were held at either the St. Pierre course near Chepstow or Woburn. The first time St. Pierre was chosen, in 1971, it was the first ever sponsored tournament in Wales and did much to put that very popular venue on the map.

That quality of the entry also ensured there would be many of the world's leading players in the list of 'Dunlop Master Golfers'. Bobby Locke was a joint winner of the first tournament – with James Adams – and was one of 10 players to win twice, his second victory coming at Prince's, Sandwich in 1954. Another double winner was Tony Jacklin, whose 1967 victory at Royal St. George's included the first hole-in-one to be seen live on British television. In fact the viewers saw it before he did! Among other notable winners were Dai Rees, Max Faulkner, Harry Weetman, Peter Thomson, Neil Coles, Bob Charles, Bernard Gallacher, Graham Marsh, Bernhard Langer and Greg Norman.

Organising the tournament, and the thousand and one details involved, was virtually a twelve month operation involving many people in the Sports Company, especially the Golf Division staff led by managers like Eric Hays, Richard Brown and Robin English. They worked closely with the management and staff of the selected clubs, with the PGA European Tour staff and, frequently, with members of neighbouring clubs who provided invaluable help during the week of the tournament. However, throughout its history the success of the Dunlop Masters was very much based on the in house team effort.

Other parts of the Dunlop Group contributed to the cost of the event and made excellent use of it as a much sought after occasion for entertaining major customers. In 1977 a Pro Am event was introduced, which provided the opportunity for some customers, preferably those with the lower handicaps, to play against leading golfers and personalities like Bruce Forsyth, Jimmy Tarbuck and Eric Sykes.

The final tournament was held at St. Pierre in 1982 and was particularly

The photo sequence of Tony Jacklin's historic hole-in-one in 1967

£1.50

10-13 June 1982   St Pierre Golf & Country Club

Bernhard Langer on the front cover of the 1982 (and final) tournament at St Pierre

memorable because the programme included golf clinics conducted by two of the best known and most respected figures in the UK game, John Jacobs and the three times Open Champion forever associated with the 65, Henry Cotton, by then in his seventies.

The principle of a company run event on this scale was briefly extended to a South African Dunlop Masters and in 1974 saw Dunlop Japan stage the first of its Phoenix Tournaments, which developed into one of the world's leading championships, which, every year, attracts the cream of the world's leading players. The Australian, Graham Marsh, holds the unique record of winning both the Phoenix (1976) and the Dunlop Masters (1979).

And the spirit of the Dunlop Masters will be very much alive in 2004 when the 25th Maxfli Champions event is staged at the Rancho Murieta Country Club, near Sacramento in California. This is a 36 hole event, which pairs club professionals with their own club champions as they compete for the title of the California State Club Pro and Club Champion Championship. This tournament was founded and always organised by Hershel Noonkester, whose whole working life has been devoted to golf in California, including more than 30 years as a territory manager for Dunlop and, more recently, TaylorMade Maxfli. Interestingly the more than 250 competitors for the 2004 event will be competing for a very similar amount of prize money to that offered for the final Dunlop Masters at Chepstow.

Greg Norman, the 1981 championship winner

Packed stands at Woburn in 1981

Definitely in the 'Stop Press' category is the very recent news that the heritage of this great event will be revived in May 2005. The new owners of Dunlop Slazenger, Sports World International, have decided to stage the *Daily Telegraph* Dunlop Masters at the Marriott Forest of Arden course from 12th to 15th May, preceded by a Pro-Am event on the 11th. In addition to the *Daily Telegraph* and Marriott other important sponsors of this addition to the European Tour will include Jaguar, Omega and International Sports Management Limited. More than 150 of Europe's top golfers will compete for this Masters title and, as the company's announcement vividly suggested, will be "Walking in the footsteps of giants".

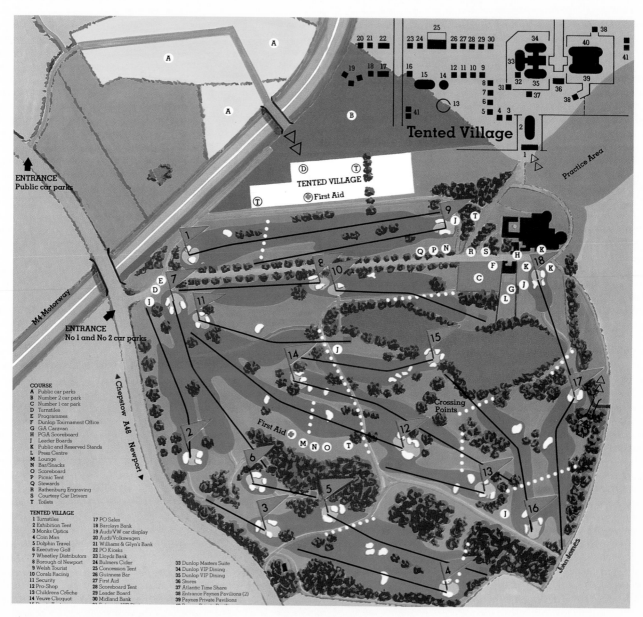

The layout of the course and tented village for the 1982 tournament at St Pierre

1984 – 1998

THE BTR YEARS, INTERNATIONAL EXPANSION, MANAGEMENT BUY OUT AND TOWARDS THE NEW MILLENNIUM

Alan Finden-Crofts

For the most part, and for well over 100 years, the history of the Dunlop and Slazenger companies had been an account of the formation and development of individual businesses. And of the process of building strong brand images within the expanding and worldwide sports equipment market; Gradidge with its focus on cricket, Sykes for leather, football and cricket, Ayres for archery, Slazenger primarily for tennis and the late comer, Dunlop, with a balance between golf and racket sports. Certainly after the amalgamation of Slazenger, Sykes, Ayres and Gradidge in the 1940s the Slazenger management had successfully welded the strength of those four companies into the single Slazenger presence, but it remained a key element of the ISC policy, for nearly 20 years after the Dunlop and Slazenger merger, to maintain the separate identities, organisation structures and brand images of its constituent units. That had been especially true in the case of Dunlop and Slazenger, which recalls the instruction from the Dunlop board to George Carr to 'keep an eye on Slazenger' rather than fully absorb it into the parent company's organisation.

Even as late as 1983, as Alan Finden-Crofts was getting to grips with the Dunlop consumer companies (Dunlopillo, Footwear and Semtex as well as ISC), Dunlop, Slazenger, Litesome, Letters and Carlton still had their own managing directors, head offices, sales forces and marketing philosophies to support their differing brand images. And ISC was still a mainly UK business with no accountability for the more important overseas sports operations.

But all of this would now change and the years ahead would present a very different story. The pattern of the two main businesses being managed for generally quite long periods by a small number of managing directors; five for Slazenger in 100 years and the same number for Dunlop in more than 70; would give way to there being four in the twenty years from 1983. Management by individual company and brand would end and be replaced, successively, by organisations based on management by product, then by a product and territory matrix, back to mainly product, then by function and, finally, by a mix of territory and function. Ownership of the business would move first from Dunlop to BTR, and, second, to a management buy out supported by venture capital, a consortium of banks and a BTR loan. Possibly the most significant difference from the past was the 1984 decision to create Dunlop Slazenger International as the single management vehicle for the more than thirty separate sports operations located in the UK, Europe, North America, the Far East, and, from 1996, South Africa. In terms of brands

Litesome and Letters soon departed, and the Puma UK franchise would later return to its parent company in 1999. Maxfli, the famous brand that developed into a separate division during this period, would be sold at the end of 2002. The rationalisation of the business, and especially of its manufacturing facilities, which had started with the 1979 closures of Speke and Waltham Abbey, would continue throughout this period and the number of personnel employed would be more than halved. And, at the end of all this, there would be a new focus on the core Dunlop and Slazenger names in their golf, racket and cricket sectors with Carlton retained for its powerful badminton presence.

Returning to the start of this re-shaping process, at the beginning of 1984, when the operating and management entity was still ISC, Finden-Crofts initial organisation changes in the UK had reflected a focus on product management. Then the principal appointments were Findlay Picken for rackets, Peter Wycherley for golf and Ian Peacock remaining as MD of Slazenger. Separate responsibilities were established for clothing (John Usher), Puma (Brian Waters), and a multi-product operation (Geoff Mortimer). Laurie Roberts in the Hong Kong sales and sourcing office also reported to Finden-Crofts and closer links were established with South Africa (Colin Van Jarsveldt), France (Roy Sherwin) and Germany (Detlef Grosse). At this stage the Dunlop Footwear general manager, Len Thompson, also reported to him but had not been brought into the sports group of companies.

During this evolutionary period Finden-Crofts had been armed with the findings of the Boston Consulting Group, which, among other things, had been asked to review the perception and market status of all the consumer companies. The main recommendation of their report was that it was essential that all of them, and most certainly the sports businesses, should establish individual identities in their main markets, which should be more clearly separated from the parent Dunlop company with its mainly tyre and industrially oriented images. This was accompanied by the recommendation that even greater emphasis be placed on the development and promotion of new products, which should have increased impact in the areas of performance and fashion. The former was well understood within ISC, the latter would require much more prominence than in the past.

With the arrival of Sir Michael Edwardes at Dunlop House in St. James's, in November, 1984, the pace of change quickened, which certainly suited Finden-Crofts as he was generally keen to turn proposals into actions as quickly as possible. He now learned his energies were to be entirely focused on the sports and leisure business. Within a week of becoming executive chairman of Dunlop, Sir Michael announced a major restructuring of the company into profit centres, or business groups, which, in the case of the non-tyre operations, were intended to allow each of them 'to grow profitably on a worldwide basis'. The emphasis on profitability wasn't new, to seek it on a truly worldwide basis was.

In the same month, with Sir Michael himself as the pro tem chairman, Finden-Crofts became chief executive (a new title within Dunlop) of Dunlop Slazenger International, which included not only the sports businesses, but also all clothing and leisure footwear. This arrangement embraced Dunlop Footwear Limited, and its additional ranges of protective footwear and slippers, so, for the first time, management of sports equipment and sports footwear was combined. The announcement of the formation of these new

Sir Michael Edwardes

202

business groups emphasised that each of the chief executives involved would be responsible for operations 'throughout the world', with the single exception, at that time, of the South African company, which continued to be responsible for all its local operations.

Also at this time the newly formed Dunlop Slazenger, with its already established management resources in Hong Kong, assumed responsibility for all other sports businesses in the Far East and for the Dunlopillo bedding factories and sales activities in Thailand and Indonesia.

Of greater significance was the decision that the Dunlop Tire & Rubber Company in Buffalo would, in future, be concerned only with tyres. Among its other product divisions the Greenville based sports business, which had just assumed responsibility for the Canadian Sportlines company, would become part of Finden-Crofts new sports empire and, after more than 50 years of reporting to Buffalo, became part of the new Dunlop Slazenger, thereby consolidating the transition towards an international sports operation. It was certainly more international than ever before though it did not include the now separately owned Australian and Japanese sports businesses, the latter as large as the whole of Dunlop Slazenger International.

Only three months later Sir Michael wrote to all Dunlop employees to advise that following the considerable work done to restructure the company, and to begin its financial recovery, it had been agreed to accept a BTR offer of £101 million for the issued share capital. This brought the end of a very difficult six months for all Dunlop employees, which had been a mixture of uncertainty about their and the company's future, and also the pressures created by the major reorganisation.

Against that background the takeover by BTR, which was generally regarded as a highly successful and very profitable company, offered the prospect of a brighter future for Dunlop Slazenger. Finden-Crofts was quick to highlight this to his new, worldwide team. He stressed the positive aspects of the change of ownership, in particular that Dunlop Slazenger, as the only sports business in the BTR portfolio – apart from a dormant Goudie squash company – would be given the opportunity and resources to develop 'an extremely good future', provided, of course, it met the objectives and targets of its new strategic plans. For its part BTR had recognised that the recent creation of the worldwide sports and leisure business group provided an operating unit that fitted comfortably into its overall structure. This meant that while overall direction and accountability remained in the UK centre, now located in the old Slazenger office in Croydon, there would also be support from BTR's local resources in overseas territories. This was to prove particularly important in the USA where its personnel and systems specialists were able to provide much needed assistance to replace the services previously provided by the Buffalo tyre operation, and which were terminated on an almost overnight basis when that business became an MBO in 1985.

From April, 1985 Finden-Crofts reported to Hugh Laughland, who had joined the BTR board when his previous company, Thomas Tilling, had been taken over the by the expanding conglomerate. He now had two main tasks. First, to continue the process of establishing and rationalising the new sports structure, and, second, to quickly adapt all the systems and procedures in the numerous individual units to fit the BTR accounting and reporting requirements. His principal lieutenant for this complex and considerable operation was Mike Dowie, a Dunlop executive with experience of both head office and operational controls, in the latter case during a spell as an accountant with Dunlop Footwear. It had quickly become apparent to both Finden-Crofts and Dowie, as well as to BTR, that the recovery already visible in the vital USA market signalled the opportunity for much greater expansion there than anywhere else in the business, and that it would be necessary to provide additional resources to accelerate this progress.

BTR's support for this approach not only in the USA, but throughout the business was acknowledged by Finden-Crofts in a March, 1986 interview he gave to *Harper's Sports and Leisure*, under the heading 'Dunlop – a new professionalism'. By then the company's markedly improved performance had made it possible to finance its continuous restructuring from current trading profits and the magazine's reporter was told this process had been driven by "The basic strategy to centralise all activities in the UK and reduce overheads as the main route to maintaining complete control over what had become a multi-armed and unmanageable creature". Evidence of this approach could be seen in the decisions to dispose of the John Letters golf club business, which was sold back to the Letters family, and also the Litesome company, which was sold to the Peter Black organisation. A more traumatic move had been the 1986 closure of the famous Horbury plant, 50 years after the Sykes company had moved there and 120 years after William Sykes had brought the sports industry to the town when he made his first six soccer balls for the boys at the Whitsun holiday treat.

The organisation structure introduced to 'maintain complete control' was based on a matrix combining product and territory management and brought to an end the long established approach by brand and individual company. In particular this had meant that Dunlop and Slazenger ceased to exist as separate trading units and while the public could still see separate golf and racket ranges for each of the brands, the regional managers in Europe (Brian Jenkins), North America (Brian Simpson) and the Far East (Laurie Roberts) were responsible for all activities in these areas. Brian Jenkins was also responsible for the Carlton badminton business. Both Jenkins and Simpson were responsible for the R & D and manufacturing functions in their regions and Laurie Roberts combined management of the six sales offices in the Far East with control of the sourcing operation. The latter had expanded dramatically as the closure of Waltham Abbey and Horbury had meant that the bulk of the group's rackets, golf clubs, golf accessories and clothing were now produced in this region, then mainly in Taiwan and South Korea. Dunlop Footwear retained control of its own external sourcing arrangements for sports and leisure shoes and of its UK factories for protective footwear, in Liverpool, and for slippers, in Blackburn.

In the UK golf and tennis ball production continued at Normanton and Barnsley respectively. Westminster and Hartwell supplied the North American region, and Hanau continued to make tennis balls for the German market. In the Far East the Philippines tennis ball plant was supplying both Dunlop Slazenger and the Australian market, the Indonesian operation produced tennis balls and Dunlopillo beds for the local market, and the Thailand company combined sports distribution and bedding manufacture. This streamlining of manufacture to the six main plants in the three regions would not be the end of a rationalisation process that continued into the next century but it compared with the seventeen wholly owned Dunlop sports manufacturing units that had existed in the 1970s, plus a further six operating in

Eric Loxton's workbench in the
Barnsley factory and his traditional bat
making tools

Australia, South Africa and Japan.

Within Dunlop Slazenger the parent BTR was viewed with a mixture of respect and wariness. Respect for the rigorous financial disciplines and obviously successful record over a 20-year period of profitable growth. The wariness, or reserve, was based on the perception that a company viewed primarily as an industrial conglomerate would not be so comfortable when operating in a consumer market environment. It would also be fair to say that a number of those who had previously worked only for Dunlop or Slazenger had to quickly adjust to a more demanding management style based largely on tough financial targets agreed at legendary annual plan challenge meetings with BTR main board directors, and the subsequent performance monitoring on a monthly and very detailed basis.

For most of the period that BTR owned Dunlop Slazenger (1985–1996), and contrary to those early concerns among the sports management team, BTR did demonstrate a willingness to invest very substantially in its development. Most importantly, and this could have been expected of a company that understood the importance of continuously improving manufacturing efficiency, investment in plant modernisation was massively increased, and sustained over a ten year period. The fact that today the company's two remaining plants at Westminster and in the Philippines are world class is almost entirely due to the funds made available to Finden-Crofts and his successors, Patrick Austen and David Jacobs, from 1985 onwards. Those present when John Cahill, BTR's chief executive, first visited Westminster were left in no doubt about his intentions to remedy the years of under investment in that facility. That situation had left the USA business extremely vulnerable due to its inability to consistently produce golf balls to match the quality standards of its leading USA based competitors.

The BTR approach to promotional expenditure was less open handed, at least in the opinion of the Dunlop Slazenger management. The new owner's mainly industrial market orientation, plus its preference for increased manufacturing efficiency as the more reliable route to profit improvement, made it inherently reluctant to support the

Alec Stewart keeps a close watch as
Eric Loxton prepares a new bat to
exactly meet his requirements

scale of A & P spending generally deployed within the sports industry, and certainly by the majority of the main competitors in that market. Not surprisingly successive sports management teams during the period of BTR ownership regarded this tight control of the promotional purse-strings as a handicap, and not least because, if anything, competitor expenditure was rising.

However, it should be observed that BTR did agree advertising expenditure above the levels that had been available during the final, embattled years within Dunlop, but that whatever the amounts agreed each year they still had to be spread across three main brands.

Additionally, the decision in the mid 1980s to focus on Maxfli as the worldwide premium golf brand inevitably required a major investment in the USA and mainly in high cost network TV. This meant that resources to support Dunlop and Slazenger, and for rackets and other product categories, were even more restricted. Certainly the USA golf ball market was correctly identified as the company's most obvious growth opportunity – and that objective was achieved in terms of a significantly increased volume of business – but given the overall spending limits both Dunlop and Slazenger were inevitably diminished in terms of brand strength in the majority of their market sectors.

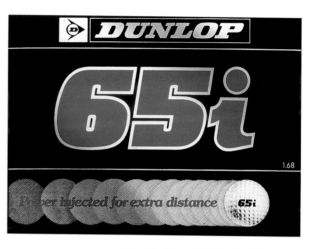

The 65i the only Dunlop ball in the main UK golf catalogue in 1987

The priority given to the Maxfli brand, within a much larger promotional budget, would continue after the 1996 management buy out, but in the early years of the new century the rebuilding process for Dunlop and Slazenger has steadily gather momentum.

The investment in manufacturing was not restricted to the Westminster golf ball plant, though that was certainly the main project. Gary Roulston, with previous experience of golf ball production at Spalding, became vice-president in charge of USA manufacturing and laid the foundations for a complete transformation of the South Carolina operation including what would eventually be the group's main R & D unit for golf balls, as well as an almost completely modernised production complex with hugely increased capacity operating with unprecedented standards of quality control. In Europe the Normanton golf ball plant and both the Hanau and Barnsley tennis ball units were steadily upgraded. Following the closure of Horbury the latter would become the new home for Eric Loxton and the cricket bat plant with its combination of modern wood preparation equipment and the traditional skills and hand tools required to prepare the large number of very individual bats required by the leading Slazenger players. Viv Richards, Mark Waugh, Alec Stewart, Mark Butcher and Jacques Kallis are just a few of the many international stars to have stood alongside Eric's rather cluttered bench as he fine-tuned their bats to meet their exact requirements. Graeme Hick probably spoke for all of them when he wrote to Eric, in 1999, on the occasion of his 40th anniversary of joining Slazenger, to say, quite simply, "Congratulations, you are the best in the business".

WINNERS IN ACTION

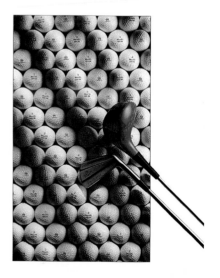

The 'Winners in Action' theme on a 1987 golf catalogue

The strategic decision to look for significant growth in the USA golf market required a degree of increased marketing investment to match that being made in the Westminster plant. Although Maxfli had been the lead sub-brand in the USA for many years, and presented as 'Maxfli by Dunlop', the decision to make it the worldwide premium golf mark meant that, for the first time, sufficient funds were available to allow both an effective use of TV, and also an increased investment in secur-

Patrick Austen

ing endorsements by Tour professionals. Previously the much smaller budgets available to the completely separate US sports operation had meant choosing one or the other. With Maxfli soon, and accurately, being promoted as 'the fastest growing ball on the US PGA Tour' the other Dunlop Slazenger operations around the world co-ordinated their golf advertising with this message, which featured leading players like Fuzzy Zoeller, Hubert Green, Larry Nelson and Fred Couples. A considerable boost was given to this programme by the decision of the Japanese Dunlop sports operation, owned by Sumitomo, to co-ordinate their promotion of the brand in conjunction with the very strong Tour in their own country, and also to provide financial support for the US TV campaign.

A quite separate attack on the US market was the establishment, in 1986, of the Slazenger Golf operation, also based in Greenville, which was managed by the former Dunlop executives, David Branon and Geoffrey Gorman, whose names were used to create the separate company known as David Geoffrey and Associates. The business was located in one of the city's former textile mills and its exclusively pro shop distribution policy featured a product range based not only on premium golf balls but also a very high quality range of apparel sourced from Hong Kong.

Both the worldwide Maxfli programme and a co-ordinated approach to utilising the powerful value of John McEnroe playing the 200G racket, again including the Japanese market, were early examples of the benefit of the 'truly international' organisation now in place. And although still separately owned the Australian and South African sports businesses were quick to utilise the worldwide impact of these campaigns.

By the end of 1986 it was clear that Dunlop Slazenger International had built up considerable momentum since its formation three years earlier. Total sales had increased by more than 50% and, more importantly from a BTR perspective, profitability, while not quite meeting the required target, had moved into percentage double figures for the first time for many years. In both product and territory terms expansion and performance improvement were the norms. Sales in North America and the Far East had trebled over a four year period. Driven by the investment focus in the USA golf sales had exploded on the way to becoming the largest product sector by the early 1990s. Sales of rackets and tennis balls had shown comparatively modest growth but profitability had more than doubled. Dunlop Footwear had maintained its previous record for consistent profitability and sales of the Puma franchise had more than

Challenge Court at Leatherhead

doubled.

At the start of 1987 the USA golf team was strengthened by the recruitment of Mike Orr as vice president responsible for marketing both the Dunlop and Maxfli ranges. He brought with him previous experience in the golf business as a senior marketing executive with Spalding and would play a major role in the international development of the Maxfli brand.

The fact that during this period the bulk of the company's total sales growth was derived from the expansion in the golf sector – mainly in USA but also very significantly in Europe – fully justified the dual investment programme that made possible the much larger expenditure on media and players, and also the improving quality of the ball range as standards at both Westminster and Normanton were steadily improved. The much higher production volume at both these plants significantly reduced manufacturing costs for the bulk of the range, and the availability of the Sumitomo balata ball provided what was probably then the highest quality and best performing product for the Tour professionals and low handicap players. At this stage the DDH dimple pattern, introduced in 1980, was used on most of the

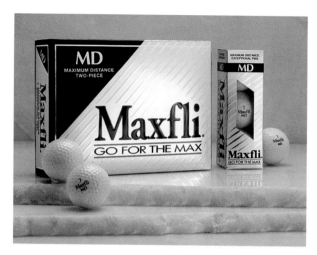

The 'Go for the Max' theme on a Maxfli MD box in the early 1990s

balls produced in USA and UK and also on the Kobe made balata Tour Limited. Maxfli had become the predominant brand for all premium balls with the UK catalogue listing only the 65i as a Dunlop product.

The less spectacular, but very important improvement in the racket business was based on the continuing strength of Dunlop and Slazenger tennis ball sales in all the main markets and the outstanding success of the UK made 200G injection moulded frame. And by now the well developed working relationships between the company's product managers, the enlarged sourcing operation in Hong Kong and the high quality Taiwan based producers of graphite frames meant the flagship 200G was supported by a strong range for both Dunlop and Slazenger brands, which was much better co-ordinated internationally.

The main advertising theme chosen for 1987, 'Winners in Action', was not an idle boast. At the start of this period John McEnroe was at the height of his considerable powers and in 1987 Steffi Graf, who had been supported by the company's German sports business, and especially by its general manager, Detlef Grosse, since her first endorsement contract signed when she was seven years old, won the first of her 22 Grand Slam titles at the French Open. And between 1983 and 1987 the combination of Seve Ballesteros, Larry Nelson, Hal Sutton, Fuzzy Zoeller, Sandy Lyle, Hubert Green and Greg Norman used Dunlop or Slazenger balls and equipment to win nine golf majors. In 1987 Ian Woosnam, who had always played Dunlop and Maxfli balls, became the first golfer to win £1 million in one year.

Early in that same year Hugh Laughland had the task of phoning the senior Dunlop Slazenger managers with the news that Alan Finden-Crofts had decided to take up a fresh challenge to revive the fortunes of the famous Raleigh cycle business. He left the company, after just over four years as chief executive, with the satisfaction of seeing that the international structure he had put in place had quickly demonstrated its ability to significantly improve the performance of what had now become known as the BTR Sports Group.

Hugh Laughland's next task was to appoint a new chief executive. The choice made was Patrick Austen, who had joined the Thomas Tilling company from ICI to run the Pretty Polly hosiery business and took up that assignment on virtually the same day Tilling was acquired by BTR. In the role of BTR's group chief executive for consumer products he continued to be responsible for Pretty Polly, until it was sold for a considerable premium in

After more than 50 years as a Dunlop ball the 65 is branded Maxfli

1991, and for a group of furniture manufacturers, also previously part of Tilling, which was sold in 1993.

However, Austen's main task was to continue the development of the sports business. Almost immediately he took over – and this reflects the degree of support by then being provided by BTR – the company made a strong bid for the Prince racket business, which didn't succeed because a management buy out route was preferred. This was a disappointment because it was clear that acquisition of the Prince brand would have given the group a much stronger position internationally and especially in North America. In the latter case it was proving much more difficult to make progress with the Dunlop brand in the tennis sector than in the golf market, where the large scale investments in both manufacturing and marketing had revitalised the Maxfli brand.

For Austen the Prince bid, which took place nearly 20 years after ISC had last made an acquisition (Carlton in 1968), signalled one of the main themes of his six years as chief executive. With the continuing BTR support further bids would be either explored in detail, or actually put forward for Wilson, Hogan, the main Puma company based in Germany, and, in 1991, a second attempt to acquire Prince was only frustrated by a 'shut out' offer from Benetton. In the latter case the company's own effort was supported by BTR director, Mike Smith, who had succeeded Hugh Laughland as the board member responsible for the sports group.

The absorption of the business into BTR was given solid, 'bricks and mortar' reality when, in 1988, its headquarters was transferred from the old Slazenger office in Croydon to a brand new office complex on the outskirts of Leatherhead in Surrey, which would be shared with other BTR companies for the next eight years. The Slazenger connection was maintained by naming the new site Challenge Court.

The priority objective for the Sports Group was to bring its profitability closer to the average for the whole of BTR, which, during the six years up to 1993 ran close to 15% while total sales had more than doubled to nearly £10 billion. That target wasn't reached but the growth pattern established since the formation of Dunlop Slazenger International was maintained. By the early 1990s total sales worldwide had reached nearly £300 million, which was more than double the starting figure in 1984. Within that total the sales of the core sports operation, i.e. excluding the Puma franchise and Dunlop Footwear, increased by more than 50% between 1986 and 1993. The basis of this growth remained the expansion in the golf market and, in the USA, the very significant market share increases achieved by the Maxfli and Slazenger combination. The Maxfli ball line had been further strengthened by the successful introduction of a new, 432 dimple design licensed from Dunlop Japan. The Maxfli brand, with its theme 'Go for the Max', had become completely dominant for premium products, so much so that the '65' was now the 'Maxfli 65'. In the golf market Dunlop was being deployed, with relatively low promotional support, as the value brand across a full range of balls, clubs and accessories, and in the USA the Detroit based licensing operation, Bilgrets – later to be re-named Focus and moved to Greenville – was driving sales of Dunlop clubs to higher volume levels than ever previously reached.

In contrast to the steady growth of golf through the 1980s and into the early 1990s tennis struggled to maintain its popularity and share of the sports equipment market. Companies supplying all forms of tennis equipment, large and small and especially in the USA, devoted considerable time and expenditure to devising numerous programmes to promote the game to the public, and there's little doubt the decline in the number of participants would have been much more serious had those efforts not been made. Although this situation worked against the company making significant progress with either sales or profitability, and would be a contributory factor to the closure of the Hartwell plant in 1992, the total volume of business, and market shares were maintained in the majority of territories. A major problem was the inability to develop a new 'flagship' racket to match the phenomenal success of the 200G.

Reference has been made to BTR's reluctance to sanction increases in promotional expenditure, and the pressure this created in terms of maintaining brand strengths as competitor spends did rise. The era of $1 million per annum player endorsements had arrived for both golf and tennis stars at a time when it was necessary to invest more heavily than ever in network TV to maintain an effective presence in the vital, and still growing USA golf market. The contrast between the buoyant golf market and the static tennis scene almost inevitably meant that the priority allocation of limited funds was given to the former and could also lead to the latter being first in line when expenditure cuts were demanded to protect against any profit shortfalls.

This limited availability of advertising money had also been a serious problem for Dunlop Footwear, especially in relation to the sports shoe range since the advent, in the 1970s, of the new breed of specialist manufacturers offering more sophisticated designs endorsed by individual star players paid almost as much as the total annual spend behind Dunlop sports shoes. By the 1990s the once supreme Green Flash tennis shoes was being marketed, albeit successfully, as a retro canvas casual. And the years of minimal investment in Dunlop as a footwear brand was one of the reasons for a sharp decline in volume as the multiple retailers, who had become the company's main customers, began not only to promote their own brands but also to deal direct with the overseas suppliers the company had fostered for so many years.

Dunlop Footwear, which operated mainly in the shoe trade rather than sports, had never fitted comfortably with either ISC or Dunlop Slazenger. After many years of successful trading its sudden and severe profit downturn in 1992 brought an extra strategic challenge for the Sports Group, which, ultimately, would be solved by closure of the UK operation and a switch to licensing the brand, rather than by attempting a recovery programme requiring the use of scarce resources in an unfamiliar sector.

While Austen had been making good progress with the sports equipment companies Puma joined Dunlop Footwear on the 'sick list' at about the same time (1991/92) with the result that more than £40 million of sales disappeared over a two year period accompanied by a very severe hit to the group's bottom line. However, the 100% sports and leisure related Puma operation, and the group's contractual commitments to the German owned brand, demanded an effective response to this setback, which was largely brought about by a failure to react quickly enough to styling changes in the sportswear sector. Austen recruited Andrew Peters, who had managed both rackets sports and cricket for Slazenger in the 1970s before becoming managing

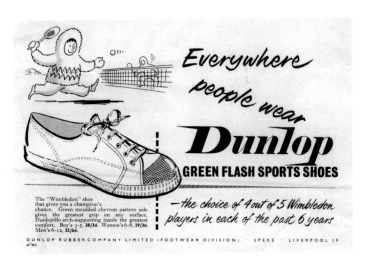

Dunlop footwear's famous Green Flash – the number one tennis shoe in the 1956 ad

director of a major sports retailer. Over a two year period, following his return as managing director of Puma, he was able to restore sales and profits to the previous 1990 peak, mainly by re-positioning both the brand and product line much more clearly in the performance category.

The shape of the business continued to evolve during Austen's stewardship. In conjunction with the 1992 closure of the Hartwell tennis ball plant the decision was made to move the Philippines plant to a much larger factory only a few hundred yards from the original unit opened in 1977. Much of the Hartwell production equipment was also transferred to the new site as part of the longer term consolidation of tennis ball manufacture, and the decision taken then made possible the subsequent concentration of all Dunlop Slazenger production there.

In the Far East the decision was taken to move the regional headquarters and main sourcing office from Hong Kong to Kuala Lumpur. This move, which combined cost reduction with concern about the future of Hong Kong, was completed in 1990 by Ronnie Downie, who had taken over the dual sales and sourcing role from Laurie Roberts. At the same time the increasingly important sourcing operation was reorganised in line with the major structural change introduced by Austen in 1989. This involved a switch from the previous territory/product matrix established by Finden-Crofts to a product led set-up with Brian Jenkins and Mike Orr as the respective international racket and golf directors supported by territory sales and distribution organisations.

In Europe, as an extension of the number of territory sales operations, local distributors were superseded by company owned businesses in Vianen, Holland, which covered the Benelux countries, and Barcelona. This pattern would be repeated later with the establishment of Dunlop Slazenger in Italy and, very importantly, the company returned to France at the end of 1993 when Sumitomo agreed to transfer the Dunlop trade marks for sports goods in that country, which they had acquired in 1984. Shortly after that move Sumitomo took the decision to close the tennis ball plant in their Montlucon factory, which had started up, in true Dunlop style, alongside the tyre-making equipment in the early 1920s.

Changes among the senior management team during the early 1990s had seen Finance Director, Mike Dowie, who had worked alongside Finden-Crofts during the creation of Dunlop Slazenger International and its integration into BTR, succeeded, on a temporary basis, by Tom Barber, who was followed by Charles Marchetti. He, in turn, was replaced by Gordon Moodie. On returning from the USA Brian Simpson had become the Strategic Planning Director, and the two original international

The Green Flash plimsoll

Forget lightweight hi-tech trainers or Prada-style fashion-cum-sports shoes with moulded soles – the truly modish consider these so out of date. Instead, stylish boys and girls are donning their Green Flash plimsolls by Dunlop to visit Top Shop and Hennes. OK, so the last time you wore these white lace-ups was probably during school PE lessons but, believe me, they're now as cool as Britney in a gym skirt. Better still, this time around you can ditch the embarrassing home-made pump bag. Just be sure to do up those laces ... *Dunlop Green Flash, from £19-99, nationwide inquiries, 01606 592 041.*

Molly Gunn

In the 1990s, Green Flash re-invented as a retro casual

product directors, Brian Jenkins and Mike Orr, had been succeeded by two BTR senior managers. Phil Wragg from International Radiator Services (Serck) taking over the racket responsibility and Dick Dodson, an American, who had been running the UK based dust control operation (DCE), returning to the USA to lead the golf business.

The high level of visibility provided for the company's brands during the early and mid 1980s by leading tennis players and golfers was maintained well into the 1990s. Player contracts were subject to as much financial discipline as all other areas of expenditure so it was obviously essential to continue to select 'winners'. Between 1987 and 1993 Steffi Graf, using the 200G, won 11 Grand Slam titles and Arantxa Sanchez-Vicario notched up a win for the Slazenger 'Mystique' racket at the 1989 French Open. Sandy Lyle was the first British winner of the US Masters and Slazenger and Maxfli equipment was used by such as Seve Ballesteros, Ian Woosnam, Ian Baker-Finch, Fred Couples, Greg Norman and Curtis Strange to win numerous key events, including six majors.

Under the headings 'Consumer Related' and 'Sports and Fashion' successive BTR annual reports at this time regularly summarised the performance of the sports business (and Pretty Polly) with considerable prominence given to high quality photographs and attractive layouts. The tournament successes of the leading players were regularly listed, new products were described in some detail, especially if they had a hi-tech content, and the emphasis on the individual brands was such that the impression given was that Dunlop and Slazenger were still operating as separate units. Indeed, the 1989 report declared that Slazenger had its own plants in the UK and Germany, and the growing success of the licensing division – 60 licensees in over 30 countries' – was largely attributed to Slazenger.

Another consistent theme throughout the second half of the 1980s and into the 1990s was an almost continuous and very necessary preoccupation with legal issues, all of which were extremely time consuming and generally very expensive in terms of lawyers' fees. Alan Finden-Crofts had found himself involved in a predatory pricing dispute almost immediately he took over Dunlop Slazenger. This was a successful action initiated by Dunlop Tire & Rubber Company in the early 1980s – on behalf of their sports division – against a major USA tennis ball competitor. In his turn Patrick Austen had to contend with several patent related issues, mainly defensively, involving golf ball design and construction and racket head design. The most important of these, which had seriously threatened the company's premium golf ball position, was successfully resolved at the highest judicial level – an appeal to the USA Supreme Court – but only after a two year battle, which had to be given priority attention over that length of time by several key members of the senior management team both in the UK and USA.

A very different issue was the need to defend a European Commission charge of infringement of competition rules in relation to tennis and squash balls. The investigation into the Commission's 'Statement of Objections' commenced in Autumn, 1986, and, three years later, resulted in a ruling against the company accompanied by a fine of £3.5 million. With the bulk of the work throughout falling on the shoulders of the sales director of the UK rack-

Steffi Graf in action with her 200G

BTR's Annual Report for 1994
showcases a successful Sports Group

et business, Peter Warren-Tape, the company decided to appeal to the European Court of First Instance against both the judgement and fine, which had to be paid immediately to avoid a considerable interest penalty. This decision was vindicated to the extent that the Court, in 1992, accepted the argument that there was little evidence of 'abuse of dominant power' within the tennis ball market, and that the squash ball market was effectively quite small and specialised. Although the Court did uphold the Commission's view that the company had attempted to restrict competition between EC markets the fine was reduced to £1.5 million. This was a very expensive lesson, which had revealed not only to Dunlop Slazenger but also to many other BTR companies, that there was very little understanding at the time of the requirements for operating across the EC markets. This omission was quickly rectified by an intensive education programme across the whole BTR group.

Early in 1993 Patrick Austen departed to become chief executive of Liberty plc, the famous Regent Street based luxury retailer and textile manufacturer. The total sales had been increased by nearly 40% since his arrival and those of the sports equipment operations by more than 50%. The expansion of the key USA business had continued and by 1993 it accounted for 32% of total sales, compared with 19% in 1986. Within that the USA golf business had expanded more than threefold, which was well ahead of the growth rate for the whole market during the same period, but racket sales both in total and in the USA had been virtually static. Profitability had declined in 1990 – the BTR annual report declaring 'Dunlop Slazenger continued to experience very difficult market conditions' – and had collapsed in 1991/92, mainly because of the problems with Puma and Dunlop Footwear. Dunlop Footwear would not recover but the combination of a return to sales growth and the corrective action taken with Puma laid the foundation for profit recovery from 1993 onwards.

As no immediate successor to Austen was appointed the business was managed throughout 1993 by a combination of its senior managers (Wragg, Dodson, Moodie and Peters) and BTR directors, Robert Quarta and Robert Faircloth. This 'management committee' was able to report on a modest sales increase but a trebling of profits. This trend was maintained and the BTR annual report on 1994 was able to declare that 'Sports' had again improved profitability despite depressed demand in many of its key markets.

Reference in this report was also made to the continuing decline in the number of people playing tennis, which had forced increased attention to cost reduction in that sector. This 'defensive' approach was in contrast to 'another successful year for the golf division' with an emphasis on new product development and the tournament successes of Ballesteros, Couples and Norman plus two new names for the company, Jack Nicklaus and Laura Davies. Cricket also featured with the news that activities in that market had been expanded by introducing clothing and footwear into the Slazenger range and by relaunching the newly acquired Stuart Surridge range of equipment, which was endorsed by Graham Gooch. The 'Consumer Related' section in this particular report was dominated by a double page 'Sports' spread with a series of photographs illustrating the golf ball design and manufacturing process alongside a panoramic view of a perfectly manicured Australian golf course. Sadly, Steffi Graf's victory at the Australian Open couldn't be mentioned as her contract had not been renewed and she was now playing with a competitor's racket.

At the start of 1994 the gap at the top of the company was filled. 'Next into bat' as chief executive was David Jacobs, a great sports enthusiast, especially for rugby (both codes) and cricket. He brought with him considerable experience, as a senior manager and director, of a number of leading consumer sector companies including Cadbury Schweppes, Gillette, Imperial Group and Grand Metropolitan. In the latter case, and immediately before moving to Dunlop Slazenger, he had been managing director of the Chef and Brewer restaurant group.

David Jacobs

He would quickly demonstrate he had very clear ideas about the future direction for the company. In particular he had seen that in order to achieve the very ambitious sales and profit objectives that both he and BTR had set for the business it would be essential to establish a 'Sports Group Culture', rather than the individual and unit cultures he felt were too prevalent. And he was well aware that while the business operated in the very specific and highly competitive environment of the sports equipment market, and must shape its policies and actions accordingly, it also had to observe, even if sometimes reluctantly, the existence of another influence, that of BTR, with its own objectives and disciplines. His previous experience of managing clearly identified business units, developing their own brand strengths, would prove invaluable in maintaining that balance between the ambitions of the Sports Group and of its much larger parent conglomerate. His commitment to the development of a 'Sports Culture' was soon apparent as his search for a fresh intake of young managers focused mainly on individuals from outside BTR. And, regardless of where they had been working, he was likely to be more impressed by their track records than whether or not they had previous sports trade experience.

In parallel with the search for 'new blood' he was insistent that the basis of developing the international character of the business should be the definition and execution of much clearer and consistent brand positions for each worldwide product range and across all markets. This would be reflected in his approach to changing the basic organisation structure of the business, and also in his choice of individuals for key appointments, especially in the marketing function, which he saw as the cutting edge of the whole operation.

While David Jacobs developed his plans for the business the recovery from the lows of 1991 and 1992 continued. Boosted by the steadily rising income from the licensing division, which was running at around £3 million per annum, profits in 1994 were the highest for six years. The licensing activity, directed during this period by John Rees from the Leatherhead office, would continue to grow through the 1990s as a steady stream of new licencees, for either the Slazenger or Dunlop brand, would be recruited for mainly clothing and accessories in those countries where a direct sales approach was not practical. And great care was taken to make sure that those applying to work with the company in this way could demonstrate their ability to work within the strict guidelines laid down regarding exactly how the brands could be presented. This approach had originally been established in line with the very detailed manuals published by the parent Dunlop company, which set out minute details on how to display both the 'Dunlop' word and the famous

'Flying D' symbol, and especially in relation to its application to the wide range of sports and leisure products involved. Dunlop Slazenger had successfully extended this principle to also cover the use of the Slazenger brand.

Jacobs, with his marketing and product background, had made clear the importance of 'developing a constant stream of innovative new products'. In this context he was probably delighted with a full page feature in the Winter 1994 edition of 'BTR News', which, under the heading 'Capitalising on high performance products', showcased 'The 1995 range of high technology sports equipment from the Sports Group' with the promise that the launch of many new products would be supported by an 'aggressive marketing campaign designed to capitalise on some of the world's leading brands'.

At first sight this particular montage, which combined a selection of key products with a detailed supporting text, represented an impressive snapshot of the overall shape of the business at that time. John McEnroe re-appears for Dunlop in the role of helping to promote the new 'Revelation' rackets, and Jack Nicklaus does the same for 'the expanded family of HT golf balls. Dunlop isn't mentioned in relation to golf but Maxfli gets another mention for its appearance on the VHL (variable hosel length) club line plus the Tad Moore designed range of putters. Slazenger is strongly presented in the golf market, with its 'Fat Cat' driver, Slazenger Plus club, new SFC range of putters and wedges developed with Seve Ballesteros, and wound golf ball. The brand's stronger connections with cricket and tennis are underlined by, respectively, the V600 bats and equipment, an upgraded 'Mystique' racket and the ever present Wimbledon tennis balls. The Dunlop Footwear 'Revelation' tennis shoe is featured and although its revolutionary design was the result of a collaboration with the Brunel Institute of Bioengineering there were virtually no promotional funds available to give it any chance of succeeding in the fiercely competitive tennis shoe sector. The Carlton badminton range is not included but to complete the parade of brands in the feature there are references to a revamped cricket bat range carrying the Surridge brand, and to the reviving Puma operation highlighted by its new ranges of footwear and clothing for street soccer, 'Puma King' football boots, new kit designs for the 1995 Great Britain and Wales rugby league teams, and 'Puma Aeroskip', a new fitness concept centred on skipping.

BTR *News* 1994 special feature on performance products

Although applied in this case to the 1995 range the closing paragraph of this feature pretty well encapsulates the story of Dunlop Slazenger. 'Whether putting or batting, hitting forehand drives or kicking goals, the impressive 1995 product range is designed to please – improving performance at all skill levels'. However, as suggested, the initial reaction to this in house promotional feature, which was not repeated externally, could be misleading, or, at least inclined to overstate the 'newness' of the products on display. Certainly, in terms of the main core golf and tennis ranges, and especially the balls, it fell short of meeting the Jacobs criteria of offering a stream of innovative products. For the most part the equipment on show represented the result of evolutionary, rather than revolutionary technical development and the choice of two legends, John McEnroe and Jack Nicklaus, to appear as, respectively, the Dunlop and Maxfli 'promoters', rather than as 'players' could have been seen as an admission that it was difficult to come up with current champions. In the absence of anything to match the iconic products of the past, like the Maxply and 200G in the tennis market, and Maxfli (as a product and not a brand), 65 and DDH in golf, the range lacked 'flagships'. And with Dunlop, as a brand, given less prominence than Maxfli, Slazenger and even Puma the 'BTR Sports Group' could have been seen as losing sight of a major element of its heritage.

Another characteristic of the business neither apparent in the 'BTR News' piece, nor in most of the literature produced by the company over the years was that its existence, and, more importantly, its profitability rested on the core ball operations. For all the success over the years with tennis rackets and golf clubs, and with many other products for virtually every sport, it was always the main 'consumable' products; golf and tennis balls, squash balls and shuttlecocks; that accounted for by far the largest proportion of sales and that had driven the spread of manufacturing units around the world. At the time of the BTR feature, in 1995, balls were nearly 60% of sales, by 1999 well over 60% and in the early years of the new century close to 70%. And at every stage the proportion of the profits would have been even greater. Annual sales of rackets are still close to 2 million, of golf clubs well over half a million but sales of balls and shuttles for golf and racket sports exceeded half a million PER DAY, or close to 150 million every year.

And it was the very important golf ball business that was badly disrupted by the earthquake that devastated Kobe in January, 1995. The almost total destruction of Sumitomo's factory close to the centre of the city meant that, for a period, the Dunlop Japan supremacy in the local premium golf ball market was extremely vulnerable and it would be at least two years before they completely recovered. For Dunlop Slazenger it meant that the supply of Maxfli balata balls quickly dried up, and for Slazenger Golf in the USA the loss of Kobe output meant they had to endure a period, at the start of a new season, without supplies of any type of ball. In the midst of these major supply problems it's worth noting that staff in Greenville were quick to organise the despatch of clothing and blankets to Kobe for those who had lost their homes.

Although total golf ball sales in 1995 were badly hit by the loss of Kobe products, with a particularly severe impact on Slazenger Golf, the overall profitability for the year was protected by insurance cover. However, a more important, longer term and much more positive impact for both Maxfli and Slazenger was the acceleration of the product development programme to introduce a much higher volume of premium quality balls from Westminster for both brands. And an integral element of that programme was the decision to develop what would prove to be the next 'iconic' product, the 'Revolution' urethane cover golf ball.

The continuous investment in the Westminster plant, over a ten year peri-

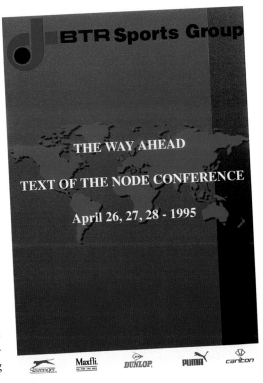

The 'Book' of the 1995 Way Ahead Conference

od, had transformed the earlier, definitely outdated facility into a state-of-the-art operation. By 1995 it was capable of turning out product of the highest quality, and a parallel investment programme in the golf ball research and development function now centred there meant that the company was in a stronger position than it had been for some years to take the heritage of Maxfli, 65 and DDH to new levels of quality and performance. The R & D team at Westminster, led by John Calabria, charged with creating the new generation of premium balls to replace the now too expensive balata product could be confident that whatever they came up with, their manufacturing colleagues had the tools to translate even the most radical of design or construction changes into high quality bulk production. As David Jacobs continually reminded his management team 'breakthrough products are key'. At the same time his determination to create a 'Can do culture' within the Sports Group was particularly appropriate in this context and not least because there would be setbacks and disappointments before the combination of new materials, new constructions and markedly different manufacturing techniques created the revolutionary new balls.

These factors were among a number that constituted not so much a wind but a 'hurricane of change' introduced at 'The Way Ahead' conference held at the Node Conference Centre in Hertfordshire in April, 1995. The purpose of the 'first senior managers' conference for the Sports Group in living memory' was to focus on the 'Vision strategy and direction of the Group', which had been developed during Jacobs first year in charge of the business and, within this framework, show how to combine lessons learned from the past with the action plans for the future.

During an intensive three days virtually every aspect of the business was reviewed in considerable detail. Many of the objectives either brought to the meeting for examination, or developed during conference sessions, established a blueprint for the business, which influenced the revised organisation structure that would be introduced less than a year later. In particular, and for the first time, the conclusion of the conference supported Jacobs' own philosophy of creating centralised, worldwide responsibilities for manufacturing and R & D, and for purchasing and marketing.

The principal guest speaker at the conference was the BTR main board director then responsible for Sports, Paul Buysse. Addressing speculation about the future of the business within BTR, he was very clear that the parent company did still want a 'global, international and highly professional sports business', and that Dunlop Slazenger was not for sale. Aware of the rumours at that time that BTR could be moving to a policy of concentrating on its core industrial businesses, and also that a number of enquiries had been made about the availability of the sports operations it's possible the conference delegates were not entirely convinced their long term future within BTR was quite so certain as had been indicated.

An interested party, also far from convinced that Dunlop Slazenger's future lay with BTR, was the venture capitalist, Cinven. Their repeatedly expressed interest in leading a management buy out of the business eventually persuaded the BTR board, and, in particular, its chief executive, Alan Jackson to accept an offer reported at the time as being £300 million, but in numerous subsequent analyses in the financial columns assumed to be much higher after taking account of 'various forms of debt the company had been loaded with'. Alan Jackson commented at the time that the business had not been actively marketed, but that Cinven had come to BTR with a good offer. He added "We took a very cautious approach to selling it because the people are very valuable". That was a pleasing compliment but 'the people' would have been more encouraged by Cinven's pledge that the business 'will have supportive shareholders with the ability to make capital and promotional expenditure where appropriate'. They would also have agreed with the view that 'it would benefit substantially from being an independent business', but, in view of the limited investment in advertising expenditure throughout nearly twenty years of both Dunlop and BTR ownership not felt so comfortable with the assessment that 'Dunlop's brands had been well maintained'. David Jacobs was quite clear about the benefits of the buy out when he told the nearly 3,000 employees that negotiations had been completed and that "This marks a new beginning for Dunlop Slazenger International and a tremendous opportunity for the Group to move forward in the future, concentrating on its own destiny".

The news that the 'Buy Out' was complete was released on 8th March, 1996. This quiet statement was in contrast to the furious pace and pressure of the negotiations during the preceeding six months. Much of that pressure was created by the need to conclude the deal in time to meet a BTR deadline related to their 1995 accounts. In addition to the company's management team the main parties involved, Cinven, BTR and a consortium of banks, each with a formidable array of legal and specialist advisers, had to wrestle with the complex legal and financial structure of the business. This had been developed over many years by the original Slazenger companies, by the Dunlop Rubber Company, and, of course, by BTR, and involved nearly 40 live or dormant companies in 14 countries. Additionally there were external partners in several of the overseas companies and the vital factor of the current and ongoing ownership of the Dunlop mark for sports goods around the world required very detailed attention, including the close involvement of Sumitomo, who had retained the mark in the important territories of Japan, Taiwan and South Korea. That factor alone necessitated a series of meetings in Tokyo and Singapore as well as in London.

Known within Ashurst, Morris and Crisp – Cinven's legal advisers – as 'Project Driver' this prolonged, 'night and day' process acquired a near legendary status for its pace and complexity. It was only appropriate that the final piece of the negotiating jigsaw fell into place, in Ashurst's offices, in the early hours of the morning during that first week of March. Under the heading 'BTR disposal' the following short announcement in the financial press on 12th March, scarcely did justice, at least for those involved, to what was arguably the most important event in the company's history.

Industrial manufacturer, BTR, yesterday completed the sale of its Dunlop Slazenger sports equipment business to a management buy-out team for up to £330 million. Some £240 million of the sum is in cash and loan notes and the rest is conditional on performance.

Pausing for a moment before getting down to the new challenge of 'concentrating only on their own destiny', the UK based members of the management buy out team enjoyed a memorable dinner with their wives and partners at a famous Berkshire hotel. David Jacobs had selected his team from the existing senior managers in the business but his decision to make a fundamental change in the organisation structure meant that several would have new roles. His analysis of the strengths and weaknesses of the business, first signalled at the Node conference the previous April, and, in particular, his belief in the importance of improving the worldwide co-ordination of the business, led to the conclusion that certain key functions should be managed across the group. Among those around the dinner table that March were Philip Wragg, with the new responsibility for worldwide manufacturing, R & D and purchasing, and Philip Jansen, who had held senior marketing positions in UK Golf and the Rackets division since joining the company from Procter & Gamble, and who now became Group Marketing Director.

Also there that evening were Gordon Moodie, who continued as Finance Director, Andrew Peters, who would continue to run Puma UK, Gordon Baird, MD of UK rackets and golf, and Brian Simpson, MD of Europe. There in spirit, to complete the team, were David Branon, who continued as President of Slazenger Golf in the USA, his neighbour in Greenville, Tom Bryant, who had succeeded Dick Dodson as president of Maxfli, USA rackets and Sportlines and Scott Brown, who had been appointed the MD in the Far East in 1995. The roles of the regional managing directors had been redefined, within David Jacobs new structure, to focus on the local sales and distribution operations, with the manufacturing and marketing support provided by Wragg and Jansen. The board of the new company comprised Jacobs, Moodie, Wragg and Peters with Cinven represented by Charles Nicholson and Brent Wheeler. Its first chairman, who joined the board in the Autumn of 1996, was Sir Michael Perry, the former Chairman of Unilever.

The new company faced immediate difficulties in 1996, due mainly to problems in the USA. There the loss of premium golf ball sales because of the 1995 supply shortages caused by the Kobe earthquake, and serious under-budgetting of a golf promotion campaign meant that total group sales, did not expand as anticipated and profits were halved compared with the previous year. With the exception of Puma, sales in Europe were also disappointing and the closure of the Dunlop Footwear business resulted in further losses. On the brighter side the Far East business continued to produce higher sales and profits and the South African sports operation became part of Dunlop Slazenger.

The downward trend continued in 1997, when an operating loss was recorded for the first time since the 1962 formation of International Sports Company. The business would return to profit in 1998 but it was apparent that the business plans prepared at the time of the MBO, which projected substantial sales and profit growth to 2002, were very challenging. Hindsight suggests that the targets then set, when related either to the company's track record over the previous ten years, or the expansion potential within the sports equipment market, were optimistic. It might also be argued that the price paid for the business reflected those projections from 1996 to 2002, and their supporting strategies, rather more than the recent performance record of the core sports equipment business, which did not suggest that substantial annual sales and profit growth would, from then on, become the norm within what was becoming and increasingly competitive market place.

These disappointments were obviously extremely costly for Cinven, Invensys (which acquired BTR in 1999) and the banks. They were also a background element in the departures, over a six year period, of the original MBO team. Phil Wragg left at the end of 1996, to take up a chief executive position in the automotive components industry, Tom Bryant, Gordon Moodie, Gordon Baird, Scott Brown and Philip Jansen moved on to new appointments and there were retirements by David Jacobs (1998), Brian Simpson (1999) and David Branon (2002). Phil Wragg was succeeded by Stan Ainsley, who joined from Black & Decker, Gordon Moodie by Alan Lovell from Costain, Tom Bryant in the USA by Bill Olson, who in turn passed the North American baton to Mike Rizzo, and Philip Jansen by Graeme Derby. Andrew Griffiths was recruited by David Jacobs to run both the UK and the European businesses and K.L Choong became the first locally recruited

Maxfli Court at Camberley

executive to be responsible for the Far East region. Andrew Peters remained as MD of Puma UK when that business returned to Puma AG control at the beginning of 1999.

However, the period between 1996 and the early years of the new century has been much more than just a story of early disappointment and subsequent management changes. The immediate pressure on the original MBO team, because of the disappointing results in 1996 and 1997, did not distract them from implementing key elements of their business plan. The continuing rationalisation of manufacturing – a process that had started 20 years earlier – saw further investment in both R & D and production at the Westminster plant, which would make possible not only the introduction of a new generation of golf balls but also the capability to take over the supply of balls to the Australian company when they closed their own factory. At the same time, and again with the support of the Australians, the production capacity of the Philippines tennis ball plant was increased, which was a prerequisite for the eventual concentration of all production at the Bataan site.

Stan Ainsley continued the work Phil Wragg had started to completely re-invent the supply and distribution systems, which had not previously received anything like the same degree of rationalisation and modernisation as applied to manufacturing. And Philip Jansen's marketing teams developed the updated and much more clearly differentiated brand definitions, for Dunlop, Maxfli, Slazenger and Carlton, that had been signalled at the Node conference a year earlier. In the case of Slazenger this process included the introduction of a completely re-designed Panther now leaping from left to right, instead of the right to left style that had been consistent for the previous 35 years.

Alan Lovell and Philip Parnell in action in the Sunday Times in 2002

And, crucially, the intensive work by John Calabria and his R & D team in Westminster to develop a replacement for the balata golf ball was nearing completion in the second half of 1997. The introduction, at the end of that year, of a urethane cover ball made it possible for the company to reclaim its position in the forefront of golf ball technology. The critical decision to use

Bernhard Langer

Fred Couples

polyurethane for the cover material was taken in 1995, when the choice facing the marketing and technical teams was between reintroducing balata production to Westminster, or finding a completely new cover material with matching or better performance to replace the HT balata balls no longer available from Sumitomo.

The introduction of the urethane cover, which ultimately made it possible for Maxfli, with the 'Revolution' and 'A10', Slazenger with 'Tourethane, 'Select' and 'Black Label' and Dunlop with the '65u' to offer the most technically advanced products, was as significant a moment in the company's history as the previous triumphs with the original Maxfli, the first 65 and the DDH. What was different, in development terms, from these earlier breakthrough balls was that the urethane covers required a completely new manufacturing process. This meant that John Calabria and his technicians not only had to formulate the ball construction and material content from scratch, but also had to work with the plant engineers to design a new production line. Small wonder that the development process alone required an investment of more than $2 million before a single ball was produced. 'Money well spent' would be the final assessment of this project, which secured the company's future in the premium sector of the market. However, there was considerable frustration with the significant delays in building the production level required to meet the very strong market demand that quickly developed. This setback obviously resulted in a serious loss of sales and profit and slowed the market penetration of this outstanding new ball.

An event of less significance in 1997, but of considerable interest to those directly involved, was the transfer of the company headquarters from the BTR site at Leatherhead, which had been its home since 1988, to a newly built business park on the edge of Camberley. The Slazenger related Challenge Court address stayed in Leatherhead and the new building was named Maxfli Court. The tennis theme had given way to the more dominant golf element of the business.

Despite the improved results in 1998 the business remained under severe pressure from its backers to reduce its borrowings. And, more importantly, to take whatever action was necessary to secure its longer term future. Despite its almost unique heritage and apparent strength across the spectrum of rackets, golf and cricket it was apparent that time could be running out for Dunlop Slazenger unless the weight of operating costs and interest payments could be reduced. At this stage Alan Lovell had become the main link between the company and its range of investors, and he would have welcomed the arrival, early in 1998, of Philip Parnell as the new chief executive.

Driven by the imperative to quickly improve the financial position Parnell and Lovell would not only apply an accelerated rationalisation programme to the structure of the business, but also make an early decision that 'the rejuvenation of Dunlop as a sports brand' was essential. Previous analyses of the relative profitability of the brands had shown that Maxili, with its high cost sales, marketing and advertising requirements, was the least profitable in the company's portfolio, but this would be the first time that this major imbalance would be addressed together with a more determined assault on the perceived operating inefficiencies of the business. In the latter case the development of carefully structured systems and processes, for each main area of activity, was approached on the basis it would provide the essential foundation for the success of the revitalised and streamlined 'New Dunlop

Slazenger'. Both Parnell and Lovell felt very strongly that the benefits of the earlier stages of the evolution towards an increasingly centralised management structure had not been fully realised because the systems and processes required to support that policy had not been developed and implemented with either the necessary speed or strength.

In fact these two key objectives – the restoration of Dunlop as THE brand for the business and the proper completion of the rationalisation process - have been, respectively, the external and internal priorities for the last six years. Combined they have made the elimination of inefficiencies a much simpler task, and the overall effect of this approach was to restore the financial stability of the company.

The last section of this history will describe the completion of the overall restructuring process. This was finalised in 2004 and laid the foundation for a new owner to develop the unique Dunlop Slazenger heritage based largely on rebuilding the strength of the two main brands that form the company's name. However, before coming to that final, or latest chapter of the history it is appropriate to look at the separate account of how the brands achieved considerable success in their main overseas markets. For most of the hundred and more years since the Slazenger companies and the Dunlop sports business were founded their ability to build substantial and enduring businesses in these key areas has been unrivalled in the sports trade. The 'Abroad' section that follows will show how this was achieved in a number of very different ways but with the common factor of the great strength of these two world famous brands.

Jose Rivero

DUNLOP AND SLAZENGER 'ABROAD'

INTRODUCTION

The history of the Dunlop and Slazenger companies is unique among sports equipment businesses for the scope and reach of its overseas trading. From the earliest days of their existence the various companies that eventually became the Slazenger group were sending their representatives, often members of their founding families, to every country where golf, cricket, tennis and many other sports were expanding as fast as in the UK. In 1895 Frank Slazenger had established a business in New York that first sold golf clubs and later a much wider range of golf and tennis products. William Sykes's son, Henry, made his first sales visit to South Africa in 1904, and made an annual visit to the USA and Canada for the next 30 years. It's certainly possible that he would have introduced the Sykes 'Roy Kilner' bat to Australia, one of which was selected by the seventeen-year-old Don Bradman in 1926 as a reward for a match winning triple century in an important club match.

Their early price lists gave details of the cable and telegraphic ordering codes for both 'Home' and 'Colonial' customers. The locations of their distributors and agents, as might be expected, included such places as New York, Paris and Cape Town, but one can only imagine the travelling and other difficulties involved in establishing representatives in such as Nairobi, Colombo, Buenos Aires and Istanbul – as early as the mid 1920s. No wonder, then, that when business began to recover after the second world war the newly formed combination of Slazenger-Sykes-Ayres-Gradidge was able to claim their overseas organisation 'spans the globe, and there is no area of importance where there is not to be found a resident representative'. The accompanying map of the world showed eighty-five distributors in eighty countries plus their own manufacturing units in Australia, New Zealand, South Africa and Canada.

Exporting was always a priority for the Slazenger companies and frequently accounted for half the company's total sales. Dunlop also built a substantial overseas business but the approach was different and much more concentrated on golf and tennis balls. The main reason for this was the rubber technology link that made it attractive to develop ball-making facilities in many of the tyre plants the company estab-

The William Sykes ordering code details for 'Home and Colonial' customers

lished around the world. That pattern, which was first seen when golf balls were produced in one of the early Birmingham tyre factories, was the blueprint for similar operations in North America, Japan, Australia, South Africa, Malaysia, Ireland, Germany and France and usually led to the local Dunlop company setting up its own sports division, which would then import racket and golf equipment from the UK. It would be some forty years after those first overseas plants were commissioned, along-side the tyre moulds, that separate ball making plants were opened at Westminster and Hartwell in the USA, and in Japan, the Philippines and Indonesia.

The Slazenger factory in New Zealand opened in 1939

It was never likely to be a practical or economic proposition for either Dunlop or Slazenger to set up their own factories in every country where there was likely to be a demand for their products. Where that demand was sufficiently large, in areas like North America, the larger European countries and Australasia, a sports dedicated unit could make good financial sense. For one thing it provided a valuable local focus for customers, rather than the thought of dealing over long distances with remote headquarters sales offices. And in the case of Dunlop the economics of a relatively small golf or tennis ball plant looked much better, at least to the local management, in the smaller markets like Malaysia, or during the pioneering golf and tennis years in Japan, when slotted into an established tyre plant with its existing technical and other service resources.

Slazenger did not have the same opportunities to share site services with an existing tyre and rubber products operation so its sports-only plants were usually smaller and produced a wide range of products. Their New Zealand operation, established in 1939 as a branch of the Australian business, is a good example of that approach. Originally staffed by twelve craftsmen sent from Sydney to make tennis, squash and badminton rackets, the company extended its range to include golf clubs and accessories, soccer balls and equipment, sports bags, table tennis and softball bats, and a range of leather grips for rackets, clubs and bats. Very much an echo of the Sykes and Slazenger approach in the UK from where the New Zealand business drew tennis and golf balls and cricket and archery equipment to augment its local output.

The debate about whether or not the overall Dunlop organisational approach to its worldwide operations, based on the primacy of territorial management for all local product operations and investment, has been aired elsewhere in this chronicle. However, it should be noted that Slazenger generally took the alternative view that all their overseas operations should look to the UK for their leadership in terms of co-ordinating products and marketing activities. Even after the 1959 acquisition by Dunlop they maintained a separate management board, which, on a monthly basis, reviewed the activities of all their overseas companies with the local managing-directors frequently travelling to London or Croydon to give first hand reports.

Even if the 'conflict between geographical and product management' – highlighted in the 1983 Strategy Review – did have the effect of obscuring

Bob Howe spreading the gospel of tennis and Dunlop with a selected group of promising young Chinese players

ckung angeboten, die
t, daß die unverzichtbare
ie" auch bei längerer
ohne Qualitätsverlust
leibt. Mit dieser energie-
hergestellten und entsor-
idlichen Verpackung lei-
op zugleich einen ein-
an Beitrag zum Umwelt-

Modern and highly automated tennis ball production at the Hanau factory

from the Dunlop board the full potential of the worldwide 'Sports Opportunity', there are notable positives arising from the approach that was adopted. It's quite clear that the combination of the consistently innovative and market leading range of mainly golf and tennis products provided by the skill of Dunlop scientists and product engineers, and the company's unique ability to transfer those skills to its international network of established tyre plants in key markets was an absolutely crucial factor in establishing Dunlop as worldwide sports brand as well as one of the major tyre manufacturers.

Additionally, and putting aside the different organisation and management styles adopted by Dunlop and Slazenger, the managements of both companies had seen the overseas opportunities that existed from the increase in leisure time and the growing interest in sporting activities to fill that time. And, while the management teams involved obviously sought to profitably expand their businesses in every country where they were operating it is also absolutely clear they devoted considerable time, energy and resources to the development of sport, and often in areas like Africa and the Far East where there would have been little chance at the time of securing significant commercial return. Examples of this approach include the 'missionary' work by Victor Barna, when introducing table tennis to Africa, and Bob Howe's 1980s teach-ins to develop the tennis skills of promising young Chinese.

During the last hundred and more years the Dunlop and Slazenger sports companies have contributed very significantly to the local economies in Birmingham, South East England, Merseyside and Yorkshire. What has not been so obvious is the impact they have also had around the world. Not only by providing the means for many forms of sport to be enjoyed by more and more people, but also by adding considerably to local wealth and employment in so many overseas locations.

Nearest to home have been the extensive operations in Europe. These have been a mixture of mainly tennis ball manufacture in Germany, France and Ireland – in the latter case also a golf ball plant – and company run sales and distribution operations not only in those three countries but also in Holland, Italy and Spain, which replaced and expanded previously privately owned distributor companies. Sales by these six businesses have frequently passed the £50 million per annum mark, with Germany accounting for about half of that total.

The German Dunlop factory in Hanau started making bicycle tyres in 1893, added car tyres in 1902 and tennis balls in 1923. It was almost completely destroyed in a 1944 air raid, but re-established limited tyre production a year later with the tennis ball unit reopening in 1949. Before being closed in 2002, as part of the group's strategic consolidation of its manufacturing resources, the tennis ball production operation was continuously developed to become the most highly automated and technically advanced unit of its kind in the world and many of the techniques pioneered at Hanau have been incorporated in the main tennis ball factory in the Philippines. The quality standards of the Hanau product, probably the best in the world, allowed the company to dominate the demanding German market for many years and it has been possible to maintain this position by ensuring the Philippines plant continues to meet these standards. The 1969 purchase of the Erbacher ski factory, a move made to better balance the business with a strong winter range, led, in 1979, to that plant being the first in the Dunlop Slazenger group to produce composite tennis frames. Hanau is now the headquarters location for the Central Europe region and its managing-director, Frans Swinkels, who is responsible for the Benelux countries as well as Germany.

Barcelona is the site for the headquarters of the Southern Europe region, which covers Spain and France. Its managing-director is Federico Guallar. France, like Germany, was an early target for the rapidly expanding Dunlop tyre business, which established its first company there in 1896. During the 1920s it built a very large tyre plant at Montlucon, virtually in the centre of France, and started making tennis balls there at about the same time as in Germany. The French Dunlop company built a very significant place in the country's industrial and commercial sectors, based mainly on its tyre, wheel, Dunlopillo and sports equipment operations, but the ownership of all these activities passed to Sumitomo in 1984, which meant that for the next ten years only the Slazenger brand was available to the group for sports sales. As it happened Slazenger's only major business in Europe, first established before the second world war, was located in Paris and provided the base for a unique competitive battle, mainly for tennis ball business, between Slazenger tennis balls made in Barnsley and Dunlop balls produced in what had become the Japanese owned Montlucon plant. For many years that factory provided the balls for the French Open championships though 'anonymously' as they were branded 'Roland Garros'.

Ireland was the first home for the company originally established to develop the pneumatic bicycle tyre invented by John Boyd Dunlop and the first Dunlop business was established there, in Dublin, in 1896. Subsequently manufacturing operations, including tennis and golf ball production, were located at Cork with Dublin as the home, for many years, of a very successful sales operation now part of the Northern Europe region with its headquarters in Wakefield.

Wakefield is also the base for the company's two international sales managers, Graham Nicholas and Eric Stevenson, who are responsible for developing business around the world in those countries where Dunlop Slazenger does not have a local operation. Their particular heritage is the network of

The Dunlop France version of a famous tennis ball poster used in the 1920s

distributors and agents, which was originally established when Henry and William Sykes, both the Slazenger and Ayres families, and the early Dunlop export salesmen made their first, arduous visits to what would now be regarded as 'primitive' overseas markets.

Graham Nicholas could be forgiven for thinking his experiences in the 1980s, when trying to develop business in Eastern Europe, weren't much less challenging than those of the earliest export travellers. He recalls having to grapple with the very formidable amounts of paperwork required to get through border controls to meet the government buying agencies, and the fact he was conscious his movements were under 'fairly serious scrutiny'. The fact that both the Dunlop and Slazenger brands were not unknown from either their pre-war presence or the connection with tyres provided a valuable platform once markets in Poland, Hungary, Bulgaria and the Czech and Slovak Republics were re-opened to competitive imports from 1990 onwards. Initially, the low level of local spending power made it necessary to adopt an 'investment margin' policy, or supply clearance lines in order to go some way to meeting the pent-up consumer demand for sports goods. Today Poland and the Czech Republic have become the largest of these markets where the local distributors are business graduates with as many business plans and action programmes as Graham himself.

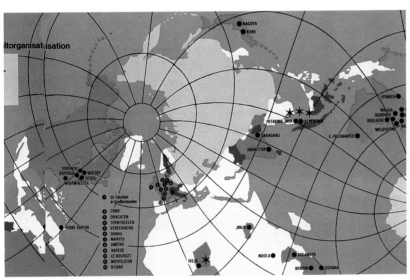

A view of the Dunlop world from a brochure produced by the German company – there are 12 ball plants on this map

And despite the longer distances involved in establishing business in Russia, where the demand is for status indicating premium racket and golf products, and the complications of the varying import duties and other regulations created by each of the separate states that were originally Yugoslavia, Dunlop Slazenger business is steadily expanding in those newly restored markets. In most of those countries the main demand is for the racket sports – squash and badminton as well as tennis – which relates to the many international successes, since the war, of their leading players, and also to the fact that the costs involved have so far limited the growth of golf courses. It's not difficult to imagine how all of this would have delighted former Dunlop 'greats', like the Hungarian Victor Barna and the Czechoslovakian Jaroslav Drobny.

Looking further afield than Europe, and rather more closely at the 'abroad' aspect of Dunlop and Slazenger, it is immediately apparent that several more and separate histories could be written with timescales of more than a hundred years. However, it is important, in terms of properly reflecting the 'truly international' character of the total business, to include in this history more important areas, or individual countries. To accomplish this, and to sketch the main events that extended the original successes achieved in the UK to virtually every corner of the globe, this narrative will now 'detour' to Australia, the Far East, Japan, South Africa, Canada and the USA.

AUSTRALIA

The history of Dunlop in Australia began as early as 1893 when a small company in Melbourne started making the new pneumatic cycle tyres patented by John Boyd Dunlop only four years earlier. In his book, *Jumping over the Wheel*, the Australian historian, Geoffrey Blainey, describes how, by the early 1990s, that very small tyre factory had grown into the multi-product, multi-brand conglomerate, Pacific Dunlop, employing nearly 50,000 people, mainly in Australia but also significant numbers in the USA, Malaysia, China, Sri Lanka, New Zealand and Thailand.

Throughout its history the company has been closely identified with Australian sport. In the 1890s the bicycle was the most popular form of transport and cycling the most popular sport. This guaranteed that the makers of the new pneumatic, or 'pudding' tyres would soon become very well known and the company was quick to accelerate this recognition by becoming involved in the major racing events. This approach was repeated as motorcycles and cars followed and the company's first publicity manager, Harry James, not only built his own reputation as the country's father figure in motor sports, but also firmly established the Dunlop brand in the minds of the sports conscious Australians.

As with motor sports Dunlop, and later Pacific Dunlop, mainly by sponsoring events and leading players has been associated with Australian Rules football, swimming, athletics, water polo, hockey, rowing, bowls, boxing and both union and league rugby. Its connections with tennis, golf and cricket, especially after the merger with Slazenger, and its substantial investments in manufacturing and marketing, resulted in both brands building major shares in the equipment markets for these hugely popular Australian sports. And because so many of the country's leading players, including a large number of 'world greats', used Dunlop and Slazenger equipment as they achieved massive international success the overall strength of both brands was given a huge boost in the world's most important markets.

A 1900 advert reflecting the early focus on Dunlop bicycle tyres in Australia

In *Jumping over the Wheel* Geoffrey Blainey acknowledges the wealth of information he received from John McClean, who was the Group Historian for Pacific Dunlop. John has also contributed to this history from his extensive research and records. His starting point for Dunlop and Slazenger in Australia is a letter written to Slazenger in the UK in April, 1900, in which a touring New Zealand tennis star, Harry Parker, expresses

A Dunlop Australia advert in 1910, possibly the first ever for the company's tennis balls

his frustrations at the lack of sports retailers in Australia, in particular the fact he couldn't find a replacement for his damaged 'Slazenger Special'. He suggested that rather than spending the money required to send a representative from England the company should appoint a local agent, who would understand the market better and be able to develop substantial sales of their tennis, golf, bowls and croquet products. It appears that Ralph and Albert Slazenger, sitting in their Laurence Pountney office, agreed with Harry, and also with his proposal he was the person best qualified to undertake this task. In 1922 Harry, who had lost in the third round at the 1901 Wimbledon championships to the eventual winner (Arthur Gore), acquired the distribution rights for Slazenger equipment and established the company's first factory in Sydney. Rackets were first produced there in 1930, to be followed by golf clubs, tennis balls and cricket bats, which led to the 1939 move to a larger factory in Bowden Street, Alexandria.

Meanwhile, Dunlop had got off to a somewhat shaky start when, in 1908, they were the first to make tennis balls in Australia. 'Shaky' because despite the fact they were 2s per dozen cheaper than the imported Ayres balls they were considered 'unsatisfactory' for some time. A more successful manufacturer was the Barnet Glass company, which made a wide range of rubber products and started to produce tennis balls in 1928, shortly before being acquired by Dunlop. In those days their ball testing routine was to employ one man whose sole task was to hit balls against a brick wall to test their quality, which included selecting the best for tournament use. Bearing in mind that in the UK the Fort Dunlop based golf and tennis ball operations were gathering momentum during the second half of the 1920s, and circulating the details of the improving quality of such as the 'Maxfli', it's not surprising to find, in 1932, they were the first to make golf balls in Australia. Only a couple of years later details of the 'sensational new "65"' would have been given to the local company, which allowed them to overtake the previously more popular 'Silver King' ball.

In 1937 Dunlop bought the Empire Racket Company and to bring together all its sporting goods activities, which it had come to see as a prime area for expansion, it formed the Dunlop Sports Company Pty. Ltd. The new company's managing-director was A. A. McPherson and one of its directors Adrian Quist, who used Dunlop rackets when playing in the Davis Cup and was a major asset to the new business, especially as a skilled promoter of its interests. He ensured that when Donald Budge came to Australia he used Dunlop equipment and, with John Bromwich, brought more glory to the company when they led the 1939 Davis Cup team to victory against USA.

Quist was also the originator of the world famous 'Volley' tennis shoe. While in the USA for the 1939 final he had seen an intriguing pair of yachting shoes in the window of a Boston ship chandler. The interesting feature that caught his eye was the herring-bone sole pattern, which he was told provided a sure grip on a wet deck. Believing that this would also work on a tennis court he bought a pair and immediately surprised his teammates, Bromwich, Harry Hopman and Jack Crawford, with his brilliant footwork. All four of them used the shoes in the final and were convinced they made a definite contribution to their success. He subsequently encouraged the Dunlop Footwear Division to use the new design, which was known as the 'Volley O.C.' (orthopaedically correct) with the 'Quist Sole'. The combination of the 'Volley' and the UK, made Green Flash would be the overwhelming choice of good tennis players, and the international stars, for over thirty years.

In 1947 the Dunlop Sports operation took over the local distribution of East Bros., who had been one of the earliest Australian golf club makers, later to be the source of a range of clubs and accessories marketed under the name of Peter Thomson, who was a director of the company.

Adrian Quist, a member of the Australia's winning Davis Cup team in 1939 and a director of the company's sports business

Back in Alexandria Slazenger expansion had been curtailed by the outbreak of war. As had happened in Horbury production was quickly switched to support the war effort by turning to the manufacture of the wooden parts for rifles and other firearms and this later expanded to include the production of marine assault craft in such large quantities that they opened their own ship-building yard. They also became sub-contractors to De Havilland for the repair of Mosquito aircraft, which could have been linked with the similar Slazenger UK operation established in High Wycombe.

A year after the war ended golf ball manufacture started, which enabled the company to share with Horbury the 1951 launch of the B51, which signalled the company's return to this sector after a gap of nearly fifty years. In 1954 they pioneered the introduction of fibreglass fishing rods and started production of shoe soles, which eventually reached 2.5 million a year supplying 83 shoe plants.

When, in 1959, Dunlop in the UK acquired the parent Slazenger company it made Slazenger in Australia a subsidiary of its local company. This move was strongly opposed by David Blacklock, who had become managing-director of Slazenger after joining the company in 1922 when Harry Parker first established the business. His proposal to take the company public was turned down and he retired shortly afterwards to be succeeded by Noel Morris, who had joined the company shortly before the war. Initially, as in the UK, Dunlop and Slazenger continued to operate as competitors and would not have been significantly affected by the formation of ISC in 1964. However, as part of a general drive for increased profitability in 1967 it was decided to merge all the sports activities under the Slazenger name and consolidate operations in their Sydney premises.

This decision to use the Slazenger name for 'The sporting goods specialist subsidiary of the Dunlop Australia Group' would have brought a wry smile to several faces in the Slazenger UK management team, which was by then operating as part of the International Sports Company formed three years earlier. However, in Australia it reflected the policy of the local company's

Lew Hoad and Ken Rosewall enjoying Australia's 1953 Davis Cup victory – with Rex Hartwig, Harry Hopman and Ashley Cooper

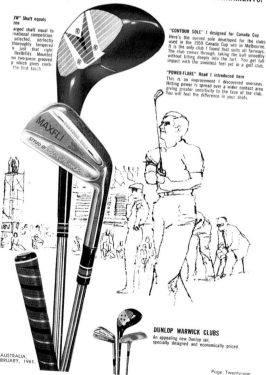

Peter Thomson, who was a director of the Australian sports business, endorsing Dunlop and Maxfli clubs in a 1961 advert

rapid expansion of its portfolio of consumer brands, which it believed should be separated from the more industrial connotations of the main products associated with the Dunlop brand.

During the next 20 years the Australian parent company would experience a complex series of expansions, mergers and retrenchment. Its name would change first to Dunlop Olympic and later to Pacific Dunlop, and it would separate completely from its original UK parent when that 'Father Dunlop' experienced its own difficulties in the late 1970s.

The links between the Australian Slazenger sports operation and both ISC, and, later Dunlop Slazenger International were maintained despite the upheavals affecting both parent companies, though, for the most part, on a 'voluntary' basis. Technical Aid agreements, facilitating the transfer of technology from the UK, remained in place, the Australians continued to contribute to the cost of player contacts when they were relevant to the Australian market, and fairly regular meetings were held, mainly in Europe or the USA, to include product and marketing co-ordination. These also included initiatives to develop joint purchasing from Far East suppliers of rackets, golf clubs and accessories. These exchanges were undoubtedly valuable but in no sense did they provide a basis for a truly uniform approach to marketing the Dunlop and Slazenger brands. The priority for ISC, and more especially Dunlop Slazenger management was to establish real co-ordination of the activities of its operations in Europe, North America and the Far East, while the Australians, not unnaturally, felt they should be concentrating their resources on their local sports market. In this respect their presentations at international meetings were characterised by an emphasis on the dominance of their shares in their relatively small market sectors.

The Australian interest in developing off-shore manufacturing for many of its product lines, in many cases in order to remain competitive in their home market, was a key factor in the 1977 decision to take a minority holding and joint management position with UK Dunlop in the Philippines tennis ball plant. Twenty years later this approach was extended when they decided against the substantial investment required to modernise their golf ball plant and, instead, negotiated a contract with Dunlop Slazenger International for the supply of balls from their high volume plant in South Carolina. This was a very specific arrangement, with significant benefits for both parties, and contrasted with earlier, less clear cut 'feelers' about closer working relationships. According to well placed sources in BTR these had included more than one enquiry from Pacific Dunlop, in the early 1990s, about acquiring Dunlop Slazenger's much larger sports operations. It's likely BTR's valuation of that business was higher than

Pacific Dunlop had anticipated.

The Australian Slazenger sports business was part of the Pacific Brands division of Pacific Dunlop, which, in 2001, was purchased by a venture capital consortium when the parent conglomerate shed all its assets except the healthcare operations. It has recently been reported that Pacific Brands is considering an Initial Public Offering for what is an entirely consumer oriented group of brands, and, in any event, is interested in selling the business. Amongst the published details of Pacific Brands activities are current annual sales volumes of 500,000 dozen golf balls and 300,000 dozen tennis balls, all of which are still supplied by the Westminster and Philippines plants respectively.

Despite all the changes of structure and ownership that have affected the UK and Australian businesses they still share a recognisably common heritage in the strength of the Dunlop and Slazenger brands, which has been embellished throughout by the many great players to have used their equipment. From the beginning of the 20th century, when not only Harry Parker was using a Slazenger racket at Wimbledon, but also the Doherty brothers and the man who beat him, Arthur Gore, through the triumphs of Perry, Austin and Pat Hughes in the 1930s, and the extraordinary twenty year Australian dominance from the 1950s led by Hoad, Rosewall, Fraser, Laver, Emerson, Newcombe, Roche, Margaret Court and Evonne Cawley to the more recent successes of McEnroe, Henman, Philippoussis and Graf. And that was just a few of the tennis names. For cricket it's almost enough just to mention Don Bradman and for golf to limit the list to such as Peter Thomson, Arnold Palmer, Jack Nicklaus and Greg Norman. Small wonder, then, these brands, and their products, remain so strong from Perth to Sydney.

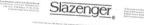

A Slazenger Australia advert for the Slazenger Bradman Collection they introduced in 1992

'BRADDLES' as a GOLFER

Bradman is a name known to thousands of cricketers. But the cricketing knight is also making a name for himself as a golfer.

BRADMAN AS A GOLFER
The famous cricketer and also prominent in South Australian golf.

FAR EAST TRADING AND SOURCING

Both Dunlop and Slazenger have been very active throughout the Far East for very many years; and especially in Hong Kong, Singapore, Malaysia, Thailand, Indonesia, the Philippines, Taiwan and China. There have been a number of different phases related initially to selling and distribution and, since the late 1950s, also to sourcing product from the region. Since the 1978 decision to establish an ISC office in Hong Kong the regional sales operations and steadily expanding purchasing activity have been directed from a single headquarters unit supported by a number of local offices in the main selling territories and a buying office in Taiwan. The regional headquarters remained in Hong Kong until 1990, when it moved, for mainly cost saving considerations, to Kuala Lumpur.

In the same year the Hong Kong office opened the Philippines tennis ball plant came on stream to be followed, ten years later, by a smaller factory in Indonesia, which mainly serviced the local market. Dunlop Footwear had started buying canvas sports shoes from Hong Kong in the late 1950s and maintained a separate purchasing operation in the area, largely managed from its Liverpool and Winsford offices, until the business was closed in the mid 1990s and licensees took over the UK marketing of sports shoes, slippers and protective footwear.

The Malaysian Dunlop company, allegedly influenced by 'high level' local golf enthusiasts, set up a golf ball plant in 1975 with an annual capacity of 24,000 dozen, which was unlikely to be sufficient for a viable operation. It was sold five years later. And to complete this Far East 'mosaic' in 1985 Dunlop Slazenger took over the management of two Dunlopillo units, in Indonesia and Thailand, which had been opened by the UK based division in the 1970s to service a growing local demand for beds, mattresses and pillows.

Both the Dunlopillo businesses have now transferred to local ownership. In the case of Thailand to the former territory manager for Dunlop Slazenger, David Lamb, who is also the local distributor for the company's sports equipment. Despite the very different technology and market sectors involved both the foam and bedding operations were run very successfully by Dunlop Slazenger managers and contributed significantly to a regional turnover that nearly tripled from the 1985 starting point and moved from 5% to 10% as a proportion of the group's worldwide sales.

An Australian, Laurie Roberts was the 'founding' regional manager, selected by Findlay Picken in 1978, to organise both the sourcing activities and what was then a much smaller sales operation. He was followed by a Scot, Ronnie Downie, who had gained considerable export sales experience with Sports Surfaces International and as export sales manager for ISC's UK business, and would be the driving force behind the move from Hong Kong to Kuala Lumpur. When Ronnie retired he was succeeded by a Canadian, Scott

Brown, an experienced sports trade executive who had worked for Spalding before running Dunlop Slazenger's Sportlines operation in Toronto, and would also manage the USA sales and distribution business based in Greenville. This 'Commonwealth' sequence was broken by the 1999 appointment of K. L. Choong as regional director.

Before the creation of a regional organisation, with its chain of local sales offices, the Groups' sales had been handled either by local distributors and agents – several of whom had very long associations with the company, and especially with Slazenger – or, as was the main route for Dunlop, through the overseas division's selling companies, the largest located in Hong Kong.

And prior to the establishment of the Hong Kong sourcing office the individual ISC companies, and some of the larger separate sports operations like USA, South Africa and Australia, organised their own buying activities in the area, mainly in Taiwan, South Korea and Hong Kong where the locally owned manufacturing facilities steadily expanded to meet the growing demand for rackets, golf club components, clothing, footwear and virtually all types of accessories. Indonesia would become a major source for footwear and the bulk of the racket manufacturers gradually migrated to China, though continued to operate there under the original Taiwan ownership. Slazenger Australia, for the most part, have maintained a separate buying operation in the region but there was a considerable degree of liaison between the ISC companies and the product managers in South Africa and USA well before the formation of Dunlop Slazenger International. And in recent years useful contacts have been made between the UK and Far East buying managers and their counter parts in Sumitomo, who have also developed a considerable purchasing presence in the region.

As the volume of goods sourced from the region increased to the point where the only manufacturing units still operating in Europe and the USA were the ball plants so the sophistication and scale of the purchasing resource was necessarily increased. In more recent years while it has been administered from the Kuala Lumpur office the main responsibility for sourcing policies and decisions has been exercised by product and function directors, generally with their own senior executives located in the region.

One of the key elements of this process, from its beginning nearly 50 years ago when Dunlop Footwear pioneered sourcing from Hong Kong, has been the emphasis on improving the quality of the products involved. Dunlop Footwear and Dunlop Slazenger quality requirements, and the strict, on the spot monitoring of production standards to meet those requirements has been a major factor in driving up general quality levels. The company's designers, technical managers and buyers have combined with the manufacturers in the region to ensure the success of what has become such an important part of the company's total

Dear Mr. Osborne.

Princess Margaret has asked me to let you know how delighted she was to be able to have the opportunity of seeing for herself the workings of your tennis ball factory. The process involved was something that Her Royal Highness had never seen before, and she found it highly interesting and instructive.

Thank you very much indeed.

I am to ask that a message of The Princess' sincerest good wishes be conveyed to all members of your Company for the future.

Private Secretary to
The Princess Margaret
Countess of Snowdon

D.A.N. Osborne, Esq.,
International Sports Co. Inc.

Princess Margaret's 1980 letter following her visit to the Bataan tennis ball plant. She is seen in the picture with Denis Osborne, Mr. Teddy Pena and Graham Lovett

Exterior of the original Philippines plant

operation. There are still a number of those early 'sourcing pioneers'; who remember how many days, rather than hours, it took to get to a Hong Kong where there were no buildings higher than four storeys, and communication was mainly by air mail or the word and numbers only language of the telex machines.

The Philippines tennis ball plant is another Far East region success story. This developed from the relatively small beginnings of the UK and Slazenger Australia joint venture first explored in 1976 by the UK's Denis Osborne, Roy Pollard and Stan Ackroyd, and the Australian, Ray Tuckerman. Their recommendation to go ahead was approved only three months later by the Dunlop main board, which authorised a £1 million investment to build a plant with a capacity of 450,000 dozen per annum. The site selected in the Bataan Export Zone is about 100 miles north of Manila in an area made famous by the ferocious battles between the Americans and Japanese during the second world war. In addition to being almost literally carved out of a surrounding jungle that still contained a number of armed guerrillas the plant could only be reached by either a four hour journey over rough roads, or a one hour boat dash across the Bay of Manila, weather permitting. The access arrangements, plus the heat and humidity, made it a tough assignment for the expatriate management team, but the logistics of bringing in raw materials and shipping out finished tennis balls were much less of a problem thanks to the port facilities built into the Export Zone.

Interior of the new plant, now the company's main tennis ball production unit

With a mixture of new and transferred plant, shipped from Australia and the UK, production started, on time, in 1978. The combination of the company's training programmes and the natural skills of the local population ensured early achievement of the required quality standards for deliveries initially to Australia and the Far East selling companies. As the volume increased to the next target of 600,000 dozen, containers were also being sent to Europe and North America but further investment was put on hold due to the fragility of the Philippines economy in the late 1980s.

The need for further capacity was met in the short term by setting up a smaller tennis ball unit in Indonesia. The individual responsible for this project was Martin Price, who had been part of the team to set up production in Bataan and had followed Denis Osborne and the Australian, John Briscoe, as president of the Philippines company. The new plant, which was located next to the Dunlopillo operation, was planned to have a maximum capacity of 600,000 dozen but was held at 200,000 for mainly local requirements as the

235

economic situation in the Philippines had improved to the point where further expansion there had become a more realistic proposition.

In 1992, following a long term strategic review of the company's tennis ball manufacturing resources, the decision was taken to close the USA Hartwell plant and transfer its equipment to the Philippines, where production was moved from the original factory to a much larger building only a few hundred yards away. The new plant came on stream in 1996 and, following the more recent closures of the Barnsley and Hanau tennis ball units, has become the main source for all Dunlop Slazenger requirements worldwide with the capability of meeting the differing product types and quality levels in all the individual markets involved, including the supply of 'perfect' balls for the Australian Open and Wimbledon. The Philippines plant has also been a factor in the relationship between the company and Sumitomo as an additional supply source for the high quality Dunlop products demanded by the Japanese consumer.

Though perhaps not immediately apparent to the casual observer it is clear that the Dunlop Slazenger presence in the Far East, and in such strength for so many years of both marketing and purchasing, has been of immense importance in the development of the total business. A lot of credit is due to those who, in often difficult and uncomfortable conditions, established the first links in what became a very powerful distribution network, searched for the new product suppliers who would help to maintain the company's competitiveness, and, as they led the new plant project teams, successfully married new technologies with local skills.

All around the Pacific Rim, from Japan in the north to Australia and New Zealand in the south, the Dunlop and Slazenger brands are widely recognised for the quality of both their operations and their products.

Ian Woosnam

Greg Rusedski

JAPAN

In the case of Japan the history is almost entirely about Dunlop. The Slazenger brand, apart from several, relatively small-scale licensing operations, has not yet been able to establish a significant presence, and it would require considerable investment to do so at this stage.

The story in Japan is one of a remarkable success for the Dunlop and 'Maxfli' brands. It also illustrates what can be achieved by a multi-product company when sufficient resources and management attention are applied to developing market opportunities even when completely different sectors are involved. In this instance a consistent focus on the merits of the main brand (Dunlop), in terms of premium quality and technical excellence allied to substantial promotional investment, overcame the potential disadvantages of using it across both the industrial and consumer markets. In many ways, and this is hardly surprising, the Dunlop business in Japan was fashioned along the lines originally established in the UK. However, the product range never became so diverse and this probably fostered the development of a successful sports operation even though, like early

Emperor Hirohito inspects tennis ball production at Kobe in 1947

Dunlop, it remained very much locked into an organisation structure primarily related to running a tyre business. For all parts of the business the Dunlop brand was of paramount importance and this philosophy was maintained by the wholly Japanese management that ultimately controlled it. In fact they believed they upheld the key attributes associated with the brand during its prime years more faithfully than anyone else.

Additionally the Japanese Dunlop company has had to deal with a number of ownership changes from the original 100% UK parentage through several sell down stages to majority local ownership with Sumitomo Electric Industries as today's largest shareholder and with its operations in the global tyre industry considerably strengthened by its 1999 alliance with the Goodyear Tire and Rubber Company.

Sumitomo's sports division accounts for around 20% of its sales in Japan and is almost entirely focused on the tennis and golf markets, especially the latter. It also markets sports goods under the Dunlop brand in Taiwan and South Korea and has developed an overseas golf

Golf ball production resumes at Kobe in 1956 wih Austen MacNally and Harry Johnson providing quality control

business under the 'Srixon' brand. Golf has been its most important sector for many years and it's interesting to note that after the USA, Japan is still the largest market in the world. It's also interesting to recall that nearly 80 years ago it was the Dunlop managers, sent from

London and Fort Dunlop to run a tyre factory, who first saw the golf potential in Japan, and who were subsequently instrumental in establishing and developing both golf and tennis ball production.

When the Dunlop Rubber Company opened its first factory in Kobe in 1908 there were only nine motor cars in the whole of Japan so it is not surprising the first production programmes scheduled tyres for rickshaws and the 100,000 bicycles then known to be the most popular form of transport. By the time a much larger Kobe plant was opened in 1931, the number of bicycles had increased to 5 million and of cars to 100,000.

During the intervening years golf and tennis had been slowly attracting the attention of the more affluent in the population. The first golf club, again in Kobe, had opened in 1903 but more than 20 years later there were still only 10. UK Dunlop announced in a 1909 issue of *Golf Trader* that the company's newly introduced golf balls had already reached Japan, probably imported from the early Birmingham production. But the key decision was taken in 1925 when the local Dunlop management decided to import both golf and tennis balls and distribute them to the trade through the Oshawa Sokai Trading Company. From then on the pace of Dunlop activity accelerated. Golf and tennis balls were first made in the Kobe plant in 1930 and quickly established the dominant position in the premium sector of the market, which has been maintained to the present day.

Putting the covers on tennis balls at Kobe in 1934

Having established the 'Dunlop Golf Ball' the range was successfully extended in 1935 by importing the sensational new '65' from the UK and also by introducing a new Kobe-made ball, which was given the name 'Green Flash', the sub brand more usually associated with the famous tennis shoes. In 1937 the pressures of the war with China brought about the prohibition of imported balls and a year later, along with many other luxury goods, the production of both golf and tennis balls was stopped.

In 1947 Emperor Hirohito visited the Kobe plant and his tour included an inspection of the tennis ball production line which had just been re-commissioned. However, it would be more than 10 years before golf balls were again in production. In 1956 the newly appointed executive director, D. B. Houghton, encouraged the then president, G. O. Saffery, to restart the golf ball operation because the increasing worldwide popularity of golf was bound to have an impact in Japan.

Dick English, who had been a tyre production manager at Fort Dunlop before the war, and had transferred to tyre production at Kobe in 1955, became part of the team that set about re-establishing

Virginia Wade for Dunlop and Sue Barker for Slazenger in action in a 1979 Dunlop Japan catalogue

John McEnroe features in a 1981 tennis catalogue for Dunlop Japan

the golf ball line. The project leaders were two other UK managers, Austen MacNally and Harry Johnson, who was a foreman in the golf ball department at Speke. A local newspaper, the *Garston Weekly News* reported that Mr. Johnson, and his wife and daughter, 'find themselves on the brink of a brand new life'. The Johnsons had decided against flying to Japan, which would have taken three days and three nights, and opted for the 'beauty of the six week sea voyage'. It was noted that as all those working in the golf ball section at Kobe only spoke Japanese he would have the services of an interpreter, and would be using photographs to explain the various stages in the manufacturing process. Harry also told the reporter that 'having received samples of the golf balls already made by Japanese firms the Dunlop company find that their products are of a much higher quality and think that their project will be a success'. He was right to be confident but would never have imagined the eventual scale of that success.

The new production line, which was 100% wound balata branded '65', made a slow start at 60 dozen per day, with initially a 40% reject rate. This was typical of the Kobe approach to quality summed up by one of the Japanese technicians in the start-up team, Mr. Horiuchi, who recalled that 'the people in factory inspected and selected good balls very carefully, and shipped only high quality good balls so we could succeed in getting good reputation afterwards'. Once satisfactory quality levels had been established Mr. Horiuchi was kept very busy redesigning the plant layout as output expanded between 20% and 30% each year in order to keep pace with what by now had become a feverish growth rate for the game in Japan. It was being fuelled by the country's rapid economic growth and the choice of golf as the game that best fitted the require-

The site of the Kobe factory before and after the 1995 earthquake

ments of corporate entertaining.

By 1963 the golf business was based largely on the '65' and a 'Maxfli' with imported Peter Thomson clubs and the tennis line featured the 'Maxply Fort' frame imported from Waltham Abbey plus a locally made 'Fort' ball. The golf club range was considerably expanded in 1964 when a team from John Letters introduced production into the Kobe factory, which was marketed under the 'Maxfli' brand. The huge interest in golf encouraged the growth of professional tournaments and the development of a Japanese Tour, which in 1973, led to the formation of Dunlop Sports Enterprise as a company to provide tournament management and promotion.

Dunlop Japan's Golf Science Centre at Ichijima opened in 1994

The golf momentum was maintained by the 1976 launch of a 'Dunlop Johnny Miller' ball – he was a Slazenger player in Europe – plus improved versions of the '65' and 'Maxfli'. In 1980 a one-piece ball was introduced for the huge driving range market and in 1982 the flow of technical aid from the UK led to the manufacture of the DDH, which was the first two-piece ball produced in Japan. By this time annual sales of tennis balls had passed the 1 million dozen mark and golf balls were heading for 4 million dozen, plus the sales of one-piece balls to driving ranges.

In 1984 Sumitomo Rubber assumed full control of Dunlop Japan and also the bulk of the worldwide Dunlop tyre operations. One effect of this change, and the BTR acquisition of the rest of Dunlop which followed shortly afterwards, was to put some distance between the UK and Japanese sports businesses, in particular the close technical relationship that had existed from the 1930 start of ball production in Kobe right through to the 1982 introduction of the DDH ball. Fortunately for both companies, a number of personal contacts between the two were maintained, which have been the basis of subsequently valuable commercial and marketing co-operation. In particular, Kobe supplies of premium quality balls during the 1980s and early 1990s were a key factor in reviving the 'Maxfli' business in North America at a time when the Westminster plant had difficulty in turning out premium quality products due to a long period of under investment. And a Kobe range of balata, wound and two-piece balls was the initial product platform for the Slazenger Golf operation launched in 1986. The most important area of marketing co-operation was the recognition by both management teams of the promotional impact, in Japan as well as in the USA, of significant visibility on the US PGA Tour. The resultant combining of resources to achieve that presence was another vital factor in the resurgence of the 'Maxfli' brand in the USA, where it had always been the 'flagship' golf mark.

Sumitomo continued to trade very successfully in Japan until the first half of the 1990s when the combination of the severe downturn in the Japanese economy and, more seriously, the destruction of the Kobe plant in the 1995 earthquake gave some of their competitors, including a number of imported brands, the opportunity to erode their share of the premium ball market. The subsequent recovery of their previous strength in the market has been based on their adherence to the highest possible quality standards and a very considerable expansion of their premium golf club business.

Their use of brands and sub-brands, particularly in the golf market, has been rather different from that of Dunlop Slazenger. Greater emphasis is given to a larger number of sub-brands, each attached to specific product and performance characteristics, and 'Dunlop', represented either in word form or by the 'Flying D', or both, is the constant corporate link. In that way the brand's sports heritage remains extremely powerful in the Japanese market as a successful part of the total Sumitomo business.

A scene from Dunlop Japan's famous Phoenix Tournament

SOUTH AFRICA

It has been said that 'Just as trade follows the flag, so golf, in due course, follows both'. Add tennis and cricket to golf and there are three of the 'imperial habits' Britain spread across the world, and which provided the opportunities for first the Slazenger companies, and, later, Dunlop to develop their international businesses.

In the case of South Africa cricket was established as early as the 1840s, and the first Test matches were played against Sir Aubrey Smith's visiting English team in 1888/89. By then golf was well established and at least a dozen South Africans entered the Men's singles event at Wimbledon before the first world war. The first was Harry Kitson in 1905.

The first reference to South Africa in this history was very 'unsporting'. As official contractors to the War Office William Sykes produced military supplies, probably rifle furniture from the Horbury factory, for the Boer War. That may or may not have fired the imagination of William 'Senior' but he certainly visited the country soon after the war had ended, and then sent William 'Junior' there for a four month stay, during which he set up an office in Cape Town. During one of his regular visits some years later he met the South African Test wicket-keeper, H. B. Cameron, and 'obtained from him his ideas and suggestions as to the most suitable designs of gauntlets and guards for efficient wicket-keeping purposes, resulting in the introduction of the splendid "Cameron" pads and gloves'. Sykes maintained their sales connections separately from Slazenger until after the second world war, working with a Johannesburg agent, Atkinson & Barker, who also handled Ayres products.

Slazenger's agents were Ross-Elliott and McKellar, with offices in Cape Town, Durban and Johannesburg, but that was only one strand of their connection. Before buying Gradidges in 1927 the McMaster twins, Michael and Humphrey, had 'cut their teeth' in the sports trade when they bought the well known South African company, Taylor & Ellis. In 1946, Tim Hadingham, who, with Michael, had been joint managing-director of the combined Slazenger and Gradidge business in the UK, moved to South Africa, came out of retirement and was 'the moving spirit' behind the construction of the country's first tennis ball plant at Mobeni, Durban. One of the first visitors to the new factory, in 1951, was none other than Denis Compton, who had also been one

Denis Compton, seen here and opposite with Jack Ellis, visits the Slazenger factory in Durban in 1951

of the famous sportsmen to visit the company's London office. His signature in the visitors' book is only a few pages away from those of the 1951, 1955 and 1959 South African cricket sides, which included other 'greats' like Roy McLean, Jackie McGlew, Eric Rowan, W. R. Endean, H. J. Tayfield, Tom Goddard, C. B. Van Ryneveld and A. D. Nourse. The cricketing connection is maintained in the present Test side with players like Jacques Kallis and

Shaun Pollock using Slazenger equipment and they are joined on the tennis court by Wayne Ferreira. The list of leading golfers is not so long but contains two of the very greatest, Bobby Locke and Gary Player, who, between them won 13 Majors.

The Dunlop story in South Africa started in 1896, when the first managing-director of the local company, Malcolm Irving, landed in Cape Town and began to lay the foundations of what would become one of the country's largest businesses. In 1934 Durban was the location chosen for the first tyre plant, and it was there, in the true Dunlop tradition, that manufacturing units for belting, hose, Dunlopillo and tennis balls were later established, the ball plant starting up in 1951. Golf balls would follow on an adjacent site in 1965.

Colin Van Jarsveldt, who joined the company in 1979, as marketing manager, and was later its managing-director, has provided a very detailed record of both the manufacturing and the marketing histories of the company during the 50 years from the opening of the first tennis ball plant, which he regards as the real beginning of the Dunlop Slazenger story. Although the brands would have been very visible before then, through the efforts of their sales agencies, they obviously took on a very definite South African presence once the Slazenger plant added tennis rackets and golf clubs to its product line and the established strength of the Dunlop brand, based largely on its dominant local tyre operation, was applied to its competing tennis ball activity.

One of the main reasons both companies chose Durban as their manufacturing location was its proximity to port facilities for importing the required raw materials. When *Harpers Sports and Games* visited the new Slazenger plant, where they were received by Tim Hadingham as deputy chairman and Jack Ellis as managing-director, both accompanied by their wives, they were obviously impressed with everything they saw. They reported that the factory, which occupied a 3-acre site, ' was surrounded by green lawns and flowering shrubs, and is the most modern of its kind'. The credit for that was due primarily to the work of the production manager, H. V. Cheetham, and John

Stirk, who had been seconded to Mobeni from Barnsley. Great credit was given in the report to the skills of the Zulu workforce and the part they had played in producing 'balls of outstanding quality, causing something of a sensation in the Union'.

When, in 1959, Dunlop acquired the parent Slazenger company in the UK its wholly owned subsidiary, Dunlop South Africa, formed Sports Equipment International as a holding company to control the operations of both brands. While this involved co-ordination of the manufacturing resources, which included the Dunlop golf ball factory making both the '65' and the Slazenger Plus in the 1.62 size, the sales organisations, as in the UK, remained competitors. However, at that stage this was more a case of splitting 100% of the market as domestic producers enjoyed the protection of stiff tariff barriers for imported sports goods.

Having started up the golf plant with the smaller sized balata balls the larger 1.68 balls were introduced in 1975 and, a year later, the '65 Fort' and 'Slazenger Duraplus' were launched as surlyn covered wound balls. In 1979 the first two-piece balls were made but the local decision was made to use the compression moulding route, which would later prove too costly when compared with the more widely used injection moulding process. By that time Sports Equipment International had decided on a policy of integrating their two main brands rather than continuing to foster direct competition. This could have reflected the need for greater discipline in a market place which had been opened up by a Government directive forcing the company to supply mass merchants rather than only using the traditional distribution route through pro-shops and sports specialists. This would lead to a backlash from the specialist outlets, who began to look for alternative brands not being supplied to the mass merchants. The initial impact for the company, as virtually the only established and domestic supplier, was a very big increase in sales but that was accompanied by severe pressure on the prices and margins as the mass merchants competed fiercely in this, for them, new sector of branded sports equipment.

This 1951 group shot of the South African Slazenger management was taken at the Mobeni tennis ball factory and includes Mr and Mrs Tim Hadingham, Mr and Mrs Jack Ellis, John Stirk and HV Cheetham

The longer term, and more damaging effect for Dunlop Slazenger was the decision by the specialist outlets to look for new, and imported brands as one means of retaliating against the mass merchants. Soon Kennex and Prince rackets, Penn tennis balls and Ram golf balls were appearing in the South African market, and creating even more pressure for Colin and his team. The mass merchants also started selling these brands as a means of achieving higher margins than those they had established with the higher volume Dunlop Slazenger lines, which became known as 'KVIs' (Known Value Items).

These market pressures had contributed to a number of changes on the manufacturing side, which would not have been possible but for the earlier decision to consolidate the previously separate businesses. Manufacture of Dunlop tennis balls moved from the tyre factory to the 'carbon black free' Slazenger plant at Mobeni. This move proved more significant than planned when, in the 1970s, the Slazenger balls, which enjoyed a 70% market share, ran into severe problems with cover material and production levels were only maintained by increasing the share held by the Dunlop balls which used material from another supplier. Squash ball manufacture, for both brands, was introduced in 1973 – Dunlop in 3 ball sleeves, Slazenger in 2 to differentiate between the brands – and became an important part of the business.

A year later Dunlop tennis racket production was also moved into Mobeni, from its previous Pinetown site. Between the two brands the company had maintained an 80% share of the market well into the 1970s and over a 20 year period sold more than 1 million each of the Maxply tennis and squash frames. Disappointed at what was perceived as a slow reaction by the UK to the advent of alternative materials for rackets aluminium frames were imported from the USA in 1976 and local product development programmes resulted in the introduction of new and lighter frames combining wood with the newly available plastic fibres and cane laminations. Sports Equipment International also claim a world first for a large head squash racket using wood strengthened with fibre facings. However, the worldwide march of the composite frames, combined with the growth of imports, led to the closure of

The paramount chief of the Zulus visits the Durban tennis ball factory in 1955

the racket plant in 1990. Uniquely within Dunlop Slazenger a reduced workforce was then employed, albeit for a short period, to use its woodworking skills to produce furniture, which was sold direct to the public.

As the whole nature of the market changed in the 1970s and 1980s, with the specialist retailers looking increasingly to footwear and apparel to compensate for the decline in the tennis sector, and the choice widening for golf outlets as Titleist and Spalding followed Ram into South Africa, the business struggled to retain its previously dominant position. The 30% tariff protection for its golf and tennis ball operations was obviously crucial but in both cases increasing pressure was being applied by the growing number of competitors, several of whom deployed more powerful promotional campaigns. The 'local manufacturer' factor, which had sustained the business for so long, would eventually be brutally demonstrated by a reduction in the golf ball market share from nearly 50% to 22% when the Durban plant was closed in the mid 1990s. For a period the Titleist attack on the premium end of the market was held at bay by adoption of the USA company's policy of promoting Maxfli balls in conjunction with Tour event successes – in this case the local Sunshine Circuit – based on using Kobe-made balata balls.

The Mobeni tennis ball plant continued to operate until very recently and this was the basis of holding on to a market share around 80% despite the increasing pressure from imports from USA and the Far East, some of them of 'rubbish' quality, all of them sold into the market at very low prices. In this context Slazenger was used as the 'fighting brand' to counter the cheap imports – exactly the opposite positioning to that maintained in the UK and elsewhere. South Africa is unique in that 60% of tennis is played at high altitude, which requires balls with lower than European or North American pressure in order to reduce the bounce in the more rarefied atmosphere. Mobeni production was based on a combination of the necessary lower pressure and a specially woven cloth which optimised flight in the thinner air.

In product terms, and seeking additional turnover from another sector when its traditional stronghold came under pressure, SEI turned to footwear production in 1974. Utilising surplus vulcanising plant made available by Dunlop Footwear in the UK men's Green Flash and women's White Flash tennis shoes were introduced with specially formulated outer soles to counter the very abrasive nature of the local all weather courts. This venture, in turn came under competitive pressure as the new wave of more sophisticated USA designs, manufactured in the Far East, reached South Africa. The limitations of the original vulcanising process were abandoned in 1986 for new soling equipment that allowed greater design variety for new ranges of tennis and squash shoes but this project was forced to cease operations in 1994.

Following the BTR takeover in 1985 SEI became part of BTR Dunlop South Africa and remained under control of the local head office of that company until 1996, when it was acquired by the newly formed Dunlop Slazenger company, which had been the management buy out vehicle earlier that year. This led to further changes which resulted in South Africa becoming essentially a sales territory based on local agents rather than a sales force, and allowed the reduction of central costs. The business was initially managed by Scott Brown, in conjunction with his responsibility for the Far East region, and later by Andrew Griffiths, who had become the managing-director for Europe in 1997. As part of the overall manufacturing rationalisation of the group the tennis ball and squash ball plants have been closed and the brands are now represented in South Africa on an agency and licencing basis.

Because of the size of the local market the scale of this business, even when it held massively dominant market shares and had the benefit of tariff protection, could never have been huge. Against that background the determination of the local, mainly tyre oriented management to establish, maintain and extend its range of sports manufacturing units is probably only justified by the existence of the tariff barriers that supported the existence of ball plants operating at relatively, if not extremely low volume levels. Possibly of equal significance was the imperfect linkage with the rest of the Dunlop and Slazenger sports businesses from the originally separate relationships with the two main companies, through the twenty years of ISC and the ten years of Dunlop Slazenger International, when local accountability to BTR Dunlop South Africa remained paramount. Direct responsibility to and amalgamation with a parent sports management may have come too late to retain a greater proportion of the brand heritage – in the form of an ongoing business – than sentiment, at least, suggests could have been the case.

Gary Player

CANADA

A page from Sykes 1919 catalogue showing details of their Toronto office and the ball range developed for Canada, including an 'American Rugger Football'

Reliable evidence exists that both the infant Dunlop sports business and the Slazenger companies were quick to identify the potential of the Canadian market. In 1911 Dunlop were advertising that the Dunlop Tire & Rubber Company depot in Toronto 'was now selling golf balls'. Immediately after the end of the first war Sykes issued a catalogue from their Lombard Street office in Toronto offering a range specifically targeted on the main North American sports, including 'American Rugger Football', and there can be little doubt that the enterprising Frank Slazenger, sitting in his New York office, would have been alert to the opportunities available to sell his golf clubs and tennis rackets north of the 49th parallel.

As the *Oxford Companion to Sports & Games* puts it 'Golf came to Canada (and Australia, New Zealand and South Africa) along with other imperial habits towards the end of the 19th century', and might even have arrived earlier if there is any truth in the tale of the Glasgow sailor, who, in 1854, is said to have 'carried his clubs to the heights of Abraham and there entertained himself in solitary contentment'. As for tennis the game had developed sufficient strength in the early years of the 20th century to allow Canada to be one of only six entrants in the 1912 Davis Cup, along with Britain, USA, Australasia, France and Germany. And 1907 had seen the first Canadian competitors at Wimbledon; Robert Powell reached the third round in the Men's singles and Violet Summerhayes the second in the Ladies. The following year Powell was a semi-finalist, losing to the eventual champion, Arthur Gore.

Fifty years after joining Slazenger, as the sales representative for Quebec, Dick Birch, by then President of Sportlines, picked up the threads of the Canadian story when he addressed the company's 1989 Awards Dinner. He reminded his audience that after the end of the first war, and for the next 40 years, Dunlop and Slazenger had remained completely separate companies and fierce competitors in the Canadian market. Dunlop were still operating as a sports division of the local Tire company with an office in Queen Street, Toronto, were making golf balls in their own factory, importing tennis balls from Fort

Dunlop and had also begun to sell rackets.

Initially the Slazenger business operated as a sales agency run by Ernest Purkis, who was also importing rackets and tennis balls from Slazenger's factories in the City of London and Woolwich. As the business expanded it was decided to form Slazengers Canada Ltd. as a subsidiary of the UK parent and the first office was opened in Lower Yonge Street, again in Toronto. At this stage, and very much in line with the development of the parent accompany, the main growth was occurring in the racket sports – tennis, badminton and squash – which were rapidly growing in popularity. The decision was taken to increase the supply of frames by establishing a small racket manufacturing unit and larger premises were obtained in Queen Street, only a few yards away from the Dunlop office.

Buzzer Hadingham and Dick Birch at the centre of this Slazenger group at a North American Trade show in the 1960s with, from left to right, Tony Wells, Bob Boomer and Saul Chavkin

Beverley Devlin, who worked in the Queen Street factory for more than eight years, remembered that in addition to a front office it had a stringing room, dry kiln and finishing area. She was 15 when she started work there in 1930 and was paid $8 for a 48 hour week. Her job was in the finishing room, with two other girls, three boys and two men. There were five other girls in the stringing room and one young man and another 8 men and boys in the rest of the factory. It seems that all went well with this 22 strong work force until, as she recalls, 'an efficiency expert was hired from England which later made the whole place a disaster'.

Nevertheless, before the start of the second world war Dunlop and Slazenger had continued to expand and, between them, completely dominated the racket sports market. Once the war had started the operations of both companies were severely restricted. Raw materials were in short supply and imports were stopped. The Dunlop golf ball plant had to shut down as all available rubber was required for tyres and other military supplies, and once all Slazenger production stopped the Queen Street factory was sold to a company making ammunition boxes. It was decided to keep the Slazenger brand alive in the Canadian market by amalgamating the company with the Campbell Manufacturing Company, which was also involved in sports goods manufacture, but for the remainder of the war their most important activity was making radio aerials for tanks.

Almost immediately the war ended Slazenger re-opened a Toronto office, this time on King Street West, but it was to be several years before adequate supplies resumed from the UK because of the time needed to recover from the destruction of the Woolwich factories and to rebuild production of rackets and balls in Horbury and Barnsley. Dunlop were having the same problems with supplies from the UK but did manage to re-start the local golf ball plant.

After completion of his military service Dick Birch was recalled to the Slazenger colours by 'Buzzer' Hadingham, who 'snatched' him from the Raleigh cycle stand at a Toronto trade show. Determined to get his man 'Buzzer' offered Dick $5,000 a year, which meant an immediate increase to $6,000 for his boss at that time, Bill Millsap. It appears that on hearing about

'Buzzer's' generosity the UK board 'went crazy', but Dick's immense contribution to the Canadian business over the next forty years fully justified that moment of madness.

By 1950 supplies from the UK were getting back to normal and the business was growing again. Larger premises were obtained in Merritton, which were used to increase the inventory range and also to house a racket finishing unit using 'frames in white' shipped from Horbury. There was also room to install the plant required to pack tennis balls in the newly introduced compressed air tins, which overcame the problem of the balls that were inclined to go 'flat' if stored too long in the previous cardboard box pack.

Dick Birch was well known in Canadian sporting circles, largely because of his status as a badminton international. He was, therefore, an ideal 'accomplice' for Bill Carlton, who, in 1952, had accidentally created a piece of plastic looking like a shuttlecock when one of his injection moulding machines exploded. Bill was also a badminton enthusiast so they made an ideal combination to develop the 'accident' into a successful synthetic shuttle. Dick's reward from the still independent Carlton operation was the exclusive sales rights in Canada for the new product.

Progress in Canada was now gathering pace. By 1954 Slazenger UK were able to send them golf balls and a good range of golf bags to service a market which was becoming the largest potential for further expansion. A major breakthrough occurred in 1956 when Slazenger Canada bought the Burke-Thumm company, which was quite small but well known locally for the very high quality clubs made by the three Martin brothers who owned it – John, Jim and Norman. This move established the company as serious players in the golf market and during the next three years it would move to a dominant position. Dick, who eventually allowed golf to take over from badminton as his main sport, was at the heart of these developments.

Two major golf club franchises were secured, possibly the two very best. First was the Canadian distributorship for Ben Hogan clubs. Hogan was not only a perfectionist on the golf course but also when it came to making clubs. He insisted that the quality of every club had to be perfect and it was a considerable credit to the Slazenger organisation that he eventually agreed their production standards were good enough to make Hogan clubs in Toronto. The company's growing reputation for supplying high quality product to the club market could have been a major factor when, in 1957, Karsten Solheim agreed Slazenger could also be the Canadian distributor for his Ping clubs. Interestingly, Slazenger in the UK also

The Slazenger Sportlines office in Toronto shortly after it opened in 1960

enjoyed a very successful distributor relationship with Hogan clubs and their Paris branch had the French rights to distribute Ping clubs for a number of years.

By 1960 the combination of the still growing racket business and the much enlarged golf operation meant it was again necessary to look for larger premises and the move was made to the custom-built complex of offices, ware-house and manufacturing area at 89, Northline Road. At almost the same moment the decision was taken to make this move the Slazenger parent in the UK was acquired by Dunlop.

For the next four years the two Canadian sports businesses continued to operate separately, in the case of Dunlop still as a subsidiary division of the local Tire company. However, in 1964, the year ISC was set up in the UK, it was decided to move the Dunlop sports business into Northline Road and combine the two operations under the Slazenger management.

In 1965 the overall business was again enlarged by the acquisition of the Raymond Lanctot distributorship for premium quality ski equipment and clothing, which brought a better trading balance by providing substantial business during the previously very quiet winter months. The 'lead' brand in the Lanctot portfolio was Rossignol. Fourteen years later that company, having seen their Canadian business expand enormously decided to set up their own organisation and it was agreed they should take over the whole Lanctot operation.

In 1968 ISC decided that the best way forward in Canada was to complete-ly integrate the Dunlop and Slazenger businesses and Sportlines International was formed as a single operating entity for both brands plus the important franchises that had been secured by the Slazenger management. The business continued to expand and the Northline premises were enlarged in 1972, and again in 1975. This proved invaluable when, in the early 1980s, Sportlines became the Canadian distributor for the Converse range of athletic footwear. The company's virtually blanket coverage of the sports market was the key element in taking Converse sales from $1 million per annum to just over $20 million in five years. However, as with Lanctot and Rossignol, it often happens that a distributor can be too successful and, in 1986, Converse decided to go their own way.

In 1984 another change was made in the reporting line for the Canadian company. Following the formation of Dunlop Slazenger International as the worldwide vehicle for managing all the sports operations still owned by Dunlop, a North American region was created, comprising the previous sports division of the Buffalo based Dunlop Tire and Rubber Company, now renamed Dunlop Slazenger Corporation, the small Slazenger business in Philadelphia and Sportlines, which would now report to the North American president based in Greenville, South Carolina. He in turn reported to Alan Finden-Crofts, the newly appointed chief executive of Dunlop Slazenger International.

At the time of that reorganisation Sportlines sales were running close to £13 million per annum, which was about half the 1984 figure for the USA. The fact that the population of the USA was more than eight times that of Canada reflects the much stronger position the Toronto based operation had established over the years. This was partly due to the close integration with first Slazenger UK and then ISC, which meant it had been reporting to a sports management board for most of its existence. And although it had held dominant shares of the Canadian racket and golf markets for many years the company's sales had been considerably expanded by the policy of maximis-ing its distribution strength by broadening the range to include brands and products; Hogan, Ping, TaylorMade, Converse, the Lanctot ski lines, string-ing machines and a large clothing range; which were complementary to what

The Canadian star, Carling Bassett, who played the 200G in the late 1980s

was available from ISC.

An interesting feature of the Sportlines structure, and another illustration of how sports managers in their various territories were allowed to make 'local' decisions, was the practice of using Slazenger on the golf side as an umbrella heading for the premium bands, like Hogan and Ping, and Dunlop as the 'value' offering. Each had its own 'brand manager' but the racket business was run with a single responsibility for both Dunlop and Slazenger except for a specialist manager dealing with badminton.

Sales peaked in 1987 at £23 million, which was the last year with the Converse distributorship, and did not reach that level again. It continued to operate profitably but later also had to deal with the loss of the Hogan and Ping franchises. These setbacks emphasised the vulnerability of relying on these brands and products as key elements of the distributor policy, and especially when Dunlop Slazenger was unable to provide suitable replacement lines. Additionally, a very extensive range of golf and tennis clothing, again multi-branded and with long lead times from Far East sources, plus a comprehensive range of accessories, e.g. separate golf bag collections for Dunlop, Slazenger, Hogan and Ping, required the financing of a substantial inventory with the attendant risk of regular end of season clearances of the 'fashion' items.

The infrastructure of the business in terms of both personnel and premises had expanded to support this relatively complex operation, which had generated sufficient revenue to maintain reasonable levels of profitability though it had proved extremely difficult to live within the tighter working capital limits that were standard practice in BTR, which had acquired Dunlop in early 1985. An inevitable process of rationalising the business around a smaller, essentially Dunlop and Slazenger portfolio of products led, in 1997, to it being absorbed in the North American operation and becoming a sales territory reporting to the Greenville headquarters.

Among the 'abroad' operations Sportlines was unique in two ways. First, from its formation in the 1920s the Slazenger business had reported directly to the UK, and that arrangement had also applied when it took over the Dunlop sports business in Canada, in 1964, to form the core of the Sportlines distribution business, which, by the mid 1980s was relying on 'non-Dunlop Slazenger' lines for half its annual sales. It only stopped reporting direct to the UK in 1984 when it became part of the North American region. Second, its status as the most powerful sports distribution operation in Canada with a chain of regional offices and warehouses and brand dedicated sales organisations, for both golf and rackets, provided the resources to build the highest per capita domestic sales for any Dunlop Slazenger business, but, at the same time, created the eventual need for radical restructuring when external decisions deprived the business of key elements of its sports trade presence. Ultimately its separate existence in the form it had built over the years could not be sustained when restricted to 'in house' products and to the more stringent disciplines now applied across the group to working capital levels.

Nevertheless, the Canadian story is of considerable success in establishing the Dunlop and Slazenger brands so firmly, and generally 'outscoring' the potentially much larger USA business in terms of market shares. It also provided the group, in its various forms, with a number of individuals who made very significant contributions to the international strength of the company. In this context the parts played by Tony Wells, John Wilson, Keith Johnson, George Bulina and Bob Hampton should be mentioned. Tony Wells, Keith Johnson and Bob Hampton 'emigrated' to senior positions in the USA business, John Wilson working closely with Dick Birch, played a major role in the expansion of the business during the 1970s and early 1980s, and George Bulina will be long remembered for his dedication to the development of the golf operation under the Slazenger banner. All these were Canadians except Keith Johnson, who, in 1986, was transferred to Toronto from Wakefield, where he had been ISC's distribution manager, and became, successively the Sportlines finance director, then president and, finally, vice-president of the USA rackets business in succession to Bob Hampton.

Another Canadian, though very much an 'internationalist', Scott Brown achieved considerable success in improving the Sportlines results in the mid 1990s, but had the unenviable task of managing the amalgamation of the business with the USA in 1997 while on secondment from his position as regional director in the Far East.

The ultimate fate of the Canadian business, i.e. becoming part of a North American regional business, was repeated many times as the separateness of the Canadian market was steadily diminished by the overwhelming presence of the much larger USA based sports operations. The combination of economics and hugely improved communication systems rendered the notion of having an independent Canadian business an expensive luxury, which the earlier 'Imperial' environment that had fostered the very British Dunlop and Slazenger brands could not be expected to withstand.

USA

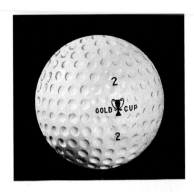

**DUNLOP
GOLD CUP**

75¢

The 'abroad' histories of Dunlop and Slazenger in Australia, South Africa, Canada and Japan differ from each other in many ways, especially which was the 'lead' brand in each of these territories; Dunlop in Japan and South Africa, Slazenger in Australia and Canada. However, they share with the UK and Europe the common factor of very strong, if not dominant market positions in tennis and golf throughout most of the 20th century.

In the USA, where, for the most part, Dunlop was the main brand the position of outright market leadership eluded the company. Had the market share levels achieved elsewhere been repeated in the USA the Dunlop Slazenger combination would have been the undisputed world leader in the racket and golf equipment sectors. And possibly the most disappointing aspect of this particular story is that the business was unable to take full advantage of the rapid expansion of both golf and tennis in the 1970s, and instead, at the end of that decade, came close to going out of existence. But it did not, and, indeed it subsequently rebuilt a substantial USA presence based on three, rather than two brands. Dunlop was primarily deployed as a racket brand, Maxfli, which had been the main golf brand since the 1920s, became a specialist division for the premium sector, and Slazenger was skilfully re-invented as a high quality, golf pro-shop only operation. Underpinning all three brands was the same heritage of technical excellence and commitment to both the playing customer and to the sports trade that has served the group so well all around the world for most of the last hundred years. As 'The Dunlop Creed' proclaims, as an introduction to the 1939 sales manual,

> 'I believe that with my customers we are a positive influence in the building of American character through sports – the inculcating of true courtesy, decency, sportsmanship and fair play ... and these ideals are as much part of my merchandise as the products themselves'.

And the 'better late than never' enlargement of the company's USA presence, which was considerably accelerated by the 1984 creation of Dunlop Slazenger International, and by BTR's subsequent major investments in the business, was the basis of the expansion of the group's turnover from £140 million in 1982 to nearly £300 million by 1989 – excluding Australia, Japan and South Africa. In that seven year period sales in the USA more than quadrupled and accounted for half the total growth of the newly established worldwide business.

The beginning, for both brands, was not quite so auspicious. Slazenger, largely due to the efforts of Frank Slazenger in his New York office on East 43 Street, had sold gutta percha golf balls and Scottish made clubs before the turn of the century, and, later advertised 'Doherty' rackets 'as used by the US Open champions' (William Larned and Molla Bjursted). However, this 'bridgehead' was not developed and it would be more than 40 years before the decision was taken to establish Slazenger Inc. in Philadelphia.

The first Dunlop venture in the USA, a cycle tyre plant set up in 1895, was sold three years later when the parent company in the UK needed to raise cash. The company did eventually, in 1920, establish itself more securely when the Buffalo tyre factory was opened. By then competitors like Firestone and Goodyear had taken a firm grip on the huge domestic market and had no intention of allowing the newcomer to make significant inroads into the businesses that had flourished as the automobile industry expanded. This shaped a Dunlop marketing policy of concentrating on premium price and specialist sectors of the market, like high performance cars, motorbikes and replacement tyres, which was the basis of its successful development and expansion over the next 80 years. It was also an approach that placed considerable emphasis on the company's well established reputation for technical excellence, which built a very appropriate brand image in advance of the launch of the sports business.

Vincent (Vinnie) Richards, who set up the Dunlop sports operation in the USA in 1929 and ran it for the next 30 years

By 1929 the company, making full use of the R & D strength based at Fort Dunlop, and of the skills of such as Albert Penfold and Sammy Ball, had firmly established its golf and tennis ball business and had just entered the wider equipment market with the purchase of F. A. Davis. The Maxply was still a couple of years in the future but the Maxfli had achieved international fame and collected a host of tournament victories around the world. It made perfect sense, and was, again, very much in the company's normal style, to locate a golf ball unit, and later tennis balls, in the Buffalo plant.

Making the balls, and importing other lines from a UK range expanded by the acquisition of the F. A. Davis company, was one thing, marketing them successfully in the well developed and very competitive USA market was quite another. As had been the case with the tyre operation the new sports business had to contend with a number of established and powerful domestic manufacturers. Additionally the Dunlop brand was nothing like as well known as in other parts of the world so it was clear someone very special would be required to lead the attack on the sports equipment market.

F. M. B. (Frank) Fisher, who had been the driving force behind the company's UK expansion into the tennis market, and was instrumental in persuading the parent company to diversify its USA operation into the sports sector, was very clear about who that special person should be. None other than the American tennis 'great' Vincent (Vinnie) Richards.

Originally tagged 'the boy wonder', because of his 1918 victory, with Bill Tilden, in the USA national doubles championships, when he was only 15, Vinnie had first met Frank Fisher at Wimbledon in 1923. They had both competed there during the next three years, including

THE DUNLOP CREED

☆

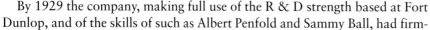

☆

THAT my contacts with my customers — and theirs with their customers — are human relationships as much as business relationship.

THAT together we have all the same goal: To help our fellow men in their pursuit of happiness.

THAT together we are a positive influence in the building of American character through sports— the inculcating of true courtesy, decency, sportsmanship, fair play.

THAT in this spirit, I can best serve, *and*

THAT to me, as a member of the Dunlop organization, these ideals are as much a part of my merchandise as the products themselves.

☆

The Vinnie Richards 'Dunlop Creed', which was page 1 in the company's sales manual in the 1930s

'Official' recognition of Howard Kinsey's one hour, eighteen minute rally with Helen Wills Moody in 1936

1924 when Vinnie was on the winning side in an all-American men's doubles final. In the same year he was the Olympic champion – winning the singles, doubles and mixed doubles gold medals – and was a member of four USA Davis Cup teams before turning professional in 1927. He then proceeded to win four USA national pro singles titles in the next seven years, and would later win doubles titles, including a 1938 success with Fred Perry.

One of his contemporaries, Howard Kinsey, would later join him at Dunlop as the Pacific Coast regional manager. Howard reached three finals at Wimbledon in 1926, sadly losing all of them. In the men's singles he was beaten by Jean Borotra, and in the men's doubles, partnered by Vinnie, the winners were two other members of the 'Four Musketeers', Cochet and Brugnon. He would later, in 1936, achieve the unique feat of a rally, with Helen Wills Moody, which lasted one hour, eighteen minutes with the ball crossing the net 2001 times.

Howard Kinsey was typical of the type of individual that Vinnie Richards recruited to the Dunlop sports management and sales teams. Vinnie's reputation as 'Mr. Tennis', his record as an outstanding player and his many contributions to the development of sport, including becoming the first Commissioner of the World's Professional Tennis League, would have appealed very strongly to the group of individuals, like Howard, with either sports trade or playing experience, or both, that he assembled to build the business. It's impossible to overstate the impact he made. When he accepted Frank Fisher's invitation to join the company he was still at the peak of his professional playing career but this didn't stop him donning overalls and spending three months in the Buffalo plant working on the golf and tennis production lines. Despite the fact Wall Street was crashing he recruited a 32 strong sales force and set up his office in the Empire State Building on New York's Fifth Avenue. His arrival there was marked by celebrations hosted by the well known sportcaster, Ted Husing, and he was welcomed by a former Governor of New York State, Alfred E. Smith, who had become the manager of what was then a brand new skyscraper.

In his first full year in charge, which was little more than a year after golf ball production had started at Buffalo, the Sports Division of the Dunlop Tire & Rubber Corporation sold $2 million worth of balls and rackets and made a handsome profit. He would run the business for thirty years, before his premature death in 1959, becoming a vice president of the USA parent organisation. It's clear that in addition to providing the outstanding leadership necessary to build the business he immersed himself in the details of the operation. He contributed to product design, especially tennis balls and rackets including a signature 'Vinnie Richards Maxply', extended the range to include golf clubs, hockey pucks, golf and tennis accessories, established the idea of golf and tennis advisory staffs and personally wrote many of the company's sales manuals and procedures, including a booklet entitled *How to play winning tennis*.

During the first 10 years virtually all the products carried the Dunlop brand. In addition to the premium Maxply and Vinnie Richards brands 'Silver Cup' and 'Speedthroat' were used for tennis, badminton and squash, and the 'Nimble' brand, first used in the UK before the first world war on 'value' golf balls, re-appeared in the States on both golf and tennis balls. The 'Nimble' golf balls were 25 cents each, for 'those who desire a 25c ball built by the unusual skill of Dunlop engineers and the unusual skill of Dunlop manufacture', the 'Dunlop Red' was 35c, the 'Dunlop Dunlop', 'with a click and feel off the club that delight most critical golfers' was 50c, the 'Gold Cup', at 75c offered 'more endurance, extra distance and stays new round after round', and the top price, 1 dollar ball was the 'Imported Dunlop', almost certainly a '65' but promoted by Fifth Avenue as 'America's aristocrat of golf balls'. Three of these balls were still available in both mesh and recess cover pattern and the 'Dunlop Red', better known as the 'Red Eye' became the most popular in the range before the start of the war.

Two leading golfers, Craig Wood and Henry Picard, were endorsing the range. Craig, who would win both the US Open and Masters in 1941, recommended the 'Gold Cup' ball and wrote *Swinging Thru – How to Play Golf* for the company, and Henry, winner of the 1938 Masters and 1939 PGA, endorsed a range of autographed woods retailing at £10 each.

Soon after America's entry into the war the Buffalo plant, exactly as had happened earlier at Fort Dunlop, concentrated all its resources on the production of tyres for war vehicles. As there were no exports of sports goods from the UK this meant the sports operation virtually went out of business but they must have retained their lease on the Empire State Building office as that same address appeared on early post war sales literature.

The front cover of Craig Wood's 1939 golf manual *Swinging Thru*

When business resumed after the war Dunlop was still used as the lead brand for a restricted range, which concentrated on the Maxply rackets (standard, Tournament and Fort), a Championship tennis ball with 'Warwick' replacing the 'Nimble' as a 'high class ball at a lower price', and the golf range initially limited to two balls, the 'Gold Cup' championship and hard cover versions. The rubber cored 'Red Eye' soon re-appeared but ran into trouble when it began to suffer from an 'out of round' condition due to breakdown of its wound rubber interior. The company's technical staff thought they had resolved the problem and the 'Maxfli' brand was used to denote the availability of the replacement 'Red Eye'. However, their modifications proved too 'successful' as USGA tests found that the ball did not conform with the official performance parameters. It was a 'hot' ball but before it could be corrected thousands were sold to golfers delighted at the sudden increase in the distances they could reach with their drivers. Illegal or not the public's awareness of both Dunlop and Maxfli had been significantly increased.

The emergence, in the 1950s, of the Maxfli as the front rank golf brand for the USA business – as it would become for the worldwide operation in the mid 1980s – signalled the start of a twenty year period of steady sales growth.

Paul Gibbs, who succeeded Vinnie Richards as the head of the USA sports business

The emphasis is on sales because, until 1985, the sports division was purely a sales operation with the parent Dunlop Tire & Rubber Company retaining control of major functions like production, purchasing and finance. In the latter case so much so that it is very difficult to identify an accurate profit result, not least because the costs of such central services were charged to the division on an allocated rather than an actual basis. This was standard practice for most of the Dunlop multi-product operations. Nevertheless, and regardless of what the 'bottom line' was showing for the sports division the two presidents of the parent US company between 1956 and 1984, Michael Billane and Neville Procter, consistently supported its ambitions and recognised the value, to the whole business, of a strong Dunlop presence in the sports and leisure sector.

The initial, and very impressive development of that sports presence by Vinnie Richards, before and after the second world war, was continued by the key managers to succeed him after his death in 1959. First was Paul Gibbs, who had been Vinnie's assistant and had worked alongside him, not only since joining Dunlop in 1936, but also as manager of the pre-war touring tennis professionals, including Perry and Tilden as well as Richards. He was followed by Vaughn Clay, who was the very much respected first plant manager at the Westminster factory and later vice president of the sports division, with Paul MacDonald as his assistant responsible for sales. They would be followed between the mid 1970s and 1982, by the Canadian, Tony Wells, and

Rod Laver stands between Paul McDonald (on his right) and Vaughn Clay at a 1960s trade show in Atlanta

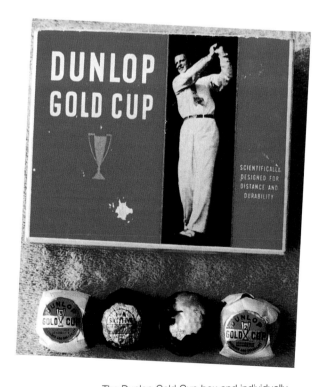

The Dunlop Gold Cup box and individually wrapped Gold Cup and 65 balls from the 1930s range

Dean Cassell, who was recruited from Titleist.

During the first half of this period Dunlop world-wide was a successful business but the difficulties it experienced from the mid 1970s onwards would have a particularly severe impact on the American sports operations. It could be said it 'ran out of steam' at a time when the participant numbers for both golf and tennis were 'exploding' and had to face the problem of a parent 'Dunlop boiler' that was no longer able to fully support it. Add to that its relative isolation from the UK based ISC, in terms of management and investment, and it is not difficult to understand why the Vinnie Richards legacy was so diminished, almost to the point of disappearance.

Less than a year after Vinnie died, and it's easy to imagine how delighted he would have been, golf ball production started at the brand new Westminster plant in South Carolina, though the cover stock was still prepared and milled at Buffalo before being shipped South by overnight road transport. The initial production capacity was 1 million dozen per annum. Although that is only a small fraction of today's figure the Buffalo manufacturing and technical team – led by Vaughn Clay and including Al Ihle, Bob Goehle and Dick Potzler – were delighted how well the local workforce adapted to what was for them a completely new technology. Like much of South Carolina the Westminster area had seen its predominantly textile based industry virtually disappear and both the State and City authorities had made a major effort to attract Dunlop as an alternative source of employment. Westminster had even organised a local referendum to approve the extension of the city limits so they would take in the whole site required for the new factory.

For those employees transferring from Buffalo, more than forty years ago, it was also something of a 'culture shock' to find themselves in what they

A 1950s advert by the Sporting Goods Division of Dunlop Tire &Rubber. Note the Fifth Avenue (Empire State Building) address

The Westminster golf ball plant shortly after its opening in 1960. Today's factory is more than twice the size of the original

A more recent shot of the Westminster plant which boasted the Hi-Tech golf ball driving range

**Play
Red Hot
Red Eye**

*...be sure
you've got
enough ball*

You can find a lot of things in the middle of golf balls
—hard glass, hard steel, hard rubber. Locked in the exact
middle of every Maxfli there's a small rubber sphere, full
of liquid. It has shock-taking flex as well as center balance
—an ideal nucleus we build Maxfli distance around. This
flexible core is surrounded by double walls of rubber, each wall

A 1968 catalogue page for the
famous 'Red Eye' golf ball

would then have regarded as the 'deep South' with relatively primitive transport arrangements to cover the 1000 mile journey between the two plants. There are memories of the first sales conference in the area, at nearby Clemson, where the only accommodation available was in the University dormitories and the only liquid refreshment offered with the evening meal a milk shake.

While the tennis business continued to rely on Maxply rackets – which for a period would be finished at Buffalo and Dunlop balls made in the same plant, Westminster production was initially concentrated on the balata covered Red and Green Maxfli balls, retailing around $14 per dozen. The Black Maxfli and cheaper 'Sprite', at $9 per dozen would soon be added. As confirmed by the regular reports in the *Dunlop Gazette* sales grew steadily and a second balata plant was opened in 1968, at nearby Hartwell in Georgia, again with a start-up capacity of 1 million dozen.

The success of the Maxfli balls encouraged the company to broaden its product line with a range of golf clubs and a very wide selection of golf bags and other accessories. Initially the clubs were manufactured in the UK by John Letters and by the American club makers, Wright and Ditson. In 1957 the supply source was switched to another USA company, the Pedersen Golf Company, who were well known for their high quality merchandise, and, with increased promotional investment, sales of Maxfli clubs continued to grow.

In 1963 a club manufacturing unit was set up in the Westminster plant and Eric Jackson, who had considerable experience of club making, was recruited from Pedersen to run the operation, which, by the early 1970s, expanded to an annual capacity of 40,000 sets. At that time 'Maxpower' woods and irons were launched using a very glamorous model to promote the 'Widowmakers' theme and a performance promise that 'each club is synchronised in flex and recovering timing to minimise torque and vibration and improve control'. US Women's Open champion, Susie Maxwell, endorsed a ladies set of woods and irons, Bob Charles a set of left-handed clubs and Peter Thomson's name appeared on a centreshaft model in a range of no less than 18 'Famous Club Putters'. Other leading players on the Advisory and Consultant staff at the time included Gary Player, David Graham, Harold Henning, Ed Furgol, Dow Finsterwald, Dave Eichelberger, Roberto De Vicenzo, Paul Hahn, JoAnne Carner and Sally Little.

Probably the best known club produced at Westminster, which first

1972 Dunlop Professional Golf Equipment

The glamorous 'Widowmaker' advertising for golf clubs in 1972

appeared in the mid 1970s, was the 'Australian Blade'. This iron, designed and first produced by Dunlop in Australia, was introduced to the USA by American touring professionals, who had spotted it when playing on the Asian Tour and sparked huge public interest when they played with it in the States because it was seen as providing an extra edge to iron play.

In 1956 Vinnie Richards had expressed his dissatisfaction with the quality of tennis balls being made at Buffalo. He claimed he would be able to more than double market share if he could import 100,000 dozen balls from Speke, with a better cover cloth, but the proposal was vetoed by the VP of production as it would have meant the closure of the tennis ball line. This incident is mentioned because it is clear from visit reports between 1956 and the 1970s that senior UK technical mangers George Mallet, Denis Osborne, Sammy Ball and Bob Haines, generally had a very high regard for the US manufacturing operations, especially the Westminster golf ball plant.

Golf club assembly at Westminster in the 1980s with Eric Jackson in the centre of the picture

In 1964, Sammy Ball, making his last business visit to the States before retiring the following year, recorded the view that 'Westminster requires less labour than at Speke, which could learn a lot from the Westminster methods, though it will require a team equally dedicated to the task and equally determined to reduce inefficiency as the one set up in Westminster to bring it about'. His report included an analysis of the operator numbers required to man each stage of the golf ball process, which showed that Westminster required only 253 to produce the same number of balls in a week compared with 341 at Speke, and he was very impressed by the general efficiency of the plant 'because supervision is quite active and also the workers appear anxious to obtain the maximum production possible, being ready to fill in for other workers who may be absent, or who need a short break'.

However, the dramatic changes in golf ball technology that occurred in the late 1960s and early 1970s, especially the introduction of surlyn covers and the advent of the two-piece ball would have as much impact on the company's USA operations as in the UK. There the dramatic reduction in the demand for balata covered balls would mean that the new Normanton plant could comfortably handle a total sales requirement previously stretching both the Speke and Normanton plants. In the USA balata production at Hartwell ceased and, in 1973, the factory started a tennis ball production line that would ship more than 20 million dozen balls before it closed in 1992. Westminster's first

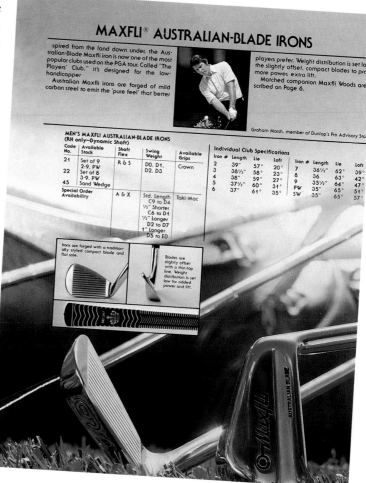

The Maxfli Australian Blade page in the 1978 catalogue

A special window feature in the Dunlop House offices in St. James's announcing the 1973 opening of the Hartwell tennis ball plant

surlyn covered ball, using the 'Gold Cup' brand, was launched in 1972 and the following year would be the lead ball in the catalogue re-named as 'Blue Max'.

The three other main balls in the 1973 catalogue were 'Improved New' versions of the Red, Green and Black Maxfli. The 'Improved New' designation was part of the effort to recover from another, even more disastrous 'out of round' situation in 1969/70. Again the fault lay with failure of the rubber thread used for the winding process. The impact was hugely damaging as it was necessary to recall a very high proportion of inventory already shipped, which severely damaged customer confidence and resulted in a severe production cutback. All of this coincided with a further large expansion in the number of golfers and increased competition from other leading ball makers, who were quicker to develop new balls utilising surlyn covers and the revolutionary two-piece construction.

The 1970s were generally difficult for the business. In addition to the golf ball setback the club manufacturing operation came under severe pressure as imports of lower cost clubs and components began to rise. The retail price of tennis balls was held down in the late 1970s, when the beginning of a decline in the game's popularity coincided with a major new manufacturer entering the market with an urgent need to build a large market share. And the company's share of the racket market fell from over 30% to less than 10% as first metal, and then the larger headed graphite frames rapidly reduced the sales of the previously all conquering wooden rackets.

By the end of the 1970s the business, by any measure, was operating at a loss. Up to that point nothing radically new had been developed in either the USA or the UK to revive the key golf ball and racket ranges. Nor were funds available from the cash strapped parent company to invest in the Westminster plant, by then much in need of modernisation to improve the quality of the surlyn wound and two-piece production replacing the original balata output. The USA tyre operation was profitable but understandably inclined to prioritise its limited capital investment resources towards the expensive new equipment required both at Buffalo and its new plant in Huntsville, Alabama. The finance department at Buffalo was not entirely averse to using the losses of its ailing sports division as a tax write off against tyre profits.

Two senior Titleist executives, Dean Cassell and David Branon, were recruited to revive the golf operation and also the overall marketing style of the business. Cassell, who had quickly recognised the urgency of being able to offer a new and competitive golf ball, 'discovered' the DDH design languishing in the UK, and he and Branon skilfully created a dramatic

Ken Johnson, Dunlop overseas director, visits the Greenville office of the USA sports business. Seen here with Brian Simpson and Michael Casazza

261

launch package based on the unique attributes of its dimple pattern. They persuaded Buffalo to more than quadruple the advertising budget to provide an effective campaign for the 1981 launch, which went a long way to restoring the company's reputation for technical and design excellence, which had never fully recovered from the 'out of round' problems ten years earlier.

Despite this undoubted success, and the impact of John McEnroe signing to play a signature Maxply in 1981, the business was still 'in the red'. In the case of racket sales the full benefit of the 'McEnroe effect' was not felt until John switched from the wooden frame to the graphite 200G in 1983. Up to that point the company had relied mainly on the Taiwanese made 'Black Max' mid-size graphite frame, developed by the VP of the racket operation, Michael Casazza, to maintain a substantial presence in the market.

At this point, with losses reaching an unacceptable level, the UK main board appointed a British executive, Brian Simpson, as president of the Dunlop Sports corporation, which had just moved its headquarters from Buffalo to Greenville, South Carolina, located about 50 miles from the Hartwell and Westminster factories. Simpson, who had joined Dunlop in 1955, as a sales trainee in the Footwear Division and had been director of the Dunlopillo foam and bedding businesses in the UK and Europe, was faced with the task of improving the operating results and also convincing the employees the business had a long term future. The operating results did improve as golf ball volume was significantly increased by widening the distribution base, sales of the 200G racket increased almost tenfold, and purchasing costs reduced. The 200G was especially notable for the fact that all Dunlop sports businesses around the world, whether or not owned by the parent company, marketed the product with completely uniform branding and presentation. This still wasn't the norm as the equally important DDH golf ball, although generally branded Dunlop, appeared in the USA under the Maxfli brand.

The improving position in America was consolidated when, in 1984, the Greenville based business became part of the newly formed Dunlop Slazenger International and, for the first time in its history, reported to a UK chief executive. At the same time a North American region was established to include all Dunlop and Slazenger operations in USA and Canada. For a short time the Tire Corporation in Buffalo continued to provide a number of support services, mainly finance and personnel related. These arrangements were abruptly terminated by the twin events of BTR acquiring Dunlop and the USA tyre operation being bought out by its management, which meant the sports business, very rapidly, had to establish its own stand alone infrastructure in Greenville, including the transfer to larger premises required to house additional, mainly finance

A typically striking USA treatment of the merits of the DDH golf ball from the 1984 catalogue

The front cover of the USA 1983 'Racquet' catalogue featuring the Maxply McEnroe, the 200G and John with the former

Over 60 PGA pros are hitting the best shots of their lives with Maxfli DDH Tour Limited. Isn't it time you moved up to Maxfli?

Row 1: Tommy Armour III, Ray Barr, Brian Claar, Bobby Clampett, Anonymous Touring Pro, Fred Couples, Jim Dent, Dave Eichelberger, Ed Fiori; Row 2: Ken Green, Anonymous Touring Pro, Jay Haas, Dan Halldorson, Mark Hayes, Anonymous Touring Pro, Lon Hinkle; Row 3: Anonymous Touring Pro, Bruce Lietzke, John Mahaffey, Anonymous Touring Pro, Blaine McCallister, Rocco Mediate, Gil Morgan, Anonymous Touring Pro; Row 4: Tom Purtzer, Mike Reid, Anonymous Touring Pro, Jack Renner, Larry Rinker, Gene Sauers, Anonymous Touring Pro, Ted Schulz; Row 5: Anonymous Touring Pro, Curtis Strange, Hal Sutton, Doug Tewell, Anonymous Touring Pro, Leonard Thompson, Howard Twitty, Anonymous Touring Pro; Row 6: Jim Gallagher, Jr., Buddy Gardner, David Graham, Hubert Green, John Inman, Kenny Knox, Anonymous Touring Pro, Gary Koch; Row 7: Bill Kratzert, Bob Murphy, Tim Simpson, Andy North, Dan Pohl, Tony Sills, Anonymous Touring Pro, Jim Simons; Row 8: Dave Stockton, Anonymous Touring Pro, Tommy Valentine, D.A. Weibring, Fuzzy Zoeller, Jim Thorpe, Rodger Davis; Not Pictured: 5 more Maxfli Pros.

DUNLOP GOLF DIVISION • DUNLOP-SLAZENGER CORPORATION • Executive Office • 131 Falls Street • P.O. Box 3070 • Greenville, SC 29602 • ORDERING HOTLINES: 1-800-845-8875 (Outside SC); 1-803-271-9767 (Within SC)

The back cover of the 1988 catalogue with pictures of the 48 US Tour pros then playing the Maxfli ball – and note the 'Bag men' to denote those playing Maxfli while contracted to competitors

staff and a new computer. Probably of greater significance was the fact that the manufacturing and development functions, led by Roger Pekrul, became the responsibility of the local sports management and no longer had a reporting line to Buffalo.

The relatively small management team in Greenville and Westminster now found they had support from both Dunlop Slazenger in the UK and BTR's North American resources. In the case of BTR, who had quickly identified the potential of the worldwide sports operation, the absolutely crucial benefit was the willingness to invest very substantially in what was virtually a ten-year modernisation programme at Westminster, which made it one of the largest and most up-to-date golf ball plants in the world.

Equally important was the agreement to significantly increase the promotional spend in the world's largest golf ball market, which, for the first time allowed the combination of substantial TV expenditure and the ability to build a highly visible presence on the PGA Tour planned and executed by Branon and the tour manager, Joe Moses. With Maxfli as the co-ordinating brand and more than fifty contract players in the USA the worldwide business, with many more players contracted in Europe, Asia and Japan, was able to challenge the previously unopposed competitor claiming the number one position on all tours.

The sports division of Dunlop Japan, by now controlled by Sumitomo Rubber Industries, and led by general manager, Hisamitsu Ohnishi, played a major role in this project by supplying its very high quality balata balls, branded Maxfli Tour Limited HT in the USA, with a 432 dimple version of the DDH design, for use on the US Tour and also as the premium product in the range available to pro shops and customers worldwide. They also contributed to the promotional investment of Maxfli in conjunction with the Tour, which was co-ordinated with their own use of the brand in conjunction with the Japanese Tour. The relationship between the USA and Japanese sports operations, no longer parts of the same parent company, was extended to the other regions of Dunlop Slazenger International and, for the first time ever, was very much marketing led. It proved extremely valuable to both companies.

By 1987 sales in the USA had trebled from the 1982 figure and would be further boosted by the separate David Geoffrey and Associates/Slazenger Golf business established the year before by David Branon and Geoffrey Gorman, both former Dunlop marketing executives. Financially backed by BTR, again demonstrating a readiness to invest in the sports equipment sector, Slazenger Golf concentrated exclusively on the on course pro shops with a premium quality product line, mainly balata and two-piece balls supplied by Sumitomo and an extensive clothing range. The professionals responded enthusiastically both to the products and marketing programme specifically designed to appeal to their requirements and ambitions, so much so that sales passed the $50 million mark in less than ten years.

A valuable additional income stream for the business was its extensive licensing programme for the Dunlop and Slazenger brands in sports and leisure sectors where the company was not directly engaged. This mainly involved clothing and footwear but also a very successful franchise for Dunlop-branded golf clubs and accessories (Focus Golf), which continues to operate from Greenville in close co-ordination with the Dunlop marketing team based there. The first major licensing programme in the US, for clothing, had been established in the early 1980s by Slazenger UK and the subsequent extension of this activity by the local management laid the foundation for what became a worldwide programme managed from the company's UK headquarters by, successively, John Rees and Richard Slater.

After a five-year existence the North American regional unit, covering Canada and the USA, was broken up in 1989 when the Dunlop Slazenger International organisation structure was changed to a product based

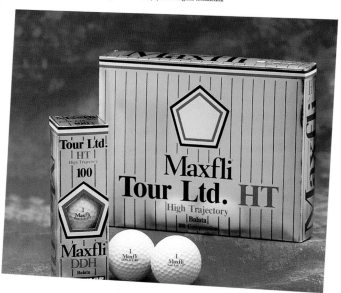

The Maxfli DDH Tour Ltd. Line

Shooting for #1

Within the past two years, the Maxfli DDH Tour Ltd. line has become the fastest growing line of golf balls in America.*

And it's no wonder. Because golfers everywhere have discovered that the Maxfli DDH Tour Ltd. line combines the PGA tour-winning design of the DDH pattern with different constructions and covers to match a style of play that's right for you.

Maxfli Tour Ltd. HT™
New for '89

The same ball that helped Sandy Lyle win the 1988 Masters and Curtis Strange win the 1988 U.S. Open Championship is fast becoming the #1 pick for pros and better golfers.

The new Maxfli Tour Ltd. HT ball is a 432 dimple ball with an icosido-decahedron (ICDDH) dimple pattern. This new dimple design combines the popular triangular icosahedral dimple pattern with Maxfli's patented dodecahedron pentagonal design. The result is a major advancement to the patented DDH dimple design of the Maxfli ball ... unsurpassed accuracy, a longer carry, and a slightly higher flight trajectory to let the low handicap golfer shoot for every pin with confidence. The new Maxfli HT has the same excellent feel, spin and consistency characteristics made famous by the regular Maxfli DDH Tour Limited Balata.

• 432 dimples
• 3-piece construction

The 1989 catalogue page for the all conquering Maxfli Tour Ltd. HT

The USA Sports offices in Greenville, on the left in Falls Road and on the right, from 1990, on North Pleasantburg Drive

The Dunlop Hole-in-One Medallion, a popular novelty item in the 1970s

approach. Having accounted for only 18% of the group's total turnover in 1982, reaching 27% by 1984, and 32% by 1989, albeit based on relatively small shares of the USA golf and tennis markets, it is at least possible that total sales in the world's largest sports equipment market could have been much bigger if it had been practical to bring greater, and internationally co-ordinated resources to bear on marketing Dunlop, Slazenger and Maxfli at an earlier stage in the golf and tennis 'boom years' of the 1960s and 1970s.

For the next six years, and separating out the Puma and Dunlop Footwear businesses, the key elements of the total business would be international racket and golf divisions. The international racket directors, first Brian Jenkins to be followed by Philip Wragg, were based in the UK. Their golf counterparts, initially Mike Orr and later Dick Dodson, operated out of the Greenville office. In both cases their responsibilities embraced worldwide R & D and manufacturing as well as marketing, which meant that in the USA the Westminster plant was the responsibility of the international golf director and the Hartwell tennis ball plant reported to Brian Jenkins. Similarly, while Mike Orr, who had joined the company in 1986, remained in charge of the USA golf business, the VP of the US racket division reported to Brian Jenkins. An exception to this general rule was that Slazenger Golf, by virtue of its existence as a completely separate business, reported direct to the group's chief executive in the UK, Patrick Austen.

The USA business would again be affected by structural change when, in 1996, and in conjunction with the management buy out from BTR, the organisational pattern would be based on functional management. As Hartwell had closed in 1992 this meant that the remaining, Westminster plant and golf R & D centre became the responsibility of a UK based manufacturing director, and worldwide marketing was managed from the UK by the group marketing director, who covered all product sectors. In the USA, as in Europe and the Far East, regional responsibility was established or maintained for sales and distribution. Once again, Slazenger Golf in the USA remained a separate entity.

Within these different forms of centralised group management the American operations, obviously, continued to be not only crucially important but also to grow. Before leaving to move into consultancy work Mike Orr, in 1990, as the golf director, had re-defined the worldwide golf activities by creating separate Maxfli and Dunlop divisions. Very much reflecting its positioning in the USA for the previous forty years Maxfli was 'promoted' from being a sub brand (Maxfli by Dunlop) to identify the company's premium product line. The Dunlop brand was still deployed in the golf market with an emphasis on 'value' products and, in the USA, occupied this position in close co-ordination with the Focus Golf licensing operation for golf clubs and accessories. When Dick Dodson succeeded his fellow countryman, Mike Orr, in the international golf role, having transferred from BTR's Dust Control division in the UK he retained Tom Bryant, who had joined the company in 1989 from Johnson & Johnson, to head the USA Maxfli operation. Tom would later be a member of the management buy out team, as president of Maxfli sales and distribution in the USA, and would be followed in that post, for two years, by Bill Olson. David Branon, as president of Slazenger Golf,

David Branon

was also a member of the buy out team and would retire in 2002 as chairman of North American operations.

The fact that since 1989 USA operations have been largely divided into separate product or functional sections should neither diminish its ongoing importance to the group, nor its huge contribution, over more than 70 years, to the heritage and existing strength of the Dunlop, Slazenger and Maxfli brands. The combination of the continuing Dunlop golf and racket businesses, based in Greenville, and the operations of the new 'brand guardians' for Maxfli and Slazenger guarantees the hard won legacy for all three of these famous names will not be devalued. And most impressive of all is the Westminster golf ball manufacturing unit, tripled in size since it was commissioned in 1960, which is producing hundreds of thousands of dozens of high quality balls every week for worldwide distribution. Westminster is also the home for a research and product engineering group that, during the most competitive and technically demanding period in golf ball history, has developed the series of groundbreaking new products absolutely essential to maintain the Dunlop Slazenger Group presence in the international market place.

The front cover of the 2001 golf catalogue showing Fred Couples with the Maxfli ball line

DUNLOP SLAZENGER

1998 – 2004

THE LATEST CHAPTER – THE NEW MANAGEMENT TEAM RESTRUCTURES THE BUSINESS AND A NEW OWNER FOR THE DUNLOP AND SLAZENGER HERITAGE

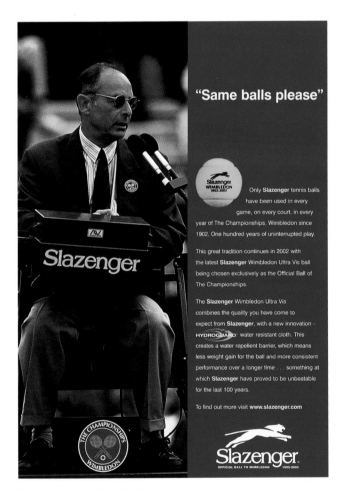

The back cover of the 2002 Wimbledon programme celebrates 100 years of Slazenger balls at the tournament

"Same balls please"

Only **Slazenger** tennis balls have been used in every game, on every court, in every year of The Championships, Wimbledon since 1902. One hundred years of uninterrupted play.

This great tradition continues in 2002 with the latest **Slazenger** Wimbledon Ultra Vis ball being chosen exclusively as the Official Ball of The Championships.

The **Slazenger** Wimbledon Ultra Vis combines the quality you have come to expect from **Slazenger**, with a new innovation – HYDROGUARD™ water resistant cloth. This creates a water repellent barrier, which means less weight gain for the ball and more consistent performance over a longer time . . . something at which **Slazenger** have proved to be unbeatable for the last 100 years.

To find out more visit www.slazenger.com

Slazenger
OFFICIAL BALL TO WIMBLEDON 1902-2002

Having looked at the different Dunlop and Slazenger 'mini-histories' around the world the last chapter of this book, though definitely not the end of the story, covers the six years from 1998 to the beginning of 2004. During this period the management team, led by Philip Parnell and Alan Lovell, restructured the business with sufficient success to attract a number of potential investors and purchasers, one of whom, Sports World Intenational, has become the new owner of the Dunlop and Slazenger brands and will provide the fresh impetus to take their unique heritage into the new Millennium.

Parnell, whose arrival at the Camberley head office early in 1998, was mentioned in the closing paragraphs of the chapter covering 1984 to 1998, had gained considerable experience in the management disciplines most relevant to his new challenge. His career with first Spillers, and, then for nearly 20 years, with United Distillers had provided experience in finance, marketing, planning and general management, including chief executive positions in North America and Europe. His belief that 'an organisation has to evolve to survive' would be reflected in many of the decisions taken over the next five years, which not only greatly accelerated the rationalisation of the total business but also brought about a fundamental change of emphasis in relation to that key element of any consumer oriented business, the brand portfolio. For many years the number of brands deployed by the company had been a strength, which allowed a focus for each by product or price category. However, despite the fact the nature and dynamics of the market place had changed very considerably, especially the scale of promotional expenditure required to maintain an effective presence for any one brand, let alone several, in a major market segment, Dunlop Slazenger had been unwilling to apply the rationalisation approach adopted for other key functions to its brand policy.

Indeed, the difficulty of spreading limited funds across the brands had been increased by the decision, in the late 1980s, to build a much stronger presence for Maxfli, as a brand rather than a product, in the premium golf sector. Although it had always featured prominently in the USA, albeit attached to 'by Dunlop', Maxfli was much less well known than either Dunlop or Slazenger in other key territories, like Europe and the Far East. This

Dunlop Golf re-emerges in the 2003 catalogue

approach meant virtually starting from scratch to establish what was effectively a new golf brand in these markets, and within the total advertising budget available it had the effect of dangerously limiting what could be spent on maintaining both Dunlop and Slazenger across all product and territory sectors. If anything, the decision, in the early 1990s, to attach 'divisional' status to Maxfli, as the premium golf operation, served to increase the promotional investment to build its position in an extremely competitive environment, which put further pressure on the budgets available for the other main brands. The negative impact of this approach on Dunlop as a golf brand has already been identified, in the chapter dealing with 1984 to 1998, by the appearance of the 65 as a Maxfli product and the make-up of the BTR in house review of the company's product range, which restricted Dunlop to rackets.

A *Times* analysis of the problems that confronted Parnell and Lovell in 1998 highlighted four main areas. Management controls had to be rebuilt, manufacturing required rationalisation (more precisely, even more rationalisation), money had to be spent on marketing, in particular on the Dunlop brand, and, as the number one priority, the company had to be put on a sound financial footing.

The first major move, in 1998, was the termination of the Puma agreement covering footwear distribution and apparel licensing in the UK. This signalled the intention to narrow the brand focus and also to concentrate on the equipment market with less involvement in footwear and apparel. 'The Link', the company's new in house newsletter, explained in a very positive way, that in addition to Puma AG wishing to have direct control of their brand throughout Europe, 'the sale also gives us the opportunity to focus on our own core brands, and there is enough happening to suggest they will keep us busy over the next few years'.

The subsequent sale of the Thailand sports distribution and Dunlopillo bedding operation to its managing director and Dunlop veteran, David Lamb, and the disposal of the Indonesian bedding business to a local investor were further evidence of the increasing focus on sports equipment, particularly as David Lamb would continue his highly successful Dunlop Slazenger activities in

Dunlop and 65 reunited on the 65U urethane cover ball

Dunlop Sport leads on the cover of 2003 racket catalogue

The 200G brand re-appears in its 'Hot Melt' version for 2003

Thailand.

Of greater significance was the decision taken at the end of 1999 to combine the North American administration of Dunlop, Maxfli and Slazenger into a single support structure. Under the chairmanship of the co-founder of Slazenger Golf in the USA, David Branon, and with the recently recruited Mike Rizzo as chief executive officer, the previously separate operations for the three brands were combined with the exception that, initially, the sales forces continued to operate independently of each other, reporting to their respective vice presidents. This ended the 14 year long separate existence of the Slazenger Golf business, which had, for the first time in the more than 100 year history of that brand, established a powerful presence in the USA. This would be maintained within the new consolidated structure, which traded as Dunlop Slazenger Group Americas, later entitled the Dunlop Sports Group America

On the wider, worldwide canvas of the total business the momentum of the 20 year rationalisation process of manufacturing resources gathered pace. The sequence of decisions as far back as the 1960 opening of the Westminster golf ball plant, and the 1977 establishment of tennis ball production in the Philippines, which had allowed the subsequent massive expansion and modernisation of both plants to world class standard, now made it possible to reap the product quality and economic benefits of having 'one plant to serve the world', which the majority of competitors had enjoyed for many years.

First to close, in 2000, was the Normanton golf ball plant, followed by the tennis ball unit at Barnsley, which brought to an end the manufacturing connection with Yorkshire started by William Sykes in 1866. The last of the major plants to close, in 2002, was Hanau, which had started making tennis balls in 1923, and provided the platform for almost total Dunlop domination of the German market for 80 years.

While these, and earlier plant closures meant the loss of local production, the group's total manufacturing capacity had been either maintained or increased by the huge investments made, over more than 20 years, in the Philippines and South Carolina More importantly the technical and engineering skills developed over many years at all the company's main factories, and the sophisticated production equipment inspired by those skills, were now incorporated in the plant layouts and processes installed in the Bataan and Westminster factories. Indeed Bataan is the only tennis ball factory in the world with the capability to simultaneously manufacture products to meet specific, and often quite different market requirements in the many countries where Dunlop and Slazenger balls are still first choice. The overall capability of the two plants is now the basis for not only maintaining the company's market leadership, but also for the establishment of strategic supply partnerships to exploit what is an unrivalled competence in golf and tennis ball research and development as well as manufacturing.

On the marketing front the company had long recognised the increasing pace of the trend to worldwide brands, several of them combining massive promotional investments with the ambitions to push their product portfolios into new, for them, equipment sectors. This has only served to confirm the urgency, for Dunlop Slazenger, of prioritising the deployment of marketing resources to support their major and core Dunlop brand. This doesn't inhibit the generation of valuable income from the tactical use of either the core brand in additional and complementary product areas by using the licensing routes or the utilisation of the still potent Slazenger and Carlton marks in their traditionally strong product and geographical areas with a combination of direct sales and licensing.

A good example of this approach is the hugely visible Slazenger presence in tennis and cricket, spearheaded by the very successful relationships with star players like Tim Henman and a whole host of leading international and county cricketers. Also the unique relationship between Slazenger and Wimbledon, which had its one hundredth anniversary celebration in 2002, simply reinforces the special nature of the connection between the

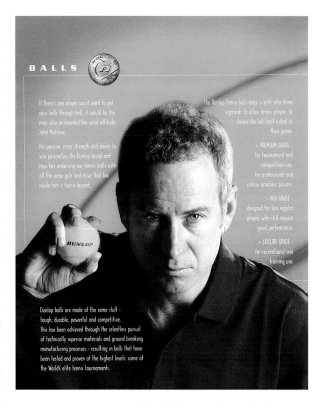

John McEnroe endorses Dunlop tennis balls for 2003

company and the sport it has supported throughout its history. And on the squash and badminton courts Dunlop and Carlton equipment and players continue to be both very visible and consistently successful.

These elements of the company's strategy for the 21st century have been most clearly visible in the USA, and it is there that the most difficult decisions were required to translate 'vision' into reality. Following the 1999 formation of the consolidated Dunlop Slazenger operation the next stage of executing the policy that the company 'should become a simpler and more focussed business' concentrating on the Dunlop brand, and which would involve 'withdrawal from the highly expensive and cash draining premium golf ball market' inevitably involved more and greater upheaval in the USA than anywhere else. This was the territory where the Dunlop brand had been most seriously neglected, and also where the bulk of the marketing investment, for more than ten years, had been put behind Maxfli and Slazenger as premium golf brands.

The corollary to that approach, as has been mentioned before, was that while the relatively large scale of expenditure on Maxfli and Slazenger still wasn't sufficient to achieve an acceptable level of return from the premium golf sector, Dunlop, historically the company's principal brand for all its main markets was being starved of even a maintenance level of support And that latter element was also more evident in the USA than anywhere else.

However, what was to prove the vital factor in resolving this apparent impasse, not only in the USA but internationally, was that the millions that had been invested in Maxfli and Slazenger had established a significant presence for both brands in their target, premium golf sector. And that was a presence with a considerable value to other businesses determined to either enter, or expand an existing involvement in that sector.

The new V200 cricket bat first seen on TV when presented to Alec Stewart on the occasion of his final Test match at the Oval in 2003

The Slazenger cricket range covers everything the player needs from shoes and socks to caps, helmet and gloves – this shows one of the legguard pages in the 2004 catalogue

The challenge to implement this next stage in the re-shaping of the business was the main preoccupation for Parnell and Lovell, supported by company secretary, Alistair Ritchie, for the next two years. Their confidence in the benefits available from either outright or licensed ownership of these two firmly established brands had to be convincingly communicated to the several companies that expressed interest in the opportunities they presented.

At the end of 2001 Parnell was able to announce the successful outcome of negotiations with the famous TaylorMade-adidas Golf Company, based in Carlsbad, California, The key elements of the alliance between the two companies were the granting of a five year licensing and distribution agreement to TaylorMade for the two brands in the golf market, and a five year supply agreement for Dunlop Slazenger to manufacture golf balls for TaylorMade. Additionally TaylorMade was given a 15 month option to buy the Maxfli brand outright and to acquire an exclusive licence for Slazenger Golf. In the company announcement giving details of the agreement Parnell was quick to acknowledge the patience and commitment of the company's employees during more than a year of complex discussions, and to declare "This is the dawn of a new era for all three of the brands".

During the following year (2002) the 'vision and strategic restructuring' continued. While the final stages of the manufacturing consolidation were completed the re-shaped Dunlop organisation in North America gathered pace. This was a combination of the company's own rackets and licensing activities and the closely co-ordinated golf market operations with Focus Golf, who had by now accumulated nearly 20 years experience as the Dunlop licensee for clubs and accessories. In Europe the marketing emphasis on the Dunlop brand was combined with the established strengths of Slazenger and Carlton, notably in tennis, cricket and badminton. At the same time work continued to complete the consolidation and modernisation of the group's administration and support systems, which included the three regions established the previous year for Northern, Central and Southern Europe, and for the newly designated Asia Pacific region with its great potential for the future expansion for both Dunlop and Slazenger. During this process it had become very clear that many of the benefits of the overall rationalisation of the business, especially the much tighter central control of its key functions had been eroded by the inadequacy of the existing business procedures and information systems. Parnell and Lovell identified this area as absolutely vital in order to maximise the improved efficiencies of the streamlined structure of the business and also to eradicate deficiencies in the customer service operations.

On the financial side, and with the vitally important assistance of the investors and bankers who had been involved in the 1996 management buy out, the total debt burden was reduced by more than half. During this period of considerable financial pressure and comprehensive management change Sir Michael Perry's enormous experience of both management at the highest level and of dealing with the financial institutions had been critical. He was succeeded as chairman at the beginning of 2002 by Robert Brooke, who presided over a board comprising Chief Executive Philip Parnell, Group Finance Director, Alasdair Marnoch, who was in his second spell with the business having previously spent three years in charge of the accounts department, and Alan Lovell, who had become Director of Strategic Business and Corporate Development. It would be difficult to overstate the importance of the part played by Lovell since he had joined the company in 1997 in his role as the principal link with the company's investors and having the main responsibility for steering it through such difficult financial circumstances.

In November 2002, and because TaylorMade had decided not to exercise their option on the Slazenger brand, the company signed a 30 year licensing agreement for Slazenger Golf in North America with Resilience Capital Partners, a Cleveland based investment company. This agreement also covered distribution in Canada, Mexico and the Caribbean Islands and included a contract for the supply of golf balls from the Westminster plant. The company's confidence there would be other approaches for Slazenger licences was fully justified in the following year when a deal was agreed with the UK sports retailer, JJB, for golf equipment and clothing and negotiations were successfully concluded with Sports Network for a similar agreement covering Japan and the Far East, and which came into operation at the start of 2004.

Meanwhile TaylorMade-adidas had exercised their option to purchase the Maxfli golf brand. This enabled Philip Parnell, at the start of 2003, to issue the following statement. This summarised the considerable efforts of his team, up to this point, to secure the future of the company, and which had achieved the priority objectives of creating the basis for the proper development, or re-development of the Dunlop brand worldwide while, at the same time, retaining the ownership of Slazenger across all sports in order to maintain a consistent approach to its expansion and presentation by both the company and its existing and new licensees.

> We have been engaged in a radical restructuring of all aspects of the business in the past five years. We have consolidated our manufacturing facilities down from seven to two principal sites, reduced the fixed cost base of the business by over 50%, introduced professional business processes and information systems and rationalised and simplified our brand portfolio. The sale of Maxfli represents the last piece of brand portfolio simplification. It paves the way for a further reduction in bank debt and a restructuring of the balance sheet and we are now on the brink of a bright new future for the Dunlop Slazenger Group.

While it probably wasn't an appropriate item to include in this statement he could have added the symbolic comment that the name of the company's headquarters in Camberley had been changed from Maxfli Court to Dunlop House.

Having looked at the progress made to address the problems, identified by *The Times*, in the areas of manufacturing, systems and finance, the change of name at Camberley signalled the priority also being given to dealing with the fourth area, the reduced visibility of the Dunlop brand. The last four years have provided numerous examples of Dunlop, and for good measure Slazenger as well, again hitting the sports headlines based, as in the past, on a combination of top quality products and the leading players and personalities.

Probably the strongest evidence of the Dunlop revival has been seen in the tennis market. Leading tour players like Tommy Haas, Cedric Pioline, Sjeng Schalken, Wayne Ferreira, James Blake, Mardy Fish, Tommy Robredo, Julien Boutter, Amelie Mauresmo, Alicia Molik and Alexandra Stevenson have enjoyed considerable success with their 200G and 300G rackets. The most notable triumph was Thomas Johansson's 2002 victory at the Australian Open, an event made even more memorable because his opponent on that

The Slazenger Pro XI racket used by Tim Henman with the re-introduced 'S' string stencilling

The Slazenger 'Ultra Vis' ball made it 102 years at Wimbledon in 2004

occasion was Marat Safin, also using a Dunlop frame.

Johansson's Melbourne win was the first Men's Grand Slam win for Dunlop since John McEnroe won the US Open in 1984. John himself had returned to the brand when, in 2001, he signed a contract to endorse the Dunlop balls he believed were the best he'd ever played with. And, more recently, in 2003, it was announced that John had agreed to be the Dunlop global ambassador for the tennis business. On that occasion he recalled that during a career that captured more than 150 singles and doubles titles he had played some of his best tennis with the Maxply Fort and the original 200G. Further recent evidence of the company's enduring strength in the game was provided by a 'USA Today Snapshot', which listed the top seven all time winners on the Women's Tour in the Open Era. Four of the seven had played with Dunlop rackets, and a fifth with Slazenger.

Rebuilding Dunlop in the golf market has been a greater challenge but the foundations have been laid. New products, like the 'Loco' (low compression ball) and the latest version of the 65 (the urethane covered 65u) have re-affirmed the company's commitment to quality and performance. Indeed the 65u was listed in the top ten balls chosen by *Today's Golfer* (two of the others were TaylorMade-Maxfli products) and the DDH Tour driving iron was featured by the same magazine among the top ten specialist clubs. At the same time, and very much in keeping with the company's tradition of supporting the development of the game it has agreed to become the official equipment supplier to the UK Golf Foundation and will also be the sponsor for that organisation's nationwide Starter Centre Network, which provides coaching opportunities for around 20,000 youngsters.

During this period Slazenger has also been very noticeable. The 2002 'Celebration of a Century' marked the centenary of the Slazenger association with Wimbledon, which is the longest relationship of its kind in sporting history. That event served to emphasise the company's hugely successful and influential involvement in tennis, which can be traced back well over 100 years to the 1870s and the very earliest beginnings of the game when Ayres were supplying everything required to enjoy the new excitement of lawn tennis. The ever present technical and quality image of the brand was renewed in the Wimbledon centenary year by the introduction of the patented 'Hydroguard' cover cloth technology, which ensures that Slazenger balls have 70% less water pick-up in damp conditions than any other tennis ball. That benefit would certainly have appealed to Albert Slazenger, whose 1887 patent made wool-covered tennis balls impervious to moisture 'by the introduction of a chemical preparation for the purpose of waterproofing'. And throughout this period, in fact since his first appearance at Wimbledon in 1994, Tim Henman's skill and style on the world's courts has given Slazenger rackets a very special kind of visibility, not to mention an impressive list of Tour titles.

The Slazenger brand has also maintained its extremely high level of visibility on cricket bats and equipment as the all seeing TV cameras, for virtually twelve months of the year, track the Panthers at work for so many of the leading players wherever in the world the game is played.

Having described how the key recovery objectives have been achieved there is one more step to report in order to bring this history up to date at the start of 2004. A *Daily Telegraph* headline on 5th February that year reported 'Game, set and match for Dunlop Slazenger' alongside a striking shot of Tim Henman in action with his Slazenger racket and revealed that the company had been acquired by the entrepreneur, Mike Ashley, and his UK based Sports World International. This would mean that Dunlop and Slazenger would be joining his sports brand and retailing empire, which already included the famous Donnay equipment and clothing brand and the combined European strengths of Lillywhites and the Sports Soccer retail chain. Under the heading 'Change of Ownership' the group's personnel were told that this acquisition by a 'Private British Investor' really was the 'Culmination of six years of restructuring and finally provides the business with a stable financial structure eliminating all debt and replacing it with equity.'

Tim Henman with his racket featuring the 'S' string stencilling

In their press release on 12th February Sports World expressed their delight in welcoming Dunlop Slazenger to their portfolio of brands. They went on to acknowledge that although the company had a tremendous heritage it had not, over the past couple of years, had the required financial backing the sports sector currently demands. Most significantly the release went on to say 'We plan to plug the gap and develop the full potential and growth of these classic British sports brands'.

For most of the 140 or more years since the formation of the first Slazenger companies the past has been as bright as the future now predicted. This history has recorded many of its successes, which have always been based on the combination of the dedication of its many thousands of employees and the brilliance of the products they have designed, developed, manufactured and marketed. The present generation of Dunlop Slazenger people, who have skilfully and patiently re-shaped the business, and the current range of exciting products provide an appropriate testimony to what is almost certainly the most potent and enduring heritage in the sports industry.

There will undoubtedly be further chapters in the history of this business. Hopefully they will report new successes to match the extraordinary achievements and adventures that have been such influential elements in the growth of so many sports around the world for nearly 150 years.

DUNLOP SLAZENGER LEADING PLAYERS

A continuous thread running through the history of the Dunlop and Slazenger companies has been their association with many of the greatest players to have thrilled millions of spectators around the world for well over one hundred years. From the days of W.G. Grace, Spencer Gore and Harold Hilton, as the 19th century gave way to the 20th, right through to the 'stars' of the 21st century the company's products have been, and still are seen, on the world's greatest sporting stages.

The records are not complete of all those to have used Dunlop and Slazenger equipment – if they were, they would contain thousands of names – but the appendix that follows lists more than 400 well known golfers, cricketers and tennis players who have been successfully associated with the company.

And in addition to the famous names from the three main sports highlighted below there have been other memorable associations with the company. Cyril Corbally, the great Irish croquet player, used Slazenger equipment and Joe Davis endorsed billiard tables produced by William Sykes in Horbury. Victor Barna was 'Mr. Table Tennis' for many years both as a player and Dunlop executive, and Jonah Barrington and Geoff Hunt were among the many hundreds to achieve great success with Dunlop squash rackets and balls. Probably less well known has been the relationship, which also involved the Dunlop Footwear Company, with soccer stars like Johnny Haynes, Charlie Cooke, Bobby Charlton, Trevor Broooking and Graeme Souness, all of whom endorsed and used the company's footwear. Denis Compton's first connection with Slazenger also involved soccer, rather than cricket, when, as an Arsenal and England star, he endorsed shin-guards!

TENNIS PLAYERS – *WINNERS OF GRAND SLAM SINGLES IN BOLD*

A Bunny Austin
J O Anderson
Vijay Armitaj

B **Sue Barker**
Bjorn Borg
John Bromwich
Geoff Brown
Angela Buxton
Maria Bueno
John Barrett
Jeremy Bates
Norman Brookes
Roper Barrett
Gerald Battrick
James Blake
Julien Bouttier
Tomas Berdych
Thomas Blake
Molla Bjurstedt

C **Jimmy Connors**
Margaret Court
Dorothea Chambers
Don Candy
Mark Cox
Gottfried Von Cramm
Charlotte Cooper

D **Reginald Doherty**
Laurie Doherty
Jaroslav Drobny
Sven Davidson
Francoise Durr
Jo Durie
Scott Draper
Phil Dent

E **Roy Emerson**
W V Eaves

F **Neale Fraser**
Wayne Ferreira
Peter Fleming
Diane Fromholtz
Mardy Fish

G Arthur Gore
Spencer Gore
Steffi Graf
Althea Gibson
Evonne Goolagong
Kitty Godfree
Andres Gimeno
Istvan Gulyas
Justin Gimelstob

H **Lew Hoad**
Willoughby Hamilton
Pat Hughes
Bob Hewitt

Bob Howe
Tim Henman
Tommy Haas
Ivo Heuberger

J Helen Jacobs
Thomas Johannson
Ann Jones
Miss J Jedrzejowska

K Billy Knight
Ramesh Krishnan

L **Rod Laver**
Herbert Lawford
William Larned
E W Lewis
Jan Lundquist
John Lloyd
David Lloyd

R Lycett
Mrs D T R Larcombe

M Dan Maskell
Buster Mottram
Angela Mortimer
John McEnroe
Amelie Maurismo
Patrick McEnroe
Martin Mulligan
Harold Mahony
Ken McGregor
Alex Metreveli
Alex Meyer
Alan Mills
Alicia Molik
Mrs R J McNair

N **John Newcombe**
Kurt Nielsen
Ilie Nastase

Martina Navratilova
B C Norton
Betty Nuthall

O **Manuel Orantes**
Tom Okker

P **Fred Perry**
Yvon Petra
Joshua Pim
Gerald Patterson
Mark Philippoussis
O Parun
Cedric Pioline
Nikki Pilic
Gianluca Pozzi
Philip Petzschber

Q **Adrian Quist**

R **William Renshaw**

Ernest Renshaw
Ken Rosewall
F L Riseley
Mervyn Rose
Dorothy Round
Tony Roche
Marty Riessen
Miss S Reynolds
Christophe Rochus
Todd Reid
Tommy Robredo
Greg Rusedski

S **Marat Safin**
Manuel Santana
Fred Stolle
Betty Stove
Mrs C Sukova
Hilde Sperling
Mike Sangster
Sjeng Schalken

Graham Stilwell
Alexandra Stevenson

T **Christine Truman**
Roger Taylor
Judy Tegart
C R D Tuckey
Michal Tabara

V **Aranxtha Sanchez-Vicario**
Guillermo Vilas
Christian Vinck

W **Tony Wilding**
Virginia Wade
Bobby Wilson
Linda Wild
George Worthington

GOLF – *WINNERS OF MAJOR GOLF CHAMPIONSHIPS IN BOLD*

A Peter Alliss
Robert Allenby
Isao Aoki
Helen Alfredsson
Tommy Armour
D Ammaccapane
Debbie Austin

B **Severiano Ballesteros**
Ian Baker-Finch
Maurice Bembridge
Hugh Baiocchi
Brian Barnes
Craig Bowden
Patrick Burke
George Burns
Kevin Burton
Pam Barton
Ray Ball
George Boutell
John Bulla
Susie Maxwell Berning
Bob Barbarossa
Lee Bonse
Al Braga
Peter Butler

C **Henry Cotton**
Neil Coles
Fred Couples

Bobby Clampett
Bob Charles
Bobby Cole
Bruce Crampton
Buster Cupit
John Cook
JoAnne Carner
Stuart Cage
John Daly

D Laura Davies
Flory Van Donck
Brian Davies
Trevor Dodds
Jean Donald
Jim Dent
Rodger Davis
Bruce Devlin

E David Eichelberger
Paul Eales

F Ed Fiori
Bill Farrell
Gene Ferrell
Mike Fetchik
Dow Finsterwald
Ed Furgol
Max Faulkner
Lauren Foye

G Malcolm Gregson
A Gallardo
Hubert Green
Dave Graham
Ignacio Garrido
Mathias Gronberg
Joakim Gronhagen
Ken Green
Jim Gallagher Jr
Buddy Gardner
Clifford Ann Gordon
Jim Goshdigian
Joann Gunderson

H **Harold Hilton**
Ben Hogan
Arthur Havers
Alex Herd
Harold Henning
Bernard Hunt
Dale Hayes
Jay Haas
John Huston
Padraig Harrington
Nancy Harvey
Mayumi Hirase
Dan Halldorson
Mark Hayes
Lon Hinkle
Jim Hahn

Herb Hooper

I John Inman

J **Tony Jacklin**
Bill Johnston

K Kenny Knox
Hideki Kase
Jerry Kelly
Hiromi Kobayashi
Gary Koch
Bill Kratzert
Takaaki Kohno
Peter Kuklinski

L **Bobby Locke**
Tony Lema
Sandy Lyle
Bernhard Langer
Bruce Lietzke
John Lively Jr
Billy Livery
Bob Lunn
Sally Little
John Lister

M **Johnny Miller**
Arnaud Massy

276

Graham Marsh
John Mahaffey
Steve Lamontagne
Blaine McAllister
Rocco Mediate
Gil Morgan
Bob Murphy
Chuck Mallory
Bill Martindale
Dennie Meyer
Larry Mowry
Margie Masters
John Mahoney
Fred Marti
Ed Merrins
Chuck Montalbo
Carl Mason

N Jack Nicklaus
   Greg Norman
   Norman Von Nida

Jack Newton
Larry Nelson
Andy North

O Peter Oosterhuis

P Arnold Palmer
   Alf Padgham
   Alf Perry
   Gary Player
   Craig Parry
   Dan Pohl
   Dicky Pride
   Tom Purtzer
   Eddie Polland
   Henry Picard
   Mike Reid

R J Rivero
   Joakim Rask
   Steve Richardson

Jack Renner
Larry Rinker
Bob Risch

S Craig Stadler
   Hal Sutton
   Curtis Strange
   Tim Simpson
   Jan Stephenson
   Mike Standly
   Dave Stockton Jr
   Mike Small
   Gene Sauers
   Ted Schulz
   Jim Simons
   Charles Sifford

T Lee Trevino
   Peter Thomson
   Doug Tewell
   Leonard Thompson

Harold Twitty
Jim Thorpe
J H Taylor

V Roberto de Vicenzo
   Tommy Valentine
   Bob Verwey

W Reg Whitcombe
   Ian Woosnam
   Tom Watson
   E Whitcombe
   Enid Wilson
   D A Weibring
   Gerta Whalen
   Craig Wood

Y Bert Yancey

Z Fuzzy Zoeller

CRICKETERS

A Leslie Ames

B Don Bradman
   Trevor Bailey
   Geoffrey Boycott
   Mark Butcher
   Alistair Brown
   Rob Bailey

C Denis Compton
   Colin Cowdrey
   Percy Chapman
   Bev Congdon
   Robert Croft
   Brian Close
   John Crawley
   Shiv Chanderpaul
   Paul Collingwood
   H B Cameron

D Phil DeFreitas
   Paul Downton
   Keith Dutch

E Godfrey Evans
   John Edrich

John Emburey

F Andrew Flintoff
   Neil Fairbrother
   Arthur Fagg

G W G Grace
   Tom Graveney
   David Graveney
   Graham Gooch
   Paul Grayson

H Len Hutton
   Kim Hughes
   Graeme Hick
   Andrew Hollioake
   Ben Hollioake
   Richard Hadlee
   Carl Hooper
   Dean Headley
   Desmond Haynes

I Colin Ingleby-
   McKenzie
   Ray Illingworth

J Steve James

K Alan Knott
   Alvin Kallicharan
   Rohan Kanhai
   Jacques Kallis
   Roy Kilner

L Allan Lamb
   Maurice Leyland
   Jason Laney

M Jackie McGlew
   John Murray
   John Morris
   Dimitri Mascarahhas

N Paul Nixon

P Peter Parfitt
   Peter Pollock
   Graeme Pollock
   Shaun Pollock
   Geoff Pullar
   Mike Proctor

R Viv Richards
   Mark Ramprakash

S Garfield Sobers
   Bobby Simpson
   Mickey Stewart
   Alec Stewart
   M J K Smith
   Ben Smith
   I Sutcliffe
   Jeff Stollemeyer

V Bryan Valentine

W Frank Woolley
   Mark Waugh
   Everton Weekes
   Clyde Walcott
   Frank Worrell
   Peter Willey
   Cyril Washbrook
   A Wells
   P Weekes

INDEX

Index does not include all Dunlop/Slazenger players. Full list on pages 275-7.

Accles & Pollock — 176
Ackroyd, Stan — 235
Adidas — 158, 173–174
Ainsley, Stan — 220
Albany Street, N.W.1. — 116–118
Albion Mill — 35, 138
Aldersgate Street — 16, 95
Alexandria, Australia — 229–230
All England Club — 15, 61, 79, 87, 96
All England Croquet Club — 1
All England tennis shoe — 48
Allam, Bert — 148, 151, 163, 175
Allington House — 148, 155–156, 160, 165–166, 175, 181
Alliss, Peter — 9, 11–13, 84–85, 92–93, 95–96, 160, 175, 232
American Rugger Football — 29, 247
An Achievement in Production — 152
Archery — 1–2, 14, 15, 17, 19, 24, 73–74, 78, 89, 169, 184, 201, 224
Argus Sports Company — 117
Ashley, Mike — 274
Aston Cross factory — 102, 105–106, 127
Atkinson & Barker — 242
Austen, Patrick — 205, 207–213, 265
Australia — 1, 4, 5, 6, 8, 16, 34, 62, 64, 68, 70, 76–78, 95, 101, 131, 137, 155, 159, 163–164, 186, 205, 223–224, 227, 228, 234–235, 247, 253, 260
Ayres — 1, 3, 4, 7, 12–14, 15, 26, 28, 33, 35, 37, 39, 43–44, 47–48, 51–54, 61, 70–71, 73, 75, 79, 82, 95, 97, 99–100, 142, 168–169, 201, 223, 227, 229, 242, 273
Ayres, Edward — 15, 24
Ayres, F. H. — 2, 3, 58, 95
Badminton — 7, 17, 19, 28, 32, 40, 51, 60, 66–67, 69, 78, 89, 115, 125, 142, 154, 157, 169–170, 172, 181, 194, 202, 204, 215, 224, 227, 248–249, 251, 255, 270–271
Badminton Association — 2
badminton rackets
  Goblin — 142
  Nimble — 142
  Nimble Shilling — 142
  Fort Maxply — 157
Badminton Tennis — 47
Badminton, Table — 52
Bagatelle — 20–21, 25
Baillieu Trophy — 176, 179
Baillieu, Lord — 151, 176
Baird, Gordon — 170, 219–220
balata — 143, 172, 177, 186–187, 208, 216–217, 220–221, 239–240, 243, 245, 259–261, 263–264
Ball, Sammy — 119, 125, 131–132, 147, 151, 154, 156, 162, 172, 177–178, 254, 260
Ballesteros, Severiano — 6, 41, 89, 92, 192, 208, 212, 213, 215
Barber, Tom — 211
Barna range — 154, 157, 159
Barna, Victor — 147, 151, 163, 175, 177–178, 225, 227, 275
Barnet Glass — 229
Barnsley — 5, 13–14, 36, 71–72, 75, 78, 84, 100, 154, 166, 169–171, 175, 180–181, 194, 204–206, 226, 236, 243, 248, 269
Barrett, John — 96, 160
Barrett, Roper — 64
Bataan — 220, 234–235, 269
Bataan Export Zone — 193, 235
Batley, Yorkshire — 92
Baum, Roland — 97
Bedford, Jack — 78
Beharrell, Sir Edward — 161–162
Beharrell, Sir George — 103, 115, 117, 136, 140, 146
Bergmann, Richard — 73, 97
Best is Best logo — 50
Billane, Michael — 257
Billiards Association — 20
Bintex — 179
Birch, Dick — 69, 95, 173–174, 176, 247–249, 252
Birmingham — 2, 5, 32, 99, 102, 104, 111, 119, 124, 127, 143,

Bjursted, Molla — 156, 179, 188, 224,–225, 238
Black, E. D. — 63, 253, 248
Blacklock, David — 28
Blainey, Geoffrey — 76, 230
Blake, Mrs. Daisy — 228
Book of the Maxfli — 127–128, 148
Boomer, Bob — 123
Boston Consulting Group — 96, 175
Bowler, Albert — 202
Bowman, Bill — 96
Bowtle, Bert — 162
Boycott, Geoff — 134
Braddon, Richard — 89, 92, 192
Bradford, Cyril — 194
Bradman, Don — 119, 162
Bradman, Don — 2, 5, 12, 33, 34, 36, 40, 43, 59, 73–75, 84, 97, 223, 232
Branon, David — 94, 187, 207, 219–220, 261, 264–265, 279
Briscoe, John — 193, 235
Bromwich, John — 5, 229
Brooke, Robert — 271
Brooke's Market, Holborn — 115–118, 140
Brookes, Norman — 25
Brown, Richard — 181, 194, 198
Brown, Scott — 219–220, 233, 245, 252–253
Bryant, Tom — 219–220, 265
Brynmawr — 152
BTR (British Thermoplastic & Rubber) — 7–9, 11, 93–94, 99, 123, 158, 179–180, 184, 191, 195, 201, 203–221, 231, 240, 245–246, 251, 253, 262–265, 268
Budge, Don — 97
Buffalo, USA — 131, 159, 162–163, 173–174, 178, 203, 250, 254–256, 258–263
Bulina, George — 252
Burden, Albert — 118, 133, 138–139, 143, 149–150, 158, 166
Burkin, George — 95
Butcher, Mark — 12, 206
Buysse, Paul — 217

C. Gibbs & Co. — 57
Cahill, John — 205
Calabria, John — 217, 220–221
Cameron, H. B. — 34, 242
Campbell Manufacturing Company — 248
Canada — 4, 62, 64, 68, 71, 87, 101, 164, 172, 174, 178, 223, 227, 247, 253, 262, 264, 272
Carlton — 7–8, 12, 93, 121, 157, 169–170, 172, 176, 183, 188, 194, 201–202, 204, 215, 220, 249–251
Carlton, Bill — 169–170, 2490
Carr, George — 83, 86–87, 97, 158, 160, 162, 165–180, 183, 196, 201
Carter, Tony — 165, 167, 170, 175, 180
Casazza, Michael — 261–262
Cassell, Dean — 187, 258, 261
'Centenary' catalogue, Slazenger — 89
Challenge House, Croydon — 82, 87, 93
Championship ball — 44, 51, 53
Chaplin, Daisy — 134
Charles, Bob — 97, 173, 198, 259
Chavkin, Saul — 88, 176, 248
Cheetham, H. V. — 243–244
Childs Greene Associates — 93
China — 144, 159, 228, 233–234, 238
Choong, K. L. — 220, 234
Church Road, Wimbledon — 54, 59
Cinven — 9, 217–219
Clarke, T. P. — 77–78
Clarke, Tom — 169–170
Clay, Vaughn — 173–174, 257–258
Clerkenwell — 2, 15–16, 22, 24, 99
Collett, David — 151
Compendium of Games — 21
Compound Chest Machine — 22
Compton, Denis — 12, 40, 73–75, 83–84, 92, 97, 242, 275
Converse — 250–251
Corbally mallet — 60, 67
Corporation Street, Manchester — 26

Cotton, Henry 6, 41, 131, 135–136, 150, 186, 199
Court, Margaret 12, 85, 92, 232
Courtaulds 94
Coventry 102, 106, 143
Cowdrey, Colin 40, 85, 92, 97, 181
Craven, Gerry 85
Crawford, McGregor and Canby 50
Croquet 1–2, 17–18, 20–22, 25, 28, 34, 45, 50–51, 53, 60, 66–67, 99–100, 115, 229, 275
Crump, John 194

Daily Express 59, 93–94, 121
dartboards 141–142, 144–145, 149, 157
David Geoffrey and Associates 94, 207, 264
Davis Ltd., Messrs. F. A. 115, 117–118, 121, 125, 134, 152, 168, 254
Davis, Joe 6, 34, 37, 275
DDH golf ball 136–137, 185–188, 191, 197, 208, 216–217, 221, 240, 261–263, 273
Dean, Colin 45
Demon brand 68
Demon racket 12–13, 47–48, 50–52, 58, 61, 66, 73
Demon tennis ball 61
Denovo 182
Derby, Graeme 220
Design Council Award 188, 190–191
Devlin, Beverley 248
Dicken, Harold 133
Dodson, Dick 212–213, 219, 265
Doherty brothers 12, 65, 79, 115, 232
Doherty racket 51–52, 60, 63, 66, 253
Doherty, H. L. 54, 65
Doherty, Laurence 79, 115, 120
Doherty, Reginald 65, 79
Dolphin, Arthur 34
Dowie, Mike 203–204, 211
Downie, Ronnie 211, 233
Duke of Edinburgh 36, 75, 154, 188, 191
Dunlop 1–13, 15–16, 20, 22, 24–25, 34, 37, 41–42, 44–45, 55, 61–62, 65, 71, 74, 76–78, 82–87, 89–90, 93–94, 95
Dunlop Archive Project 127
'Dunlop Caddie' 110–112
Dunlop Digest 123, 141, 148
Dunlop Footwear 8, 115, 159, 173, 192, 195, 202, 204, 207, 209–211, 213–215, 219, 230, 233–234, 245, 265, 275
Dunlop Footwear 8, 115, 159, 173, 192, 195, 202, 204, 207, 209–211, 213, 215, 219, 230, 233–234, 245, 265, 275
Dunlop Gazette 77, 90, 119, 135, 162, 174, 176
Dunlop Golf News 123
Dunlop in War and Peace 143
Dunlop Masters Tournament 6, 162
Dunlop Maxply 6–7
Dunlop News 176, 181, 184, 193–195
Dunlop Newsletter 114, 120, 124, 132, 137
Dunlop Olympic 231
Dunlop Pneumatic Tyre Company Limited 2
Dunlop Rubber Company 7, 12, 76, 101–103, 218, 238
Dunlop Slazenger 1–3, 5–9, 11–12, 15–16, 20, 25, 34, 37, 45, 55, 61, 74, 86, 90, 93–94, 147, 154, 168–170, 172, 179–180, 184, 187, 194–196, 200–201, 203–205, 207–219, 221–222, 226–227, 231–232, 233–234, 236, 241, 243–246, 250–251, 253, 262–266, 267, 275
Dunlop Story 142, 165, 179, 191
Dunlop Tire & Rubber Goods Co. 108, 174, 203, 212, 247, 250, 255, 257–258
Dunlop, John Boyd 4, 99, 101, 105, 112, 226, 228
Dunlopillo 8, 103, 137, 142, 149, 157, 165, 179, 195, 203–204, 226, 233, 235, 243, 262, 268
Dunning, Bill 14, 70–71, 75, 144
Dupont 96, 173, 177
Durban 65, 262
'Durolastek' 153
Duronap 136–137

E.D.B. racket 28, 30, 33
East Bros. 230
Easy Row, Broad Street 111
Eden, Les 78
Edwardes, Sir Michael 7, 172, 195, 202
Ellis, Jack 88, 97, 170, 194, 243–244
Ellis, William Webb 1
Empire Racket Company 229

English, Dick 238
English, Robin 198
Erbacher 182–183, 226
Evans, Bill 118–120, 122–123, 148–149, 151, 159, 162–163, 165, 176
Evans, Godfrey 40, 66, 73, 97

Faircloth, Robert 213
Far East 8, 9, 89, 98, 106, 157, 159, 163, 176, 182, 184, 193–196, 201, 203–204, 207, 211, 219–220, 225, 227, 231, 233, 245, 251–252, 265, 268, 272
Faulkner, Max 54, 147, 150, 198
Finden-Crofts, Alan 195–196, 201–205, 208, 211–212, 250
Firestone 103, 254
Fisher, F. M. B. (Frank) 120–121, 126, 131, 158, 160, 254–255
fishing tackle 7, 164, 169, 174, 230
'Flying D' logo 85, 158, 164–165, 192, 215, 241
Football Association 1
Fort Dunlop 5, 6, 103, 105–106, 110, 112–114, 116, 119, 123–132, 134–135, 137–138, 141, 143–145, 147–148, 151–152, 172, 229, 238, 254
Fort Dunlop Works Council 127
France 4, 6, 8, 41, 58, 64, 87, 96, 101, 124, 131, 137, 143, 162, 164, 171, 194–196, 202, 211, 224–226, 247
Fraser, Sir Campbell 179, 185, 192
Fred Hurtley & Son 77

G.A.T. racket 60, 67
Gamble, Tom 96
Gardner Brothers 117–118, 120, 142
Gathercole, Tony 79
Geddes, Sir Eric 103, 112, 114–115, 117, 126
Geddes, Sir Reay 76, 164–165, 176, 179
Germany 6, 83, 101, 121, 131, 142, 143, 162, 171, 196, 202, 209, 212, 224–226, 247
Gibbs, Paul 257
Glasgow 7, 155, 169, 175
Goehle, Bob 258
Golf 49, 102, 104–105, 166, 185
Golf Balls (Dunlop)
  '65' 41, 78, 119, 125, 131–132, 135–136, 141, 143, 145, 147–148, 150–151, 156, 161–162, 167, 172–173, 177, 180–187, 199, 206, 208–209, 216–217, 221, 229, 238–240, 243, 256–257, 268, 273
  Lattice design 110–112, 114, 132, 136, 141, 150
  Magnum 110
  Silver King 99, 110, 229
  Warwick 141, 156
Golf Balls Limited 104
Golf Heroes 160
Golf Illustrated 102, 104, 105, 166, 185
Golf Trader 112, 238
Goodrich, Mr. 117
Goodyear 103, 237, 254
Gore, A. W. 52
Gore, Spencer 25, 79, 275
Gorman, Geoffrey 94, 207, 264
Gouldson, Cissie 48
Grace, W. G. 25, 39, 51, 95
Gradidge 3–5, 7, 14, 15, 26, 37, 39, 50, 52, 61, 63–71, 73–75, 97, 99–100, 137, 140–141, 168, 201, 223, 242
Gradidge, Harry 14, 39–40
Gradidge, Tim 41
Grand National Archery Society 2
Great Chesterford 145, 149, 153–154, 157
Greenville, South Carolina 186, 203, 207, 209, 216, 219, 234, 250–251, 261–266
Griffin, Charles 123
Griffiths, Andrew 220, 245
Grosse, Detlef 202, 208
Groves, Norman 14
Guallar, Federico 226
Guardian 161
'Guinea Demon' racket 13, 47
Gully, Leila Mary 56
Gutt, Betty 46, 48
Gutta Percha 4, 49, 63, 99, 105, 107, 110, 113, 129, 136, 143, 253

Hadingham, Edward (Tim) 42, 45, 53, 59, 61, 65, 118, 242–243
Hadingham, Reginald ('Buzzer') 45, 53, 59, 65, 69, 83–84, 86–87, 95–96, 134,

	170, 175, 248–249	Johnson, Harry	237, 239
Haines, Bob	147, 150–151, 183, 185–186, 188–189, 191, 260	Johnson, Keith	252
Halligan, Mrs.	154	Johnson, Ken	261
Hammer, Erbacher	182	Jones, Professor Roy	45
Hampton, Bob	252	Joynes, Mrs.	78
Hanau	131, 204, 206, 225–226, 256, 269	Junior golf ball	104, 106–108
Hardstaff, Joe	40		
Harpers Sports and Games	36, 75, 243	Kallis, Jacques	12, 52, 206, 242
Harrison, Nora	78	Keighley	77, 169, 175
Hartbridge, James	190	Kenward, Mr. L. V.	115, 117–118
Hartley, George	90	Kenyon, Eddie	78
Hartwell, USA	180–181, 204, 210–211, 224, 236, 259–262, 265	Kilner, Roy	33, 223
Haskell	99	Kinsey, Howard	255
Haskell ball	100	Kirkham, Rodney	78
Hatfield–Smith, Mr. H.	78	Kobe	102, 119, 131, 156, 159, 162, 172–173, 196, 208, 216, 219, 237–240, 245
Hawkins, Donald	149, 170		
Haymarket Stores	116	Kuala Lumpur	211, 233–234
Hays, Eric	198	Kuzuoka, Takeshi	162
Head	158, 183		
Heathcote, John Moyer	15, 17	Lamb, David	233, 268
Heavy Dunlop ball	105, 107	Lanctot, Raymond (ski equipment)	172, 174, 250
Heavy Junior ball	105	Land and Water	51
Henman, Tim	12, 79, 94, 270, 273–274	Larcombe, Major D. R.	
Hiam, R. C. (Bob)	149	Larned, William	61
High Grade Cycles	22	Laughland, Hugh	203, 208–209
High Wycombe	69, 230	Laurence Pountney Hill	2, 13, 46, 53, 56, 59, 65, 82–84, 93, 95, 97, 156, 175
Hillington	154–155		
Hilton, Harold	4, 50, 275	Laver, Rod	6, 160, 165–166, 191, 232, 257
Hinchliffe, Shirley	78	Lawn Tennis and Badminton	79
History of Dunlop	103	Lawn Tennis Association	1, 53, 86, 98, 114, 121, 150
Hockey Association	2	Leibster, A. F	68
Hogan	209, 249–251	Lenglen/Wills Match	121
Hogan, Ben	41, 84–85, 92, 150, 249	Letters, John	7, 142, 155, 204, 240, 259
Holland	211, 225	Leyland, Maurice	33
Hong Kong	32, 89, 159, 184, 197, 202–203, 207–208, 211, 253	Line markers	17, 23
		Litesome	7, 77, 82, 87–88, 94, 169, 172–173, 194, 201–202, 204
Hopwood, Mr.	116		
Horbury	2, 4–5, 12–14, 26–27, 29, 31–32, 34–38, 43, 50, 55, 62, 70–74, 78, 82, 84–86, 89–91, 95–97, 99, 138, 144, 154, 166–172, 175–176, 185, 187–189, 191, 193–194, 204, 206, 230, 242, 248–249, 275	Locke, Bobby	41, 73–74, 84–85, 97, 147, 150, 160, 198, 243
		Lombard Street, Toronto	29, 247
		Lord's	1, 5
		Loughton factory (Dunlop)	116
		Lovell, Alan	220–222, 267–268, 271
Horiuchi, Mr.	239	Lovett, Graham	234
Howe, Bob	178, 189–190, 225	Lowe, Ronald	194
Hoylake	4, 41, 136	Loxton, Eric	72, 205–206
Hughes, Pat	64, 134, 137, 147, 149, 156, 161, 163, 166, 177–178, 232		
		MacDonald, Paul	173–174, 257
Hurstpierpoint, Sussex	69	MacNally, Austen	237, 239
Hutchin, Mary	78	Malaysia	177, 186, 196, 224, 228, 233
Hutton, Len	12, 36, 40–41, 43, 66, 68, 73–75	Mallett, George	154, 178
Hydroguard	75, 273	Marnoch, Alasdair	271
Hydroguard cover	79, 273	Manchester	2–3, 32, 45–46, 69, 76, 95, 119, 165, 189
		Manor Mills	99–100, 102–107, 109, 111–112, 127
Ihle, Al	258	Marchetti, Charles	211
Imperial Driver (cricket bat)	40–42	Market Street, Manchester	46
Inchinnan	179	Marsh, Roy	89, 185
India Rubber and Gutta		Marshall, Julian	17
Percha Company	99, 107, 110	Martin, John Stuart	104, 106, 108, 110
India Rubber Journal	123	Martin, Mrs.	78
Indonesia	8, 203, 224, 233–235	Marylebone Cricket Club	1
Infringement of Competition		Mass Production	126
Rules, Charge of	212	Maxfli	6, 8–9, 12, 93, 111–114, 123, 136, 172–174, 186–187, 196, 199, 202, 206—209, 212, 215–217, 220–221, 231, 245, 254, 256, 259–266, 268–273
injection-moulding techniques	188		
International Sports Company (ISC)	7, 34, 37, 82–84, 86–88, 156–157, 158, 168–197, 201–202, 209–210, 219, 230–235, 246, 250–252, 258		
		Maxpower golf club	181, 184, 259
Ireland	224–226	MBO	9, 203, 219–220
Irving, Malcolm	243	McCowen, Rob	96–97
		McEnroe, John	84–85, 89, 190–191, 207–208, 215–216, 239, 262, 270, 273
J. S. Moss and Sons	46		
Jackson, Alan	217	McMaster, Humphrey	34, 39, 41–42, 45, 53, 61, 65, 68–70, 75–76, 82–84, 86–89, 95, 242
Jackson, Eric	259–260		
Jacobs, David	205, 214–215, 217–220	McMaster, Michael	34, 36, 39, 41–42, 45, 53, 61, 65, 68–70, 72, 75–78, 82–83, 85–86, 95, 164, 242
James, Ken	34		
Jansen, Philip	219–220	McMaster, Peter	82
Japan	4–6, 8, 101–102, 119, 131, 136, 143–144, 159, 162, 171–173, 176, 185–187, 195–196, 199, 205, 209, 216, 218, 224, 227, 236, 237, 253, 263, 272	McMillan, James	165, 179–180, 191
		McPherson, A. A.	229
		mechanical driving machine	124, 130
		Meers, E. G.	52
		Melton Mowbray	16, 58
Jaques, John	2, 60	Merritton, Canada	249
Jefferies and Company	15, 32–33	Metalastik	180
Jenkins, Brian	204, 211–212, 265	Michie, Alan	193
Jest, Mr.	134	Miller, Johnny	41, 84, 92, 192, 240
Jewell, Richard	185	Millsap, Bill	248
Johnson, Albert	168		

Mitchell, Ian — 96
Mitchell, Joyce — 148
Mobeni, Durban — 242–245
Montlucon — 131, 211, 226
Moodie, Gordon — 211, 213, 219–220
Morgan, Alun — 163, 176
Morris, Noel — 230
Mortimer, Geoff — 202
Morton, Jack — 78, 156–157, 158–161, 164–165, 168, 170, 179

National Tyre Service — 180
New Zealand — 8, 34, 37, 41, 50, 64, 68, 87, 97, 120, 170, 196–197, 223–224, 228, 236, 247
Newcombe, John — 12, 79, 85, 92, 180–181, 192
Niblett, Mr. T. W. — 109
Nicholas, Graham — 226–227
Nicklaus, Jack — 6, 41, 84–85, 88, 92, 160, 167, 192, 213, 215–216, 232
Nike — 173–174
Noonkester, Hershel — 199
Normanton — 166, 177, 181, 183, 186–187, 193–194, 204, 206, 208, 260, 269
North America — 4, 6, 8–9, 28, 140, 160, 163, 174, 181, 183, 197, 201, 204, 207, 209, 224, 231, 235, 240, 267, 271–272
North British Rubber Company — 110
Norton, George — 95

Old Street — 22
Olson, Bill — 220
On the Road — 102
Orange Spot ball — 100, 104–106
Orr, Mike — 207, 211–212, 265
Osborne, Denis — 151, 154, 170, 178, 234–235, 260
Oshawa Sokai Trding Company — 238
Osnaburgh Street, N.W.1. — 118
Oval — 1–2, 40, 68, 271
Oxford Companion to Sports and Games — 178, 247

Pacific Dunlop — 228, 231–232
Padder Tennis — 74
Paddle Tennis — 74
Padgham, Alf — 41, 66, 136
Palmer, Archdale — 42, 45, 53–57, 61, 65, 68, 118, 122
Palmer, Arnold — 7, 160, 165, 167, 173, 232
Panther International — 87
Panther logo — 3, 40, 77, 82, 85, 87, 89, 92–95, 173, 181–182, 220, 273
Panther Press — 82
Parker, Harry — 228, 230, 232
Parnell, Philip — 220–222, 267–268, 271–272
Parr, Susan — 180
Peacock, Ian — 84, 86, 88, 95, 180, 183, 188, 202
Pekrul, Roger — 263
Pena, Teddy — 234
Penfold, Albert Edward — 110–115, 117–119, 121, 128, 131, 147, 151, 254
Perry, Fred — 12, 59, 63–64, 66–68, 71–74, 79, 84, 97, 134, 137–138, 147, 172–173, 181, 255
Perry, Sir Michael — 219, 271
Perry/Maskell Instructional Racket — 74
Persimmon golf heads — 50
Peter Black Company — 94, 204
Peters, Andrew — 210, 213, 219–220
Peters, Bill — 53, 95
Philippines — 193, 196–197, 204–205, 211, 220, 224, 226, 231–232, 233, 235–236, 269
Picken, Findlay — 86–87, 89, 158–160, 177–179, 181, 183, 190–191, 194–195, 202, 233
Ping — 249–251
Pirelli — 179, 182
Pittsburg — 178
Player, Gary — 97, 160, 243, 246, 259,
Playne, Wm., & Co. — 137
Pneumatic Tyre and Booth's Cycle Agency — 101
Pollard, Roy — 235
Pollock, Shaun — 12, 52, 243
Polydur — 186
Popplewell, Frank — 188
Potzler, Dick — 258
Pretty Polly — 208, 212
Price, Martin — 193, 235
Pridgeon, Royce — 180

Priestley, Bretton — 167
Prince — 158, 183, 209, 244
Procter, Neville — 257
Proctor, Guy — 118–119, 133–134, 143–144, 152–153
Puma — 7–8, 82, 87–89, 92, 94, 174, 184, 202, 207, 209–211, 213, 215–216, 219–220, 265, 268
Purkis, Ernest — 248

Quarta, Robert — 213
Queen's Award to Industry — 175
Quist, Adrian — 229–230

Real Tennis — 16–17, 52, 96
Redditch — 7, 163, 169
Reebok — 173–174
Rees, John — 214, 264
Reid, John — 96
Reliance waterproof football — 48
Rennocks, Len — 152, 162, 193
Renshaw racket — 12, 47
Renshaw, William — 12, 25
Repellant football — 48
Reynolds, Peter — 185
Rhymer, Ann — 180
Richards, Vincent (Vinnie) — 131, 254–255, 257–258, 260
Riggs, Charles — 60
Riseley, A. H. — 115
Riseley, Frank — 115
Ritchie, Alistair — 271
Rizzo, Mike — 220, 269
Rizzo, Mike — 220, 269
Roberton, Neil — 194
Roberts, Laurie — 184, 202, 204, 211, 233
Robinson, D. S. — 141, 149
Rochdale — 125, 165
root word — 34
Rootham, P. W. — 54
Rosewall, Ken — 79, 85, 92, 155, 231
Ross-Elliott and McKellar — 242
Rossignol — 183, 250
Roulston, Gary — 206
Royal and Ancient — 1, 40, 120
Royal Flying Corps — 4, 109, 145
Royds — 93
Rubber House, Holborn — 115
rugby — 5, 13, 19, 22, 25, 28, 32, 34, 40, 50–51, 59, 68, 73, 86, 97, 99, 165–166, 171, 214–215, 228
Rugby Football Union — 2
Rugby School — 1

Sammells, Ralph, — 156
Schlesinger — 46
Schofield, Ken — 91
Sealey — 163–164, 169–170, 172, 174
Sealey, David — 163–164, 180–181, 186
Sealey, Edgar — 7, 164
Sealeys — 163–164, 169–170, 172, 174
Selby, Charles — 134, 178, 193
Semtex flooring — 149, 152–153, 160, 170, 201
Seward, Maurice — 204
Shaw, Herbert — 78
Shaw, Mike — 185, 188
Sherwin, Roy — 170, 194, 202
shuttles/Plastic Carlton — 157
Simpson, Brian — 204, 211, 219–220, 261–262
Singapore — 179, 218, 233
Skull, Jack — 95
Slack, Bob — 115
Slater, Richard — 264
Slazenger — 1–10, 31, 99–102, 109, 113, 115, 118, 121–122, 134, 136–138, 140–142, 147, 149–150, 153–157, 158–159, 163–176, 179–184, 186–187, 192–198, 200, 201–238, 240–254, 256–266, 267–275
Slazenger et Fils — 2, 46
Slazenger history, the articles of — 97–98
Slazenger Moss, Albert — 47–48
Slazenger Moss, Joseph — 46
Slazenger Sports Club — 36
Slazenger Sports Desk Newsletter — 87
Slazenger Sports Newspaper — 87
Slazenger, Albert — 11–12, 14, 42, 45–50, 53, 55–56, 62, 65, 68–69, 75–76, 88, 95, 98, 229, 273
Slazenger, Frank — 11, 46, 50, 63, 95, 253
Slazenger, Horatio — 46, 50, 57, 95

Slazenger, Mordecai	45–46
Slazenger, Ralph	11–12, 57, 69, 75–76, 164
Slazenger, Ralph, Snr.	11–12, 45–47, 50, 53, 55–56, 68, 76, 88, 95, 229
Slazengers Ltd.	2, 58, 78
Smart, Jack	105–106
Smith, Cyril	90
Smith, Frank (F. H.)	77, 149–151. 154, 156–160, 168, 170, 179
Smith, Mike	209
Sobers, Sir Garfield	52, 75, 78, 84–85, 92, 140
Solheim, Karsten	249
South Africa	4, 6, 29, 34, 41, 45, 64–65, 68, 73–74, 87–88, 93, 97, 140, 149, 156, 163–164, 170, 174, 177, 179–180, 186, 192, 196, 199, 201–203, 205, 207, 219, 223–224, 227, 234, 242, 253
South Korea	204, 218, 234, 237
Spain	74, 98, 225–226
Spalding	41, 99, 107, 151, 158, 176, 178, 206–207, 234, 245
Speke	6, 84, 100, 119, 146–149, 151–152, 154, 157–159, 161–162, 169–173, 175, 177–178, 181, 186, 193, 202, 239, 260
Spence, Clifford	78
Sport and its Industry	13
Sporting Club de Paris	58, 62
Sportlines International	203, 219, 234, 247, 249–252
Sports Dealer	61, 121
Sports Equipment International	243–245
Sports Trader	12, 29, 41–42, 53, 56–58, 68, 72, 76, 104, 107–108, 116–117, 125–126, 132–133, 147, 157
Sports World International	10, 200
Sportsdesk	82
Squash	2, 40, 52, 66–67, 78, 89, 115, 125, 142, 148, 151, 154, 157, 159, 166–167, 169, 172, 182, 194, 203, 212–213, 216, 224, 227, 244–246, 248, 255, 270, 275
Squash Rackets Association	2
Srixon	237
St. James's Street	116–118, 172, 202, 261
Stadium soccer ball	60
Stadium tennis racket	63
Steele, Mrs. Edith	36
Stevenson, Eric	226
Stewart, Alec	12, 52, 205–206
Stirk, John	243–244
Storrs, Sir Ronald	143
Sumitomo Rubber Industries	179, 195–196, 207–208, 211, 216, 218, 221, 226, 234, 236–237, 240–241, 263–264
Sunday Times	91, 160, 192, 220
Surlyn	173, 177, 183, 243, 260–261
Surridge, Stuart	213, 215
Swingball	174, 181
Swinkels, Frans	226
Sykeometer	37
Sykes	3–7, 12–15, 18, 22–25, 39–40, 43–44, 47, 51–52, 57, 59, 70, 71–75, 78, 82–83, 89, 97, 99–100, 109, 113, 137, 144, 168–169, 174, 194, 201, 204, 223–224, 242, 247
Sykes, Henry	27–28, 174, 223, 227
Sykes, William	2, 5, 12, 14, 22, 26, 55, 58, 62, 65, 70, 72, 89–90, 95, 99, 138, 185, 204, 223, 227, 242, 269, 275
Sykes, William, Jnr.	27–29, 34
Sykraft balls	73
Szarvasy, Mr. F. A.	140
Taiwan	159, 176, 183, 188, 194, 204, 208, 218, 233–234, 237, 262
Taylor & Ellis	41, 242
TaylorMade-adidas Group	9. 119, 250, 271–273
tennis ball dating machine	124
Tennis Ball War	60
Tennis balls	
Fort	136, 141, 148, 156, 181, 240
Tennis balls (Dunlop)	
'65'	147–148, 151, 156, 162, 229
Tennis racket, 150G (Dunlop)	188–191
Tennis racket, 200G (Dunlop)	188, 190–192, 197, 207–208, 210, 212, 216, 251, 262, 269, 272–273
Tennis racket, 300G (Dunlop)	272
Tennis rackets (Dunlop)	
31	125, 134
Argus	117, 125
Blue Flash	134, 157
Courtier	125
De Luxe	125
Green Flash	134
Maxply	6–7, 65, 120, 125, 132–134, 137–138, 140, 142, 150–152, 154, 156–157, 159–160, 162, 165–166, 169, 172, 176–184, 188, 190–195, 216, 224, 254–256, 259, 262
Maxply Fort	137, 139, 142, 157, 181, 190, 240, 273
Maxply McEnroe	190, 262
Maxply Tournament	125
Popular	137
Queen Mary	137
Red Flash	134
Riseley Hexagon	115, 125, 134
Thailand	8, 203–204, 228, 233, 268–269
The Curious History of the Golf Ball	84
The Development of a Great Industry	106
The Dunlop Book	121–122
The Field	1, 15, 47, 51, 124
The Way Ahead conference	217
Theydon Hall, Essex	56
Thompson, Len	202
Thomson, Peter	150, 154–156, 159–160, 173, 198, 230–232, 240, 259
Thornhill, Mickey	175
Thornliebank	155
Thorpe, I. A. (Bunny)	156
Tinkler, George	162
Tinling, Teddy	120–121, 192
Tonbridge	40
TPI (Transpolyisoprene)	172–173
Truflite	49–50
Tuckerman, Ray	235
Tuphine footballs	31
Ullyett, Roy	93–94
Ultra Vis ball	79, 273
Underhill, Ruth	4, 50
United States Golf Association	1
urethane	216, 221, 268, 273
USA (see also North America)	5, 49, 62–64, 76, 82, 87–89, 94, 107, 110, 131, 133, 135, 157, 159, 162–164, 171, 173–174, 178–180, 183, 185–188, 190–191, 193, 196–197, 203–213, 216, 219–220, 223–224, 227–228, 231, 234, 236–237, 240, 244–245, 247, 250, 252, 253, 268–270
USA Women's Amateur Championship	4, 50
Usher, John	202
'V' floater ball	107
Van Jarsveldt, Colin	202, 243
Vaughan, George	124, 151–153, 170
'Ventiflex' canvas	142
Victory racket	44, 46, 73
Wade, Virginia	190, 192, 195, 238
Walker, Oscar	149
Waltham Abbey	6, 77–78, 115, 117–120, 125, 131–135, 137, 141–145, 147–149, 151–154, 156–158, 162–163, 167, 169, 172, 175–176, 178, 193–194, 202, 204, 240
Walton, Liverpool	125
Wandsworth factory	116
Ward, Donald	36
Warren-Tape, Peter	213
Waters, Brian	202
Watt, George	78
Waugh, Mark	12, 52, 206
Weaver, Sam	57–58
Wells, Tony	176, 248, 252, 257
Westminster, South Carolina	9, 161–163, 173, 187, 204–206, 208, 216–217, 220–221, 224, 232, 240, 257–263, 265–266, 269, 272
Whip cricket bat	48
Whitcombe, Reg	41, 66, 68, 132, 136
Wilding, Tony	25, 79
Williamson, Greta	148
Wilson Sporting Goods	164
Wilson, Jimmy	91
Wilson, John	252
Wimbledon	1, 4–6, 8, 12, 15–17, 24–25, 44, 48, 50–51, 53–55, 59–61, 64–65, 67, 79, 84, 87, 94, 96,

	100, 102, 115, 118, 120, 122–123, 131–132, 134–135, 137–138, 140–141, 147, 150, 154–155, 160, 166–167, 169, 173, 176, 180, 183, 189, 190–192, 198, 215, 229, 232, 236, 242, 247, 254–255, 267, 270, 273
Wimbledon, Parade of Champions 2000	8
Wood, Craig	256
Woodgates, Billie	181
Woodstock, Oxfordshire	29
Woolwich	2, 4–5, 15, 39, 41, 43, 46–47, 60–62, 67, 69, 71, 99, 100, 107, 115, 136, 140–141, 248
Woosnam, Ian	6, 208, 212
World Cup 1966	89, 90, 167, 174
Worple Road	15, 54
wound golf ball	40, 50, 63, 100, 107, 110, 172, 186, 215, 239–240, 243, 256, 261
Wragg, Philip	212, 219–220,265
Wright & Ditson	99
Wycherley	37, 95
Wycherley, Peter	37, 170, 188, 190, 194, 202
Yorkshire Athletic Manufactory	26–27, 31
Yorkshire Evening Post	71
Young's	163
Zig Zag football	37, 73, 83

PLAIN JERSEYS

Stock Colours :—

Scarlet	Green
Royal	Navy
White	Maroon
Amber	Sky

2 in. Vertical Stripes
Design

Stock Colours :—
Red and White
Black and Amber
Green and White
Red and Black
Royal and White
Black and White
Navy and Sky
Navy and White
Green and Black

RUGBY
2 in. Horizontal Stripes
White Collar; Button
Front

Stock Colours :—
Red and White
Black and Amber
Green and White
Red and Black
Royal and White
Black and White
Navy and Sky
Navy and White
Green and Black

QUALITY G

A. V. Design

Stock Colours :—

Maroon and Sky
Royal and White
Scarlet and White
Green and White
Navy and Sky
Black and Scarlet
Black and Amber

M. U. Design

Stock Colours :—

Royal and White
Scarlet and White
Green and White
Navy and Sky
B ack and Scarlet
Maroon and Sky
Black and Amber